AMERICAN FORUM

Speeches on Historic Issues, 1788–1900

AMERICAN FORUM

Speeches on Historic Issues, *1788–1900*

EDITED BY

ERNEST J. WRAGE
Northwestern University

BARNET BASKERVILLE
University of Washington

HARPER & ROW, PUBLISHERS

New York and Evanston

Library of Congress catalog card number: 60–7019

IT IS THE *peculiarity of some schools of eloquence that they embody and utter, not merely the individual genius and character of the speaker, but a national consciousness —a national era, a mood, a hope, a dread, a despair—in which you listen to the spoken history of the time.*

—RUFUS CHOATE

PREFACE

"AMERICAN FORUM" is a collection of representative speeches on many of the vital and urgent questions that were threshed over from the time of the ratification of the Constitution of the United States to the twentieth century. The speeches selected are of interest to students of history, government, literature, religion, speech—indeed to all readers who respond to the drama of lively exchange in ideas. For that is what this book is—a record of men and ideas jostling for public acceptance in the free competition of an American forum.

Obviously these speeches were not devised to be preserved in an anthology. Each was delivered to a specific audience on a specific occasion for a specific purpose. The speakers were not making literature; they were making history. Patrick Henry fighting to keep his beloved Virginia from joining the proposed Federal government; William Ellery Channing stating publicly for the first time the Unitarian credo; William Graham Sumner stanchly upholding rugged individualism; Susan B. Anthony demanding equal rights for women —all were transacting public business, advancing important causes, energizing significant ideas. And it is precisely because the attention of these speakers was fixed upon the job at hand, because in their utterances can be seen the clash of ideas, policies, and principles, that these real-life debates so vividly reflect the mood and temper of the times which called them forth and the scenes into which they were projected.

Anthologies of speeches tend to follow one of two patterns, neither of which does full justice to the material. Older anthologies in particular were born in an era when appreciation for the pyrotechnics of oratory was high. Anthologists were keen for heart-pounding eloquence, and each specimen they exhibited was something of a *tour de force*. Anthologies in this tradition were advertised as containing masterpieces of eloquence. Their editors winnowed out purple passages which they were sure would survive indefinitely as distinguished contributions to our national literature. Now that such compositions are no longer highly regarded as literature they have been consigned to the same limbo as lace antimacassars and cast-iron deer.

A second type of anthology attempts to select speeches alleged to have influenced the course of history. Such collections are generally more discriminating and more objective. They often contain many genuinely notable public addresses produced at moments of tension in history and acclaimed by those who heard them, speeches that have stood the test of time and that bear unmistakable marks of rhetorical excellence. Anthologies of this type have a worthy purpose, but they are too often mere miscellanies, collections of discrete items wrenched from their settings and arranged in chronological order, or assembled under a set of conventional headings such as "types of speech." Presented without adequate context or connecting links, these speeches are but surviving fragments of some obscure whole. Generations of schoolboys nourished on such a diet have memorized the exordium and peroration of Webster's "Second Reply to Hayne" without ever discovering the nature and significance of the reply or what it was a reply to.

This volume is not a garland of rhetorical flowers, a mere miscellany of eloquent passages, although many of its speeches are profoundly eloquent. Nor is its purpose that of catering to an antiquarian's sentimental attachment to monumental speeches of the past, although many of the speeches are incontestably great. Rather, we have selected and juxtaposed speeches in order to provide the substance and framework of an American forum as a venture in intellectual history through public address. We think this is a worthy enterprise for several reasons.

1. Speech-making is important business in a free society. In the democratic theory, each person is privileged to express himself on issues of concern to him and his contemporaries. Whether or not he succeeds in gaining a hearing depends upon his endowments for speaking and his ability to find or build a platform. In its history, the United States has provided an enormous number and variety of platforms, which its citizens have not been reluctant to mount. In short, public address is one of the primary means by which popular thought and action have always been developed and energized, sustained or modified.

2. Although many important speeches of the past have been lost, the number of surviving texts is enormous. The main job of the anthologist is to winnow through extant speeches, choose those that illuminate the discussion of root issues in American life and thought, and then make them accessible.

Reading speeches on critical issues brings us into direct encounter with competing schools of thought, with current assumptions, values, attitudes, and characteristic modes of address. Although a speech is primarily expressive of the mind of a speaker, it also is a gauge to the mind of his audience, both listeners and readers. What speakers choose to talk about and what listeners choose to listen to are matters esteemed by both parties. In still other ways a speech bears the impress of an audience, always covertly, often overtly. Through intuition, experience, or by precept, effective public speakers discover they must take into account the interests, belief-systems, prejudices, and caprices of their audiences. The adaptations speakers make are implicit in the formulations of their arguments, in idiomatic language, in images fashioned from life experiences of the group, and in appeals that go to the heart as well as to the head. In short, speeches on critical issues are vibrant with the immediacy of life, with the sense of interaction between speaker and listeners.

3. If a speech is to be comprehended, interpreted, and evaluated, it must be placed within the context of its time. No speech completely transcends its time, and most speeches are inextricably interwoven with the moment. Accordingly, and in broad outline, we have sketched the events and intellectual environment that constitute the backdrop for these speeches. Suggestions for acquiring additional background information may be found at the end of the volume.

For these reasons, then, we have fashioned an anthology of speeches based on issues underlying the American experience. Preparing such a collection, however, poses this vexatious question: Which issues should be included? We have focused upon basic and persistent problems that commanded widespread public interest, provoked serious controversy, and continue directly or indirectly to challenge us today. Hence we excluded evanescent excitements and concentrated upon fundamental constitutional, political, economic, social, and religious questions. If read successively, the speeches on these issues will reveal some of the major cleavages and continuities in American thought and action.

These speeches have been drawn from many sources. We exhumed them from crumbling pamphlets, from yellowing newspapers, from legislative debates and hearings, and from journals. If finally we decided to include certain speeches that also appear in standard collections (e.g., Henry and Madison on ratification of the Constitution), it is because we have satisfied ourselves that they are the best statements available, and not because they have become established. In selecting the twenty-six speeches in *American Forum* we have rejected hundreds of others. Many of those omitted have been sacrificed only with the most painful reluctance. Each reader will doubtless look in vain for some old favorite which has fallen a casualty to the limitations of space, or did not conform to the plan of this volume. Such must inevitably be the case with any collection. The anthologist can do no more and no less than to make known his standards of selection and then to stand steadfastly behind his choice.

The speeches finally selected passed a number of tests. Each speech had to be the most cogent and economical statement of a position that we could find. Each had to be significantly relevant to one specific issue. Each had to deal in essentials of the specific problem, not in its tangential aspects. Each had to be representative of the case in behalf of one side or party to a controversy. Each had to be a representative expression of a foremost spokesman from among accredited exponents of a position. Each had to convey to today's reader the authentic spirit of the occasion.

How reliable are the texts used? Admittedly, texts of speeches are often open to question, particularly in matters of stylistic detail. Texts of early speeches suffer from the crude systems of stenography used in those days, and from limited reportorial service. In each case we have identified the source of the text used, and we have, of course, tried always to choose what we considered the most reliable text available. We have corrected typographical errors and misspelled words. Here and there we took the liberty of modernizing archaic and eccentric punctuation when changes could be made without affecting meaning.

We have been compelled by the prodigious length of some speeches, particularly the earlier ones, to modify our original resolution to present only complete texts. Where we have found it necessary to cut a text, we have tried scrupulously to preserve its real substance. We have cut remarks of local reference that lend nothing to the thought and distract today's reader. We have eliminated a few long and superfluous prefatory statements. We have cut extended amplifications of a point, or disgressions from the main line of argument. In short, we have tried to retain important substantive matters and eliminate "detachable" elements whenever it was impossible to reproduce a text *in toto*. All omissions, however minor, are clearly indicated by ellipses. Where transitions were needed, explanatory notes have been provided.

American Forum, then, is made up of twenty-six speeches, arranged chronologically in relation to basic historical issues. A short introduction to each issue and the speeches related to it supplies historical context. A brief chronology of life facts identifies each of the speakers. The bibliographical notes at the end of the book open opportunities for further study. This volume constitutes, we believe, a lively chronicle of ideas in action, to be read with profit and enjoyment for its own sake, or as a source book in the history of American public address from 1788 to 1900. A second volume, following a similar format and featuring twentieth-century speeches, will be published subsequently by Harper & Brothers.

CONTENTS

xi

PART ONE

To Form a More Perfect Union

RATIFICATION OF THE
FEDERAL CONSTITUTION

THE DELIBERATIONS *leading to the ratification of the newly drawn Federal Constitution by the various state conventions constitute some of the most significant and dramatic debates in American history. In September of 1787 the Constitutional Convention finished its work and the proposed plan of government was transmitted by Congress to the states for approval. By January of the following year five states had ratified the document: Delaware, New Jersey, and Georgia by unanimous vote; Connecticut and Pennsylvania by substantial majorities. The following month the Massachusetts convention, after bitter debate, voted for ratification by the slender margin of 187 to 168, and proposed a series of amendments, thus setting a precedent which was followed by states subsequently ratifying. During the spring and summer of 1788 Maryland, South Carolina, New Hampshire, Virginia, and New York voted to support the new government, the latter state by a margin of only three votes. In September, after a year of the widest, and in some quarters the most intense, public discussion throughout the Confederation, Congress voted to put the Constitution into operation.*

The debates in the different states are unequally reported, and the accuracy of the reports is open to question. Little record remains of the proceedings of the New Hampshire convention; those of Virginia and New York are preserved in some detail. Judging from such reports as are available, it appears that the same general arguments were presented for and against the Constitution in most of the state conventions. The Federalists pointed to the weakness and general inadequacy of the Articles of Confederation and argued that the new government would provide much-needed order and security. The Antifederalists were primarily concerned about the loss of personal liberties and states' rights; the proposed organization, they were convinced, would be too strong and too remote.

In no state were both Federalist and Antifederalist cases presented with more clarity and competence than in the key state of Virginia. Here the antagonists were evenly matched, and the provisions of the new federal organization were carefully analyzed and ably discussed by friend and foe alike. When the Virginia delegates assembled on the second day of June, 1788, eight states had already ratified, and it appeared that the fate of the Constitution might be settled by the Richmond convention. Even when New Hampshire on June 21 became the ninth state to ratify, the importance of Virginia's decision was in no way lessened, since without her and without New York, the new government would have small hope of success. Virginia was the most populous, and in many ways the most important state in the Confederation, and Federalists elsewhere were anxiously awaiting the outcome of her deliberations. Alexander Hamilton, as leader of the New York Federalists, wrote to James Madison in Richmond that "Our chance of success depends on you."

The two speeches presented below were delivered during the opening days of the Virginia convention. They include many of the principal arguments for and against adoption of the Constitution, and although imperfectly reported, suggest the contrast in personality,

*style, and method between the two speakers. Henry
begins with a reference to his brief remarks of the preceding day in which he had questioned the authority of
the framers of the Constitution to use the language of
"We, the people" instead of "We, the states." The basic
change in the nature of the government implied in this
phraseology would, he believes, render all liberties insecure. Liberty, he insists, and not world power or increased trade, should be the direct end of government.
Henry then sets forth at length and with considerable
repetition his objections to the new Federal government
as opposed to a loose confederation of states. He offers
in conclusion the suggestion that Virginia consider the
possibility of remaining outside the Union, that she
"stand by a while, and see the effect of its [the Constitution's] adoption in other states." As reported, the speech
is personal and colloquial. Its loose organization and
general diffuseness are acknowledged in Henry's own
statement that he has found his mind hurried on from
subject to subject. He did not, he says, "come prepared
to speak, on so multifarious a subject, in so general a
manner."*

*The tone of Madison's reply is calmer and less emo-
tional. He seems at times to be smiling condescendingly
at Henry's vehement protest of the preceding day. His
introduction is a plea for the avoidance of appeals to the
passions and a judicious examination of the Constitution
solely on its own merits. Madison's charge that Henry
spoke too vaguely and generally of the dangers inherent
in the Constitution is unfair. Henry's enumeration of
these dangers was quite specific, as Madison's own excellent point by point refutation of them indicates. Madison concludes his carefully constructed rebuttal with
some remarks as to his conception of the general nature
of the proposed government. It is, he points out, unprecedented in form, being "of a mixed nature," in some*

respects "federal" (i.e., confederated), in others "con-
solidated." It avoids the evils of absolute consolidation
and of mere confederation, and combines the assets of
both.

    Eloquent and memorable as were the debates them-
selves, the skillful management of the convention had
much to do with determining the final outcome. The
Federalists were particularly adept at political strategy
and parliamentary tactics, and in view of the even match-
ing of the disputants, it is possible that superior general-
ship may have accounted in large measure for the
ultimate triumph of their cause. The Virginia convention
ratified the Constitution June 25, 1788, by a vote of 89
to 79. Meanwhile, a similar battle had been raging in
the New York convention between the Federalists under
Alexander Hamilton and the Antifederalists led by
Governor Clinton and Melancton Smith, where the news
of Virginia's decision may have exerted some influence
upon the final vote of 30 to 27 in favor of ratification.

Against the Federal Constitution

PATRICK HENRY

Born, Hanover County, Virginia, May 29, 1736; died, Charlotte County, Virginia, June 6, 1799. Won fame as an orator in celebrated "Parsons' Cause," 1763. Elected to House of Burgesses, 1765; author of "Virginia Resolutions" denouncing Stamp Act. Delegate to Continental Congress, 1774 and 1775, and in 1775 to second revolutionary convention of Virginia where he delivered his "Liberty or Death" speech. Governor of Virginia, 1776–1779, and again 1784–1786. Delegate to Philadelphia Constitutional Convention of 1787, but declined to serve; later led opposition to ratification in Virginia. Declined a succession of offices, among them United States Senator, Secretary of State, and Chief Justice of United States Supreme Court.

*M*r. *Chairman:* I am much obliged to the very worthy gentleman for his encomium. I wish I was possessed with talents, or possessed of any thing that might enable me to elucidate this great subject. I am not free from suspicion: I am apt to entertain doubts. I rose yesterday to ask a question which arose in my own mind. When I asked that question, I thought the meaning of my interrogation was obvious. The fate of this question and of America may depend on this. Have they said, We, the states? Have they made a proposal of a compact between states? If they had, this would be a confederation. It is otherwise most clearly a consolidated government. The question turns, sir, on that poor little thing—the expression,

Virginia Ratifying Convention, Richmond, June 5, 1788. Jonathan Elliot, ed., *The Debates in the Several State Conventions, on the Adoption of the Federal Constitution,* 2nd ed. (Philadelphia: J. B. Lippincott Company, 1901), III, pp. 43–64.

We, the *people*, instead of the *states*, of America. I need not take much pains to show that the principles of this system are extremely pernicious, impolitic, and dangerous. Is this a monarchy, like England—a compact between prince and people, with checks on the former to secure the liberty of the latter? Is this a confederacy, like Holland—an association of a number of independent states, each of which retains its individual sovereignty? It is not a democracy, wherein the people retain all their rights securely. Had these principles been adhered to, we should not have been brought to this alarming transition, from a confederacy to a consolidated government. We have no detail of these great considerations, which, in my opinion, ought to have abounded before we should recur to a government of this kind. Here is a resolution as radical as that which separated us from Great Britain. It is radical in this transition; our rights and privileges are endangered, and the sovereignty of the states will be relinquished: and cannot we plainly see that this is actually the case? The rights of conscience, trial by jury, liberty of the press, all your im-munities and franchises, all pretensions to human rights and privileges, are rendered insecure, if not lost, by this change, so loudly talked of by some, and inconsiderately by others. Is this tame relinquishment of rights worthy of freemen? Is it worthy of that manly fortitude that ought to characterize republicans? It is said eight states have adopted this plan. I declare that if twelve states and a half had adopted it, I would, with manly firmness, and in spite of an erring world, reject it. You are not to inquire how your trade may be increased, nor how you are to become a great and powerful people, but how your liberties can be secured; for liberty ought to be the direct end of your government.

Having premised these things, I shall, with the aid of my judgment and information, which, I confess, are not extensive, go into the discussion of this system more minutely. Is it necessary for your liberty that you should abandon those great rights by the adoption of this system? Is the relinquish-ment of the trial by jury and the liberty of the press necessary for your liberty? Will the abandonment of your most sacred rights tend to the security of your liberty? Liberty, the greatest of all earthly blessings—give us that precious jewel, and you may take every thing else! But I am fearful I have lived long enough to become an old-fashioned fellow. Perhaps an invincible attachment to the dearest rights of man may, in these refined, enlightened days, be deemed old-fashioned; if so, I am contented to be so. I say, the time has been when every pulse of my heart beat for American liberty, and which, I believe, had a counterpart in the breast of every true American; but suspicions have gone forth—suspicions of my integrity—publicly reported that my professions are not real. Twenty-three years ago was I supposed a traitor to my country? I was then said to be the bane of sedition, because I supported the rights of my country. I may be thought suspicious when I say our privileges and rights are in danger. But, sir, a number of the people of this country are weak enough to think these things are too true. I am happy to find that the gentleman on the other side declares they are groundless. But, sir, suspicion is a virtue as long as its object is the preservation of the public good, and as long as it stays within proper bounds: should it fall on me, I am contented: conscious rectitude is a powerful consolation. I trust there are many who think my professions for the public good to be real. Let your suspicion look to both sides. There are many on the other side, who possibly may have been persuaded to the necessity of these measures, which I conceive to be dangerous to your liberty. Guard with jealous attention the public liberty. Suspect every one who approaches that jewel. Unfortunately, nothing will preserve it but downright force. Whenever you give up that force, you are inevitably ruined. I am answered by gentlemen, that, though I might speak of terrors, yet the fact was, that we were surrounded by none of the dangers I apprehended. I conceive this new government to be one of those dangers: it has produced those horrors which distress many of our best citizens. We are come hither to preserve the poor commonwealth of Virginia, if it can be possibly done: something must be done to preserve your liberty and mine. The Confederation, this same despised government, merits, in my opinion, the highest encomium: it carried us through a long and dangerous war; it rendered us victorious in that bloody conflict with a powerful nation; it has secured us a territory greater than any European monarch possesses: and shall a government which has been thus strong and vigorous, be accused of imbecility, and abandoned for want of energy? Consider what you are about to do before you part with the government. Take longer time in reckoning things; revolutions like this have happened in almost every country in Europe; similar examples are to be found in ancient Greece and ancient Rome—instances of the people losing their liberty by their own carelessness and the ambition of a few. We are cautioned by the honorable gentleman, who presides, against faction and turbulence. I acknowledge that licentiousness is dangerous, and that it ought to be provided against: I acknowledge, also, the new form of government may effectually prevent it: yet there is another thing it will as effectually do—it will oppress and ruin the people.

There are sufficient guards placed against sedition and licentiousness; for, when power is given to this government to suppress these, or for any other purpose, the language it assumes is clear, express, and unequivocal; but when this Constitution speaks of privileges, there is an ambiguity, sir, a fatal ambiguity—an ambiguity which is very astonishing. In the clause under consideration, there is the strangest language that I can conceive. I mean, when it says that there shall not be more representatives than one for every thirty thousand. Now, sir, how easy is it to evade this privilege! "The number shall not exceed one for every thirty thousand." This may be satisfied by one representative from each state. Let our numbers be ever so great, this immense continent may, by this artful expression, be reduced to have but thirteen representatives. I confess this construction is not natural; but the ambiguity of the expression lays a good ground for a quarrel. Why was it not clearly and unequivocally expressed, that they should be entitled to have one for every thirty thousand? This would have obviated all disputes; and was this difficult to be done? What is the inference? When population increases, and a state shall send representatives in this proportion, Congress *may* remand them, because the right of having one for every thirty thousand is not clearly expressed. This possibility of reducing the number to one for each state approximates to probability by that other expression—"but each state shall at least have one representative." Now, is it not clear that, from the first expression, the number might be reduced so much that some states should have no representatives at all, were it not for the insertion of this last expression? And as this is the only restriction upon them, we may fairly conclude that they *may* restrain the number to one from each state. Perhaps the same horrors may hang over my mind again. I shall be told I am continually afraid: but, sir, I have strong cause of apprehension. In some parts of the plan before you, the great rights of freemen are endangered; in other parts, absolutely taken away. How does your trial by jury stand? In civil cases gone—not sufficiently secured in criminal—this best privilege is gone. But we are told that we need not fear; because those in power, being our representatives, will not abuse the powers we put in their hands. I am not well versed in history, but I will submit to your recollection, whether liberty has been destroyed most often by the licentiousness of the people, or by the tyranny of rulers. I imagine, sir, you will find the balance on the side of tyranny. Happy will you be if you miss the fate of those nations, who, omitting to resist their oppressors, or negligently suffering their liberty to be wrested from them, have groaned under intolerable despotism! Most of the human race are now in this deplorable condition; and those nations who have gone in search of grandeur, power, and splendor, have also fallen a sacrifice, and been the victims of their own folly. While they acquired those visionary blessings, they lost their freedom. My great objection to this government is, that it does not leave us the means of defending our rights, or of waging war against tyrants. It is urged by some gentlemen, that this new plan will bring us an acquisition of strength—an army, and the militia of the states. This is an idea extremely ridiculous; gentlemen cannot be in earnest. This acquisition will trample on our fallen liberty. Let my beloved Americans guard against that fatal lethargy that has pervaded the universe. Have we the means of resisting disciplined armies, when our only defence, the militia, is put into the hands of Congress?

The honorable gentleman said that great danger would ensue if the Convention rose without adopting this system. I ask, Where is that danger? I see none. Other gentlemen have told us, within these walls, that the union is gone, or that the union will be gone. Is not this trifling with the judgment of their fellow-citizens? Till they tell us the grounds of their fears, I will consider them as imaginary. I rose to make inquiry where those dangers were; they could make no answer: I believe I never shall have that answer. Is there a disposition in the people of this country to revolt against the dominion of laws? Has there been a single tumult in Virginia? Have not the people of Virginia, when laboring under the severest pressure of accumulated distresses, manifested the most cordial acquiescence in the execution of the laws? What could be more awful than their unanimous acquiescence under general distresses? Is there any revolution in Virginia? Whither is the spirit of America gone? Whither is the genius of America fled? It was but yesterday, when our enemies marched in triumph through our country. Yet the people of this country could not be appalled by their pompous armaments: they stopped their career, and victoriously captured them. Where is the peril, now, compared to that? Some minds are agitated by foreign alarms. Happily for us, there is no real danger from Europe; that country is engaged in more arduous business: from that quarter there is no cause of fear: you may sleep in safety forever for them.

Where is the danger? If, sir, there was any, I would recur to the American spirit to defend us; that spirit which has enabled us to surmount the greatest difficulties: to that illustrious spirit I address my most fervent prayer to prevent our adopting a system destructive to liberty. Let not gentlemen be told that it is not safe to reject this government. Wherefore is it not safe? We are told there are dangers, but those dangers are ideal; they cannot be demonstrated. To encourage us to adopt it, they tell us that there is a plain, easy way of getting amendments. When I come to contemplate this part, I suppose that I am mad, or that my countrymen are so. The way to amendment is, in my conception, shut. Let us consider this plain, easy way. "The Congress, whenever two thirds of both houses shall deem it necessary, shall propose amendments to this Constitution, or on the application of the legislatures of two thirds of the several states, shall call a Convention for proposing amendments, which, in either case, shall be valid to all intents and purposes, as part of this Constitution, when ratified by the legislatures of three fourths of the several states, or by the Conventions in three fourths thereof, as the one or the other mode of ratification may be proposed by the Congress. . . ."

Hence it appears that three fourths of the states must ultimately agree to any amendments that may be necessary. Let us consider the consequence of this. However uncharitable it may appear, yet I must tell my opinion—

that the most unworthy characters may get into power, and prevent the introduction of amendments. Let us suppose—for the case is supposable, possible, and probable—that you happen to deal those powers to unworthy hands; will they relinquish powers already in their possession, or agree to amendments? Two thirds of the Congress, or of the state legislatures, are necessary even to propose amendments. If one third of these be unworthy men, they may prevent the application for amendments; but what is destructive and mischievous, is, that three fourths of the state legislatures, or of the state conventions, must concur in the amendments when proposed! In such numerous bodies, there must necessarily be some designing, bad men. To suppose that so large a number as three fourths of the states will concur, is to suppose that they will possess genius, intelligence, and integrity, approaching to miraculous. It would indeed be miraculous that they should concur in the same amendments, or even in such as would bear some likeness to one another; for four of the smallest states, that do not collectively contain one tenth part of the population of the United States, may obstruct the most salutary and necessary amendments. Nay, in these four states, six tenths of the people may reject these amendments; and suppose that amendments shall be opposed to amendments, which is highly probable,— is it possible that three fourths can ever agree to the same amendments? A bare majority in these four small states may hinder the adoption of amendments; so that we may fairly and justly conclude that one twentieth part of the American people may prevent the removal of the most grievous inconveniences and oppression, by refusing to accede to amendments. A trifling minority may reject the most salutary amendments. Is this an easy mode of securing the public liberty? It is, sir, a most fearful situation, when the most contemptible minority can prevent the alteration of the most oppressive government; for it may, in many respects, prove to be such. Is this the spirit of republicanism?

What, sir, is the genius of democracy? Let me read that clause of the bill of rights of Virginia which relates to this: 3d clause:—that government is, or ought to be, instituted for the common benefit, protection, and security of the people, nation, or community. Of all the various modes and forms of government, that is best, which is capable of producing the greatest degree of happiness and safety, and is most effectually secured against the danger of mal-administration; and that whenever any government shall be found inadequate, or contrary to those purposes, a majority of the community hath an indubitable, unalienable, and indefeasible right to reform, alter, or abolish it, in such manner as shall be judged most conducive to the public weal.

This, sir, is the language of democracy—that a majority of the community have a right to alter government when found to be oppressive. But how different is the genius of your new Constitution from this! How different

from the sentiments of freemen, that a contemptible minority can prevent
the good of the majority!

. . . .

Let me here call your attention to that part which gives the Congress
power "to provide for organizing, arming, and disciplining the militia, and
for governing such part of them as may be employed in the service of the
United States—reserving to the states, respectively, the appointment of the
officers, and the authority of training the militia according to the discipline
prescribed by Congress." By this, sir, you see that their control over our
last and best defence is unlimited. If they neglect or refuse to discipline
or arm our militia, they will be useless: the states can do neither—this
power being exclusively given to Congress. The power of appointing officers
over men not disciplined or armed is ridiculous; so that this pretended little
remains of power left to the states may, at the pleasure of Congress, be
rendered nugatory. Our situation will be deplorable indeed: nor can we
ever expect to get this government amended, since I have already shown that
a very small minority may prevent it, and that small minority interested in
the continuance of the oppression. Will the oppressor let go the oppressed?
Was there ever an instance? Can the annals of mankind exhibit one single
example where rulers overcharged with power willingly let go the oppressed,
though solicited and requested most earnestly? The application for amendments will therefore be fruitless. Sometimes, the oppressed have got loose
by one of those bloody struggles that desolate a country; but a willing
relinquishment of power is one of those things which human nature never
was, nor ever will be, capable of.

The honorable gentleman's observations, respecting the people's right
of being the agents in the formation of this government, are not accurate,
in my humble conception. The distinction between a national government
and a confederacy is not sufficiently discerned. Had the delegates, who were
sent to Philadelphia, a power to propose a consolidated government instead
of a confederacy? Were they not deputed by states, and not by the people?
The assent of the people, in their collective capacity, is not necessary to the
formation of a federal government. The people have no right to enter into
leagues, alliances, or confederations; they are not the proper agents for this
purpose. States and foreign powers are the only proper agents for this kind
of govenment. Show me an instance where the people have exercised this
business. Has it not always gone through the legislatures? I refer you to the
treaties with France, Holland, and other nations. How were they made?
Were they not made by the states? Are the people, therefore, in their
aggregate capacity, the proper persons to form a confederacy? This, therefore,
ought to depend on the consent of the legislatures, the people having never

sent delegates to make any proposition for changing the government. Yet I must say, at the same time, that it was made on grounds the most pure; and perhaps I might have been brought to consent to it so far as to the change of government. But there is one thing in it which I never would acquiesce in. I mean, the changing it into a consolidated government, which is so abhorrent to my mind. . . .

If we admit this consolidated govenment, it will be because we like a great, splendid one. Some way or other we must be a great and mighty empire; we must have an army, and a navy, and a number of things. When the American spirit was in its youth, the language of America was different: liberty, sir, was then the primary object. We are descended from a people whose government was founded on liberty: our glorious forefathers of Great Britain made liberty the foundation of every thing. That country is become a great, mighty, and splendid nation; not because their government is strong and energetic, but, sir, because liberty is its direct end and foundation. We drew the spirit of liberty from our British ancestors: by that spirit we have triumphed over every difficulty. But now, sir, the American spirit, assisted by the ropes and chains of consolidation, is about to convert this country into a powerful and mighty empire. If you make the citizens of this country agree to become the subjects of one great consolidated empire of America, your government will not have sufficient energy to keep them together. Such a government is incompatible with the genius of republicanism. There will be no checks, no real balances, in this government. What can avail your specious, imaginary balances, your rope-dancing, chain-rattling, ridiculous ideal checks and contrivances? But, sir, we are not feared by foreigners; we do not make nations tremble. Would this constitute happiness, or secure liberty? I trust, sir, our political hemisphere will ever direct their operations to the security of those objects. . . .

When I thus profess myself an advocate for the liberty of the people, I shall be told I am a designing man, that I am to be a great man, that I am to be a demagogue; and many similar illiberal insinuations will be thrown out: but, sir, conscious rectitude outweighs those things with me. I see great jeopardy in this new government. I see none from our present one. I hope some gentleman or other will bring forth, in full array, those dangers, if there be any, that we may see and touch them.

I have said that I thought this a consolidated government: I will now prove it. Will the great rights of the people be secured by this government? Suppose it should prove oppressive, how can it be altered? Our bill of rights declares, "that a majority of the community hath an indubitable, unalienable, and indefeasible right to reform, alter, or abolish it, in such manner as shall be judged most conducive to the public weal."

I have just proved that one tenth, or less, of the people of America—a most despicable minority—may prevent this reform or alteration. Suppose the people of Virginia should wish to alter their government; can a majority of them do it? No; because they are connected with other men, or, in other words, consolidated with other states. When the people of Virginia, at a future day, shall wish to alter their government, though they should be unanimous in this desire, yet they may be prevented therefrom by a despicable minority at the extremity of the United States. The founders of your own Constitution made your government changeable: but the power of changing it is gone from you. Whither is it gone? It is placed in the same hands that hold the rights of twelve other states; and those who hold those rights have right and power to keep them. It is not the particular government of Virginia: one of the leading features of that government is, that a majority can alter it, when necessary for the public good. This government is not a Virginian, but an American government. Is it not, therefore, a consolidated government? The sixth clause of your bill of rights tells you, "that elections of members to serve as representatives of the people in Assembly ought to be free, and that all men having sufficient evidence of permanent common interest with, and attachment to, the community, have the right of suffrage, and cannot be *taxed*, or deprived of their property for public uses, without their own consent, or that of their representatives so elected, nor bound by any law to which they have not in like manner assented for the public good." But what does this Constitution say? The clause under consideration gives an unlimited and unbounded power of taxation. Suppose every delegate from Virginia opposes a law laying a tax; what will it avail? They are opposed by a majority; eleven members can destroy their efforts: those feeble ten cannot prevent the passing the most oppressive tax law; so that, in direct opposition to the spirit and express language of your declaration of rights, you are taxed, not by your own consent, but by people who have no connection with you.

The next clause of the bill of rights tells you, "that all power of suspending law, or the execution of laws, by any authority, without the consent of the representatives of the people, is injurious to their rights, and ought not to be exercised." This tells us that there can be no suspension of government or laws without our own consent; yet this Constitution can counteract and suspend any of our laws that contravene its oppressive operation; for they have the power of direct taxation, which suspends our bill of rights; and it is expressly provided that they can make all laws necessary for carrying their powers into execution; and it is declared paramount to the laws and constitutions of the states. Consider how the only remaining defence we have left is destroyed in this manner. Besides the expenses of maintaining the Senate and other house in as much splendor as they please, there is to be a great and mighty President, with very extensive powers—the powers of a king. He is to be supported in extravagant magnificence; so that the whole of our property may be taken by this American government, by laying what taxes they please, giving themselves what salaries they please, and suspending our laws at their pleasure. I might be thought too inquisitive, but I believe I should take up very little of your time in enumerating the little power that is left to the government of Virginia; for this power is reduced to little or nothing: their garrisons, magazines, arsenals, and forts, which will be situated in the strongest places within the states; their ten miles square, with all the fine ornaments of human life, added to their powers, and taken from the states, will reduce the power of the latter to nothing.

The voice of tradition, I trust, will inform posterity of our struggles for freedom. If our descendants be worthy the name of Americans, they will preserve, and hand down to their latest posterity, the transactions of the present times; and, though I confess my exclamations are not worthy the hearing, they will see that I have done my utmost to preserve their liberty; for I never will give up the power of direct taxation but for a scourge. I am willing to give it conditionally; that is, after non-compliance with requisitions. I will do more, sir, and what I hope will convince the most skeptical man that I am a lover of the American Union—that, in case Virginia shall not make punctual payment, the control of our custom-houses, and the whole regulation of trade, shall be given to Congress, and that Virginia shall depend on Congress even for passports, till Virginia shall have paid the last farthing, and furnished the last soldier. Nay, sir, there is another alternative to which I would consent;—even that they should strike us out of the Union, and take away from us all federal privileges, till we comply with federal requisitions: but let it depend upon our own pleasure to pay our money in the most easy manner for our people. Were all the states, more terrible than the mother country, to join against us, I hope Virginia could defend herself; but, sir, the dissolution of the Union is most abhorrent to my mind. The first thing I have at heart is American liberty: the second thing is American union; and I hope the people of Virginia will endeavor to preserve that union. The increasing population of the Southern States is far greater than that of New England; consequently, in a short time, they will be far more numerous than the people of that country. Consider this, and you will find this state more particularly interested to support American liberty, and not bind our posterity by an improvident relinquishment of our rights. I would give the best security for a punctual compliance with requisitions; but I beseech gentlemen, at all hazards, not to give up this unlimited power of taxation. The honorable gentleman has told us that these powers, given to Congress, are accompanied by a judiciary which will correct all. On examination, you will find this very judiciary oppressively constructed; your jury trial destroyed, and the judges dependent on Congress.

In this scheme of energetic government, the people will find two sets of tax-gatherers—the state and the federal sheriffs. This, it seems to me, will produce such dreadful oppression as the people cannot possibly bear. The federal sheriff may commit what oppression, make what distresses, he pleases, and ruin you with impunity; for how are you to tie his hands? Have you any sufficiently decided means of preventing him from sucking your blood by speculations, commissions, and fees? Thus thousands of your people will be most shamefully robbed: our state sheriffs, those unfeeling bloodsuckers, have, under the watchful eye of our legislature, committed the most horrid and barbarous ravages on our people. It has required the most constant vigilance of the legislature to keep them from totally ruining the people; a repeated succession of laws has been made to suppress their iniquitous speculations and cruel extortions; and as often has their nefarious ingenuity devised methods of evading the force of those laws: in the struggle they have generally triumphed over the legislature.

It is a fact that lands have been sold for five shillings, which were worth one hundred pounds: if sheriffs, thus immediately under the eye of our state legislature and judiciary, have dared to commit these outrages, what would they not have done if their masters had been at Philadelphia or New York? If they perpetrate the most unwarrantable outrage on your person or property, you cannot get redress on this side of Philadelphia or New York; and how can you get it there? If your domestic avocations could permit you to go thither, there you must appeal to judges sworn to support this Constitution, in opposition to that of any state, and who may also be inclined to favor their own officers. When these harpies are aided by excise-men, who may search, at any time, your houses, and most secret recesses, will the people bear it? If you think so, you differ from me. Where I thought there was a possibility of such mischiefs, I would grant power with a niggardly hand; and here there is a strong probability that these oppressions shall actually happen. I may be told that it is safe to err on that side, because such regulations may be made by Congress as shall restrain these officers, and because laws are made by our representatives, and judged by righteous judges: but, sir, as these regulations may be made, so they may not; and many reasons there are to induce a belief that they will not. I shall therefore be an infidel on that point till the day of my death.

This Constitution is said to have beautiful features; but when I come to examine these features, sir, they appear to me horribly frightful. Among other deformities, it has an awful squinting; it squints towards monarchy; and does not this raise indignation in the breast of every true American?

Your President may easily become king. Your Senate is so imperfectly constructed that your dearest rights may be sacrificed by what may be a small minority; and a very small minority may continue forever unchangeably this government, although horridly defective. Where are your checks in this government? Your strongholds will be in the hands of your enemies. It is on a supposition that your American governors shall be honest, that all the good qualities of this government are founded; but its defective and imperfect construction puts it in their power to perpetrate the worst of mischiefs, should they be bad men; and, sir, would not all the world, from the eastern to the western hemisphere, blame our distracted folly in resting our rights upon the contingency of our rulers being good or bad? Show me that age and country where the rights and liberties of the people were placed on the sole chance of their rulers being good men, without a consequent loss of liberty! I say that the loss of that dearest privilege has ever followed, with absolute certainty, every such mad attempt.

If your American chief be a man of ambition and abilities, how easy is it for him to render himself absolute! The army is in his hands, and if he be a man of address, it will be attached to him, and it will be the subject of long meditation with him to seize the first auspicious moment to accomplish his design; and, sir, will the American spirit solely relieve you when this happens? I would rather infinitely—and I am sure most of this Convention are of the same opinion—have a king, lords, and commons, than a government so replete with such insupportable evils. If we make a king, we may prescribe the rules by which he shall rule his people, and interpose such checks as shall prevent him from infringing them; but the President, in the field, at the head of his army, can prescribe the terms on which he shall reign master, so far that it will puzzle any American ever to get his neck from under the galling yoke. I cannot with patience think of this idea. If ever he violates the laws, one of two things will happen: he will come at the head of his army, to carry every thing before him; or he will give bail, or do what Mr. Chief Justice will order him. If he be guilty, will not the recollection of his crimes teach him to make one bold push for the American throne? Will not the immense difference between being master of every thing, and being ignominiously tried and punished, powerfully excite him to make this bold push? But, sir, where is the existing force to punish him? Can he not, at the head of his army, beat down every opposition? Away with your President! we shall have a king: the army will salute him monarch: your militia will leave you, and assist in making him king, and fight against you: and what have you to oppose this force? What will then become of you and your rights? Will not absolute despotism ensue? . . .

What can be more defective than the clause concerning the elections? The control given to Congress over the time, place, and manner of holding elections, will totally destroy the end of suffrage. The elections may be held at one place, and the most inconvenient in the state; or they may be at remote distances from those who have a right of suffrage: hence nine out of ten must either not vote at all, or vote for strangers; for the most influential characters will be applied to, to know who are the most proper to be chosen. I repeat, that the control of Congress over the *manner*, &c., of electing, well warrants this idea. The natural consequence will be, that this democratic branch will possess none of the public confidence; the people will be prejudiced against representatives chosen in such an injudicious manner. The proceedings in the northern conclave will be hidden from the yeomanry of this country. We are told that the yeas and nays shall be taken, and entered on the journals. This, sir, will avail nothing: it may be locked up in their chests, and concealed forever from the people; for they are not to publish what parts they think require secrecy: they *may* think, and *will think*, the whole requires it.

Another beautiful feature of this Constitution is, the publication from time to time of the receipts and expenditures of the public money. This expression, *from time to time*, is very indefinite and indeterminate: it may extend to a century. Grant that any of them are wicked; they may squander the public money so as to ruin you, and yet this expression will give you no redress. I say they may ruin you; for where, sir, is the responsibility? The yeas and nays will show you nothing, unless they be fools as well as knaves; for, after having wickedly trampled on the rights of the people, they would act like fools indeed, were they to publish and divulge their iniquity, when they have it equally in their power to suppress and conceal it. Where is the responsibility—that leading principle in the British government? In that government, a punishment certain and inevitable is provided; but in this, there is no real, actual punishment for the grossest mal-administration. They may go without punishment, though they commit the most outrageous violation on our immunities. That paper may tell me they will be punished. I ask, By what law? They must make the law, for there is no existing law to do it. What! will they make a law to punish themselves?

This, sir, is my great objection to the Constitution, that there is no true responsibility—and that the preservation of our liberty depends on the single chance of men being virtuous enough to make laws to punish themselves.

In the country from which we are descended, they have real and not imaginary responsibility; for their mal-administration has cost their heads to some of the most saucy geniuses that ever were. The Senate, by making treaties, may destroy your liberty and laws for want of responsibility. Two thirds of those that shall happen to be present, can, with the President, make treaties that shall be the supreme law of the land; they may make the most ruinous treaties; and yet there is no punishment for them. Whoever shows me a punishment provided for them will oblige me. So, sir, notwithstanding there are eight pillars, they want another. Where will they make another? I trust, sir, the exclusion of the evils wherewith this system is replete in its present form, will be made a condition precedent to its adoption by this or any other state. The transition, from a general unqualified admission to offices, to a consolidation of government, seems easy; for, though the American states are dissimilar in their structure, this will assimilate them. This, sir, is itself a strong consolidating feature, and is not one of the least dangerous in that system. Nine states are sufficient to establish this government over those nine. Imagine that nine have come into it. Virginia has certain scruples. Suppose she will, consequently, refuse to join with those states; may not she still continue in friendship and union with them? If she sends her annual requisitions in dollars, do you think their stomachs will be so squeamish as to refuse her dollars? Will they not accept her regiments? They would intimidate you into an inconsiderate adoption, and frighten you with ideal evils, and that the Union shall be dissolved. 'Tis a bugbear, sir: the fact is, sir, that the eight adopting states can hardly stand on their own legs. Public fame tells us that the adopting states have already heart-burnings and animosity, and repent their precipitate hurry: this, sir, may occasion exceeding great mischief. When I reflect on these and many other circumstances, I must think those states will be found to be in confederacy with us. If we pay our quota of money annually, and furnish our ratable number of men, when necessary, I can see no danger from a rejection.

The history of Switzerland clearly proves that we might be in amicable alliance with those states without adopting this Constitution. Switzerland is a confederacy, consisting of dissimilar governments. This is an example which proves that governments of dissimilar structures may be confederated. That confederate republic has stood upwards of four hundred years; and, although several of the individual republics are democratic, and the rest aristocratic, no evil has resulted from this dissimilarity; for they have braved all the power of France and Germany during that long period. The Swiss spirit, sir, has kept them together; they have encountered and overcome immense difficulties with patience and fortitude. In the vicinity of powerful and ambitious monarchs, they have retained their independence, republican simplicity, and valor. . . .

The most valuable end of government is the liberty of the inhabitants. No possible advantages can compensate for the loss of this privilege. Show me the reason why the American Union is to be dissolved. Who are those eight adopting states? Are they averse to give us a little time to consider, before we conclude? Would such a disposition render a junction with them eligible; or is it the genius of that kind of government to precipitate people hastily into measures of the utmost importance, and grant no indulgence? If it be, sir, is it for us to accede to such a government? We have a right to have time to consider; we shall therefore insist upon it. Unless the government be amended, we can never accept it. The adopting states will doubtless accept our money and our regiments; and what is to be the consequence, if we are disunited? I believe it is yet doubtful, whether it is not proper to stand by a while, and see the effect of its adoption in other states. In forming a government, the utmost care should be taken to prevent its becoming oppressive; and this government is of such an intricate and complicated nature, that no man on this earth can know its real operation. The other states have no reason to think, from the antecedent conduct of Virginia, that she has any intention of seceding from the Union, or of being less active to support the general welfare. Would they not, therefore, acquiesce in our taking time to deliberate—deliberate whether the measure be not perilous, not only for us, but the adopting states?

Permit me, sir, to say, that a great majority of the people, even in the adopting states, are averse to this government. I believe I would be right to say, that they have been egregiously misled. Pennsylvania has, *perhaps*, been tricked into it. If the other states who have adopted it have not been tricked, still they were too much hurried into its adoption. There were very respectable minorities in several of them; and if reports be true, a clear majority of the people are averse to it. If we also accede, and it should prove grievous, the peace and prosperity of our country, which we all love, will be destroyed. This government has not the affection of the people at present. Should it be oppressive, their affections will be totally estranged from it; and, sir, you know that a government, without their affections, can neither be durable nor happy. I speak as one poor individual; but when I speak, I speak the language of thousands. But, sir, I mean not to breathe the spirit, nor utter the language, of secession.

I have trespassed so long on your patience, I am really concerned that I have something yet to say. The honorable member has said, we shall be properly represented. Remember, sir, that the number of our representatives is but ten, whereof six is a majority. Will those men be possessed of sufficient information? A particular knowledge of particular districts will not suffice. They must be well acquainted with agriculture, commerce, and a great variety of other matters throughout the continent; they must know not only the actual state of nations in Europe and America, the situations of their farmers, cottagers, and mechanics, but also the relative situations and inter-course of those nations. Virginia is as large as England. Our proportion of representatives is but ten men. In England they have five hundred and fifty-eight. The House of Commons, in England, numerous as they are, we are told, are bribed, and have bartered away the rights of their con-stituents: what, then, shall become of us? Will these few protect our rights? Will they be incorruptible? You say they will be better men than the English commoners. I say they will be infinitely worse men, because they are to be chosen blindfolded: their election (the term, as applied to their appointment, is inaccurate) will be an involuntary nomination, and not a choice.

I have, I fear, fatigued the committee; yet I have not said the one hundred thousandth part of what I have on my mind, and wish to impart. On this occasion, I conceived myself bound to attend strictly to the interest of the state, and I thought her dearest rights at stake. Having lived so long—been so much honored—my efforts, though small, are due to my country. I have found my mind hurried on, from subject to subject, on this very great occasion. We have been all out of order, from the gentleman who opened to-day to myself. I did not come prepared to speak, on so multifarious a subject, in so general a manner. I trust you will indulge me another time. Before you abandon the present system, I hope you will consider not only its defects, most maturely, but likewise those of that which you are to substitute for it. May you be fully apprized of the dangers of the latter, not by fatal experience, but by some abler advocate than I!

For the Federal Constitution

JAMES MADISON

> Born, Port Conway, Virginia, March 16, 1751; died,
> Montpelier, Virginia, June 28, 1836. Graduate of College
> of New Jersey. Elected to Virginia convention 1776,
> helped draft new state constitution. Served in Continen-
> tal Congress 1780–1783 and 1787–1788, and in Virginia
> legislature 1784–1786. Worked with Hamilton to have
> Federal Constitutional Convention called. Because his was
> the chief hand in actual drafting of Constitution, has
> been called "the father of the Constitution." Contributed
> with Hamilton and Jay to Federalist Papers and led fight
> for ratification in Virginia. Representative to Congress,
> 1789. Secretary of State in Jefferson's cabinet. President
> of United States, 1809–1817.

M^r. Chairman: I shall not attempt to make impressions by any ardent professions of zeal for the pub-
lic welfare. We know the principles of every man will, and ought to be,
judged, not by his professions and declarations, but by his conduct; by that
criterion I mean, in common with every other member, to be judged; and
should it prove unfavorable to my reputation, yet it is a criterion from which I
will by no means depart. Comparisons have been made between the friends of
this Constitution and those who oppose it: although I disapprove of such comparisons, I trust that, in point of truth, honor, candor, and rectitude of motives,
the friends of this system, here and in other states, are not inferior to its opponents. But professions of attachment to the public good, and comparisons of

Virginia Ratifying Convention, Richmond, June 6, 1788. Jonathan Elliot, ed.,
*The Debates in the Several State Conventions, on the Adoption of the Federal Con-
stitution*, 2nd ed. (Philadelphia: J. B. Lippincott Company, 1901), III, pp. 86–97.

parties, ought not to govern or influence us now. We ought, sir, to examine the Constitution on its own merits solely: we are to inquire whether it will promote the public happiness: its aptitude to produce this desirable object ought to be the exclusive subject of our present researches. In this pursuit, we ought not to address our arguments to the feelings and passions, but to those understandings and judgments which were selected by the people of this country, to decide this great question by a calm and rational investigation. I hope that gentlemen, in displaying their abilities on this occasion, instead of giving opinions and making assertions, will condescend to prove and demonstrate, by a fair and regular discussion. It gives me pain to hear gentlemen continually distorting the natural construction of language; for it is sufficient if any human production can stand a fair discussion.

Before I proceed to make some additions to the reasons which have been adduced by my honorable friend over the way, I must take the liberty to make some observations on what was said by another gentleman [Mr. Henry]. He told us that this Constitution ought to be rejected because it endangered the public liberty, in his opinion, in many instances. Give me leave to make one answer to that observation: Let the dangers which this system is supposed to be replete with be clearly pointed out: if any dangerous and unnecessary powers be given to the general legislature, let them be plainly demonstrated; and let us not rest satisfied with general assertions of danger, without examination. If powers be necessary, apparent danger is not a sufficient reason against conceding them. He has suggested that licentiousness has seldom produced the loss of liberty; but that the tyranny of rulers has almost always effected it. Since the general civilization of mankind, I believe there are more instances of the abridgment of the freedom of the people by gradual and silent encroachments of those in power, than by violent and sudden usurpations; but, on a candid examination of history, we shall find that turbulence, violence, and abuse of power, by the majority trampling on the rights of the minority, have produced factions and commotions, which, in republics, have, more frequently than any other cause, produced despotism. If we go over the whole history of ancient and modern republics, we shall find their destruction to have generally resulted from those causes. If we consider the peculiar situation of the United States, and what are the sources of that diversity of sentiment which pervades its inhabitants, we shall find great danger to fear that the same causes may terminate here in the same fatal effects which they produced in those republics. This danger ought to be wisely guarded against. Perhaps, in the progress of this discussion, it will appear that the only possible remedy for those evils, and means of preserving and protecting the principles of republicanism, will be found in that very system which is now exclaimed against as the parent of oppression.

I must confess I have not been able to find his usual consistency in the gentleman's argument on this occasion. He informs us that the people of the country are at perfect repose,—that is, every man enjoys the fruits of his labor peaceably and securely, and that every thing is in perfect tranquillity and safety. I wish sincerely, sir, this were true. If this be their happy situation, why has every state acknowledged the contrary? Why were deputies from all the states sent to the general Convention? Why have complaints of national and individual distresses been echoed and reechoed throughout the continent? Why has our general government been so shamefully disgraced, and our Constitution violated? Wherefore have laws been made to authorize a change, and wherefore are we now assembled here? A federal government is formed for the protection of its individual members. Ours has attacked itself with impunity. Its authority has been disobeyed and despised. I think I perceive a glaring inconsistency in another of his arguments. He complains of this Constitution, because it requires the consent of at least three fourths of the states to introduce amendments which shall be necessary for the happiness of the people. The assent of so many he urges as too great an obstacle to the admission of salutary amendments, which, he strongly insists, ought to be at the will of a bare majority. We hear this argument, at the very moment we are called upon to assign reasons for proposing a constitution which puts it in the power of nine states to abolish the present inadequate, unsafe, and pernicious Confederation! In the first case, he asserts that a majority ought to have the power of altering the government, when found to be inadequate to the security of public happiness. In the last case, he affirms that even three fourths of the community have not a right to alter a government which experience has proved to be subversive of national felicity! nay, that the most necessary and urgent alterations cannot be made without the absolute unanimity of all the states! Does not the thirteenth article of the Confederation expressly require that no alteration shall be made without the unanimous consent of all the states? Could any thing in theory be more perniciously improvident and injudicious than this submission of the will of the majority to the most trifling minority? Have not experience and practice actually manifested this theoretical inconvenience to be extremely impolitic? Let me mention one fact, which I conceive must carry conviction to the mind of any one: the smallest state in the Union has obstructed every attempt to reform the government; that little member has repeatedly disobeyed and counteracted the general authority; nay, has even supplied the enemies of its country with provisions. Twelve states had agreed to certain improvements which were proposed, being thought absolutely necessary to preserve the existence of the general government; but as these improvements, though really indispensable, could not, by the Confederation, be introduced into it without the consent of every state, the refractory dissent of that little state prevented their adoption. The inconveniences resulting from this requisition, of unanimous concurrence in alterations in the Confederation, must be known to every member in this Convention; it is therefore needless to remind them of them. Is it not self-evident that a trifling minority ought not to bind the majority? Would not foreign influence be exerted with facility over a small minority? Would the honorable gentleman agree to continue the most radical defects in the old system, because the petty state of Rhode Island would not agree to remove them?

He next objects to the exclusive legislation over the district where the seat of government may be fixed. Would he submit that the representatives of this state should carry on their deliberations under the control of any other member of the Union? If any state had the power of legislation over the place where Congress should fix the general government, this would impair the dignity, and hazard the safety, of Congress. If the safety of the Union were under the control of any particular state, would not foreign corruption probably prevail, in such a state, to induce it to exert its controlling influence over the members of the general government? Gentlemen cannot have forgotten the disgraceful insult which Congress received some years ago. When we also reflect that the previous cession of particular states is necessary before Congress can legislate exclusively any where, we must, instead of being alarmed at this part, heartily approve of it.

But the honorable member sees great danger in the provision concerning the militia. This I conceive to be an additional security to our liberty, without diminishing the power of the states in any considerable degree. It appears to me so highly expedient that I should imagine it would have found advocates even in the warmest friends of the present system. The authority of training the militia, and appointing the officers, is reserved to the states. Congress ought to have the power to establish a uniform discipline throughout the states, and to provide for the execution of the laws, suppress insurrections, and repel invasions: these are the only cases wherein they can interfere with the militia; and the obvious necessity of their having power over them in these cases must convince any reflecting mind. Without uniformity of discipline, military bodies would be incapable of action: without a general controlling power to call forth the strength of the Union to repel invasions, the country might be overrun and conquered by foreign enemies: without such a power to suppress insurrections, our liberties might be destroyed by domestic faction, and domestic tyranny be established.

The honorable member then told us that there was no instance of power once transferred being voluntarily renounced. Not to produce European examples, which may probably be done before the rising of this Convention, have we not seen already, in seven states (and probably in an eighth state), legislatures surrendering some of the most important powers they possessed? But, sir, by this government, powers are not given to any particular set of men; they are in the hands of the people; delegated to their representatives chosen for short terms; to representatives responsible to the people, and whose situation is perfectly similar to their own. As long as this is the case we have no danger to apprehend. When the gentleman called our recollection to the usual effects of the concession of powers, and imputed the loss of liberty generally to open tyranny, I wish he had gone on farther. Upon his review of history, he would have found that the loss of liberty very often resulted from factions and divisions; from local considerations, which eternally lead to quarrels; he would have found internal dissensions to have more frequently demolished civil liberty, than a tenacious disposition in rulers to retain any stipulated powers. . . .

The power of raising and supporting armies is exclaimed against as dangerous and unnecessary. I wish there were no necessity of vesting this power in the general government. But suppose a foreign nation to declare war against the United States; must not the general legislature have the power of defending the United States? Ought it to be known to foreign nations that the general government of the United States of America has no power to raise and support an army, even in the utmost danger, when attacked by external enemies? Would not their knowledge of such a circumstance stimulate them to fall upon us? If, sir, Congress be not invested with this power, any powerful nation, prompted by ambition or avarice, will be invited, by our weakness, to attack us; and such an attack, by disciplined veterans, would certainly be attended with success, when only opposed by irregular, undisciplined militia. Whoever considers the peculiar situation of this country, the multiplicity of its excellent inlets and harbors, and the uncommon facility of attacking it,—however much he may regret the necessity of such a power, cannot hesitate a moment in granting it. One fact may elucidate this argument. In the course of the late war, when the weak parts of the Union were exposed, and many states were in the most deplorable situation by the enemy's ravages, the assistance of foreign nations was thought so urgently necessary for our protection, that the relinquishment of territorial advantages was not deemed too great a sacrifice for the acquisition of one ally. This expedient was admitted with great reluctance, even by those states who expected advantages from it. The crisis, however, at length arrived, when it was judged necessary for the salvation of this country to make certain cessions to Spain; whether wisely or otherwise is not for me to say; but the fact was, that instructions were sent to our representative at the court of Spain, to empower him to enter into negotiations for that purpose. How it terminated is well known. This fact shows the extremities to which nations will go in cases of imminent danger, and demonstrates the necessity of making ourselves more respectable. The necessity of making dangerous cessions, and of applying to foreign aid, ought to be excluded.

The honorable member then told us that there are heart-burnings in the adopting states, and that Virginia may, if she does not come into the measure, continue in amicable confederacy with the adopting states. I wish as seldom as possible to contradict the assertions of gentlemen; but I can venture to affirm, without danger of being in an error, that there is the most satisfactory evidence that the satisfaction of those states is increasing every day, and that, in that state where it was adopted only by a majority of nineteen, there is not one fifth of the people dissatisfied. There are some reasons which induce us to conclude that the grounds of proselytism extend every where; its principles begin to be better understood; and the inflammatory violence wherewith it was opposed by designing, illiberal, and unthinking minds, begins to subside. I will not enumerate the causes from which, in my conception, the heart-burnings of a majority of its opposers have originated. Suffice it to say, that in all they were founded on a misconception of its nature and tendency. Had it been candidly examined and fairly discussed, I believe, sir, that but a very inconsiderable minority of the people of the United States would have opposed it. With respect to the Swiss, whom the honorable gentleman has proposed for our example, as far as historical authority may be relied on, we shall find their government quite unworthy of our imitation. I am sure, if the honorable gentleman had adverted to their history and government, he never would have quoted their example here; he would have found that, instead of respecting the rights of mankind, their government (at least of several of their cantons) is one of the vilest aristocracies that ever was instituted: the peasants of some of their cantons are more oppressed and degraded than the subjects of any monarch in Europe; nay, almost as much so as those of any Eastern despot. It is a novelty in politics, that from the worst of systems the happiest consequences should ensue. Their aristocratical rigor, and the peculiarity of their situation, have so long supported their union: without the closest alliance and amity, dismemberment might follow; their powerful and ambitious neighbors would immediately avail themselves of their least jarrings. As we are not circumstanced like them, no conclusive precedent can be drawn from their situation. I trust the gentleman does not carry his idea so far as to recommend a separation from the adopting states. This government may secure our happiness; this is at least as probable as that it shall be oppressive. If eight states have, from a persuasion of its policy and utility, adopted it, shall Virginia shrink from it, without a full conviction of its danger and inutility? I hope she will never shrink from any duty; I trust she will not determine without the most serious reflection and deliberation.

I confess to you, sir, were uniformity of religion to be introduced by this system, it would, in my opinion, be ineligible; but I have no reason to conclude that uniformity of government will produce that of religion. This subject is, for the honor of America, perfectly free and unshackled. The government has no jurisdiction over it: the least reflection will convince us there is no danger to be feared on this ground.

But we are flattered with the probability of obtaining previous amendments. This calls for the most serious attention of this house. If amendments are to be proposed by one state, other states have the same right, and will also propose alterations. These cannot but be dissimilar, and opposite in their nature. I beg leave to remark, that the governments of the different states are in many respects dissimilar in their structure; their legislative bodies are not similar; their executive are more different. In several of the states, the first magistrate is elected by the people at large; in others, by joint ballot of the members of both branches of the legislature; and in others, in other different manners. This dissimilarity has occasioned a diversity of opinion on the theory of government, which will, without many reciprocal concessions, render a concurrence impossible. Although the appointment of an executive magistrate has not been thought destructive to the principles of democracy in many of the states, yet, in the course of the debate, we find objections made to the federal executive: it is urged that the President will degenerate into a tyrant. I intended, in compliance with the call of the honorable member, to explain the reasons of proposing this Constitution, and develop its principles; but I shall postpone my remarks till we hear the supplement which, he has informed us, he intends to add to what he has already said.

Give me leave to say something of the nature of the government, and to show that it is safe and just to vest it with the power of taxation. There are a number of opinions; but the principal question is, whether it be a federal or consolidated government. In order to judge properly of the question before us, we must consider it minutely in its principal parts. I conceive myself that it is of a mixed nature; it is in a manner unprecedented; we cannot find one express example in the experience of the world. It stands by itself. In some respects it is a government of a federal nature; in others, it is of a consolidated nature. Even if we attend to the manner in which the Constitution is investigated, ratified, and made the act of the people of America, I can say, notwithstanding what the honorable gentleman has alleged, that this government is not completely consolidated, nor is it entirely federal. Who are parties to it? The people—but not the people as composing one great body; but the people as composing thirteen sovereignties. Were it, as the gentleman asserts, a consolidated government, the assent of a majority of the people would be sufficient for its establishment; and, as a majority have adopted it already, the remaining states would be bound by the act of the majority, even if they unanimously reprobated it. Were it such a government as is suggested, it would be now binding on the people of this state, without having had the privilege of deliberating upon it. But, sir, no state is bound by it, as it is, without its own consent. Should all the states adopt it, it will be then a government established by the thirteen states of America, not through the intervention of the legislatures, but by the people at large. In this particular respect, the distinction between the existing and proposed governments is very material. The existing system has been derived from the dependent derivative authority of the legislatures of the states; whereas this is derived from the superior power of the people. If we look at the manner in which alterations are to be made in it, the same idea is, in some degree, attended to. By the new system, a majority of the states cannot introduce amendments; nor are all the states required for that purpose; three fourths of them must concur in alterations; in this there is a departure from the federal idea. The members to the national House of Representatives are to be chosen by the people at large, in proportion to the numbers in the respective districts. When we come to the Senate, its members are elected by the states in their equal and political capacity. But had the government been completely consolidated, the Senate would have been chosen by the people in their individual capacity, in the same manner as the members of the other house. Thus it is of a complicated nature; and this complication, I trust, will be found to exclude the evils of absolute consolidation, as well as of a mere confederacy. If Virginia was separated from all the states, her power and authority would extend to all cases: in like manner, were all powers vested in the general government, it would be a consolidated government; but the powers of the federal government are enumerated; it can only operate in certain cases; it has legislative powers on defined and limited objects, beyond which it cannot extend its jurisdiction.

But the honorable member has satirized, with peculiar acrimony, the powers given to the general government by this Constitution. I conceive that the first question on this subject is, whether these powers be necessary; if they be, we are reduced to the dilemma of either submitting to the inconvenience or losing the Union. Let us consider the most important of these reprobated powers; that of direct taxation is most generally objected to. With respect to the exigencies of government, there is no question but the most easy mode of providing for them will be adopted. When, therefore, direct taxes are not necessary, they will not be recurred to. It can be of little advantage to those in power to raise money in a manner oppressive to the people. To consult the conveniences of the people will cost them nothing, and in many respects will be advantageous to them. Direct taxes will only be recurred to for great purposes. What has brought on other nations those immense debts, under the pressure of which many of them labor? Not the expenses of their governments, but war. If this country should be engaged in war,—and I conceive we ought to provide for the possibility of such a case,—how would it be carried on? By the usual means provided from year to year? As our imports will be necessary for the expenses of government and other common exigencies, how are we to carry on the means of defence? How is it possible a war could be supported without money or credit? and would it be possible for a government to have credit without having the power of raising money? No; it would be impossible for any government, in such a case, to defend itself. Then, I say, sir, that it is necessary to establish funds for extraordinary exigencies, and to give this power to the general government; for the utter inutility of previous requisitions on the states is too well known. Would it be possible for those countries, whose finances and revenues are carried to the highest perfection, to carry on the operations of government on great emergencies, such as the maintenance of a war, without an uncontrolled power of raising money? Has it not been necessary for Great Britain, notwithstanding the facility of the collection of her taxes, to have recourse very often to this and other extraordinary methods of procuring money? Would not her public credit have been ruined, if it was known that her power to raise money was limited? Has not France been obliged, on great occasions, to use unusual means to raise funds? It has been the case in many countries, and no government can exist unless its powers extend to make provisions for every contingency. If we were actually attacked by a powerful nation, and our general government had not the power of raising money, but depended solely on requisitions, our condition would be truly deplorable: if the revenue of this commonwealth were to depend on twenty distinct authorities, it would be impossible for it to carry on its operations. This must be obvious to every member here; I think, therefore, that it is necessary, for the preservation of the Union, that this power shall be given to the general government.

But it is urged that its consolidated nature, joined to the power of direct taxation, will give it a tendency to destroy all subordinate authority; that its increasing influence will speedily enable it to absorb the state governments. I cannot think this will be the case. If the general government were wholly independent of the governments of the particular states, then, indeed, usurpation might be expected to the fullest extent. But, sir, on whom does this general government depend? It derives its authority from these governments, and from the same sources from which their authority is derived. The members of the federal government are taken from the same men from whom those of the state legislatures are taken. If we consider the mode in which the federal representatives will be chosen, we shall be convinced that the general will never destroy the individual governments; and this conviction must be strengthened by an attention to the construction of the

Senate. The representatives will be chosen probably under the influence of the members of the state legislatures; but there is not the least probability that the election of the latter will be influenced by the former. One hundred and sixty members represent this commonwealth in one branch of the legislature, are drawn from the people at large, and must ever possess more influence than the few men who will be elected to the general legislature. . . . Those who wish to become federal representatives must depend on their credit with that class of men who will be the most popular in their counties, who generally represent the people in the state governments; they can, therefore, never succeed in any measure contrary to the wishes of those on whom they depend. It is almost certain, therefore, that the deliberations of the members of the federal House of Representatives will be directed to the interest of the people of America. As to the other branch, the senators will be appointed by the legislatures; and, though elected for six years, I do not conceive they will so soon forget the source from whence they derive their political existence. This election of one branch of the federal by the state legislatures, secures an absolute dependence of the former on the latter. The biennial exclusion of one third will lessen the facility of a combination, and may put a stop to intrigues. I appeal to our past experience, whether they will attend to the interests of their constituent states. Have not those gentlemen, who have been honored with seats in Congress, *often signalized themselves by their attachment to their seats?* I wish this government may answer the expectation of its friends, and foil the apprehension of its enemies. I hope the patriotism of the people will continue, and be a sufficient guard to their liberties. I believe its tendency will be, that the state governments will counteract the general interest, and ultimately prevail. The number of the representatives is yet sufficient for our safety, and will gradually increase; and, if we consider their different sources of information, the number will not appear too small.

THE BASIS OF POLITICAL SOCIETY: A SPECTRUM OF VIEWS

How MUCH *popular government did the new nation require, how much could it tolerate? How far could the people be trusted to manage their political affairs so as to reconcile liberty with order and to secure both? Bothersome questions such as these—sometimes openly exposed, sometimes half-concealed—lie at the heart of much political discussion from the time of the Constitutional Convention to the present day.*

During pre-Civil War history individuals and political parties often divided sharply on the trustworthiness of the democratic thrust. Federalists inclined toward minority rule and looked to men of substance, accredited talent, and public virtue for energetic leadership in public councils. Fisher Ames, arch-Federalist orator from Boston, defined democracy as "A government by the passions of the multitude, or, no less correctly, according to the vices and ambitions of their leaders. . . ." In 1798, Timothy Dwight, President of Yale University, catalogued in a public address the sins of the French Jacobins, hinted darkly that the party of Jefferson was filled with blood-brothers of the revolutionists, and put these chilling questions:

Shall we, my brethren, become partakers of these sins? Shall we introduce them into our government, our schools, our families? Shall we become the disciples of Voltaire, and the dragoons of Marat; or our daughters the concubines of the Illuminati?

The rule of the Federalist party was short-lived, but its outlook was inherited by the Whig party, a conglomeration of conservatives who were forced to assume a popular guise in order to compete with the Democratic party during the era of Jackson. On many matters Jefferson's Republican party, which was later called the Democratic party, contested with their rivals over expedients. Then as now, interest blocs and not ideology were foremost in the struggle for power. Even so, the party of Jefferson and Jackson separated from the Federalist-Whig tradition on at least one fundamental value: it encouraged extensions in popular rule. The great impact of Jacksonian democracy in particular was to broaden the base of popular government and to promote the open society.

Public discussion on the basis of political society went on around pot-bellied stoves, in constitutional conventions, in legislative chambers, and from the platform. Often it was an outcropping of debate on practical devices of government. The contributions of Daggett, Jefferson, Webster, and Bancroft suggest variety in perspective and were part of a continuing discussion in various situations and accents.

In 1799 David Daggett, stanch new England Federalist, but more urbane than Ames or Dwight, tilted at the specter of Jeffersonian democracy, and alleged its unsubstantial Utopian idealism. Satirically, in the vein of Jonathan Swift, he sought to expose through his speech "Sun-Beams May Be Extracted from Cucumbers, But the Process Is Tedious" what he regarded as Jefferson's soft-headedness toward foreign intellectual influences, and to lay bare follies that were anathema to conservatives—wild experimentation, Deism, democracy, naive confidence in human reason, and sundry auguries. Daggett placed his faith in tradition as the keystone in the arch of the Republic.

But Daggett and his fellow Federalists could not stop

*the tide then running, and on March 4, 1801, Jefferson
replaced John Adams, the Federalist, and delivered the
first presidential inaugural address given at the new seat
of government in Washington. Jefferson openly declared
his faith in majority rule and free discussion as unqualified
principles of popular government. At the same time the
conciliatory tone of his remarks did much to prove that
Federalists had been terrorized by phantoms of their own
creation when they had represented him as a French
Jacobin thinly disguised and bent on revolution under
banners that flaunted doctrinaire slogans on the rights of
man.*

*Throughout the colonial and early national periods,
property tests for voting and office-holding were applied
as brakes on democracy. Increasingly such tests came
under attack by artisans and mechanics. Between 1810
and 1820, six states entered the Union with constitutions
that eliminated property qualifications for voting. One
by one the older states were forced to divest themselves
of property tests. In the Massachusetts Constitutional
Convention of 1820, radical delegates challenged provisions in the old Constitution that fixed the number
of representatives in the Senate on the basis of taxable
wealth in the districts rather than upon population. In
this setting, Daniel Webster, the great conservative, rose
to speak for property and the status quo. "Not indeed,"
said Webster, "that every man's power should be in exact
proportion to his property, but that, in a general sense,
and in a general form, property as such should have
its weight and influence in political arrangements." Webster's views did not prevail, but his speech, rooted in
political thought and experience, has remained one of
the most informed and cogent statements ever delivered
in a deliberative assembly on the inexorable relationships
between political society and the economic interests that
lie at the heart of it.*

Fifteen years later, George Bancroft, distinguished historian and political figure, spoke in a new key. In his "The Office of the People in Art, Government, and Religion," Bancroft challenged conservatives by insisting upon the superiority of the collective or "common mind" over that of either the individual or an elite, holding that "the best government rests on the people and not on the few, on persons and not on property, on the free development of public opinion and not on authority."

Views on man and his political society voiced by conservatives such as John Adams and Daniel Webster were shaped by the assumptions of economic realism. Those of George Bancroft were the product of emergent transcendental idealism fused with the more radical strains of Jacksonian democracy. Out of this fusion, Bancroft uttered his optimistic declaration in behalf of man's intellectual and moral capabilities for self-government. Spanning the decades, his encomium of a people's culture and government stirred the imagination of William Jennings Bryan, the first great popular leader of the Democratic party since Jackson. In his Memoirs Bryan urged young speakers seeking political careers to turn to Bancroft's address as the best introduction to the true spirit of democracy. The speaker who heeds Bancroft, advised Bryan, becomes the authentic voice of the people.[1]

---

[1] *The Memoirs of William Jennings Bryan* (Philadelphia: The John C. Winston Company, 1925), pp. 259–260.

Sun-Beams May Be Extracted from Cucumbers, But the Process Is Tedious

DAVID DAGGETT

> *Born, Attleborough, Massachusetts, December 31, 1764; died, New Haven, Connecticut, April 12, 1851. Member of the Connecticut legislature for many years. United States Senator from Connecticut, 1813–1819. Chief Justice of Connecticut Supreme Court. Professor of Law at Yale. Mayor of New Haven. Celebrated man of wit, of vigorous intellect and speech. His extant orations still communicate his lively polemical spirit.*

*H*istory informs us that at Lagado, in Laputa, there was a grand academy established, in which there was a display of much curious learning.

One artist, of a very philosophic taste, was racking his invention to make a pin-cushion out of piece of marble.

Another had formed an ingenious project to prevent the growth of wool upon two young lambs, by a composition of gums, minerals and vegetables, applied inwardly, and thus he hoped in a reasonable time to propagate the breed of naked sheep throughout the Kingdom.

A third had contrived a plan to entirely abolish words; and this was urged as a great advantage in point of health as well as brevity. For it is plain that every word we speak is an injury to our lungs, by corrosion, and consequently contributes to the shortening of our lives. An expedient was therefore offered, that since words were only names for things, it would be more convenient for all men to carry about them such things as were necessary to express the particular business on which they were to discourse.

An Oration Pronounced On the Fourth of July, 1799, At The Request of the Citizens of New-Haven, 2nd ed. (New Haven: Thomas Green and Son, 1799).

And the historian adds

. . . that he had often beheld two of these sages almost sinking under the weight of their packs, who when they met in the streets would lay down their loads, open their sacks, and hold conversation for an hour together; then put up their implements, help each other to resume their burdens, and take their leave.

A fourth appeared with sooty hands and face, his hair and beard long, ragged and singed in several places. His clothes, shirt and skin were all of the same colour. He had been eight years upon a project for extracting sun-beams out of cucumbers, which were to be put into vials, hermetically sealed, and let out to warm the air in raw inclement summers. He said he did not doubt but that in *eight years more* he should be able to supply the Governor's gardens with sunshine at a reasonable rate.

These Theorists were very patient, industrious and laborious in their pursuits—had a high reputation for their singular proficiency, and were regarded as prodigies in science. The common laborers and mechanics were esteemed a different race of beings, and were despised for their stupid and old-fashioned manner of acquiring property and character. If the enquiry had been made whether any of these projects had succeeded, it would have been readily answered that they had not; but that they were reasonable— their principles just—and of course, that they must ultimately produce the objects in view. Hitherto no piece of marble had been made into a pin-cushion, and few, very few sun-beams had been extracted from cucumbers, but what then? Are not all great and noble and valuable things accomplished with immense exertion, and with an expense of much time? If a farther enquiry had been made what would be the great excellence of marble pin-cushions, or the superior advantage of a breed of naked sheep, the answer would have been, it is unphilosophical to ask such questions.

In more modern times we have witnessed projects not unlike those of the learned of Laputa, above mentioned. A machine called an *Automaton,* was not long since constructed. This was designed to transport from place to place, by land, any load without the aid of horses, oxen, or any other animal. The master was to sit at helm, and guide it up hill and down, and over every kind of road. This machine was completed, and proved demonstrably capable of performing the duties assigned to it, and the only difficulty which attended it, and which hath hitherto prevented its universal use was, *that it would not go.*—Here, if any ignorant fellow had been so uncivil, he might have doubted why, if wood and iron were designed to go alone and carry a load, the whole herd of oxen, horses, and camels were created.

A few years ago the learned insisted that it was grovelling to travel either by *land* or *water,* but that the truly *philosophical* mode was to go by air. Hence, in all parts of the world speculatists were mounted in balloons, with the whole apparatus of living and dying, and were flying through the Heavens, to the utter astonishment and mortification of those poor illiterate wretches who were doomed to tug and sweat on the earth. To be sure this method of travelling was somewhat precarious.—A flaw of wind, regardless of the principles of this machine, might destroy it, or by the giving way of one *philosophical pin, peg or rope*, it might be let into the sea, or dashed against a rock, and thus its precious contents miserably perish. But doubtless reason will in time provide sufficient checks against all these casualties. Here again some "busy body in other men's matters" might ask, if it was intended that men should fly through the air, why were they not made with feathers and wings, and especially why are there so many who are justly called *heavy-moulded men?*

Another class of the literati of our age, scorning to travel either *on* the *sea*, or on the *land*, or in the *air*, have constructed a *submarine* boat or *diving machine*, by which they were constantly *groping* among shark, sturgeon and sea-horses. To say nothing of the hazard which these gentlemen encounter of running on rocks or shoals, or of being left in the lurch, on the bottom of the sea, by a leak, may we not wonder that they were not made with fins and scales, and may they not esteem themselves very fortunate that they have hitherto escaped being cut up to be made into oil?

These are a few among many modern inventions. All the principles of these various machines are capable of defence, and the inventors are all great, and learned, and ingenious men. Yet strange as it may seem, the stupid, foolish plodding people of this and other countries still keep their oxen and their horses—their carriages are still made as they were an hundred years ago, and our coasters will still go to New York on the surface of the Sound, instead of sinking to the bottom or rising into the clouds—and they still prefer a fair wind and tide to the greatest profusion of steam, produced in the most scientific manner.

[Daggett illustrates further from the fields of agriculture and medicine.]

. . . .

A more extensive field for the operation of these principles has been opened, in the new theories of the education of children. It has lately been discovered that the maxim, "Train up a child in the way he should go, and when he is old he will not depart from it," is an erroneous translation, and should read thus—"Let a child walk in his own way, and when he is old he will be perfect." Volumes have been written, and much time and labor expended, to shew that all reproof, restraint and correction, tend directly to extinguish the fire of genius, to cripple the faculties and enslave the understanding. Especially we are told (and the system of education now adopted in the Great Gallic nursery of arts is entirely on this plan) that the prejudices of education, and an inclination to imitate the example of parents and other ancestors, is the great bane of the peace, dignity and glory of young men, and that reason will conduct them, if not fettered with habits, to the perfection of human nature. Obedience to parents is expressly re-probated, and all the tyranny and despotism in the world ascribed to parental authority. This sentiment is explicitly avowed by Mr. Volney, who is the friend and associate of many distinguished men in the United States, and who has, in this opinion, shewed that Paul was a fool or knave when he said, "Children obey your parents in the Lord, for this is right."

If any person, groping in darkness, should object to these sentiments and enquire, how it is possible that children should become thus excellent if left entirely to themselves, when the experience of ages has been that with great and continued exertions, no such facts have existed, it may be replied, *the projector of Laputa had not been able in* EIGHT YEARS *to extract sun-beams from Cucumbers, but he was certain it would be done* IN EIGHT YEARS MORE.

We all recollect when these principles began to impress our Colleges—when it was seriously contended that the study of mathematics and natural philosophy was ruinous to the health, genius and character of a young gentle-man—that music and painting, and dancing and fencing, and *speaking French,* were the only accomplishments worth possessing; and that Latin and Greek were fitted only for stupid divines or black-letter-lawyers. An indispen-sable part of this *philosophical,* and *polite,* and *genteel* and *pretty* education was, to travel into foreign countries, and there reside long enough to forget all the early habits of life—to forget all domestic connexions—to forget the school-house where he was first taught his New England primer—to forget the old-fashioned meeting-house where he was first led to worship God, and especially to forget his native country, and to *remember* only, but remember always and effectually, that he was a polished cosmopolite, or citizen of the world.

The system of morals which has been reared by the care, anxiety and wis-dom of ages, has, in its turn, been assailed by these Theorists. The language of modern reformers to those who venerate ancient habits, ancient manners, ancient systems of morals and education, is, "O fools, when will ye be wise?" To first shake, and then destroy the faith of every man on these interesting subjects, has been attempted by many distinguished men, with an industry, labor and perseverance which deserved a better cause, and has been for many years a prime object of pursuit in that nation which has been the great hot-bed of premature and monstrous productions. To particularize on this subject would be impossible, but I cannot forbear to hint at a few of those doctrines now strenuously supported.

That men should love their children precisely according to their worth, and that if a neighbor's child be more deserving, it should be preferred.

That men are to regard the general good in all their conduct, and of course to break promises, contracts and engagements, or perform them, as will conduce to this object.

That to refuse to lend a sum of money, when possible, and when the applicant is in need of it, is an act equally criminal with theft or robbery, to the same amount.

If a difficulty should here be started, that men may judge erroneously as to the desert of a neighbor's child—the demands of the public as to the fulfilment of a promise, or the necessity for the loan in the case mentioned, the answer is ready, *reason*, mighty reason, will be an infallible guide. A plain old-fashioned man will say, this is indeed a beautiful system, but there appears one difficulty attending it, that is, it is made for a race of beings entirely different from men. Again, says he—Why for six thousand years the love of parents to children has been considered as the only tie by which families have been connected; and families have been considered as the strongest band and most powerful cement of society—destroy then this affection, and what better than miserable vagabonds will be the inhabitants of the earth?—This part of the project really strikes me, he adds, *like the attempt to propogate the breed of naked sheep*. Then again, it is quite doubtful whether parents of ordinary nerves can, at once, divest themselves of natural affection.—Indeed, there is a strong analogy between this part of the scheme, and *making a pin-cushion out of a piece of marble*.—But to the cosmopolite, who belongs nowhere, is connected with nobody, and who has been from his youth progressing to perfection, these sentiments are just, and the exercise of them quite feasible.

But these modern theories have appeared in their native beauty, and shone with the most resplendent lustre, in the science of politics. We are seriously told that men are to be governed only by reason. *Instruct* men and there will be an end of punishment. It is true, since the world began, not a family, a state or a nation has been, on these principles, protected; but this is because reason has not been properly exercised. The period now approaches when reason unfolds itself—one more *hot-bed* will mature it, and then behold the glorious harvest!

But it may be *stupidly* asked what shall be done in the mean time? Men are now *somewhat imperfect*—Theft, burglary, robbery and murder are now and then committed, and it will be some years before the perfection of human nature will shield us from these evils. This interregnum will be somewhat calamitous.—And also, is it certain that the commission of crimes has a tendency to refine and perfect the perpetrator? These questions never should be asked at the close of the eighteenth century.—They are manifestly too uncivil.

Again, say modern theories, men are all equal, and of course no *restraints* are imposed by society—no *distinctions* can exist, except to gratify the pride of the *ambitious*, the cruelty of the *despotic*. Hence it is the plain duty of every individual, to hasten the reign of liberty and equality. It is not a novel opinion, that men are by nature possessed of equal rights, and that "God hath made of one blood all nations of men to dwell on the face of the earth," but 'tis somewhat doubtful whether every man should be permitted to do as he pleases.—Such *liberty*, it may be said, is *unsafe* with men who are not perfect.—A cosmopolite, to be sure, will not abuse it, because he loves all mankind in an equal degree: but the expediency of the general principle may be questioned—any opinion of great and learned men in any wise, to the contrary notwithstanding.

If, however, by liberty and equality is intended the power of acting with as much freedom as is consistent with the public safety—and that each man has the same right to the protection of law as another, there is no controversy; but these terms, as now explained, advocated and adopted, mean the power of acting without any other restraint than reason, and the levelling all distinctions by right or wrong, and thus understood, they are of rather too suspicious a character for men of *ordinary talents* to admit.

But these principles extend still farther—their grasp is wider. They aim at the actual destruction of every government on earth.

Kings are the first object of their attack—then a nobility—then commons.

To prepare the way for the accomplishment of these objects, all former systems of thinking and acting must be annihilated, and the reign of reason firmly established.

But it will be enquired, where have these novel theories appeared? I answer—They have dawned upon New England—they have glowed in the southern states—they have burnt in France. We have seen a few projectors in Boats, Balloons and Automatons—A few philosophical farmers—A few attempts to propagate the breed of naked sheep—and we have at least one Philosopher in the United States, who has taken an accurate mensuration of the Mammoth's bones—made surprising discoveries in the doctrine of vibrating pendulums, and astonished the world with the precise gauge and dimensions of all the aboriginals in America.

But in France, for many years, these speculations in agriculture, the mechanic arts, education, morals and government, have been adopted and pursued. It is there declared and established by law, that ancient habits, customs and manners, modes of thinking, reasoning and acting, ought to be ridiculed, despised and rejected, for that a totally new order of things has taken place. All those rules of action which civilized nations have deemed necessary to their peace and happiness, have been declared *useless* or *arbitrary*, *unnecessary* or *unjust*. The most distinguished treatises on the laws of nations —treatises which have been considered as containing rules admirably adapted to the situation of different countries, and therefore of high authority, have not only been disregarded, but publicly contemned as musty, worm-eaten productions. Even that accomplished Cosmopolite, Mr. Genet, who came the messenger of *peace* and *science* to this guilty and deluded people, and who treated us precisely according to those assumed characters, opened his budget with an explicit renunciation of the principles of Puffendorf, Vattel, and other writers of that description, and declared that his nation would be governed by none of their obsolete maxims.

Indeed, this learned nation has yielded implicitly to the sentiments of Mr. Volney, Mr. Paine, and Mr. Godwin, in all questions of morals and policy; and in all matters of religion there is associated with them that learned and pious divine the Bishop of Autun [Talleyrand], who had the Cosmopolitism to boast that he had preached twenty years, under an oath, without believing a word which he uttered.

To aid the establishment of these projects, the credulity of the present age has become truly astonishing. There appears to be a new machinery for the mind, by which its capacity at believing certain things is perfect. It is believed that Socrates, and Plato and Seneca—Bacon, Newton and Locke, and all who lived and died prior to the commencement of the French Revolution, were either fools or slaves. That in no country but France is there *science* or *virtue*. That the body of the people in England are now groaning under the most oppressive bondage and tyranny. That this was precisely the case in Holland, Italy and Switzerland, till France introduced them to their present happy condition. It is believed by all the Cosmopolites in Europe, and by many in America—by all genuine Jacobins, by many Democrats, by the greater part of the readers of the *Aurora*, the *Argus* and the *Bee*, and by an innumerable multitude who don't read at all, that the citizens of these States, and particularly of New England, are miserable, benighted, enslaved and wretched dupes; and that the President and his adherents are in a firm league to injure and destroy them. That our members of Congress, and the heads of departments, are bribed with British gold, and are exerting all their faculties to forge chains for their posterity. That all in any way connected with the government are constantly plundering the Treasury—amassing wealth—becoming independent—and thus establishing an abominable, cruel, wicked, despotic and devilish aristocracy, which is to continually enlarge its grasp till it shall embrace all the valuable interests of America, and leave the people "destitute, afflicted, tormented." And finally, it is believed by many that John Adams has entered into copartnership with John Q. Adams, his son, now Minister at Berlin, for the express purpose of importing Monarchy, by wholesale, into this country. And to increase and perpetuate the stock of the house, that the son is to marry one of the daughters of the King of England.

If you enquire respecting the truth of these things, they cite Gallatin, Nicholas and Lyon—they quote from the *Aurora*, the *Argus* and the *Bee*; and who can doubt these sources of information, since the various publications, within a year past, respecting Connecticut, this City, and our College?

But it may be asked, where is your proof that the sentiments and theories which you have been describing, in fact, have an existence? Where is your proof, Sir, that the modern Literati are attempting to extract sun-beams from Cucumbers—to travel without exertion—to reap without sowing—to educate children to perfection—to introduce a new order of things as it respects *morals* and *politics, social* and *civil duties,* and to establish this strange species of credulity? I reply—those who have not yet become Cosmopolites need no proof. They have seen and heard and read these wild vagaries, and are therefore satisfied of their existence. As to the others, I have only to remark that this same new machinery of the mind, by which *certain* things are believed, necessarily, and by the plain axiom that action and reaction are equal, produces *absolute* incredulity as to certain other things, and of course *no testimony* will have any effect. Thus genuine Jacobins do not believe a word published in the *Spectator,* the *Connecticut Journal,* the *Connecticut Courant,* or the *Sentinel.* They do not believe that France has any intention to destroy the government of this country.—They do not believe that our ministers at Paris were treated with any neglect or contempt.—Indeed some doubt whether Mr. Pinckney ever was in France. They do not believe that Italy or Holland or Germany has ever been pillaged by the armies of the Republic, or that the path of those armies has been marked with any scenes of calamity and distress. In short, they do not believe but that the Directory, with their associates, are a benevolent society established in that regenerate country, for the great purpose of propagating religion and good government through the world; and that their armies are their missionaries to effect these glorious objects.

And now my Fellow-Citizens, let me ask, what effects have been produced by these theoretic, speculative and delusive principles? France has made an experiment with them. Under pretence of making men perfect—of establishing perfect liberty—perfect equality—and an entirely new order of things, she has become one great Bedlam, in which some of the inhabitants are falling into the water, some into the fire, some biting and gnashing themselves with their teeth, and others beholding these acts, are chanting "RIGHTS OF MAN! CA-IRA!"

With the pleasant but deceptive sounds of *Liberty* and *Rights* of *Man* on their tongues, they have made an open and violent war upon all the valuable interests of society.

Their own country, Italy, Belgium, Batavia and Switzerland, making together the fairest portion of Europe, have been despoiled by the arms of these reformers, and they are now plundering the wretched Arabs.

No place has been too sacred for them to defile—no right too dear for them to invade—no property too valuable for them to destroy.

. . . .

We have seen the treatment of the Republic towards other nations—we have experienced it towards ourselves. There is no man, except the slaves of the credulity or incredulity, which I have mentioned, who doubts but their wish and object is, to destroy our government and subject us entirely to their control.

They have robbed us on the sea, without law or pretence of law.

They have declared, by a legislative act, that they will treat us as we may be compelled to suffer other nations to treat us.

They have attempted to influence the election of our great officers, and particularly of President and Vice President.

They have, through their Ministers and other agents, been creating a party in this country which has once and again, threatened us with the horrors of a civil war, and which has smitten us with a disease worse than the plague.

From the day Mr. Genet landed on this Continent 'till the poisonous, debauching diplomatic intercourse between us and France was prohibited, French emissaries and American Jacobins have been constantly plotting and executing treasons against our government, which according to the laws of every well regulated society, would subject the authors to the punishment of death.

When we have complained, the Directory have, with the most pointed abuse or sullen contempt, rejected our complaints.

One minister has been refused an audience, and three were met with a mixture of the most foul and debasing intrigue.

They demand, in terms, that the speeches of the President should be accommodated to a Directorial ear. Yes, Americans! They demand that the speeches of your President, delivered at the opening of Congress in conformity to the Constitution, and in which it is his duty to declare the state of the Union, should be modified and accommodated to the ear of a *juggling* Directory.

And why this imperious conduct?—Why this insufferable insolence? Come thou MAGNANIMOUS REPUBLIC, "Shew thy strong reasons!"—Let us hear them!—

The *Republic is great! Terrible to its enemies!—Beneficent to its friends!* BENEFICENT TO REPUBLICANS! *Witness the blood and groans and universal desolation of Switzerland!* BLOOD AND GROANS AND DESOLATION ARE THE TROPHIES OF THY BENEFICENCE, THOU MAGNANIMOUS REPUBLIC.

But the Republic is *irresistible* to support the *rights of man!—She will cause the rights of man every where to be respected!—Rights of Man!* I am astonished that the utterance of those words *don't blister their tongues.* Since the combination against France was defeated, she has uniformly been the aggressor, and Europe has become one great slaughter-house. Within this period, it is computed that more than four millions of people have perished by the revolution, and this mighty destruction has been effected in ways, by means and under circumstances so afflicting and distressing, that 'tis hardly possible to conceive how four millions of people could have perished with more infamy to the Republic.

But the Directory proclaim, *Liberty* and *Equality*. *Liberty* and *Equality!*—Was the earth ever before insulted with such mockery!—The Directory, each of whom assumes a haughtiness, and appears with a pomp and splendor unequalled by any potentate in Europe, insult the world by the pretence of establishing *Liberty* and *Equality!*

But they "have opened prisons and bastiles, given freedom to the miserable captive, broken down the images of idolatry, and driven error and superstition from the earth." That they have unloosed bands is not denied—that they have destroyed the strongest ligaments by which individuals and societies were connected, is not denied, but that the cause of genuine liberty is promoted, I do deny. Is there a single country in Europe, in which their arms have triumphed, less oppressed, or less wretched now than ten years ago?

That they have driven men from one species of error and superstition to another, is agreed. But what consolation is it to the wretched worshippers of stones to forget these gods, and adore reason, fortitude and virtue?

If they found in Egypt those who were bowing down to *onions* and *leeks,* have they rendered them any essential service, by telling them henceforth to believe in the liberty and equality of man—in the perfectability of human nature, and in the eternal sleep of death? Paul, whose character they so heartily despise, acted a much more civil and kind (not to say Christian) part. He found an altar among the Athenians, inscribed "To the Unknown God;" and beholding their devotions, cried, "Whom therefore, ye ignorantly worship, him declare I unto you." Let the advocates for the reformation in religion, which this nation are effecting, compare the plain and unadorned account of Paul's God, with the address of the French Apostle, Buonaparte, to the ignorant Egyptians. "There is no God but God. He has no son or associate in his kingdom."

But 'tis said, these mighty events, which now astonish the world, are in exact conformity to the will of Heaven. What do the asserters of this proposition mean? That 'tis, in itself, right, and therefore agreeable to the will of Heaven, for one nation to destroy the government of another, be that government ever so bad?—If they mean this, I answer directly, the proposition is false. All writers on the laws of nations, without an exception, teach a directly opposite doctrine. Nay, this principle would place France above reproach.—It would give her the ground she has assumed, viz. That power is the only rule of action. This is her creed.—This her friends (I have once and again heard them) declare to be her standard. And what is this but a principle which has ever been the single rule of conduct in Hell!—

But 'tis said, these events tend directly to fulfil a great plan for the good of the Universe. Do these apologists for Frenchmen mean, that the Directory,

and their subordinates, are commissioned by God to destroy all the governments on earth? If they mean this, I beg them to shew, first, that they are the
privy counsellors of Heaven; and secondly, that such commissions have actually issued. But do they mean that these horrid acts of plunder, treachery
and murder are under the divine control, and therefore we must acquiesce
and rejoice? If they mean this, I congratulate them on their resignation, and
wish that it may increase, till it produces a spirit of reconciliation to our own
government. But is it a just principle, that we are to be thankful for all
events, because they are under the divine control? I think the friends of this
new theory should praise God for all the evil and misery which men commit,
and suffer, and they will be entitled, then, to the credit of being consistent.

But is it meant that these events WILL produce good, and therefore are
the subject of rejoicing?—Thunder and lightning, volcanos and earthquakes,
pestilence and famine, which *affrighten, astonish* and *destroy,* may produce
good! The fire and plague, of 1665 and 1666, which desolated the first city in
the world, probably have been followed with salutary consequences! But what
assembly ever yet seriously engaged in mutual congratulation, that the
pestilence was slaying its thousands, or that millions of old and young, innocent and guilty, were consumed by a conflagration, or swallowed up by an
earthquake?

. . . .

If many of our countrymen approve the measures of France, and applaud
them in their mad career of domination, I speak with confidence, the body of
our citizens entertain different opinions. Such will cordially join in protecting
our government, and in supporting an energetic administration. They will,
particularly as a mean to accomplish this object, and the only one I shall now
urge, discountenance that unparalleled abuse of all those to whom is entrusted
the management of our national interests, which is now so prevalent.

Not a man, tho' his private character were like tried gold, has escaped the
most malignant censure.—The President, each head of department, each
member of the Legislature, and every other man who supports the administration, is daily charged with the most vile and degrading crimes. They are
openly vilified, as parties to a conspiracy against the peace, the dignity, and
the happiness of the United States.

And who are these reformers, that exhibit these charges?—Are they the
virtuous, meek, unspotted and holy of the earth?

Who are these thus reproached? They are your neighbors, chosen to protect your interests.—What is their object? Wealth?—If so, they are miserably
employed. There is not a man among them who can, with the utmost
economy, secure as much money as hundreds of merchants, lawyers, physi-
cians, masters of vessels, and farmers, annually make by their various pursuits.

But alas! they wish to enslave us. Is this their character in private life? Have they not, with you, houses and lands, character and liberty to defend?—Have they not wives and children, whose happiness is near their hearts?—And do they, indeed, labour and toil to forge chains and fetters for their children, and children's children, that their names and memories may go down to future generations covered with the bitterest curses?

I have made these observations, my Fellow-Citizens, that we may, on this anniversary of our National existence, a day which I hope may be kept sacred to that solemn employment, contemplate the labours, the exertions and the characters of those venerable men who founded, and have hitherto, protected this nation. I wish them to be seen, and compared with the speculating theorists and mushroom politicians of this age of reason.

It is now less than two hundred years since the first settlement of white people was effected, in these United States; less than one hundred and eighty, since the first settlement was made in New England, and less than one hundred and seventy, since the first settlement was made in Connecticut. The place where we are now assembled was then a wild waste. Instead of cultivated fields, *dens and caves*. Instead of a flourishing city, *huts and wigwams*. Instead of polite, benevolent, and learned citizens, *a horde of savages*. Instead of a seat of science, full of young men qualifying to adorn and bless their country, here was only taught the art of tormenting *ingeniously*, and here were only heard the groans of the dying.

What is here said of New Haven may, with little variation, be said of all New England, and of many other parts of the United States.

We have now upwards of four millions of inhabitants, cultivating a fertile country, and engaged in a commerce, with 876,000 tons of shipping, and second only to that of Great Britain.

How has this mighty change been effected?—Was it by magic? By supernatural aid? Or was it by ingenious theories in morals, economics and government? My Fellow-Citizens, it was accomplished by the industry, the labour, the perseverance, the sufferings and virtues of those men from whom we glory in being descended.

These venerable men spent no time in extracting sun-beams from cucumbers—in writing letters to Mazzei, or perplexing the world with the jargon of the perfectability of human nature.

They and their illustrious descendants pursued directly, and by those means which always will succeed, for they always have succeeded, those which common sense dictates, the erection and support of good government and good morals. To effect these great objects they stood like monuments, with their wives, their children, and their lives in their hands.—They fought— they bled—they died.—At this expense of ease, happiness and life, they made establishments for posterity—they protected them against savages—they cemented them with their blood—they delivered them to us as a sacred deposit, and if we suffer them to be destroyed by the tinselled refinements of this age, we shall deserve the reproaches, with which impartial justice will cover such a pusillanimous race.

Look particularly at the various complaints, remonstrances and petitions made by these States, on various occasions, from the first settlement of this country to the 4th of July 1776, and compare them with the state papers of the great Republic. In the one you will see the plain, pointed language of injured innocence, demanding redress—in the other, the sly, wily, ambiguous, chameleon dialect of Jesuits, curiously wrought up to mean everything and nothing, by a set of mountebank politicians, headed by a perjured Bishop of Autun.

At this day there exist two parties in these United States. At the head of one are Washington, Adams and Ellsworth.—The object of this party is to protect and defend the government from that destruction with which they believe it threatened, by its enemies. To preserve and transmit to posterity those establishments which they believe important to the happiness of society.

At the head of the other, is the gentleman who drank toasts at Fredericksburgh in May 1798, in direct contempt of our government, who wrote the letter to Mazzei, with Gallatin and Nicholas, and *Lyon,* and to grace the company they shine, with the borrowed lustre of Talleyrand, that dissembler to God and Man. The object of this party is to destroy ancient systems— ancient habits—ancient customs—to introduce a new liberty, new equality, new rights of man, new modes of education, and a new order of things.

Let them meet and make a full, fair, and perfect exposition of their principles—their objects, and the means by which they are to be accomplished— And let there be present at this display, the departed spirits of Davenport, Hooker, Winthrop, Wolcott, Hopkins, Haynes and Heaton, and let there also appear a Lawrence, a Warren, a Mercer, and a Wooster, and to which of these parties would they give their blessing?—For which of these causes, if it were possible to bleed and die again in the cause of America, would the beloved WARREN AGAIN BLEED AND DIE?

First Inaugural Address

THOMAS JEFFERSON

*Born, Shadwell, Albemarle County, Virginia, April 13,
1743; died, Monticello, July 4, 1826. Graduate of William and Mary. Studied and practiced law. Member of
the House of Burgesses, 1769–1775. Delegate to the Continental Congress, 1775–1776; drafted the Declaration
of Independence. Served in the Virginia legislature from
1776–1779. Governor of Virginia, 1779–1781. Returned
to the Congress, 1783–1784. Minister to France, 1785–
1789; witnessed the outbreak of the French Revolution.
Washington's first Secretary of State until 1793, when he
resigned in protest to Hamiltonian policies. Vice-President under John Adams. Third President of United
States, 1801–1809. Founded University of Virginia, 1819.
Jefferson was a philosopher-statesman of the Enlightenment. His First Inaugural Address ranks among the foremost statements in this quadrennial tradition.*

Friends and Fellow-Citizens: Called upon to undertake the duties of the first executive office of our
country, I avail myself of the presence of that portion of my fellow-citizens
which is here assembled to express my grateful thanks for the favor with
which they have been pleased to look toward me, to declare a sincere
consciousness that the task is above my talents, and that I approach
it with those anxious and awful presentiments which the greatness of the
charge and the weakness of my powers so justly inspire. A rising nation,
spread over a wide and fruitful land, traversing all the seas with the rich

Washington, D.C., March 4, 1801. *Inaugural Addresses of the Presidents of the
United States,* House Document No. 540 (Washington: Government Printing Office,
1952), pp. 11–14.

productions of their industry, engaged in commerce with nations who feel power and forget right, advancing rapidly to destinies beyond the reach of mortal eye—when I contemplate these transcendent objects, and see the honor, the happiness, and the hopes of this beloved country committed to the issue and the auspices of this day, I shrink from the contemplation, and humble myself before the magnitude of the undertaking. Utterly, indeed, should I despair did not the presence of many whom I here see remind me that in the other high authorities provided by our Constitution I shall find resources of wisdom, of virtue, and of zeal on which to rely under all difficulties. To you, then, gentlemen, who are charged with the sovereign functions of legislation, and to those associated with you, I look with encouragement for that guidance and support which may enable us to steer with safety the vessel in which we are all embarked amidst the conflicting elements of a troubled world.

During the contest of opinion through which we have passed the animation of discussions and of exertions has sometimes worn an aspect which might impose on strangers unused to think freely and to speak and to write what they think; but this being now decided by the voice of the nation, announced according to the rules of the Constitution, all will, of course, arrange themselves under the will of the law, and unite in common efforts for the common good. All, too, will bear in mind this sacred principle, that though the will of the majority is in all cases to prevail, that will to be rightful must be reasonable; that the minority possesses their equal rights, which equal law must protect, and to violate would be oppression. Let us, then, fellow-citizens, unite with one heart and one mind. Let us restore to social intercourse that harmony and affection without which liberty and even life itself are but dreary things. And let us reflect that, having banished from our land that religious intolerance under which mankind so long bled and suffered, we have yet gained little if we countenance a political intolerance as despotic, as wicked, and capable of as bitter and bloody persecutions. During the throes and convulsions of the ancient world, during the agonizing spasms of infuriated man, seeking through blood and slaughter his long-lost liberty, it was not wonderful that the agitation of the billows should reach even this distant and peaceful shore; that this should be more felt and feared by some and less by others, and should divide opinions as to measures of safety. But every difference of opinion is not a difference of principle. We have called by different names brethren of the same principle. We are all Republicans, we are all Federalists. If there be any among us who would wish to dissolve this Union or to change its republican form, let them stand undisturbed as monuments of the safety with which error of opinion may be tolerated where reason is left free to combat it. I know, indeed, that some honest men fear that a republican government can not be strong, that this Government is not strong enough;

but would the honest patriot, in the full tide of successful experiment, abandon a government which has so far kept us free and firm on the theoretic and visionary fear that this Government, the world's best hope, may by possibility want energy to preserve itself? I trust not. I believe this, on the contrary, the strongest Government on earth. I believe it the only one where every man, at the call of the law, would fly to the standard of the law, and would meet invasions of the public order as his own personal concern. Sometimes it is said that man can not be trusted with the government of himself. Can he, then, be trusted with the government of others? Or have we found angels in the forms of kings to govern him? Let history answer this question.

Let us, then, with courage and confidence pursue our own Federal and Republican principles, our attachment to union and representative government. Kindly separated by nature and a wide ocean from the exterminating havoc of one quarter of the globe; too high-minded to endure the degradations of the others; possessing a chosen country, with room enough for our descendents to the hundredth and thousandth generation; entertaining a due sense of our equal right to the use of our own faculties, to the acquisitions of our own industry, to honor and confidence from our fellow-citizens, resulting not from birth, but from our actions and their sense of them; enlightened by a benign religion, professed, indeed, and practiced in various forms, yet all of them inculcating honesty, truth, temperance, gratitude, and the love of man; acknowledging and adoring an overruling Providence, which by all its dispensations proves that it delights in the happiness of man here and his greater happiness hereafter—with all these blessings, what more is necessary to make us a happy and a prosperous people? Still one thing more, fellow-citizens—a wise and frugal Government, which shall restrain men from injuring one another, shall leave them otherwise free to regulate their own pursuits of industry and improvement, and shall not take from the mouth of labor the bread it has earned. This is the sum of good government, and this is necessary to close the circle of our felicities.

About to enter, fellow-citizens, on the exercise of duties which comprehend everything dear and valuable to you, it is proper you should understand what I deem the essential principles of our Government, and consequently those which ought to shape its Administration. I will compress them within the narrowest compass they will bear, stating the general principle, but not all its limitations. Equal and exact justice to all men, of whatever state or persuasion, religious or political; peace, commerce, and honest friendship with all nations, entangling alliances with none; the support of the State governments in all their rights, as the most competent administrations for our domestic concerns and the surest bulwarks against antirepublican tendencies; the preservation of the General Government in its whole constitutional vigor, as the sheet anchor of our peace at home and safety abroad; a jealous care of the right of election by the people—a mild and safe corrective of abuses which are lopped by the sword of revolution where peaceable remedies are unprovided; absolute acquiescence in the decisions of the majority, the vital principle of republics, from which is no appeal but to force, the vital principle and immediate parent of despotism; a well-disciplined militia, our best reliance in peace and for the first moments of war, till regulars may relieve them; the supremacy of the civil over the military authority; economy in the public expense, that labor may be lightly burthened; the honest payment of our debts and sacred preservation of the public faith; encouragement of agriculture, and of commerce as its handmaid; the diffusion of information and arraignment of all abuses at the bar of the public reason; freedom of religion; freedom of the press, and freedom of person under the protection of the habeas corpus, and trial by juries impartially selected. These principles form the bright constellation which has gone before us and guided our steps through an age of revolution and reformation. The wisdom of our sages and blood of our heroes have been devoted to their attainment. They should be the creed of our political faith, the text of civic instruction, the touchstone by which to try the services of those we trust; and should we wander from them in moments of error or of alarm, let us hasten to retrace our steps and to regain the road which alone leads to peace, liberty, and safety.

I repair, then, fellow-citizens, to the post you have assigned me. With experience enough in subordinate offices to have seen the difficulties of this the greatest of all, I have learnt to expect that it will rarely fall to the lot of imperfect man to retire from this station with the reputation and the favor which bring him into it. Without pretentions to that high confidence you reposed in our first and greatest revolutionary character, whose preeminent services had entitled him to the first place in his country's love and destined for him the fairest page in the volume of faithful history, I ask so much confidence only as may give firmness and effect to the legal administration of your affairs. I shall often go wrong through defect of judgment. When right, I shall often be thought wrong by those whose positions will not command a view of all the whole ground. I ask your indulgence for my own errors, which will never be intentional, and your support against the errors of others, who may condemn what they would not if seen in all its parts. The approbation implied by your suffrage is a great consolation to me for the past, and my future solicitude will be to retain the good opinion of those who have bestowed it in advance, to conciliate that of others by doing them all the good in my power, and to be instrumental to the happiness and freedom of all.

Relying, then, on the patronage of your good will, I advance with obedience to the work, ready to retire from it whenever you become sensible how much better choice it is in your power to make. And may that Infinite Power which rules the destinies of the universe lead our councils to what is best, and give them a favorable issue for your peace and prosperity.

Basis of the Senate

DANIEL WEBSTER

*Born, Salisbury, New Hampshire, January 18, 1782;
died, Marshfield, Massachusetts, October 24, 1852.
Graduate of Dartmouth College. Studied law in Boston,
practiced in New Hampshire until 1816, when he moved
to Boston. A Federalist, he served New Hampshire in
United States House of Representatives, 1812–1816. After
1816 he became a foremost constitutional lawyer and
an orator of national rank. Sent to Congress from Massachusetts in 1823 and to United States Senate, 1827. In
1836 and 1840 he sought unsuccessfully the Whig
nomination for the Presidency. Secretary of State in the
Harrison-Tyler administrations until 1843. Served in
United States Senate, 1844–1850. Secretary of State,
1850–1852. Webster's political career is identified with
the conservative tradition and political parties, supremacy
of the federal Constitution, and national unity; his greatest
orations are expressive of these commitments.*

I know not, Sir, whether it be probable that any opinions
or votes of mine are ever likely to be of more permanent importance, than those which I may give in the discharge of my
duties in this body. And of the questions which may arise here, I anticipate
no one of greater consequence than the present. I ask leave, therefore, to submit a few remarks to the consideration of the committee.

Massachusetts Constitutional Convention, December 15, 1820, on the resolution
to divide the Commonwealth into districts for choosing Senators according to population. *The Works of Daniel Webster*, 13th ed. (Boston: Little, Brown and Company, 1864), III, pp. 8–25.

The subject before us is the manner of constituting the legislative department of government. We have already decided that the legislative power shall exist as it has heretofore existed, in two separate and distinct branches, a Senate and a House of Representatives. We propose also, at least I have heard no intimation of a contrary opinion, that these branches shall, in form, possess a negative on each other. I presume I may also take it for granted, that the members of both these houses are to be chosen annually. The immediate question now under discussion is, In what manner shall the senators be elected? They are to be chosen in districts; but shall they be chosen in proportion to the number of inhabitants in each district, or in proportion to the taxable property of each district, or, in other words, in proportion to the part which each district bears in the public burdens of the State? The latter is the existing provision of the constitution; and to this I give my support.

The resolution of the honorable member from Roxbury proposes to divide the State into certain legislative districts, and to choose a given number of senators, and a given number of representatives, in each district, in proportion to population. This I understand. It is a simple and plain system. The honorable member from Pittsfield and the honorable member from Worcester support the first part of this proposition, that is to say, that part which provides for the choice of senators according to population, without explaining entirely their views as to the latter part, relative to the choice of representatives. They insist that the questions are distinct, and capable of a separate consideration and decision. I confess myself, Sir, unable to view the subject in that light. It seems to me, there is an essential propriety in considering the questions together; and in forming our opinions of them, as parts respectively of one legislative system. The legislature is one great machine of government, not two machines. The two houses are its parts, and its utility will, as it seems to me, depend not merely on the materials of these parts, or their separate construction, but on their accommodation, also, and adaptation to each other. Their balanced and regulated movement, when united, is that which is expected to insure safety to the State; and who can give any opinion on this, without first seeing the construction of both, and considering how they are formed and arranged with respect to their mutual relation? I cannot imagine, therefore, how the member from Worcester should think it uncandid to inquire of him, since he supports this mode of choosing senators, what mode he proposes for the choice of representatives.

It has been said that the constitution, as it now stands, gives more than an equal and proper number of senators to the county of Suffolk. I hope I may be thought to contend for the general principle, without being influenced by any regard to its local application. I do not inquire whether the senators whom this principle brings into the government will come from the county of Suffolk, from the valley of Housatonic, or the extremity of Cape

Cod. I wish to look only to the principle; and as I believe that to be sound and salutary, I shall give my vote in favor of maintaining it.

In my opinion, Sir, there are two questions before the committee. The first is, Shall the legislative department be constructed with any other *check* than such as arises simply from dividing the members of this department into two houses? The second is, If such other and further check ought to exist, *in what manner* shall it be created?

If the two houses are to be chosen in the manner proposed by the resolutions of the member from Roxbury, there is obviously no other check or control than a division into separate chambers. The members of both houses are to be chosen at the same time, by the same electors, in the same districts, and for the same term of office. They will of course all be actuated by the same feelings and interests. Whatever motives may at the moment exist to elect particular members of one house, will operate equally on the choice of the members of the other. There is so little of real utility in this mode, that, if nothing more be done, it would be more expedient to choose all the members of the legislature, without distinction, simply as members of the legislature, and to make the division into two houses, either by lot or otherwise, after these members thus chosen should have come up to the capital.

I understand the reason of checks and balances, in the legislative power, to arise from the truth, that, in representative governments, that department is the leading and predominating power; and if its will may be at any time suddenly and hastily expressed, there is great danger that it may overthrow all other powers. Legislative bodies naturally feel strong, because they are numerous, and because they consider themselves as the immediate representatives of the people. They depend on public opinion to sustain their measures, and they undoubtedly possess great means of influencing public opinion. With all the guards which can be raised by constitutional provisions, we are not likely to be too well secured against cases of improper, or hasty, or intemperate legislation. It may be observed, also, that the executive power, so uniformly the object of jealousy to republics, has in the States of this Union been deprived of the greater part both of its importance and its splendor, by the establishment of the general government. While the States possessed the power of making war and peace, and maintained military forces by their own authority, the power of the State executives was very considerable and respectable. It might then even be an object, in some cases, of a just and warrantable jealousy. But a great change has been wrought. The care of foreign relations, the maintenance of armies and navies, and their command and control, have devolved on another government. Even the power of appointment, so exclusively, one would think, an executive power, is, in very many of the States, held or controlled by the legislature; that department either making the principal appointments itself, or else surrounding the chief executive magistrate with a council of its own election, possessing a negative upon his nominations.

Nor has it been found easy, nor in all cases possible, to preserve the judicial department from the progress of legislative encroachment. Indeed, in some of the States, all judges are appointed by the legislature; in others, although appointed by the executive, they are removable at the pleasure of the legislature. In all, the provision for their maintenance is necessarily to be made by the legislature. As if Montesquieu had never demonstrated the necessity of separating the departments of governments; as if Mr. Adams had not done the same thing, with equal ability, and more clearness, in his Defence of the American Constitutions; as if the sentiments of Mr. Hamilton and Mr. Madison were already forgotten; we see, all around us, a tendency to extend the legislative power over the proper sphere of the other departments. And as the legislature, from the very nature of things, is the most powerful department, it becomes necessary to provide, in the mode of forming it, some check which shall insure deliberation and caution in its measures. If all legislative power rested in one house, it is very problematical whether any proper independence could be given, either to the executive or the judiciary. Experience does not speak encouragingly on that point. If we look through the several constitutions of the States, we shall perceive that generally the departments are most distinct and independent where the legislature is composed of two houses, with equal authority, and mutual checks. If all legislative power be in one popular body, all other power, sooner or later, will be there also.

I wish, now, Sir, to correct a most important mistake in the manner in which this question has been stated. It has been said, that we propose to give to property, merely as such, a control over the people, numerically considered. But this I take not to be at all the true nature of the proposition. The Senate is not to be a check on the people, but on the House of Representatives. It is the case of an authority, given to one agent, to check or control the acts of another. The people, having conferred on the House of Representatives powers which are great, and, from their nature, liable to abuse, require, for their own security, another house, which shall possess an effectual negative on the first. This does not limit the power of the people; but only the authority of their agents. It is not a restraint on their rights, but a restraint on that power which they have delegated. It limits the authority of agents in making laws to bind their principals. And if it be wise to give one agent the power of checking or controlling another, it is equally wise, most manifestly, that there should be some difference of character, sentiment, feeling, or origin in that agent who is to possess this control. Otherwise, it is not at all probable that the control will ever be exercised. To require the consent of two agents to the validity of an act, and yet to appoint agents so similar, in all respects, as to create a moral certainty that what one does the other will do also, would be inconsistent, and nugatory. There can be no effectual control, without some difference of origin, or character, or interest, or feeling, or sentiment. And the great question in this country has been, where to find, or how to create, this difference, in governments entirely elective and popular.

Various modes have been attempted in various States. In some, a difference of qualification has been required in the persons to be elected. This obviously produces little or no effect. All property qualification, even the highest, is so low, as to produce no exclusion, to any extent, in any of the States. A difference of age in the persons elected is sometimes required; but this is found to be equally unimportant. Neither has it happened, that any consideration of the relative rank of the members of the two houses has had much effect on the character of their constituent members. Both in the State governments, and in the United States government, we daily see persons elected into the House of Representatives who have been members of the Senate. Public opinion does not attach so much weight and importance to the distinction, as to lead individuals greatly to regard it. In some of the States, a different sort of qualification in the electors is required for the two houses; and this is probably the most proper and efficient check. But such has not been the provision in this Commonwealth, and there are strong objections to introducing it. In other cases, again, there is a double election for senators; electors being first chosen, who elect senators. Such is the case in Maryland, where the senators are elected for five years, by electors appointed in equal numbers by the counties; a mode of election not unlike that of choosing representatives in the British Parliament for the boroughs of Scotland. In this State, the qualification of the voters is the same for the two houses, and there is no essential difference in that of the persons chosen. But, in apportioning the Senate to the different districts of the State, the present constitution assigns to each district a number proportioned to its public taxes. Whether this be the best mode of producing a difference in the construction of the two houses, is not now the question; but the question is, whether this be better than no mode.

The gentleman from Roxbury called for authority on this subject. He asked, what writer of reputation had approved the principle for which we contend. I should hope, Sir, that, even if this call could not be answered, it would not necessarily follow that the principle should be expunged. Governments are instituted for practical benefit, not for subjects of speculative reasoning merely. The best authority for the support of a particular principle or provision in government is experience; and of all experience, our own, if it have been long enough to give the principle a fair trial, should be most decisive. This provision has existed for forty years, and while so many gentlemen contend that it is wrong in theory, no one has shown that it has been either injurious or inconvenient in practice. No one pretends that it has caused a bad law to be enacted, or a good one to be rejected. To call on us, then, to strike out this provision, because we should be able to find no authority for it in any book on government, would seem to be like requiring a mechanic to abandon the use of an implement, which had always answered all the purposes designed by it, because he could find no model of it in the patent-office.

But, Sir, I take the *principle* to be well established, by writers of the greatest authority. In the first place, those who have treated of natural law have maintained, as a principle of that law, that, as far as the object of society is the protection of something in which the members possess unequal shares, it is just that the weight of each person in the common councils should bear a relation and proportion to his interest. Such is the sentiment of Grotius, and he refers, in support of it, to several institutions among the ancient states.

Those authors who have written more particularly on the subject of political institutions have, many of them, maintained similar sentiments. Not, indeed, that every man's power should be in exact proportion to his property, but that, in a general sense, and in a general form, property, as such, should have its weight and influence in political arrangement. Montesquieu speaks with approbation of the early Roman regulation, made by Servius Tullius, by which the people were distributed into classes, according to their property, and the public burdens apportioned to each individual according to the degree of power which he possessed in the government. By this regulation, he observes, some bore with the greatness of their tax because of their proportionable participation in power and credit; others consoled themselves for the smallness of their power and credit by the smallness of their tax. One of the most ingenious of political writers is Mr. Harrington, an author not now read so much as he deserves. It is his leading object, in his Oceana, to prove, that power *naturally* and *necessarily* follows property. He maintains that a government founded on property is legitimately founded; and that a government founded on the disregard of property is founded in injustice, and can only be maintained by military force. "If one man," says he, "be sole landlord, like the Grand Seignior, his empire is absolute. If a few possess the land, this makes the Gothic or feudal constitution. If the *whole people* be landlords, then is it a commonwealth." "It is strange," says an ingenious person in the last century, "that Harrington should be the first man to find out so evident and demonstrable a truth as that of property being the true basis and *measure* of power." In truth, he was not the first. The idea is as old as political science itself. It may be found in

Aristotle, Lord Bacon, Sir Walter Raleigh, and other writers. Harrington seems, however, to be the first writer who has illustrated and expanded the principle, and given to it the effect and prominence which justly belong to it. To this sentiment, Sir, I entirely agree. It seems to me to be plain, that, in the absence of military force, political power naturally and necessarily goes into the hands which hold the property. In my judgment, therefore, a republican form of government rests, not more on political constitutions, than on those laws which regulate the descent and transmission of property.

If the nature of our institutions be to found government on property, and that it should look to those who hold property for its protection, it is entirely just that property should have its due weight and consideration in political arrangements. Life and personal liberty are no doubt to be protected by law; but property is also to be protected by law, and is the fund out of which the means for protecting life and liberty are usually furnished. We have no experience that teaches us that any other rights are safe where property is not safe. Confiscation and plunder are generally, in revolutionary commotions, not far before banishment, imprisonment, and death. It would be monstrous to give even the name of government to any association in which the rights of property should not be completely secured. The disastrous revolutions which the world has witnessed, those political thunder-storms and earthquakes which have shaken the pillars of society to their very deepest foundations, have been revolutions against property. Since the honorable member from Quincy* has alluded on this occasion to the history of the ancient states, it would be presumption in me to dwell upon it. It may be truly said, however, I think, that Rome herself is an example of the mischievous influence of the popular power when disconnected with property and in a corrupt age. It is true the arm of Caesar prostrated her liberty; but Caesar found his support within her very walls. Those who were profligate and necessitous, and factious and desperate, and capable, therefore, of being influenced by bribes and largesses, which were distributed with the utmost prodigality, outnumbered and outvoted, in the tribes and centuries, the substantial, sober, prudent, and faithful citizens. Property was in the hands of one description of men, and power in those of another; and the balance of the constitution was destroyed. Let it never be forgotten that it was the popular magistrates, elevated to office where the bad outnumbered the good,—where those who had not a stake in the commonwealth, by clamor and noise and numbers, drowned the voice of those who had,— that laid the neck of Rome at the feet of her conqueror. When Caesar, manifesting a disposition to march his army against the capital, approached that little stream which has become so memorable from its association with his history, a decree was proposed in the Senate declaring him a public

* Ex-President Adams.

enemy if he did not disband his troops. To this decree the popular tribunes, the sworn protectors of the people, interposed their negative; and thus opened the high road to Rome, and the gates of the city herself, to the approach of her conqueror.

The English Revolution of 1688 was a revolution in favor of property, as well as of other rights. It was brought about by the men of property for their security; and our own immortal Revolution was undertaken, not to shake or plunder property, but to protect it. The acts of which the country complained were such as violated rights of property. An immense majority of all those who had an interest in the soil were in favor of the Revolution; and they carried it through, looking to its results for the security of their possessions. It was the property of the frugal yeomanry of New England, hard earned, but freely given, that enabled her to act her proper part and perform her full duty in achieving the independence of the country.

I would not be thought, Mr. Chairman, to be among those who underrate the value of military service. My heart beats, I trust, as responsive as any one's, to a soldier's claim for honor and renown. It has ever been my opinion, however, that while celebrating the military achievements of our country-men in the Revolutionary contest, we have not always done equal justice to the merits and the sufferings of those who sustained, on their property, and on their means of subsistence, the great burden of the war. Any one, who has had occasion to be acquainted with the records of the New England towns, knows well how to estimate those merits and those sufferings. Nobler records of patriotism exist nowhere. Nowhere can there be found higher proofs of a spirit that was ready to hazard all, to pledge all, to sacrifice all, in the cause of the country. Instances were not infrequent, in which small freeholders parted with their last hoof, and the last measure of corn from their granaries, to supply provisions for the troops, and hire service for the ranks. The voice of Otis and of Adams in Faneuil Hall found its full and true echo in the little councils of the interior towns; and if within the Continental Congress patriotism shone more conspicuously, it did not there exist more truly, nor burn more fervently; it did not render the day more anxious, or the night more sleepless; it sent up no more ardent prayer to God, for succor; and it put forth in no greater degree the fulness of its effort, and the energy of its whole soul and spirit, in the common cause, than it did in the small assemblies of the town. I cannot, therefore, Sir, agree that it is in favor of society, or in favor of the people, to constitute government with an entire disregard to those who bear the public burdens in times of great exigency. This question has been argued as if it were proposed only to give an advantage to a few rich men. I do not so understand it. I consider it as giving property, generally, a representation in the Senate, both because it is just that it should have such representation, and because it is a convenient mode of providing that *check* which the constitution of the legislature requires. I do not say that such check might not be found in some other provision; but this is the provision already established, and it is, in my opinion, a just and proper one.

I will beg leave to ask, Sir, whether property may not be said to deserve this portion of respect and power in the government? It pays, at this moment, I think, five sixths of all the public taxes; one sixth only being raised on persons. Not only, Sir, do these taxes support those burdens which all governments require, but we have, in New England, from early times held property to be subject to another great public use; I mean the support of schools. Sir, property, and the power which the law exercises over it for the purpose of instruction, are the basis of the system. It is entitled to the respect and protection of government, because, in a very vital respect, it aids and sustains government. The honorable member from Worcester, in contending for the admission of the mere popular principle in all branches of the government, told us that our system rested on the intelligence of the community. He told us truly. But allow me, Sir, to ask the honorable gentleman, what, but property, supplies the means of that intelligence? What living fountain feeds this ever-flowing, ever-refreshing, ever-fertilizing stream of public instruction and general intelligence? If we take away from the towns the power of assessing taxes on property, will the school-houses remain open? If we deny to the poor the benefit which they now derive from the property of the rich, will their children remain on their forms, or will they not, rather, be in the streets, in idleness and in vice?

I might ask again, Sir, how is it with religious instruction? Do not the towns and parishes raise money by vote of the majority, assessed on property, for the maintenance of religious worship? Are not the poor as well as the rich benefited by the means of attending on public worship, and do they not equally with the rich possess a voice and vote in the choice of the minister, and in all other parish concerns? Does any man, Sir, wish to try the experiment of striking out of the constitution the regard which it has hitherto maintained for property, and of foregoing also the extraordinary benefit which society among us for near two centuries has derived from laying the burden of religious and literary instruction of all classes upon property? Does any man wish to see those only worshipping God who are able to build churches and maintain ministers for themselves, and those children only educated whose parents possess the means of educating them? Sir, it is as unwise as it is unjust to make property an object of jealousy. Instead of being, in any just sense, a popular course, such a course would be most injurious and destructive to the best interests of the people. The nature of our laws sufficiently secures us against any dangerous accumulations; and, used and diffused as we have it, the whole operation of property is in the highest degree useful, both to the rich and to the poor. I rejoice, Sir, that every man in this community may call all property his own, so far as he has occasion for it, to furnish for himself and his children the blessings of religious instruction and the elements of knowledge. This heavenly and this earthly light he is entitled to by the fundamental laws. It is every poor man's undoubted birthright, it is the great blessing which this constitution has secured to him, it is his solace in life, and it may well be his consolation in death, that his country stands pledged, by the faith which it has plighted to all its citizens, to protect his children from ignorance, barbarism, and vice.

I will now proceed to ask, Sir, whether we have not seen, and whether we do not at this moment see, the advantage and benefit of giving security to property, by this and all other reasonable and just provisions. The constitution has stood on its present basis forty years. Let me ask, What State has been more distinguished for wise and wholesome legislation? I speak, Sir, without the partiality of a native, and also without intending the compliment of a stranger; and I ask, What example have we had of better legislation? No violent measures affecting property have been attempted. Stop laws, suspension laws, tender laws, all the tribe of these arbitrary and tyrannical interferences between creditor and debtor, which, wheresoever practiced, generally end in the ruin of both, are strangers to our statute-book. An upright and intelligent judiciary has come in aid of wholesome legislation; and general security for public and private rights has been the result. I do not say that this is peculiar, I do not say that others have not done as well. It is enough that, in these respects, we shall be satisfied that we are not behind our neighbors. No doubt, Sir, there are benefits of every kind, and of great value, in an organization of government, both in legislative and judicial administration, which well secures the rights of property; and we should find it so, by unfortunate experience, should that character be lost. There are millions of personal property now in this Commonwealth which are easily transferable, and would be instantly transferred elsewhere, if any doubt existed of its entire security. I do not know how much of this stability of government, and of the general respect for it, may be fairly imputed to this particular mode of organizing the Senate. It has, no doubt, had some effect. It indicates a respect for the rights of property, and may have operated on opinion as well as upon measures. Now to strike out and obliterate it, as it seems to me, would be in a high degree unwise and improper.

As to the *right* of apportioning senators upon this principle, I do not understand how there can be a question about it. All government is a modification of general principles and general truths, with a view to practical utility. Personal liberty, for instance, is a clear right, and is to be provided for; but it is not a clearer right than the right of property, though it may be more important. It is, therefore, entitled to protection. But property is also to be protected; and when it is remembered how great a portion of the people of this State possess property, I cannot understand how its protection or its influence is hostile to their rights and privileges. For these reasons, Sir, I am in favor of maintaining that check, in the constitution of the legislature, which has so long existed there.

[In the remainder of his speech—less than one-third of the text—Webster deals primarily with local issues as they bear on the resolution before the convention.]

The Office of the People in Art, Government, and Religion

GEORGE BANCROFT

Born, Worcester, Massachusetts, October 3, 1800; died,
Washington, D.C., January 17, 1891. Graduated from
Harvard University, received a Ph.D. degree from the
University of Göttingen. Teacher and author of 10-volume
History of the United States. An active Jacksonian
Democrat, he was an unsuccessful candidate for the
governorship of Massachusetts. Secretary of Navy,
1845–1846. United States Minister to Great Britain,
1846–1849; United States Minister to Germany, 1867–
1874. Throughout his years of public service, he was
tireless in his research, writing, and public speaking.

I

*T*he material world does not change in its masses or in its powers. The stars shine with no more lustre than when they first sang together in the glory of their birth. The flowers that gemmed the fields and the forests, before America was discovered, now bloom around us in their season. The sun that shone on Homer shines on us in unchanging lustre. The bow that beamed on the patriarch still glitters in the clouds. Nature is the same. For her no new forces are generated; no new capacities are discovered. The earth turns on its axis, and perfects its revolutions, and renews its seasons, without increase or advancement.

The Adelphi Society, Williamstown College, August [?], 1835. George Bancroft, *Literary and Historical Miscellanies* (New York: Harper & Brothers, 1855), pp. 408–435.

But a like passive destiny does not attach to the inhabitants of the earth. For them the expectations of social improvement are no delusion; the hopes of philanthropy are more than a dream. The five senses do not constitute the whole inventory of our sources of knowledge. They are the organs by which thought connects itself with the external universe; but the power of thought is not merged in the exercise of its instruments. We have functions which connect us with heaven, as well as organs which set us in relation with earth. We have not merely the senses opening to us the external world, but an internal sense, which places us in connexion with the world of intelligence and the decrees of God.

There is a *spirit in man:* not in the privileged few; not in those of us only who by the favor of Providence have been nursed in public schools: IT IS IN MAN: it is the attribute of the race. The spirit, which is the guide to truth, is the gracious gift to each member of the human family.

Reason exists within every breast. I mean not that faculty which deduces inferences from the experience of the senses, but that higher faculty, which from the infinite treasures of its own consciousness, originates truth, and assents to it by the force of intuitive evidence; that faculty which raises us beyond the control of time and space, and gives us faith in things eternal and invisible. There is not the difference between one mind and another, which the pride of philosophers might conceive. To them no faculty is conceded, which does not belong to the meanest of their countrymen. In them there can not spring up a truth, which does not equally have its germ in every mind. They have not the power of creation; they can but reveal what God has implanted in every breast.

The intellectual functions, by which relations are perceived, are the common endowments of the race. The differences are apparent, not real. The eye in one person may be dull, in another quick, in one distorted, and in another tranquil and clear; yet the relation of the eye to light is in all men the same. Just so judgment may be liable in individual minds to the bias of passion, and yet its relation to truth is immutable, and is universal.

In questions of practical duty, conscience is God's umpire, whose light illumines every heart. There is nothing in books, which had not first, and has not still its life within us. Religion itself is a dead letter, wherever its truths are not renewed in the soul. Individual conscience may be corrupted by interest, or debauched by pride, yet the rule of morality is distinctly marked; its harmonies are to the mind like music to the ear; and the moral judgment, when carefully analyzed and referred to its principles, is always founded in right. The eastern superstition, which bids its victims prostrate themselves before the advancing car of their idols, springs from a noble root, and is but a melancholy perversion of that self-devotion, which enables the Christian to bear the cross, and subject his personal passions to the will of

God. Immorality of itself never won to its support the inward voice; conscience, if questioned, never forgets to curse the guilty with the memory
of sin, to cheer the upright with the meek tranquillity of approval. And this
admirable power, which is the instinct of Deity, is the attribute of every
man; it knocks at the palace gate, it dwells in the meanest hovel. Duty, like
death, enters every abode, and delivers its message. Conscience, like reason
and judgment, is universal.

That the moral affections are planted every where, needs only to be
asserted to be received. The savage mother loves her offspring with all
the fondness that a mother can know. Beneath the odorous shade of the
boundless forests of Chili, the native youth repeats the story of love as
sincerely as it was ever chanted in the valley of Vaucluse. The affections of
family are not the growth of civilization. The charities of life are scattered
every where; enamelling the vales of human being, as the flowers paint
the meadows. They are not the fruit of study, nor the privilege of refinement, but a natural instinct.

Our age has seen a revolution in works of imagination. The poet has
sought his theme in common life. Never is the genius of Scott more
pathetic, than when, as in the Antiquary, he delineates the sorrows of a
poor fisherman, or as in the Heart of Mid Lothian, he takes his heroine
from a cottage. And even Wordsworth, the purest and most original poet of
the day, in spite of the inveterate character of his political predilections,
has thrown the light of genius on the walks of commonest life; he finds a
lesson in every grave of the village churchyard; he discloses the boundless
treasures of feeling in the peasant, the laborer and the artisan; the strolling
peddler becomes, through his genius, a teacher of the sublimest morality;
and the solitary wagoner, the lonely shepherd, even the feeble mother of
an idiot boy, furnishes lessons in the reverence for Humanity.

. . . .

I speak for the universal diffusion of human powers, not of human at-
tainments; for the capacity for progress, not for the perfection of undisciplined
instincts. The fellowship which we should cherish with the race, receives
the Comanche warrior and Caffre within the pale of equality. Their functions may not have been exercised, but they exist. Immure a person in a
dungeon; as he comes to the light of day, his vision seems incapable of
performing its office. Does that destroy your conviction in the relation
between the eye and light? The rioter over his cups resolves to eat and drink
and be merry; he forgets his spiritual nature in his obedience to the senses;
but does that destroy the relation between conscience and eternity? "What
ransom shall we give?" exclaimed the senators of Rome to the savage Attila.
"Give," said the barbarian, "all your gold and jewels, your costly furniture

and treasures, and set free every slave." "Ah," replied the degenerate Romans, "what then will be left to us?" "I leave you your souls," replied the unlettered invader from the steppes of Asia, who had learnt in the wilderness to value the immortal mind, and to despise the servile herd, that esteemed only their fortunes, and had no true respect for themselves. You cannot discover a tribe of men, but you also find the charities of life, and the proofs of spiritual existence. Behold the ignorant Algonquin deposit a bow and quiver by the side of the departed warrior; and recognise his faith in immortality. See the Comanche chieftain, in the heart of our continent, inflict on himself severest penance; and reverence his confession of the needed atonement for sin. The Barbarian who roams our western prairies has like passions and like endowments with ourselves. He bears within him the instinct of Deity; the consciousness of a spiritual nature; the love of beauty; the rule of morality.

And shall we reverence the dark-skinned Caffre? Shall we respect the brutal Hottentot? You may read the right answer written on every heart. It bids me not despise the sable hunter, that gathers a livelihood in the forests of Southern Africa. All are men. When we know the Hottentot better, we shall despise him less.

II

If it be true, that the gifts of mind and heart are universally diffused, if the sentiment of truth, justice, love, and beauty exists in every one, then it follows, as a necessary consequence, that the common judgment in taste, politics, and religion, is the highest authority on earth, and the nearest possible approach to an infallible decision. From the consideration of individual powers I turn to the action of the human mind in masses.

If reason is a universal faculty, the universal decision is the nearest criterion of truth. The common mind winnows opinions; it is the sieve which separates error from certainty. The exercise by many of the same faculty on the same subject would naturally lead to the same conclusions. But if not, the very differences of opinion that arise prove the supreme judgment of the general mind. Truth is one. It never contradicts itself. One truth cannot contradict another truth. Hence truth is a bond of union. But error not only contradicts truth, but may contradict itself; so that there may be many errors, and each at variance with the rest. Truth is therefore of necessity an element of harmony; error as necessarily an element of discord. Thus there can be no continuing universal judgment but a right one. Men cannot agree in an absurdity; neither can they agree in a falsehood.

If wrong opinions have often been cherished by the masses, the cause always lies in the complexity of the ideas presented. Error finds its way into the soul of a nation, only through the channel of truth. It is to a truth that men listen; and if they accept error also, it is only because the error is for the time so closely interwoven with the truth, that the one cannot readily be separated from the other.

Unmixed error can have no existence in the public mind. Wherever you see men clustering together to form a party, you may be sure that however much error may be there, truth is there also. Apply this principle boldly; for it contains a lesson of candor, and a voice of encouragement. There never was a school of philosophy, nor a clan in the realm of opinion, but carried along with it some important truth. And therefore every sect that has ever flourished has benefited Humanity; for the errors of a sect pass away and are forgotten; its truths are received into the common inheritance. To know the seminal thought of every prophet and leader of a sect, is to gather all the wisdom of mankind.

> By heaven! there should not be a seer, who left
> The world one doctrine, but I'd task his lore,
> And commune with his spirit. All the truth
> Of all the tongues of earth, I'd have them all,
> Had I the powerful spell to raise their ghosts.

The sentiment of beauty, as it exists in the human mind, is the criterion in works of art, inspires the conceptions of genius, and exercises a final judgment on its productions. For who are the best judges in matters of taste? Do you think the cultivated individual? Undoubtedly not; but the collective mind. The public is wiser than the wisest critic. In Athens, the arts were carried to perfection, when "the fierce democracie" was in the ascendant; the temple of Minerva and the works of Phidias were planned and perfected to please the common people. When Greece yielded to tyrants, her genius for excellence in art expired; or rather, the purity of taste disappeared; because the artist then endeavored to gratify a patron, and therefore, humored his caprice; while before he had endeavored to delight the race.

. . . .

Demosthenes of old formed himself to the perfection of eloquence by means of addresses to the crowd. The great comic poet of Greece, emphatically the poet of the vulgar mob, is distinguished above all others for the incomparable graces of his diction; and it is related of one of the most skilful writers in the Italian, that when inquired of where he had learned the purity and nationality of his style, he replied, from listening to the country people, as they brought their produce to market.

At the revival of letters a distinguishing feature of the rising literature was the employment of the dialect of the vulgar. Dante used the language of the populace and won immortality; Wickliffe, Luther, and at a later day Descartes, each employed his mother tongue, and carried truth directly to all who were familiar with its accents. Every beneficent revolution in letters has the character of popularity; every great reform among authors has sprung from the power of the people in its influence on the development and activity of mind.

The same influence continues unimpaired. Scott, in spite of his reverence for the aristocracy, spurned a drawing-room reputation; the secret of Byron's superiority lay in part in the agreement which existed between his muse and the democratic tendency of the age. German literature is almost entirely a popular creation. It was fostered by no monarch; it was dandled by no aristocracy. It was plebian in its origin, and therefore manly in its results.

III

In like manner the best government rests on the people and not on the few, on persons and not on property, on the free development of public opinion and not on authority; because the munificent Author of our being has conferred the gifts of mind upon every member of the human race without distinction of outward circumstances. Whatever of other possessions may be engrossed, mind asserts its own independence. Lands, estates, the produce of mines, the prolific abundance of the seas, may be usurped by a privileged class. Avarice, assuming the form of ambitious power, may grasp realm after realm, subdue continents, compass the earth in its schemes of aggrandizement, and sigh after other worlds; but mind eludes the power of appropriation; it exists only in its own individuality; it is a property which cannot be confiscated and cannot be torn away; it laughs at chains; it bursts from imprisonment; it defies monopoly. A government of equal rights must, therefore, rest upon mind; not wealth, not brute force, the sum of the moral intelligence of the community should rule the State. Prescription can no more assume to be a valid plea for political injustice; society studies to eradicate established abuses, and to bring social institutions and laws into harmony with moral right; not dismayed by the natural and necessary imperfections of all human effort, and not giving way to despair, because every hope does not at once ripen into fruit.

The public happiness is the true object of legislation, and can be secured only by the masses of mankind themselves awakening to the knowledge and the care of their own interests. Our free institutions have reversed the false and ignoble distinctions between men; and refusing to gratify the pride of caste, have acknowledged the common mind to be the true material for a commonwealth. Every thing has hitherto been done for the happy few. It is not possible to endow an aristocracy with greater benefits than they have already enjoyed; there is no room to hope that individuals will be more highly gifted or more fully developed than the greatest sages of past times. The world can advance only through the culture of the moral and intellectual powers of the people. To accomplish this end by means of the people themselves, is the highest purpose of government. If it be the duty of the individual to strive after a perfection like the perfection of God, how much more ought a nation to be the image of Deity. The common mind is the true Parian marble, fit to be wrought into likeness to a God. The duty of America is to secure the culture and the happiness of the masses by their reliance on themselves.

The absence of the prejudices of the old world leaves us here the opportunity of consulting independent truth; and man is left to apply the instinct of freedom to every social relation and public interest. We have approached so near to nature, that we can hear her gentlest whispers; we have made Humanity our lawgiver and our oracle; and, therefore, the nation receives, vivifies and applies principles, which in Europe the wisest accept with distrust. Freedom of mind and of conscience, freedom of the seas, freedom of industry, equality of franchises, each great truth is firmly grasped, comprehended and enforced; for the multitude is neither rash nor fickle. In truth, it is less fickle than those who profess to be its guides. Its natural dialectics surpass the logic of the schools. Political action has never been so consistent and so unwavering, as when it results from a feeling or a principle, diffused through society. The people is firm and tranquil in its movements, and necessarily acts with moderation, because it becomes but slowly impregnated with new ideas; and effects no changes, except in harmony with the knowledge which it has acquired. Besides, where it is permanently possessed of power, there exists neither the occasion nor the desire for frequent change. It is not the parent of tumult; sedition is bred in the lap of luxury, and its chosen emissaries are the beggared spendthrift and the impoverished libertine. The government by the people is in very truth the strongest government in the world. Discarding the implements of terror, it dares to rule by moral force, and has its citadel in the heart.

Such is the political system which rests on reason, reflection, and the free expression of deliberate choice. There may be those who scoff at the suggestion, that the decision of the whole is to be preferred to the judgment of the enlightened few. They say in their hearts that the masses are ignorant; that farmers know nothing of legislation; that mechanics should not quit their workshops to join in forming public opinion. But true political science does indeed venerate the masses. It maintains, not as has been perversely asserted, that "the people can make right," but that the people can DISCERN right. Individuals are but shadows, too often engrossed by the pursuit of shadows; the race is immortal: individuals are of limited sagacity; the common mind is infinite in its experience: individuals are languid and blind; the many are ever wakeful: individuals are corrupt; the race has been redeemed: individuals are time-serving; the masses are fearless: individuals may be false; the masses are ingenuous and sincere: individuals claim the divine sanction of truth for the deceitful conceptions of their own fancies; the Spirit of God breathes through the combined intelligence of the people. Truth is not to be ascertained by the impulses of an individual; it emerges from the contradictions of personal opinions; it raises itself in majestic serenity above the strifes of parties and the conflict of sects; it acknowledges neither the solitary mind, nor the separate faction as its oracle; but owns as its only faithful interpreter the dictates of pure reason itself, proclaimed by the general voice of mankind. The decrees of the universal conscience are the nearest approach to the presence of God in the soul of man.

Thus the opinion which we respect is, indeed, not the opinion of one or of a few, but the sagacity of the many. It is hard for the pride of cultivated philosophy to put its ear to the ground, and listen reverently to the voices of lowly humanity; yet the people collectively are wiser than the most gifted individual, for all his wisdom constitutes but a part of theirs. When the great sculptor of Greece was endeavoring to fashion the perfect model of beauty, he did not passively imitate the form of the loveliest woman of his age; but he gleaned the several lineaments of his faultless work from the many. And so it is, that a perfect judgment is the result of comparison, when error eliminates error, and truth is established by concurring witnesses. The organ of truth is the invisible decision of the unbiased world; she pleads before no tribunal but public opinion; she owns no safe interpreter but the common mind; she knows no court of appeals but the soul of humanity. It is when the multitude give counsel, that right purposes find safety; theirs is the fixedness that cannot be shaken; theirs is the understanding which exceeds in wisdom; theirs is the heart, of which the largeness is as the sand on the sea-shore.

It is not by vast armies, by immense natural resources, by accumulations of treasure, that the greatest results in modern civilization have been accomplished. The traces of the career of conquest pass away, hardly leaving a scar on the national intelligence. The famous battle grounds of victory are, most of them, comparatively indifferent to the human race; barren fields of blood, the scourges of their times, but affecting the social condition as little as the raging of a pestilence. Not one benevolent institution, not one ameliorating principle in the Roman state, was a voluntary concession of the aristocracy; each useful element was borrowed from the Democracies of Greece, or was a reluctant concession to the demands of the people. The same is true in modern political life. It is the confession of an enemy to Democracy, that "ALL THE GREAT AND NOBLE INSTITUTIONS OF THE WORLD HAVE COME FROM POPULAR EFFORTS."

It is the uniform tendency of the popular element to elevate and bless Humanity. The exact measure of the progress of civilization is the degree in which the intelligence of the common mind has prevailed over wealth and brute force; in other words, the measure of the progress of civilization is the progress of the people. Every great object, connected with the benevolent exertions of the day, has reference to the culture of those powers which are alone the common inheritance. For this the envoys of religion cross seas, and visit remotest isles; for this the press in its freedom teems with the productions of maturest thought; for this the philanthropist plans new schemes of education; for this halls in every city and village are open to the public instructor. Not that we view with indifference the glorious efforts of material industry; the increase in the facility of internal intercourse; the accumulations of thrifty labor; the varied results of concentrated action. But even there it is mind that achieves the triumph. It is the genius of the architect that gives beauty to the work of human hands, and makes the temple, the dwelling, or the public edifice, an outward representation of the spirit of propriety and order. It is science that guides the blind zeal of cupidity to the construction of the vast channels of communication, which are fast binding the world into one family. And it is as a method of moral improvement, that these swifter means of intercourse derive their greatest value. Mind becomes universal property; the poem that is published on the soil of England, finds its response on the shores of lake Erie and the banks of the Missouri, and is admired near the sources of the Ganges. The defence of public liberty in our own halls of legislation penetrates the plains of Poland, is echoed along the mountains of Greece, and pierces the darkest night of eastern despotism.

The universality of the intellectual and moral powers, and the necessity of their development for the progress of the race, proclaim the great doctrine of the natural right of every human being to moral and intellectual culture. It is the glory of our fathers to have established in their laws the equal claims of every child to the public care of its morals and its mind. From this principle we may deduce the universal right to leisure; that is, to time not appropriated to material purposes, but reserved for the culture of the moral affections and the mind. It does not tolerate the exclusive enjoyment of leisure by a privileged class; but defending the rights of labor, would suffer none to sacrifice the higher purposes of existence in unceasing toil for that which is not life. Such is the voice of nature; such the conscious claim of the human mind. The universe opens its pages to every eye; the music of creation resounds in every ear; the glorious lessons of immortal truth, that are written in the sky and on the earth, address themselves to every mind, and claim attention from every human being. God has made man upright, that he might look before and after; and he calls upon every one not merely to labor, but to reflect; not merely to practise the revelations of divine will, but to contemplate the displays of divine power.

. . . .

Yes, reforms in society are only effected through the masses of the people, and through them have continually taken place. New truths have been successively developed, and, becoming the common property of the human family, have improved its condition. This progress is advanced by every sect, precisely because each sect, to obtain vitality, does of necessity embody a truth; by every political party, for the conflicts of party are the war of ideas; by every nationality, for a nation cannot exist as such, till humanity makes it a special trustee of some part of its wealth for the ultimate benefit of all. The irresistible tendency of the human race is therefore to advancement, for absolute power has never succeeded, and can never succeed, in suppressing a single truth. An idea once revealed may find its admission into every living breast and live there. Like God it becomes immortal and omnipresent. The movement of the species is upward, irresistibly upward. The individual is often lost; Providence never disowns the race. No principle once promulgated, has ever been forgotten. No "timely tramp" of a despot's foot ever trod out one idea. The world cannot retrograde; the dark ages cannot return. Dynasties perish; cities are buried; nations have been victims to error, or martyrs for right; Humanity has always been on the advance; gaining maturity, universality, and power.

Yes, truth is immortal; it cannot be destroyed; it is invincible, it cannot long be resisted. Not every great principle has yet been generated; but when once proclaimed and diffused, it lives without end, in the safe custody of the race. States may pass away; every just principle of legislation which has been once established will endure. Philosophy has sometimes forgotten God; a great people never did. The skepticism of the last century could not uproot Christianity, because it lived in the hearts of the millions. Do you think that infidelity is spreading? Christianity never lived in the hearts of so many millions as at this moment. The forms under which it is professed may decay, for they, like all that is the work of man's hands, are subject to the changes and chances of mortal being; but the spirit of truth is incorruptible; it may be developed, illustrated, and applied; it never can die; it never can decline.

No truth can perish; no truth can pass away. The flame is undying, though generations disappear. Wherever moral truth has started into being, Humanity claims and guards the bequest. Each generation gathers together the imperishable children of the past, and increases them by new sons of light, alike radiant with immortality.

RELIGIOUS LIBERALISM VS.
ORTHODOXY

It HAD BEEN *the hope of early New England leaders to establish in America a virtual theocratic state, governed by a Calvinist clergy. But by the end of the seventeenth century there were evidences of rebellion against the Calvinist system. Its stern doctrines did not appear to square with the realities of American life: many Americans found difficulty in convincing themselves that they and their neighbors were totally depraved; and such authoritarian dogmas as that of special election clashed sharply with nascent tendencies toward individualism and democracy. To some, theological absolutism seemed as abhorrent as the political absolutism against which they had been contending. The eighteenth century brought a series of revolts against Calvinism ranging from modification to outright repudiation. Liberalizing influences had been felt even before the Whitefield revivals of the 1740's; it was Jonathan Edwards' hatred and fear of Arminianism which impelled him to preach the terrifying sermons which began the Great Awakening. The Deism which claimed so many influential adherents at the time of the American Revolution was one manifestation of an increasing rationalism in religion, as was the Unitarianism which succeeded it.*

By the beginning of the nineteenth century, ministers and laymen were being designated as either "liberal" or "orthodox," although there was little open hostility and no sign of actual separation of the two groups. There were, indeed, many degrees of both orthodoxy and liberalism; each camp contained men with a variety of opinions. Even those who considered themselves good Calvinists were far from agreement on such doctrinal matters as total depravity, the vicarious atonement, and the degree of Christ's divinity. However, the chief division within the Calvinist ranks at this time seems to have been that between the evangelical, revivalistic "Hopkinsians," and the more moderate "Old Calvinists." The liberals were united chiefly by their anti-Calvinism. They professed indifference to dogma, being in general opposed to man-made creeds, and advocating mental freedom in religion and the use of reason in interpreting the Bible. They were called by different names—the terms "Arian," "Arminian," and "Socinian," being used more or less indiscriminately by their enemies to designate those who questioned the doctrine of the trinity or emphasized man's free will.

Unitarianism, then, was merely one aspect of a general liberal reaction against what were regarded as the excesses of Calvinism. Its American roots are difficult to trace, for the term was not generally used before 1800. It has been suggested that the New England parsons who preached revolution from 1750 to 1775, as the theological liberals of their time, were in a sense pre-Unitarian. Boston ministers Jonathan Mayhew and Charles Chauncy had long before the Revolution questioned the doctrines of the trinity and original sin. But it was not until 1785 that the first American Unitarian Church was established (although the name "Unitarian" was not actually used until eleven years later when the First Unitarian Church of Philadelphia was founded). In this year James Freeman, Harvard graduate and liberal minister of King's Chapel, Boston, struck from the Anglican order of service all prayers to Christ and all references to the Trinity.

During the first decade of the 1800's Unitarian influence increased, particularly in the Boston area, and Unitarianism began to emerge as a denomination distinct from Calvinistic Congregationalism. In 1805, after a divisive controversy, Henry Ware, a liberal, was chosen over the orthodox candidate, Jesse Appleton, as Hollis Professor of Divinity at Harvard College. With the election of a liberal president and several other liberal professors, Harvard soon became a Unitarian stronghold. The orthodox retaliated by establishing their own theological seminary at Andover—a move made possible largely through the efforts of Jedidiah Morse, who had opposed Ware's election, and who succeeded in establishing a working agreement between the Hopkinsians and the Old Calvinists.

By 1810 the lines were beginning to be drawn. Some orthodox ministers discontinued the practice of exchanging pulpits with liberals. An increasingly bitter discussion developed between the orthodox journal, The Panoplist, founded by Morse in 1805, and the liberal Christian Disciple, published by Noah Worcester. When the crisis came, it turned loose on New England a flood of controversy which was to continue for fifteen years.

The crisis was precipitated by a review article in The Panoplist in June, 1815. Earlier in that year Jedidiah Morse had published as a pamphlet a chapter from a biography of Theophilus Lindsey written by the English Unitarian, Thomas Belsham. This pamphlet, entitled American Unitarianism, contained letters from American correspondents, some of them connected with King's Chapel, discussing liberal sentiments in this country. The review of the pamphlet in The Panoplist accused American liberals of cowardice and dishonesty in concealing their Unitarian leanings. The Unitarians found it im-

possible to ignore this direct challenge, and their reply
was made public in a letter written by William Ellery
Channing and addressed to the Reverend Samuel C.
Thacher. Channing acknowledged the failure of Unitarians to declare themselves openly, but attributed it not
to cowardice, but to a desire to avoid controversy. He
denied that the liberals were trying to divide the church
and he closed his letter with a warning to Unitarians
not to be betrayed by the review into any sort of sectarian
revolt. Dr. Samuel Worcester of Salem published an
answer to Channing, which evoked a pamphlet entitled
"Are You a Christian or a Calvinist?" published anony-
mously by John Lowell, a member of the Harvard
Corporation, denouncing Morse and Worcester and defending Channing.

Despite Channing's warning against sectarianism, the
trend toward a separate denomination continued. By 1819
Channing himself was preaching militant Unitarianism.
In May of that year he preached a sermon at the ordination of Jared Sparks in the elegant First Unitarian
Church of Baltimore. This eloquent statement of the
Unitarian credo, which established the young Channing
as undisputed leader of the liberal movement, proved
to be one of the most influential pulpit utterances in
American history. It is said to have had the widest
circulation of any printed speech of its time until Webster's "Reply to Hayne." Elizabeth Peabody recalled that
it was read extensively by laymen everywhere, especially
by young men, and that "it made multitudes conscious
that they were Unitarians." But if this manifesto rallied
many to the liberal standard, it also drew bitter criticism
from the orthodox. The controversy grew more heated,
fanned by a series of public letters, articles, and sermons.
As parish after parish was divided and the offended
factions seceded to form new congregations, legal difficulties arose over ownership of the church property.

In the celebrated Dedham case of 1820 the Supreme Court of Massachusetts ruled that church property was vested in the voters of the parish rather than in the actual communicants or members of the church. Since in most cases the liberals constituted a majority in the parish (although they were frequently in the minority among the communicants) this decision favored the liberal cause. In a large number of parishes the meeting house and church property were turned over to the Unitarians, as the orthodox departed to set up new churches. One of the most important of these was the Hanover Street Church in Boston to which Dr. Lyman Beecher was called in 1826.

Beecher had been a student at Yale when Channing was at Harvard. There he had studied theology under the dedicated Calvinist Timothy Dwight, and had come to regard Unitarianism as a deadly foe. From the time it first began to show itself, he said, "it was a fire in my bones." His correspondence at the time of Channing's Baltimore sermon reveals the depth of his feeling. He was profoundly troubled by the apathy of the orthodox and he burned to stamp out the heresies of the liberals. He waged unceasing warfare on infidelity— carrying on vigorous correspondence with his fellow-ministers, preaching and conducting revivals in various parts of New England, and driving himself beyond the limits of his strength. In September, 1823, he wrote his children that he was preparing an ordination sermon to preach at Worcester "which, I believe, as near as I can guess, will be a good one." In the spring of that year, while participating in a revival at the Park Street Church of Boston, Beecher had noted in his letters that Unitarians were in many cases people of weak beliefs, who knew only that they did not believe in Calvinism. But the Calvinism which repelled them, said Beecher, was a caricature. "When the truth, divested of obnoxious terms, is mildly, and kindly, and luminously explained and earnestly applied, they have no shield, and are easily impressed and awakened. . . ."[1] It was in this spirit that Beecher began the preparation of his Worcester sermon.

Jedidiah Morse, in the preface to the first issue of The Panoplist, had issued this call to arms: "It is the duty of the friends of evangelical truth and Christian morality . . . to 'contend earnestly for the faith once delivered to the saints.'" In the Worcester sermon Lyman Beecher took the offensive in this battle by placing the two systems in contrast and pointing out that the liberal system was not the faith delivered to the saints. It was a long sermon, and he was able to deliver only half of it, but he set about immediately to prepare it for printing. Liberal reaction came early in 1824 when the Christian Examiner (successor to the Disciple) printed a thirty-page review, which began by expressing agreement with much Beecher had said and accusing him of not being a real Calvinist at all. To this Dr. Beecher replied that he had preached these doctrines for twenty years without opposition from Calvinists, that since publication of the sermon he had not been denounced for heresy by the orthodox, that Unitarians had not offered to distribute editions of this "anti-Calvinist" sermon, and that the reviewer, having accused him of anti-Calvinism, had gone on to smite him "as if he were contending with a real antagonist."[2]

Shortly after delivering his Worcester sermon, Dr. Beecher was called from his Litchfield, Connecticut, church to the pulpit of the new Hanover Street Congregational Church in Boston. For more than six years he continued to contend for the faith delivered to the saints, and through his preaching and writing to denounce

[1] Charles Beecher, ed., Autobiography and Correspondence of Lyman Beecher (New York: Harper & Bros., 1865, 2 vols.), I, p. 542.
[2] Ibid., pp. 560–563.

Unitarian infidelity. Surrounded by liberal congregations, the Hanover church was an island of orthodoxy from which Beecher carried on an almost continuous revival. But the great Unitarian Controversy which had split the Congregational Church in two was practically at an end. The founding of the American Unitarian Association in 1825 made the separation complete; where once had been two factions within one church were now two churches. And in the Boston area at least, the Unitarians, who controlled the College, the Divinity School, and a large majority of the pulpits, held unquestioned command of the field.

Unitarian Christianity

WILLIAM ELLERY CHANNING

Born, Newport, Rhode Island, April 7, 1780; died, Ben-
nington, Vermont, October 2, 1842. Grandson of Wil-
liam Ellery, one of the Sons of Liberty and signer of
the Declaration of Independence. Graduated from Har-
vard, 1798. Ordained and installed as minister, Federal
Street Church, Boston, June 1, 1803; continued in this
pastorate for 40 years until his death. A small, mild man
of delicate health, known for his sweetness of spirit and
hatred of factionalism, he was drawn against his will into
one of the great religious controversies of his time.
Through his speaking and writing, particularly during
his later years, he exerted an important influence on the
social issues of his day. The inscription on his statue in
the Boston Public Gardens notes: "He breathed into
theology a humane spirit."

Prove all things, hold fast that which is good.
                                                        I Thess., 21

*T*he peculiar circumstances of this occasion not only justify, but seem to demand a departure from the course
generally followed by preachers at the introduction of a brother into the sacred
office. It is usual to speak of the nature, design, duties, and advantages of the
Christian ministry; and on these topics I should now be happy to insist, did I not
remember that a minister is to be given this day to a religious society, whose peculiarities of opinion have drawn upon them much remark, and may I not add,

Baltimore, Maryland, May 5, 1819. *The Works of William E. Channing, D.D.*
(Boston: American Unitarian Association, 1889), pp. 367–384.

much reproach. Many good minds, many sincere Christians, I am aware, are apprehensive that the solemnities of this day are to give a degree of influence to principles which they deem false and injurious. The fears and anxieties of such men I respect; and, believing that they are grounded in part on mistake, I have thought it my duty to lay before you, as clearly as I can, some of the distinguishing opinions of that class of Christians in our country, who are known to sympathize with this religious society. I must ask your patience, for such a subject is not to be despatched in a narrow compass. I must also ask you to remember, that it is impossible to exhibit, in a single discourse, our views of every doctrine of Revelation, much less the differences of opinion which are known to subsist among ourselves. I shall confine myself to topics on which our sentiments have been misrepresented, or which distinguish us most widely from others. May I not hope to be heard with candor? God deliver us all from prejudice and unkindness, and fill us with the love of truth and virtue.

There are two natural divisions under which my thoughts will be arranged. I shall endeavor to unfold, 1st, The principles which we adopt in interpreting the Scriptures. And 2dly, Some of the doctrines which the Scriptures, so interpreted, seem to us clearly to express.

I. We regard the Scriptures as the records of God's successive revelations to mankind, and particularly of the last and most perfect revelation of his will by Jesus Christ. Whatever doctrines seem to us to be clearly taught in the Scriptures, we receive without reserve or exception. We do not, however, attach equal importance to all the books in this collection. Our religion, we believe, lies chiefly in the New Testament. The dispensation of Moses, compared with that of Jesus, we consider as adapted to the childhood of the human race, a preparation for a nobler system, and chiefly useful now as serving to confirm and illustrate the Christian Scriptures. Jesus Christ is the only master of Christians, and whatever he taught, either during his personal ministry, or by his inspired Apostles, we regard as of divine authority, and profess to make the rule of our lives.

This authority, which we give to the Scriptures, is a reason, we conceive, for studying them with peculiar care, and for inquiring anxiously into the principles of interpretation, by which their true meaning may be ascertained. The principles adopted by the class of Christians in whose name I speak need to be explained, because they are often misunderstood. We are particularly accused of making an unwarrantable use of reason in the interpretation of Scripture. We are said to exalt reason above revelation, to prefer our own wisdom to God's. Loose and undefined charges of this kind are circulated so freely, that we think it due to ourselves, and to the cause of truth, to express our views with some particularity.

Our leading principle in interpreting Scripture is this, that the Bible

is a book written for men, in the language of men, and that its meaning is
to be sought in the same manner as that of other books. We believe that
God, when he speaks to the human race, conforms, if we may so say, to
the established rules of speaking and writing. How else would the Scriptures
avail us more than if communicated in an unknown tongue?

Now all books, and all conversation, require in the reader or hearer the
constant exercise of reason; or their true import is only to be obtained by
continual comparison and inference. Human language, you well know,
admits various interpretations; and every word and every sentence must
be modified and explained according to the subject which is discussed,
according to the purposes, feelings, circumstances, and principles of the writer,
and according to the genius and idioms of the language which he uses. These
are acknowledged principles in the interpretation of human writings; and a
man whose words we should explain without reference to these principles,
would reproach us justly with a criminal want of candor, and an intention
of obscuring or distorting his meaning.

Were the Bible written in a language and style of its own, did it consist
of words which admit but a single sense, and of sentences wholly detached
from each other, there would be no place for the principles now laid down.
We could not reason about it as about other writings. But such a book would
be of little worth; and perhaps, of all books, the Scriptures correspond least
to this description. The Word of God bears the stamp of the same hand
which we see in his works. It has infinite connections and dependences.
Every proposition is linked with others, and is to be compared with others,
that its full and precise import may be understood. Nothing stands alone.
The New Testament is built on the Old. The Christian dispensation is a
continuation of the Jewish, the completion of a vast scheme of providence,
requiring great extent of view in the reader. Still more, the Bible treats
of subjects on which we receive ideas from other sources besides itself—
such subjects as the nature, passions, relations, and duties of man; and it
expects us to restrain and modify its language by the known truths which
observation and experience furnish on these topics.

We profess not to know a book which demands a more frequent exercise
of reason than the Bible. In addition to the remarks now made on its
infinite connections, we may observe that its style nowhere affects the
precision of science, or the accuracy of definition. Its language is singularly
glowing, bold, and figurative, demanding more frequent departures from
the literal sense than that of our own age and country, and consequently
demanding more continual exercise of judgment. We find, too, that the
different portions of this book, instead of being confined to general truths,
refer perpetually to the times when they were written, to states of society,
to modes of thinking, to controversies in the church, to feelings and usages

which have passed away, and without the knowledge of which we are constantly in danger of extending to all times, and places, what was of temporary and local application. We find, too, that some of these books are strongly marked by the genius and character of their respective writers, that the Holy Spirit did not so guide the Apostles as to suspend the peculiarities of their minds, and that a knowledge of their feelings, and of the influences under which they were placed, is one of the preparations for understanding their writings. With these views of the Bible, we feel it our bounden duty to exercise our reason upon it perpetually, to compare, to infer, to look beyond the letter to the spirit, to seek in the nature of the subject and the aim of the writer his true meaning; and, in general, to make use of what is known for explaining what is difficult, and for discovering new truths.

Need I descend to particulars to prove that the Scriptures demand the exercise of reason? Take, for example, the style in which they generally speak of God, and observe how habitually they apply to him human passions and organs. Recollect the declarations of Christ, that he came not to send peace, but a sword; that unless we eat his flesh, and drink his blood, we have no life in us; that we must hate father and mother, and pluck out the right eye; and a vast number of passages equally bold and unlimited. Recollect the unqualified manner in which it is said of Christians, that they possess all things, know all things, and can do all things. Recollect the verbal contradiction between Paul and James, and the apparent clashing of some parts of Paul's writings with the general doctrines and end of Christianity. I might extend the enumeration indefinitely; and who does not see that we must limit all these passages by the known attributes of God, of Jesus Christ, and of human nature, and by the circumstances under which they were written, so as to give the language a quite different import from what it would require had it been applied to different beings, or used in different connections.

Enough has been said to show in what sense we make use of reason in interpreting Scripture. From a variety of possible interpretations, we select that which accords with the nature of the subject and the state of the writer, with the connection of the passage, with the general strain of Scripture, with the known character and will of God, and with the obvious and acknowledged laws of nature. In other words, we believe that God never contradicts in one part of Scripture what he teaches in another; and never contradicts in revelation what he teaches in his works and providence. And we therefore distrust every interpretation which, after deliberate attention, seems repugnant to any established truth. We reason about the Bible precisely as civilians do about the constitution under which we live; who, you know, are accustomed to limit one provision of that venerable instrument by others, and to fix the precise import of its parts by inquiring into its general spirit, into the intentions of its authors, and into the prevalent feelings, impressions, and circumstances of the time when it was framed. Without these principles of interpretation, we frankly acknowledge that we cannot defend the divine authority of the Scriptures. Deny us this latitude, and we must abandon this book to its enemies.

. . . .

II. Having thus stated the principles according to which we interpret Scripture, I now proceed to the second great head of this discourse, which is, to state some of the views which we derive from that sacred book, particularly those which distinguish us from other Christians.

1. In the first place, we believe in the doctrine of God's UNITY, or that there is one God, and one only. To this truth we give infinite importance, and we feel ourselves bound to take heed, lest any man spoil us of it by vain philosophy. The proposition that there is one God seems to us exceedingly plain. We understand by it, that there is one being, one mind, one person, one intelligent agent, and one only, to whom underived and infinite perfection and dominion belong. We conceive that these words could have conveyed no other meaning to the simple and uncultivated people, who were set apart to be the depositaries of this great truth, and who were utterly incapable of understanding those hair-breadth distinctions between being and person, which the sagacity of later ages has discovered. We find no intimation that this language was to be taken in an unusual sense, or that God's unity was a quite different thing from the oneness of other intelligent beings.

We object to the doctrine of the Trinity, that, whilst acknowledging in words, it subverts in effect, the unity of God. According to this doctrine, there are three infinite and equal persons, possessing supreme divinity, called the Father, Son, and Holy Ghost. Each of these persons, as described by theologians, has his own particular consciousness, will, and perceptions. They love each other, converse with each other, and delight in each other's society. They perform different parts in man's redemption, each having his appropriate office, and neither doing the work of the other. The Son is mediator, and not the Father. The Father sends the Son, and is not himself sent; nor is he conscious, like the Son, of taking flesh. Here, then, we have three intelligent agents, possessed of different consciousnesses, different wills, and different perceptions, performing different acts, and sustaining different relations; and if these things do not imply and constitute three minds or beings, we are utterly at a loss to know how three minds or beings are to be formed. It is difference of properties, and acts, and consciousness, which leads us to the belief of different intelligent beings, and if this mark fails us, our whole knowledge falls; we have no proof that all the agents and persons in the universe are not one and the same mind. When we attempt to conceive of three Gods, we can do nothing more than represent to ourselves three agents, distinguished from each other by similar marks and peculiarities to those which separate the persons of the Trinity; and when common Christians hear these persons spoken of as conversing with each other, loving each other, and performing different acts, how can they help regarding them as different beings, different minds?

We do, then, with all earnestness, though without reproaching our brethren, protest against the irrational and unscriptural doctrine of the Trinity. "To us," as to the Apostle and the primitive Christians, "there is one God, even the Father." With Jesus, we worship the Father, as the only living and true God. We are astonished that any man can read the New Testament, and avoid the conviction that the Father alone is God. We hear our Saviour continually appropriating this character to the Father. We find the Father continually distinguished from Jesus by this title. "God sent his Son." "God anointed Jesus." Now, how singular and inexplicable is this phraseology, which fills the New Testament, if this title belong equally to Jesus, and if a principal object of this book is to reveal him as God, as partaking equally with the Father in supreme divinity! We challenge our opponents to adduce one passage in the New Testament, where the word God means three persons, where it is not limited to one person, and where, unless turned from its usual sense by the connection, it does not mean the Father. Can stronger proof be given that the doctrine of three persons in the Godhead is not a fundamental doctrine of Christianity?

[Channing develops this idea further, and objects to the doctrine of the Trinity on the ground that it sets before the Christian not one, but three distinct objects of supreme adoration.]

. . . .

2. Having thus given our views of the unity of God, I proceed, in the second place, to observe that we believe in the unity of Jesus Christ. We believe that Jesus is one mind, one soul, one being, as truly one as we are, and equally distinct from the one God. We complain of the doctrine of the Trinity, that, not satisfied with making God three beings, it makes Jesus Christ two beings, and thus introduces infinite confusion into our conceptions of his character. This corruption of Christianity, alike repugnant to common sense and to the general strain of Scripture, is a remarkable proof of the power of a false philosophy in disfiguring the simple truth of Jesus.

According to this doctrine, Jesus Christ, instead of being one mind, one conscious intelligent principle, whom we can understand, consists of two souls, two minds; the one divine, the other human; the one weak, the other almighty; the one ignorant, the other omniscient. Now we maintain that this is to make Christ two beings. To denominate him one person, one being, and yet to suppose him made up of two minds, infinitely different from each other, is to abuse and confound language, and to throw darkness over all our conceptions of intelligent natures. According to the common doctrine, each of these two minds in Christ has its own consciousness, its own will, its own perceptions. They have, in fact, no common properties. The divine mind feels none of the wants and sorrows of the human, and the human is infinitely removed from the perfection and happiness of the divine. Can you conceive of two beings in the universe more distinct? We have always thought that one person was constituted and distinguished by one consciousness. The doctrine that one and the same person should have two consciousnesses, two wills, two souls, infinitely different from each other, this we think an enormous tax on human credulity.

We say that if a doctrine so strange, so difficult, so remote from all the previous conceptions of men, be indeed a part, and an essential part, of revelation, it must be taught with great distinctness, and we ask our brethren to point to some plain, direct passage, where Christ is said to be composed of two minds infinitely different, yet constituting one person. We find none. Other Christians, indeed, tell us that this doctrine is necessary to the harmony of the Scriptures, that some texts ascribe to Jesus Christ human, and others divine properties, and that to reconcile these, we must suppose two minds, to which these properties may be referred. In other words, for the purpose of reconciling certain difficult passages, which a just criticism can in a great degree, if not wholly, explain, we must invent an hypothesis vastly more difficult, and involving gross absurdity. We are to find our way out of a labyrinth by a clue which conducts us into mazes infinitely more inextricable.

Surely, if Jesus Christ felt that he consisted of two minds, and that this was a leading feature of his religion, his phraseology respecting himself would have been colored by this peculiarity. The universal language of men is framed upon the idea that one person is one person, is one mind, and one soul; and when the multitude heard this language from the lips of Jesus, they must have taken it in its usual sense, and must have referred to a single soul all which he spoke, unless expressly instructed to interpret it differently. But where do we find this instruction? Where do you meet, in the New Testament, the phraseology which abounds in Trinitarian books, and which necessarily grows from the doctrine of two natures in Jesus? Where does this divine teacher say, "This I speak as God, and this as man; this is true only of my human mind, this only of my divine"? Where do we find in the

Epistles a trace of this strange phraseology? Nowhere. It was not needed in that day. It was demanded by the errors of a later age.

We believe, then, that Christ is one mind, one being, and, I add, a being distinct from the one God. That Christ is not the one God, not the same being with the Father, is a necessary inference from our former head, in which we saw that the doctrine of three persons in God is a fiction. But on so important a subject, I would add a few remarks. We wish that those from whom we differ would weigh one striking fact. Jesus, in his preaching, continually spoke of God. The word was always in his mouth. We ask, does he by this word, ever mean himself? We say, never. On the contrary, he most plainly distinguishes between God and himself, and so do his disciples. How this is to be reconciled with the idea that the mani festation of Christ, as God, was a primary object of Christianity, our adversaries must determine.

. . . .

We are also told that Christ is a more interesting object, that his love and mercy are more felt, when he is viewed as the Supreme God, who left his glory to take humanity and to suffer for men. That Trinitarians are strongly moved by this representation, we do not mean to deny; but we think their emotions altogether founded on a misapprehension of their own doctrines. They talk of the second person of the Trinity's leaving his glory and his Father's bosom, to visit and save the world. But this second person, being the unchangeable and infinite God, was evidently incapable of parting with the least degree of his perfection and felicity. At the moment of his taking flesh, he was as intimately present with his Father as before, and equally with his Father filled heaven, and earth, and immensity. This Trinitarians acknowledge; and still they profess to be touched and overwhelmed by the amazing humiliation of this immutable being! But not only does their doctrine, when fully explained, reduce Christ's humiliation to a fiction, it almost wholly destroys the impressions with which his cross ought to be viewed. According to their doctrine, Christ was comparatively no sufferer at all. It is true, his human mind suffered; but this, they tell us, was an infinitely small part of Jesus, bearing no more proportion to his whole nature, than a single hair of our heads to the whole body, or than a drop to the ocean. The divine mind of Christ, that which was most properly himself, was infinitely happy at the very moment of the suffering of his humanity. Whilst hanging on the cross, he was the happiest being in the universe, as happy as the infinite Father; so that his pains, compared with his felicity, were nothing. This Trinitarians do, and must, acknowledge. It follows necessarily from the immutableness of the divine nature which they ascribe to Christ; so that their system, justly viewed, robs his death of interest,

weakens our sympathy with his sufferings, and is, of all others, most unfavorable to a love of Christ, founded on a sense of his sacrifices for
mankind. We esteem our own views to be vastly more affecting. It is our
belief that Christ's humiliation was real and entire, that the whole Saviour,
and not a part of him, suffered, that his crucifixion was a scene of deep
and unmixed agony. As we stand round his cross, our minds are not distracted, nor our sensibility weakened, by contemplating him as composed
of incongruous and infinitely differing minds, and as having a balance of
infinite felicity. We recognize in the dying Jesus but one mind. This, we
think, renders his sufferings, and his patience and love in bearing them,
incomparably more impressive and affecting than the system we oppose.

3. Having thus given our belief on two great points, namely, that there
is one God, and that Jesus Christ is a being distinct from and inferior to
God, I now proceed to another point, on which we lay still greater stress.
We believe in the *moral perfection of God*. We consider no part of
theology so important as that which treats of God's moral character; and we
value our views of Christianity chiefly as they assert his amiable and
venerable attributes.

It may be said that in regard to this subject all Christians agree, that all
ascribe to the Supreme Being infinite justice, goodness, and holiness. We
reply, that it is very possible to speak of God magnificently, and to think
of him meanly; to apply to his person high-sounding epithets, and to his
government, principles which make him odious. The Heathens called
Jupiter the greatest and the best; but his history was black with cruelty and
lust. We cannot judge of men's real ideas of God by their general language,
for in all ages they have hoped to soothe the Deity by adulation. We must
inquire into their particular views of his purposes, of the principles of his
administration, and of his disposition towards his creatures.

We conceive that Christians have generally leaned towards a very injurious view of the Supreme Being. They have too often felt as if he
were raised, by his greatness and sovereignty, above the principles of morality,
above those eternal laws of equity and rectitude to which all other beings are
subjected. We believe that in no being is the sense of right so strong,
so omnipotent, as in God. We believe that his almighty power is entirely
submitted to his perceptions of rectitude; and this is the ground of our
piety. It is not because he is our Creator merely, but because he created
us for good and holy purposes; it is not because his will is irresistible, but
because his will is the perfection of virtue, that we pay him allegiance.
We cannot bow before a being, however great and powerful, who governs
tyrannically. We respect nothing but excellence, whether on earth or in
heaven. We venerate not the loftiness of God's throne, but the equity and
goodness in which it is established.

We believe that God is infinitely good, kind, benevolent, in the proper sense of these words; good in disposition as well as in act; good not to a few, but to all; good to every individual, as well as to the general system.

We believe, too, that God is just; but we never forget that his justice is the justice of a good being, dwelling in the same mind and acting in harmony, with perfect benevolence. By this attribute, we understand God's infinite regard to virtue or moral worth, expressed in a moral government; that is, in giving excellent and equitable laws, and in conferring such rewards, and inflicting such punishments, as are best fitted to secure their observance. God's justice has for its end the highest virtue of the creation, and it punishes for this end alone; and thus it coincides with benevolence; for virtue and happiness, though not the same, are inseparably conjoined.

God's justice thus viewed appears to us to be in perfect harmony with his mercy. According to the prevalent systems of theology, these attributes are so discordant and jarring, that to reconcile them is the hardest task and the most wonderful achievement of infinite wisdom. To us they seem to be intimate friends, always at peace, breathing the same spirit, and seeking the same end. By God's mercy, we understand not a blind instinctive compassion, which forgives without reflection, and without regard to the interests of virtue. This, we acknowledge, would be incompatible with justice, and also with enlightened benevolence. God's mercy, as we understand it, desires strongly the happiness of the guilty; but only through their penitence. It has a regard to character as truly as his justice. It defers punishment, and suffers long, that the sinner may return to his duty, but leaves the impenitent and unyielding to the fearful retribution threatened in God's Word.

To give our views of God in one word, we believe in his Parental character. We ascribe to him, not only the name, but the dispositions and principles of a father. We believe that he has a father's concern for his creatures, a father's desire for their improvement, a father's equity in proportioning his commands to their powers, a father's joy in their progress, a father's readiness to receive the penitent, and a father's justice for the incorrigible. We look upon this world as a place of education, in which he is training men by prosperity and adversity, by aids and obstructions, by conflicts of reason and passion, by motives to duty and temptations to sin, by various disciplines suited to free and moral beings, for union with himself, and for a sublime and ever-growing virtue in heaven.

Now, we object to the systems of religion which prevail among us, that they are adverse, in a greater or less degree, to these purifying, comforting, and honorable views of God; that they take from us our Father in heaven, and substitute for him a being whom we cannot love if we would, and whom we ought not to love if we could. We object, particularly on this ground, to that system which arrogates to itself the name of Orthodoxy, and which is now industriously propagated through our country. This system indeed takes various shapes, but in all it casts dishonor on the Creator. According to its old and genuine form, it teaches that God brings us into life wholly depraved, so that under the innocent features of our childhood is hidden a nature averse to all good and propense to all evil, a nature which exposes us to God's displeasure and wrath, even before we have acquired power to understand our duties or to reflect upon our actions. According to a more modern exposition, it teaches that we came from the hands of our Maker with such a constitution, and are placed under such influences and circumstances, as to render certain and infallible the total depravity of every human being from the first moment of his moral agency; and it also teaches that the offence of the child, who brings into life this ceaseless tendency to unmingled crime, exposes him to the sentence of everlasting damnation. Now, according to the plainest principles of morality, we maintain that a natural constitution of the mind, unfailingly disposing it to evil and to evil alone, would absolve it from guilt; that to give existence under this condition would argue unspeakable cruelty; and that to punish the sin of this unhappily constituted child with endless ruin would be a wrong unparalleled by the most merciless despotism.

This system also teaches that God selects from this corrupt mass a number to be saved, and plucks them, by a special influence, from the common ruin; that the rest of mankind, though left without that special grace which their conversion requires, are commanded to repent, under penalty of aggravated woe; and that forgiveness is promised them on terms which their very constitution infallibly disposes them to reject, and in rejecting which they awfully enhance the punishments of hell. These proffers of forgiveness and exhortations of amendment, to beings born under a blighting curse, fill our minds with a horror which we want words to express.

That this religious system does not produce all the effects on character which might be anticipated, we most joyfully admit. It is often, very often, counteracted by nature, conscience, common sense, by the general strain of Scripture, by the mild example and precepts of Christ, and by the many positive declarations of God's universal kindness and perfect equity. But still we think that we see its unhappy influence. It tends to discourage the timid, to give excuses to the bad, to feed the vanity of the fanatical, and to offer shelter to the bad feelings of the malignant. By shocking, as it does, the fundamental principles of morality, and by exhibiting a severe and partial Deity, it tends strongly to pervert the moral faculty, to form a gloomy, forbidding, and servile religion, and to lead men to substitute censoriousness, bitterness, and persecution, for a tender and impartial charity. We think, too, that this system, which begins with degrading human nature, may be expected to end in pride; for pride grows out of a consciousness of high distinctions, however obtained, and no distinction is so great as that which is made between the elected and abandoned of God.

The false and dishonorable views of God which have now been stated, we feel ourselves bound to resist unceasingly. Other errors we can pass over with comparative indifference. But we ask our opponents to leave to us a GOD, worthy of our love and trust, in whom our moral sentiments may delight, in whom our weaknesses and sorrows may find refuge. We cling to the Divine perfections. We meet them everywhere in creation, we read them in the Scriptures, we see a lovely image of them in Jesus Christ; and gratitude, love, and veneration call on us to assert them. Reproached, as we often are, by men, it is our consolation and happiness, that one of our chief offences is the zeal with which we vindicate the dishonored goodness and rectitude of God.

4. Having thus spoken of the unity of God; of the unity of Jesus, and his inferiority to God; and of the perfections of the Divine character; I now proceed to give our views of the mediation of Christ, and of the purposes of his mission. With regard to the great object which Jesus came to accomplish, there seems to be no possibility of mistake. We believe that he was sent by the Father to effect a moral or spiritual deliverance of mankind; that is, to rescue men from sin and its consequences, and to bring them to a state of everlasting purity and happiness. We believe, too, that he accomplishes this sublime purpose by a variety of methods; by his instructions respecting God's unity, parental character, and moral government, which are admirably fitted to reclaim the world from idolatry and impiety, to the knowledge, love, and obedience of the Creator; by his promises of pardon to the penitent, and of divine assistance to those who labor for progress in moral excellence; by the light which he has thrown on the path of duty; by his own spotless example, in which the loveliness and sublimity of virtue shine forth to warm and quicken as well as guide us to perfection; by his threatenings against incorrigible guilt; by his glorious discoveries of immortality; by his sufferings and death; by that signal event, the resurrection, which powerfully bore witness to his divine mission, and brought down to men's senses a future life; by his continual intercession, which obtains for us spiritual aid and blessings; and by the power with which he is invested of raising the dead, judging the world, and conferring the everlasting rewards promised to the faithful.

We have no desire to conceal the fact that a difference of opinion exists among us in regard to an interesting part of Christ's mediation; I mean, in regard to the precise influence of his death on our forgiveness. Many suppose that this event contributes to our pardon, as it was a principal means of confirming his religion, and of giving it a power over the mind;

in other words, that it procures forgiveness by leading to that repentance and virtue which is the great and only condition on which forgiveness is bestowed. Many of us are dissatisfied with this explanation, and think that the Scriptures ascribe the remission of sins to Christ's death with an emphasis so peculiar that we ought to consider this event as having a special influence in removing punishment, though the Scriptures may not reveal the way in which it contributes to this end.

Whilst, however, we differ in explaining the connection between Christ's death and human forgiveness,—a connection which we all gratefully acknowledge,—we agree in rejecting many sentiments which prevail in regard to his mediation. The idea which is conveyed to common minds by the popular system, that Christ's death has an influence in making God placable, or merciful, in awakening his kindness towards men, we reject with strong disapprobation. We are happy to find that this very dishonorable notion is disowned by intelligent Christians of that class from which we differ. We recollect, however, that not long ago, it was common to hear of Christ as having died to appease God's wrath, and to pay the debt of sinners to his inflexible justice; and we have a strong persuasion that the language of popular religious books, and the common mode of stating the doctrine of Christ's mediation, still communicate very degrading views of God's character. They give to multitudes the impression that the death of Jesus produces a change in the mind of God towards man, and that in this its efficacy chiefly consists. No error seems to us more pernicious. We can endure no shade over the pure goodness of God. We earnestly maintain that Jesus, instead of calling forth in any way or degree, the mercy of the Father, was sent by that mercy, to be our Saviour; that he is nothing to the human race but what he is by God's appointment; that he communicates nothing but what God empowers him to bestow; that our Father in heaven is originally, essentially, and eternally placable, and disposed to forgive; and that his unborrowed, underived, and unchangeable love is the only fountain of what flows to us through his Son. We conceive that Jesus is dishonored, not glorified, by ascribing to him an influence which clouds the splendor of Divine benevolence.

. . . .

5. Having thus stated our views of the highest object of Christ's mission, that it is the recovery of men to virtue, or holiness, I shall now, in the last place, give our views of the nature of Christian virtue, or true holiness. We believe that all virtue has its foundation in the moral nature of man, that is, in conscience, or his sense of duty, and in the power of forming his temper and life according to conscience. We believe that these moral faculties are the grounds of responsibility, and the highest distinctions of

human nature, and that no act is praiseworthy any farther than it springs from their exertion. We believe that no dispositions infused into us without our own moral activity are of the nature of virtue, and therefore we reject the doctrine of irresistible divine influence on the human mind, moulding it into goodness as marble is hewn into a statue. Such goodness, if this word may be used, would not be the object of moral approbation, any more than the instinctive affections of inferior animals, or the constitutional amiableness of human beings.

By these remarks, we do not mean to deny the importance of God's aid or Spirit; but by his Spirit, we mean a moral, illuminating, and persuasive influence, not physical, not compulsory, not involving a necessity of virtue. We object, strongly, to the idea of many Christians respecting man's impotence and God's irresistible agency on the heart, believing that they subvert our responsibility and the laws of our moral nature, that they make men machines, that they cast on God the blame of all evil deeds, that they discourage good minds, and inflate the fanatical with wild conceits of immediate and sensible inspiration.

Among the virtues, we give the first place to the love of God. We believe that this principle is the true end and happiness of our being, that we were made for union with our Creator, that his infinite perfection is the only sufficient object and true resting-place for the insatiable desires and unlimited capacities of the human mind, and that, without him, our noblest sentiments, admiration, veneration, hope, and love, would wither and decay. We believe, too, that the love of God is not only essential to happiness, but to the strength and perfection of all the virtues; that conscience, without the sanction of God's authority and retributive justice, would be a weak director; that benevolence, unless nourished by communion with his goodness, and encouraged by his smile, could not thrive amidst the selfishness and thanklessness of the world; and that self-government, without a sense of the divine inspection, would hardly extend beyond an outward and partial purity. God, as he is essentially goodness, holiness, justice, and virtue, so he is the life, motive, and sustainer of virtue in the human soul.

But, whilst we earnestly inculcate the love of God, we believe that great care is necessary to distinguish it from counterfeits. We think that much which is called piety is worthless. Many have fallen into the error that there can be no excess in feelings which have God for their object; and, distrusting as coldness that self-possession without which virtue and devotion lose all their dignity, they have abandoned themselves to extravagances which have brought contempt on piety. Most certainly, if the love of God be that which often bears its name, the less we have of it the better. If religion be the shipwreck of understanding, we cannot keep too far from it. On this subject, we always speak plainly. We cannot sacrifice our reason to the reputation of zeal. We owe it to truth and religion to maintain that fanaticism, partial insanity, sudden impressions, and ungovernable transports, are any thing rather than piety.

We conceive that the true love of God is a moral sentiment, founded on a clear perception, and consisting in a high esteem and veneration of his moral perfections. Thus, it perfectly coincides, and is in fact the same thing, with the love of virtue, rectitude, and goodness. You will easily judge, then, what we esteem the surest and only decisive signs of piety. We lay no stress on strong excitements. We esteem him, and him only, a pious man, who practically conforms to God's moral perfections and government; who shows his delight in God's benevolence by loving and serving his neighbour; his delight in God's justice by being resolutely upright; his sense of God's purity by regulating his thoughts, imagination, and desires; and whose conversation, business, and domestic life are swayed by a regard to God's presence and authority. In all things else men may deceive themselves. Disordered nerves may give them strange sights, and sounds, and impressions. Texts of Scripture may come to them as from Heaven. Their whole souls may be moved, and their confidence in God's favor be undoubting. But in all this there is no religion. The question is, Do they love God's commands, in which his character is fully expressed, and give up to these their habits and passions? Without this, ecstacy is a mockery. One surrender of desire to God's will is worth a thousand transports. We do not judge of the bent of men's minds by their raptures, any more than we judge of the natural direction of a tree during a storm. We rather suspect loud profession, for we have observed that deep feeling is generally noiseless, and least seeks display.

We would not, by these remarks, be understood as wishing to exclude from religion warmth, and even transport. We honor, and highly value, true religious sensibility. We believe that Christianity is intended to act powerfully on our whole nature, on the heart as well as the understanding and the conscience. We conceive of heaven as a state where the love of God will be exalted into an unbounded fervor and joy; and we desire, in our pilgrimage here, to drink into the spirit of that better world. But we think that religious warmth is only to be valued when it springs naturally from an improved character, when it comes unforced, when it is the recompense of obedience, when it is the warmth of a mind which understands God by being like him, and when, instead of disordering, it exalts the understanding, invigorates conscience, gives a pleasure to common duties, and is seen to exist in connection with cheerfulness, judiciousness, and a reasonable frame of mind. When we observe a fervor called religious in men whose general character expresses little refinement and elevation, and whose piety seems at war with reason, we pay it little respect. We honor religion too much to give its sacred name to a feverish, forced, fluctuating zeal, which has little power over the life.

Another important branch of virtue we believe to be love to Christ. The greatness of the work of Jesus, the spirit with which he executed it, and the sufferings which he bore for our salvation, we feel to be strong claims on our gratitude and veneration. We see in nature no beauty to be compared with the loveliness of his character, nor do we find on earth a benefactor to whom we owe an equal debt. We read his history with delight, and learn from it the perfection of our nature. We are particularly touched by his death, which was endured for our redemption, and by that strength of charity which triumphed over his pains. His resurrection is the foundation of our hope of immortality. His intercession gives us boldness to draw nigh to the throne of grace, and we look up to heaven with new desire when we think that, if we follow him here, we shall there see his benignant countenance, and enjoy his friendship for ever.

I need not express to you our views on the subject of the benevolent virtues. We attach such importance to these, that we are sometimes reproached with exalting them above piety. We regard the spirit of love, charity, meekness, forgiveness, liberality, and beneficence, as the badge and distinction of Christians, as the brightest image we can bear of God, as the best proof of piety. On this subject I need not and cannot enlarge; but there is one branch of benevolence which I ought not to pass over in silence, because we think that we conceive of it more highly and justly than many of our brethren. I refer to the duty of candor, charitable judgment, especially towards those who differ in religious opinion. We think that in nothing have Christians so widely departed from their religion, as in this particular. We read with astonishment and horror the history of the church; and sometimes, when we look back on the fires of persecution, and on the zeal of Christians in building up walls of separation, and in giving up one another to perdition, we feel as if we were reading the records of an infernal, rather than a heavenly kingdom. An enemy to every religion, if asked to describe a Christian, would, with some show of reason, depict him as an idolator of his own distinguishing opinions, covered with badges of party, shutting his eyes on the virtues, and his ears on the arguments, of his opponents, arrogating all excellence to his own sect and all saving power to his own creed, sheltering under the name of pious zeal the love of domination, the conceit of infallibility, and the spirit of intolerance, and trampling on men's rights under the pretence of saving their souls.

. . . .

To all who hear me, I would say, with the Apostle, Prove all things, hold fast that which is good. Do not, brethren, shrink from the duty of searching God's Word for yourselves, through fear of human censure and denunciation. Do not think that you may innocently follow the opinions which prevail around you, without investigation, on the ground that Christianity is now so purified from errors, as to need no laborious research. There is much reason to believe that Christianity is at this moment dishonored by gross and cherished corruptions. If you remember the darkness which hung over the Gospel for ages; if you consider the impure union which still subsists in almost every Christian country between the church and state, and which enlists men's selfishness and ambition on the side of established error; if you recollect in what degree the spirit of intolerance has checked free inquiry, not only before, but since the Reformation; you will see that Christianity cannot have freed itself from all the human inventions which disfigured it under the Papal tyranny. No. Much stubble is yet to be burned; much rubbish to be removed; many gaudy decorations which a false taste has hung around Christianity must be swept away; and the earth-born fogs which have long shrouded it must be scattered, before this divine fabric will rise before us in its native and awful majesty, in its harmonious proportions, in its mild and celestial splendors. This glorious reformation in the church, we hope, under God's blessing, from the progress of the human intellect, from the moral progress of society, from the consequent decline of prejudice and bigotry, and, though last not least, from the subversion of human authority in matters of religion, from the fall of those hierarchies, and other human institutions, by which the minds of individuals are oppressed under the weight of numbers, and a Papal dominion is perpetuated in the Protestant church. Our earnest prayer to God is that he will overturn, and overturn, and overturn the strong-holds of spiritual usurpation, until HE shall come whose right it is to rule the minds of men; that the conspiracy of ages against the liberty of Christians may be brought to an end; that the servile assent so long yielded to human creeds may give place to honest and devout inquiry into the Scriptures; and that Christianity, thus purified from error, may put forth its almighty energy, and prove itself, by its ennobling influence on the mind, to be indeed "the power of God unto salvation."

The Faith Once Delivered to the Saints

LYMAN BEECHER

Born, New Haven, Connecticut, October 12, 1775; died, Brooklyn, New York, January 10, 1863. Graduated from Yale, 1797. Ordained a Presbyterian minister in 1799. Pastor East Hampton, Long Island, 1799–1810; Litchfield, Connecticut, 1810–1826; Hanover Street, Boston, 1826–1832. Left Boston in 1832 to become first president and professor of theology at Lane Theological Seminary and pastor of the Second Presbyterian Church of Cincinnati. Became involved in a theological controversy; was accused of heresy; tried and acquitted. Resigned from Lane in 1850. A Calvinist, but a believer in free will, Beecher devoted his pastorates to a continuous religious revival. Called by Theodore Parker "the father of more brains than any other man in America," Beecher had thirteen children, the most famous being Henry Ward Beecher and Harriet Beecher Stowe.

Beloved, when I gave all diligence to write unto you of the common salvation, it was needful for me to write unto you, and exhort you that ye should earnestly contend for the faith which was once delivered to the saints.

Jude, 3

*B*y the faith once delivered to the saints is to be understood the doctrines of the Gospel. These were delivered to the saints by holy men, who spake as they were moved by the Holy

A Sermon Delivered at Worcester, Mass., Oct. 15, 1823, at the Ordination of the Rev. Loammi Ives Hoadly, Lyman Beecher, D.D., 2nd ed. (Boston: Crocker and Brewster, 1824), 40 pp. Basic doctrinal points are presented in approximately the first half of the sermon reproduced here.

Ghost. The saints to whom they were delivered were those who constituted the church under the Old dispensation, and the New.

The exhortation to contend for them earnestly supposes that they would be powerfully assailed; and yet that they might be known and defended.

It is proposed, in this discourse, to give an epitome of what is supposed to be the faith delivered to the saints;—to state the reasons for believing it such;—and to point out the manner in which it becomes the churches of our Lord to contend for it.

The faith once delivered to the saints included, it is believed, among other doctrines, the following:—

That men are free agents; in the possession of such faculties, and placed in such circumstances, as render it practicable for them to do whatever God requires; reasonable that he should require it; and fit that he should inflict, literally, the entire penalty of disobedience,—such ability is here intended, as lays a perfect foundation for government by law, and for rewards and punishments according to deeds.

That the divine law requires love to God with all the heart, and impartial love for men; together with certain overt duties to God and men, by which this love is to be expressed; and that this law is supported by the sanctions of eternal life and eternal death.

That the ancestors of our race violated this law; that, in some way, as a consequence of their apostasy, all men, as soon as they become capable of accountable action, do, *of their own accord, most freely,* and *most wickedly,* withhold from God the *supreme love,* and from man the *impartial love,* which the law requires, beside violating many of its practical precepts: and that the obedience of the heart, which the law requires, has ceased entirely from the whole race of man.

That, according to the principles of moral government, obedience, either antecedent or subsequent to transgression, cannot avert the penalty of law; and that pardon, upon condition of repentance merely, would destroy the efficacy of moral government.

That an atonement has been made for sin by Jesus Christ; with reference to which God can maintain the influence of his law and forgive sin, upon condition of repentance towards God and faith in our Lord Jesus Christ:—that all men are invited sincerely, in this way to return to God, with an assurance of pardon and eternal life if they comply.

That a compliance with these conditions is practicable, in the regular exercise of the powers and faculties given to man as an accountable creature; and is prevented only by the exercise of a voluntary, criminal aversion to God, so inflexibly obstinate that, by motives merely, men are never persuaded to repent and believe.

That God is able, by his Spirit, to make to the mind of man such an application of the truth, as shall unfailingly convince him of sin, render him willing to obey the gospel, and actually and joyfully obedient.

That this special influence of the Holy Spirit is given according to the supreme discretion or good pleasure of God; and yet, ordinarily, is so inseparably associated with the use of means by the sinner, as to create ample encouragement to attend upon them, and to render all hopes of conversion, while neglecting or rejecting the truth, or while living in open sin, eminently presumptuous.

That believers are justified by the merits of Christ through faith; and are received into a covenant with God, which secures their continuance in holiness forever;—while those who die in their sins will continue to sin wilfully, and to be punished justly, for ever.

That God exercises a providential government; which extends to all events in such a manner, as to lay a just foundation for resignation to his will in afflictions brought upon us by the wickedness of men, and for gratitude in the reception of good in all the various modes of human instrumentality;—that all events shall illustrate his glory, and be made subservient to the good of his kingdom;—and that this government is administered in accordance with a purpose or plan known and approved of by him from the beginning.

Finally, that the God of the universe has revealed himself to us as existing in three persons, the Father, the Son, and the Holy Ghost; possessing distinct and equal attributes, and, in some unrevealed manner, so united as to constitute *one God*.

These are the doctrines, which, it is believed, were delivered to the saints, and which have been held, substantially, though with some variety of modification, by the true church of God in all ages. To prevent circumlocution, I shall, in this discourse, call them *the Evangelical System,* and for the same reason I shall call the opposite doctrines *the Liberal System.*

It has been common to support these doctrines by the quotation of proof texts. But to these a different exposition is given, more reasonable, it is said, and carrying with it a higher probability of truth; which leads to critical exposition, and opens a wide field for evasion, and creates perplexity and indecision.

My design at present is to avail myself of collateral evidence only; with the view of attempting to decide, in this way, which is the correct exposition of the proof texts, the evangelical, or the liberal exposition.

For the sake of argument, I shall suppose the evidence from exposition to be, on each side, exactly balanced; and proceed to lay into the scale of evangelical exposition those arguments which seem to furnish evidence of its correctness. I observe, then,

1. That the doctrines of the evangelical system are in accordance with the most direct and obvious meaning of the sacred text. By *obvious meaning,*

I intend that which is actually suggested, without note or comment, to the minds of honest and unlettered men. That the proof texts teach the doctrines of the evangelical system in this manner is alleged by learned infidels as a reason for rejecting the inspiration of the Bible; by Unitarian commentators and writers, as a reason for restraining, modifying, and turning aside, the text; and by critics, who translate or expound without reference to theological opinions; and by the better part of the Unitarian German critics, after having denied the inspiration of the Bible. No translators have been able to maintain a reputation for classical literature, and to sink, in a translation, the obvious meaning below, and bring up the philosophical meaning upon, the surface. The editors of the "Improved Version" have manifested as much good will, with as little conscience, in the attempt, as has ever appeared; and yet have been compelled to allow the proof texts, in most instances, to speak the offensive doctrines, and to content themselves with a simple contradiction of them in notes and comments. Interpretation according to the obvious import has always resulted in the evangelical system; while expositors according to the supposed rational and philosophical mode of exposition have differed indefinitely. It is not the evangelical, but the liberal rule of interpretation, which has filled the world with divers doctrines, perplexity and doubt. All versions, and all expositions according to the obvious meaning, of whatever country or age, do substantially agree in the evangelical system; and agree with the understanding of mankind at large who read the Bible. The Bible, for the most part, was written also by men who understood language only according to its obvious import;— and for the use of men to whom it must have been a sealed book upon any other principle of interpretation. Add to this the testimony of the Bible to its own plainness: that it can be read by him that runs; and understood by the wayfaring man though a fool; that it is a lamp to the path; that it furnishes the man of God thoroughly; that it is profitable for doctrine; that it is able to make wise to salvation; that it creates obligation to know the truth, and renders error inexcusable. Now if the obvious meaning of the proof texts be not the true one; and if the true meaning be one which can be seen only by men of classical and philosophical vision; then the common people have *no Bible*. For the book itself teaches *them* nothing; and the critical expositions of uninspired men are not a revelation. The character of God is also implicated, as having practiced on his subjects a most deplorable deception; as having taught them falsehood in their own tongue, and the truth in an unknown tongue; for, to the common people, the obvious is the only meaning of terms. If, therefore, the truth is not contained in the obvious meaning, it is not revealed to them in any form. Indeed, if the obvious be not the true import, the Bible teaches them falsehood. And yet, with a book, whose only intelligible meaning on the subject of doctrines is false, and whose real import is necessarily unknown, the common people are required, upon pain of his eternal displeasure, to abhor error, and to love and obey the truth.—Was the glorious God ever more scandalized than by such an imputation? We have heard of his having made a great part of mankind on purpose to damn them, and of his sending to hell infants and helpless victims, for the nonperformance of impossibilities: and, if such were indeed his character and conduct, I know not what other Bible we could expect, than one impossible to be understood, and framed to deceive. But, on this subject, we adopt the language of a distinguished advocate of the liberal system. "It is impossible that a teacher of infinite wisdom should expose those, whom he would teach, to infinite error. He will rather surpass all other instructors in bringing down truth to our apprehension. A revelation is a gift of light; it cannot thicken and multiply our perplexities."*

2. It is the uniform testimony of the Bible that the righteous love the truth, and that the wicked are opposed to it.

If then, we can decide who are the wicked, in the Scriptural sense, which system they approve, and which they oppose; we have an inspired decision which is the faith delivered to the saints. But the Scriptures have decided that the irreligious and profane, and all persons of confirmed vicious habits, are wicked men. They have placed in the same class the ambitious, who love the praise of men more than the praise of God; and the voluptuous, who love pleasure more than God. Now that some of this description of sinners are found among the professed believers of both systems is admitted; but which system do they, as a body, prefer; and against which do they manifest unequivocal hostility? It requires no proof, but universal observation, to support the position that the irreligious, immoral and voluptuous part of the community prefer the liberal system, and are vehement in their opposition to the evangelical system.† If this assertion needs confirmation; assemble the pleasure-loving and licentious community of the world;—the patrons of balls and theatres and masquerades:—and let the doctrines of the evangelical system be preached plainly to them. Would they be pleased with them? Would they endure them? Do this class of the community, where their numbers or influence preponderate, any where, in the wide world, settle and support an evangelical minister; and if they support the preaching of any system of doctrines, is it not substantially the liberal system? Go to the

* Channing's Sermon, second Baltimore ed., pp. 12, 13.

† The reader will observe, that we do not say, nor do we believe it to be true, that all, or even the majority, who professedly embrace the liberal system are wicked in the sense explained. . . . Our assertion is, that those who are wicked, in the Scripture sense of that term, do, as a body, whatever preaching they attend, and with whatever denomination they are classed, dislike the doctrines of the evangelical faith and prefer those of the liberal system.

voluntary evening association for conference and prayer; and which system will you hear breathed out in supplication? Then go to the voluntary evening association for gambling or inebriation, and which system, with its patrons, will you hear loaded with execration and ridicule? When a division is made in a town or parish, by the settlement of a minister of liberal or evangelical opinions; which side do a majority of the pious take, if there be on earth any such thing as piety manifested by credible evidence; and which side do the wicked take, if there be on earth any such class of persons as wicked men—proved to be such by their deeds? If a majority is obtained against evangelical opinions, was it ever known to be done by the most pious and moral part of the community, in opposition to the suffrages of the most irreligious and flagitious?* There is, then, some powerful cause, of universal operation, which arrays the irreligious part of the community against the evangelical system. But, according to the Bible, of two opposing systems, one of which must be true, that which the wicked approve is false, and that which they oppose and hate is true;—"for he that doeth evil hateth the light, neither cometh to the light, lest his deeds should be reproved."

3. The evangelical system produces the same effects, universally, as were produced by the faith delivered to the saints.

The maxim, that *the same cause, in the same circumstances, will produce the same effect,* is as true in the moral as in the natural world; the laws of mind, and the operation of moral causes, being just as uniform as the laws of matter. The Gospel, the greatest moral cause which ever operated in the world, is the same now as in the apostolic age; and the heart of man, civilized or uncivilized, is also the same. So that this great cause is operating now, in substantially the same circumstances as it did in the primitive age;— for the heart of man is the moral world, and is the same now as then. If there be a system of doctrines, then, at the present time, whose effects are universally the same with those produced by the faith once delivered to the saints; that system, demonstrably, *is the faith* which was once delivered to the saints. Identity of moral effect proves identity of moral cause.

* It may not be known to all who read this discourse, that, according to a late construction given to the laws of Massachusetts, the town, or society, may dispose of the funds which were given to the church; and dismiss or settle a minister without the concurrence, and in opposition to, the suffrage of the church. And that, in consequence of this decision, Unitarian ministers have often been settled by towns and societies, in opposition to the efforts of evangelical churches: by which means, they have been stripped of their funds, and exiled from their place of worship; and subjected to the necessity of forming a new society, and erecting another house of worship, unless they would consent to set under Unitarian ministrations, and forego that instruction which they considered an important means of salvation.

Now, in every one of these instances, it is believed, that the immoral and irreligious part of the town or society, have united with Unitarians; and sometimes, if not always, have contributed to the formation of a majority which could not have been obtained without them. . . .

The illustration of the argument from effects must consist of many particulars, and of matters of fact. The argument, therefore, can only be stated concisely, without attempting to answer every possible objection. The facts, too, may be regarded by some as invidious. I have only to say that no fact will be stated, as such, which is not believed to be notoriously true, and, if denied, capable of unequivocal proof; and as to the invidious bearing of matters of fact, or of arguments, I am persuaded it is both a false delicacy, and an unsound cause, which would shrink from this test, and shield itself under forms of alleged decorum. But I must be allowed to believe also, that no real decorum is violated by the statement of facts, or the pressure of arguments, where the object is important, the design honest, and the manner sober and respectful. Systems of religion, as well as of natural philosophy, may be brought to the test of actual experiment. "By their fruits shall ye know them." But if the moral world were, by the laws of decorum, closed against us; and we might only theorise without upon practical tendencies, and not enter it to collect and appeal to facts; we might contend earnestly, but certainly should contend to very little purpose. To the word and testimony of God, and to matters of fact, we appeal.

I observe then, that the evangelical system occasions the same objections, precisely, now, which were occasioned by the faith once delivered to the saints.

Such an exhibition was given of old of the particular Providence of God, as occasioned on the part of thieves, and liars, and adulterers, and idolaters, the extenuating plea, "We are delivered to do all these abominations." God governs the moral world by such irresistible influence that crimes are as much a matter of physical necessity as rain and sunshine. Do I need to say to this audience that the charge constantly urged against the Decrees of God, as an article of the evangelical system, is that it destroys accountable agency, and makes men machines, and all actions necessary by an irresistible fatality? The faith delivered to the saints then, and the evangelical faith, are perverted, in this article, exactly alike.

The ancient faith included an article which led the wicked, among the Jews, to extenuate their crimes by the allegation, "The fathers have eaten sour grapes, and the children's teeth are set on edge"; i.e., 'Sin in man is a physical property, transmitted from father to son, as bones and sinews are, and alike inconsistent with choice or blame.' And is not the objection urged against the doctrine of Original Sin, as contained in the evangelical system, the same? The inspired answer to the objection of old was, That children are accountable only for their own voluntary exercises and deeds; and this is the reply returned now by the patrons of the evangelical system.

The degree of human Depravity, as taught in the Bible, led the people, in a time of great wickedness, to say, "If our transgressions and our sins be

upon us, and we pine away in them and die, how should we then live?"
i.e., 'If we be dead in sin, to the exclusion of all spiritual life, how can we
be free agents, and how can we help ourselves, or be justly blamed?' And,
as if they had been told by the prophet that their death in sin was voluntary
and criminal, though entire, and certain in its efficacy; they seem to say,
'Well, if we are so wicked that we certainly shall pine away and die in our
sins, how can we be to blame? If we shall not turn of ourselves, how can we
turn; and of what use is ability that will never be exerted?' Now are not
these precisely the objections which are at this day alleged, constantly,
against the doctrines of man's entire depravity, and moral inability, as articles
of the evangelical system?

Our Saviour asserts the necessity of some great change to qualify a man
for the kingdom of heaven; which, to a ruler in Israel, appeared mysterious,
and even impossible. And is there not a great change insisted on, in the
evangelical system, as indispensable to salvation; to which masters in Israel
now confess that they are strangers; and which they regard as impossible,
without the destruction of free agency and accountability?

The manner of a sinner's Justification was delivered to the saints in such
terms, as occasioned the objection that it made void the law; superseding
the obligations and motives to a moral life, and leading to licentiousness.
"Do we then make void the law through faith?" "Shall we continue in sin
that grace may abound?" And is not this precisely the objection which has
been urged against the doctrine of justification by faith, as contained in
the evangelical system, from the time of the Reformation to this day?

The saints were taught something concerning the Sovereignty of God,
as having mercy on whom he would, and punishing whom he would;—
which produced the objection, "Why then doth he yet find fault; for who
hath resisted his will?" 'If wicked men receive their destination as God ap-
points; why does he blame them? If it be his will that they perish, and they
do perish; are they not obedient? and why does he find fault?' And is not
this the objection which is urged, unceasingly, against the doctrine of Election, as taught in the evangelical system? To our reply, that the will of
God, as a moral rule to man, and the will of God, as a rule of administration
to himself in disposing of rebels, are distinct; the answer is, 'Metaphysics!
metaphysics! The will of God is the will of God; and if sinners, *in any
sense*, act in accordance with any will of God, they are obedient; and he has
no cause to find fault.' Now did the liberal exposition of the ninth of Romans
ever produce, in the whole history of man, the objection which this chapter
produced as written by the Apostle? or do liberal preachers ever have occasion
to adopt the reply of Paul to objections produced by their exposition? But
the evangelical exposition produces, invariably, the same objection which
the Apostle encountered, and this objection receives, invariably, the same

reply. "Nay, but O man, who art thou that repliest against God?" 'Shall a being of yesterday arraign the conduct of his Maker? Shall a rebel sit in judgment upon his God? Are not men rebels, justly doomed to die; and, in reference to their character and condition as condemned criminals, all clay of the same lump? And is not the discretion of God, to pardon or reprieve, as absolute as that of the potter over his clay, to make one vessel to honor and another to dishonor?' Do you object, that the punishment threatened is unjust? But how could God make a vessel of *mercy* of one whose punishment would be unjust; or a vessel of *wrath* of one whose punishment would be undeserved? Do you call men impotent because they are compared to clay; or assert that the sovereignty of God, in saving some, *causes,* and renders unavoidable, the destruction of others? We reply, those who perish, perish *for their sins,* for which they might have been punished, justly, without an offer of pardon. They might, if they would, comply with the terms of pardon, and are punished for rejecting them. Nor are they cut down in haste. With much long-suffering they are endured, while, by despising the riches of the goodness of God, they *fit themselves* for destruction. Such is the evangelical reply; and such, as we understand his language and argument, is the reply of Paul. . . .

The faith delivered to the saints occasioned a virulent hatred. It was not hatred of it as false, arising from an ardent love of truth: for Pharisees and Sadducees could tolerate each other; and Pagans could tolerate thirty thousand gods, with all their lust and blood. And is not the evangelical system encountered by a virulence of opposition, in circumstances which show that it cannot arise from the love of truth or hatred of error? None will pretend that the effects of the evangelical system are as deplorable as the effects of idolatry in its present forms. The evangelical system has produced no temple of impure resort; no gratifications of lust enjoined as acts of worship; no blood of human victims; no burning of widows, or drowning of infants; no self-inflicted penal tortures. And yet, such is the hatred of many to the evangelical system, that they oppose, deliberately, all attempts to extend it to the heathen; and on the ground, avowedly, that they had rather the heathen would remain as they are, than adopt the evangelical system. . . .

The faith delivered to the saints produced a stricter morality than any contemporaneous system. Whether this be true of the evangelical system is not to be decided by a comparison of the best characters on one side with the most defective on the other; or of individuals of good moral character on both sides, of which it is admitted there are many. Nor can the moral efficacy of the two systems be decided by the standard of public morality, where the evangelical system has prevailed in the early period of life, and exerted its influence upon the conscience, and in the formation of moral habits; or where it still prevails to such an extent as to exert a powerful modifying influence; and, especially, where the opposite system is of but recent public notoriety, and of limited extent. Great moral causes do not produce their effects immediately; nor, upon every individual, exactly the same effect. Their tendency and efficacy is to be looked for in those communities where the influence of the two systems has been the most unmingled, and of the longest duration; and also, in those obvious changes in a community, which, as one or the other prevails, become apparent. With these explanations in view, I remark that the superior moral efficacy of the evangelical system is a matter of unequivocal concession. In an article on predestination in the British Encyclopedia, written, it is said, by Robert Forsyth, Esq., a learned civilian, and an infidel; after giving an account of the Calvinistic and Arminian system, and the preference to the latter, it is said, "There is one remark which we think ourselves in justice bound to make. It is this; that, from the earliest ages, down to our own days, if we consider the character of the ancient Stoics, the Jewish Essenes, the modern Calvinists and Jansenists, compared with that of their antagonists, the Epicurians, the Sadducees, the Arminians and the Jesuits; we shall find that they have excelled, in no small degree, in the practice of the most rigid and respectable virtues; and have been the highest honor to their own age, and the best models for imitation to every succeeding age." This is the testimony of a philosopher, to the different moral effects of the two systems, from the time of Augustine, at least, to the present day.

. . . .

The accusations brought against evangelical writers and professors as requiring too much, or making no sufficient allowance for the weakness of human nature; as rigid, austere, enemies to innocent amusements; as setting themselves up as better than their neighbors; as righteous over much, are also concessions in point: as are also the topics of ridicule, having reference, as they do, to the fastidious strictness of our ancestors, and of evangelical professors: to which we may add the invidious names given to them, of Puritan, Methodist, &c. It appears then, as a matter of fact, that sound morality has never, in any country or age, been so elevated, and so extensively prevalent, as in those communities where the evangelical doctrines have been most universally believed, and most diligently taught, in families and schools, and in the sanctuary. It has been said, I am sensible, that these salutary effects of the evangelical system are produced by the truths contained in it in common with the liberal system, and in spite of the errors it embraces, and not *by* them. Does the truth, then, mingled with absurdity and falsehood, produce better effects than the truth simple and undefiled, as in the liberal system it is claimed to be? If it is the truth, held in common by the evangelical and liberal systems, which produces these good effects, why does not the liberal system alone produce the same effects? Allow me to suggest another solution. The evangelical system *requires* a stricter morality, enforced by more powerful motives. It adopts, as its rule, the moral law, unmitigated; and its sanctions, of eternal life and eternal death. A law which the opposite system regards as too strict, and as set aside or mitigated, in accommodation to human frailty; and whose sanctions are regarded as nothing;—or as a salutary temporary discipline;—or as annihilation;—or as a matter of entire uncertainty. Now is it strange that lax requisitions, and feeble, uncertain sanctions, do not produce the strict and vigorous morality of the law of God? What would human laws avail, should expositors and judges say, 'Men are too wicked to allow of our interpreting the laws strictly: they must not be understood to mean exactly what they say, or to threaten exactly what they speak: perfect honesty, or truth, or purity, is not to be expected; a little fraud, and theft, and perjury, and violence, they allow, in accommodation to human weakness; and threaten the *greater crimes* with *no punishment,* or only a beneficial temporary discipline, or exile from the state, or—we know not what'?

Again, the evangelical system produces the best attendance on the public worship of God, and, of course, if the moral tendency of each were the same, that would produce the strictest and most general morality, which commanded, most extensively and deeply, the attention of men. That the doctrines of the evangelical system do this, is claimed by Witherspoon as true, in his day, in Scotland; and by Overton as true in England; and is admitted by English Unitarian writers, and denied by no one. It is also admitted in this country recently, as a matter of notoriety "which none will question." It is accounted for, it must be acknowledged, in a way not favorable to the moral tendency of evangelical sentiments. It is on the ground of the intolerable strictness of liberal preaching; so strict and terrifying that few, besides the more pious and exemplary, can abide it. The whole pleasure-loving, voluptuous and dissipated community being driven, panic-struck, by Unitarian denunciation, to the horns of the altar in evangelical churches; where, by "smooth preaching," and the hope of impunity in sin, their fears may be allayed, and their consciences quieted.

The faith delivered to the saints produced revivals of religion. The preaching of it was attended with sudden anxieties, and deep convictions of sin, and sudden joy in believing; followed by reformation and a holy life. Nor was this the effect of miracles, or itself a miraculous event, in the common acceptation of the term. Miracles, merely, produced no such effects. It was under the preaching of the word that men were pricked in their hearts, and cried out, "Men and brethren, what shall we do to be saved?" And it was by the moral transformation, which attended the apostolic answer to this question, and not by the power of miracles, that the Gospel defied opposition, and spread during the first three hundred years. There was no resisting it. Conviction attended the word; and a joyful obedience to the faith followed. The very chiefs of opposition exchanged their weapons of annoyance for the shield of faith, and the sword of the Spirit. And do not the same convictions of sin attend the preaching of the evangelical system; and does it not extend its victories in the same manner? By argument, merely, we convince few, and reclaim none. But there is an efficacy in evangelical preaching on the conscience and on the heart; against which neither learning, nor talents, nor prejudice, nor wrath itself, afford effectual protection. Multitudes who virulently hated, and verily thought that they ought to oppose, evangelical doctrines and revivals of religion have been convinced of their mistake, and sin; and have embraced, joyfully, the doctrines which they reviled. Many who preach the liberal system can bear witness that they have lost, in this way, again and again, the very pillars of their societies. Defections of the same kind are frequent still, and clothe evangelical doctrines and revivals of religion with a terrifying power.

The faith delivered to the saints was efficacious in the sudden reformation of those who had been long under the dominion of vicious habits. The apostle enumerates the habits of crime which prevailed among Pagans; and then, writing to the church of Corinth, says, "And such were some of you." But, while the liberal system despairs, professedly, of any sudden reformation from vicious habits, as against the established laws of the moral world; and is unable to produce an instance in which a vicious person has been reformed, by *abandoning the evangelical and adopting the liberal system*; and while reformation from vicious habits is a rare event, if it exist at all, under liberal preaching; it is a frequent event for profligates, on *abandoning their confidence in the liberal system and adopting the evangelical, to manifest a most salutary and abiding change of character and conduct*. . . .

The faith delivered to the saints produced a spirit of missions. On the day of Pentecost the number of disciples was one hundred and twenty. And on that day the scales of Jewish prejudice fell from their eyes; and the spirit of missions descended upon their hearts; and, in three hundred years, without colleges, or theological seminaries, or the press, or governmental aid, but in opposition to its dire hostility, they evangelized the world. And are not the great movements now making to evangelize the world, conducted chiefly under the auspices and by the charities of those who adopt substantially the evangelical system? Are not all the denominations in the world, who believe in the Divinity of Christ and his atonement, in the depravity of man and his need of a moral renovation by the Spirit; and in the doctrine of justification by faith, and future eternal punishment, more or less engaged in the work of missions? And is there, in the wide world, a denomination which rejects these doctrines, that is thus engaged? And is this system, which does nothing to evangelize the world, the Gospel; and that, which does all that is done in accordance with the efforts of the primitive church, not the Gospel?

The faith delivered to the saints produced a piety of great solemnity, and ardor, and decision. It was a piety which took delight in the public worship of God, and in frequent private association for religious conference and prayer; a piety which included a deep solicitude, and made vigorous exertions, for the conversion of sinners, and experienced peculiar joy in the event; a piety which espoused openly the cause of Christ, encountered obloquy and the loss of all things, and stood undaunted in the face of danger, and produced joy unspeakable in the hour of death. And is not this, precisely, the same cast of piety which the evangelical system does, and which the liberal system does not, produce? Is not the deeply serious cast of the one regarded as constituting the evangelical a gloomy religion; and the lighter cast of the other as giving to it vastly the preference on the score of cheerfulness? Is not the ardor of the one stigmatized as enthusiasm; and the cool, deliberate, intellectual cast of the other regarded as giving to it the enviable preeminence of a rational religion? Does not the one delight in, and the other deprecate, frequent voluntary associations for religious conference and prayer? Does not the one ridicule the supposed work of sudden conversion by the Spirit of God, and the other hold it in the highest estimation? . . .

The faith delivered to the saints was attended, from the beginning to the end, with an unwavering confidence of its truth. False christs and false prophets arose; but they could not "deceive the elect." Winds of false doctrine blew, but they scattered only the chaff; some also made shipwreck of the faith, but it was not the saints. There were heresies early; and it was needful there should be, that they which were approved might be manifest. And they were manifest; for the last Apostle that remained testified, "They went out from us, but they were not of us; for if they had been of us, they would no doubt have continued with us." But to those who adhered to the faith, he said, "Ye have an unction from the Holy One, and know all things": i.e., 'You know the truth of all those doctrines which some have rejected.' Now it is admitted that some patrons of the evangelical system abandon it. But it will not be denied that, as a general fact, they hold the same system of truth to the end; modified, explained, and proved, with some variation; but the same system undeniably. But can it be said of the patrons of the liberal system, as a body, that their system, first and last, is the same? Can it be said of an individual scarcely, that he continues to embrace the same system through life? . . .

4. A departure from the faith delivered to the saints, producing divisions in the church, was denominated a heresy during the three first centuries.

This does not prove those doctrines to be false which the churches condemned, because churches and councils are not infallible. But it does prove the opinions denominated heretical to be novelties, and in opposition to the received opinion of the church until the time of their condemnation. The declaration of the primitive church that a doctrine is a heresy is a public formal testimony as to what had been, until then, the received opinion of the churches.

The heretics themselves admitted, sometimes, that their opinions were novel, but contended that they were nevertheless true; or, more commonly, so explained them as to claim that they were not a departure from the received faith. Uniting, of course, the testimony of heretics to that of the church, as to what had been the received opinion.

From the nature, then, and the known era of the several heresies in the primitive church, we may ascertain what was the antecedent faith of the church, on the points to which they relate.

The doctrine of the Incarnation of Christ was, then, the received opinion of the church, when denied by the Gnostics, towards the close of the first century. The Divinity of Christ was the received opinion of the church when denied by Arius, A.D. 315; who, soon after, was condemned as a heretic in a council of 380 Fathers. And the doctrines of original sin, entire depravity, regeneration by special grace, and justification by faith, continued to be the received doctrines of the church until the time of Pelagius, about A.D. 400.

The doctrines of the evangelical system, then, commenced their journey down to us from the apostolic age: and as each doctrine of the liberal system encountered any one of them, *that* was declared by the church to be a novelty, and the other the antecedently received opinion of the church. Can this fact be reconciled with the supposition that the liberal system was the faith *first* delivered to the saints? Did all the churches, from the beginning, misunderstand the import of the Gospels and Epistles, and all the apostolic expositions of them; and misunderstand, systematically, and exactly alike, on all points, and in direct opposition to what Jesus Christ and the Apostles intended to teach; and this too, without concert, and throughout the Roman Empire? Or if the liberal was the system first delivered to the saints, could all the churches have exchanged it for the opposite system, so early, so silently, so unitedly, as to have the *whole truth* regarded as a novelty, and denounced as a heresy, in the second and third and fourth centuries? Dr. Priestley has, indeed, attempted to show that the liberal system was that which was actually delivered by Christ and his Apostles to the saints, and that such a change as we have supposed did happen in the progress of two or three hundred years. But, beside the utter failure of his proof, he might as well have attempted to show that the course of all the rivers in the Roman Empire was reversed during the three first centuries of the Christian era, in opposition to the testimony of all the historians and naturalists of the empire, convened by public authority on purpose to inquire into the matter of fact.

5. It is a point decided by inspiration that the Martyrs who suffered under Pagan and Papal persecutions held the same faith; and that the faith which they held, and for which they suffered, is the faith which was delivered to the saints. The Apostle John saw in vision "under the altar, the souls of them that were slain for the word of God, and for the testimony which they held." It is called in another place, "the commandments of God, and the testimony of Jesus Christ." These are the Martyrs under Pagan Rome. But with reference to those who suffered afterwards, under Papal Rome, it is said: "Here is the patience of the saints: here are they that keep the commandments of God, and the faith of Jesus." The faith, then, which the Martyrs held, under Pagan and Papal Rome, and for which they suffered, was the same, and was the WORD OF GOD AND THE FAITH OF JESUS. But we know, by evidence unequivocal and undeniable, that the doctrinal opinions of the Martyrs under Papal Rome were the doctrines of the evangelical system, and not those of the liberal system. They exist now upon historical records, and in public creeds; and are denominated the doctrines of the Reformation. The doctrines of the Reformation then, which we denominate the evangelical system, have the seal of heaven impressed upon them, as being the WORD OF GOD AND THE FAITH OF JESUS, THE FAITH WHICH WAS ONCE DELIVERED TO THE SAINTS.

THE ESSENTIAL NATURE OF
THE CONSTITUTION

IT WAS the autumn of 1832 when South Carolina legislators summoned a state convention to exercise its right
as a sovereign power to veto an act of the United States
Congress. The Convention quickly drafted an Ordinance
of Nullification that declared the Tariff Acts of 1828 and
1832 unconstitutional, forbade collection of duties at
South Carolina ports, imposed a test or loyalty oath on
state officials, and threatened secession if the Federal
Government tried to enforce the Acts.

Nullification had been bubbling ominously for years.
When it boiled over, no one was caught by surprise, least
of all the President of the United States. Andrew Jackson
promptly issued a ringing proclamation, warning the
people of South Carolina that they had been led by designing leaders to the brink of treason, and that the
Federal Government would use troops to collect duties
and maintain the Union. At once, South Carolina set
about raising troops to repel "invasion."

Jackson was dead sure that the Vice-President of the
United States, John C. Calhoun, was the arch-traitor and
villain in the piece. There had been bad blood between
the two for years; the feud was personal and political. A
Southerner himself, Jackson was a states-rights man up to
a point, but he would countenance no threat to the nation's sovereignty. This he had made clear at a Jefferson
birthday dinner in 1830, when, with his eyes fixed on the

*Vice-President, he offered a toast: "Our Federal Union—
it must be preserved!" Calhoun replied: "The Union—
next to our liberty, the most dear!"*

Through the years, Calhoun had undergone political
metamorphosis. In 1811 he entered Congress an ardent
nationalist. After the War of 1812, he was all for unify-
ing the nation and strengthening its economy through a
protective tariff, a national bank, and a program of internal improvements. Out of Congress between 1817 and
1832, Calhoun served successively as Secretary of War
and Vice-President, and Henry Clay took over leadership
of the grandiose program of national development, which
he called The American System. In 1824 and 1828 Congress enacted further tariff legislation that hiked rates,
the 1828 Act being the famous or infamous Tariff of
Abominations. This did it.

Antiprotection sentiment was rife in the South; South
Carolina was explosive. The state had failed to develop
the balanced economy Calhoun hoped for when he
pushed the 1816 Tariff Act. By 1828 its economic position
had deteriorated badly, principally because of its land-
destroying cotton culture. Mulling over their declining
position, South Carolinians viewed with jaundiced eyes
the growing prosperity among manufacturing states. Inflated pride and empty pocketbooks goaded them into
seeking some external reason for their plight. They
reached the settled conviction that it was discriminatory
tariff legislation that made them a tributary to the North.

As Calhoun's political views shifted to coincide with
those dominant in his state, the former nationalist captured the intellectual and political leadership of the states-
rights movement. While occupying the Vice-President's
chair he secretly wrote The South Carolina Exposition in
1828, a doctrine of nullification for the benefit of South
Carolina legislators. It contained two basic propositions:
The Federal Constitution is a compact between states, not

an instrument of "we the people"; and each sovereign state retains its power to judge the constitutionality of an act of Congress. In short, the Federal Government was only an agent of the states; each state had the authority to veto an act of its agent. A nullified law would become binding only if it were subsequently adopted as an interpretative amendment by three-fourths of the states.

Calhoun and his henchmen succeeded in holding the lid on South Carolina while they looked westward for friends in Congress to help roll back the tariff. The West, too, had its grievances against the manufacturing East. Western congressmen chafed with suspicion that industrial states were blocking migration to the land of Eden. These suspicions seemed justified when, on December 29, 1829, Senator Foote of Connecticut offered a resolution to inquire into the expediency of limiting the sale of lands in the public domain to those already on the market, and to abolish the office of Surveyor-General. Senator Benton of Missouri, quick to denounce this resolution as an Eastern plot to keep exploited laborers from settling in the West, openly invited the South to make common cause against the East. Responding to Benton's overture, Senator Robert Y. Hayne of South Carolina flirted with Benton and his friends while making as much mischief as he could between West and East. Hayne's attacks on New England and his defense of nullification brought Daniel Webster into the act. Webster pulled the debate from its wayward course and placed it on an ideological basis. For years he had expounded constitutional theory before the Supreme Court. Now, in his Second Reply to Hayne, he was out to win his case for Federal sovereignty in Congress and before the bar of public opinion. Although Webster's patriotic plea for national unity resounded through the country, it fell on deaf ears in South Carolina.

The Tariff Act of 1832 dashed southern hopes for sub-

stantial downward revision. With no further faith in Jackson or sectional alliances, South Carolina plumped for nullification. Calhoun, too, had come to the fork in his political roads. He resigned from the Vice-Presidency in December, 1832, whereupon South Carolina promptly sent him to the United States Senate to replace Robert Hayne, now Governor.

Amidst rumors that he would be arrested for treason, Calhoun returned to Washington filled wtih apprehension. On January 4, 1833, this gaunt, intense man walked unfalteringly into the tense Senate chamber, over which he had presided for nearly eight years, presented his credentials and took a solemn oath to uphold and defend the Constitution. The ice broken, he plunged into legislative business.

Against the background of nullification the Congress busied itself with two matters of overriding importance. Compromise tariff legislation was in the making. Success was assured when Henry Clay, great in reputation for The American System and as engineer of compromise, took charge. Amidst this promising activity, Jackson requested sweeping authority to use force against South Carolina if it resisted Federal authority. Since everyone knew that South Carolina would revoke its Ordinance of Nullification when a tariff bill with lower rates was passed, and since everyone knew that Jackson would not be called upon to use force, the request was inflammatory. It brought Calhoun to his feet. On January 22, he introduced three resolutions which pinpointed his constitutional theory and which, if adopted, would compel the rejection of Jackson's "force bill."

Senators jockeyed for position in the unfolding debate. Not until February 15, 1833 was it possible for Calhoun to launch his major speech against the force bill and in behalf of his January 22 resolutions. Meanwhile congressional and public anticipation mounted. Symboli-

cally, the worst storm of the winter raged outside the capitol building on February 15, when Calhoun opened his two-day argument inside the densely packed Senate chamber. On the first day he pursued a thread of constitutional argument while rationalizing his past political career, particularly his part in the Tariff Act of 1816. With passion, he denounced the force bill:

And how is it proposed to preserve the Union? By force! Does any man in his senses believe that this beautiful structure, this harmonious aggregate of States, produced by joint consent of all, can be preserved by force? Its very introduction will be certain destruction of this Federal Union. No, no; you cannot keep the States united in their constitutional and federal bonds by force. Force may, indeed, hold the parts together; but such union would be the bond between master and slave; a union of exaction on one side, and of unqualified obedience on the other.

The next day, February 16, Calhoun focused sharply upon constitutional theory by which this "aggregate of States, produced by joint consent of all" could be maintained. His answer revolved about the question, how may a minority protect its rights against the tyranny of the majority? The question was ancient, but never before had it been pressed with such vigor or rigor in public debate. Although the nub of his states-rights doctrine derived from the Virginia and Kentucky resolves of 1798, Calhoun's brilliant mind expanded the doctrine by projecting an elaborate system for distibuting power through the methods of nullification and concurrent majorities.

The logic of events cast Daniel Webster into the role of Calhoun's chief opponent. Webster's stirring replies to Hayne in 1830 had won for him the title Defender of the Constitution. Now he faced a serious psychological hazard, however, for his reply to Calhoun might turn out to be an anticlimax to his Second Reply to Hayne. Now, too, he faced the real intellectual leader of the South Carolina doctrine. Webster spoke for one hour immedi-

*ately after Calhoun had finished, and then the Senate
recessed. At five o'clock, Webster resumed his argument
and completed the address at eight in the evening.*

Wisely, Webster attempted no tour de force *for popular consumption. Wisely, he directed his shafts at Calhoun's interpretative resolutions and arguments on constitutional theory, eschewing argument on particulars of
the force bill itself. Step by step, Webster pursued his
sober legal analysis of the Constitution to prove that it
was truly the organic law of the land and the foundation
for federal sovereignty. He dissected Calhoun's premises
and their consequences to show that they led backwards
toward the feeble and impotent Confederacy that preceded the Constitution, and ultimately to revolution.*

*The controversy between Calhoun and Webster over
the Constitution was the high point in the debate, which
petered out in February. Congress passed Clay's compromise tariff bill which in turn opened the way for
South Carolina's repeal of its Ordinance of Nullification.
Congress also passed Jackson's force bill, which South
Carolina promptly nullified without reprisal.*

*The tempest subsided temporarily, but clouds hung
oppressively at the horizon. Ultimately the entire South
was swept up into the currents of Calhoun's thinking and
driven onto the rocks of secession. It was Webster's constitutional theory that weathered the storms of the century.*

The Compact Theory of the Constitution

JOHN CALDWELL CALHOUN

*Born, Abbeville district, South Carolina, March 18, 1782;
died, Washington, D.C., March 30, 1850. Graduated
from Yale, 1804; attended law school, Litchfield, Connecticut. Admitted to South Carolina bar, 1807. Member of
South Carolina legislature, 1808–1809; of United States
House of Representatives, 1811–1817. Secretary of War,
1817–1825. Vice-President of United States, 1825–1832.
United States Senator, 1832–1844. Secretary of State,
1844–1845. United States Senator, 1845–1850. Foremost
exponent of states-rights doctrine after 1828.*

*H*aving supplied the omissions of yesterday, I now
resume the subject at the point where my remarks
then terminated. The Senate will remember that I stated, at their close, that
the great question at issue is, whether ours is a federal or a consolidated
system of government; a system in which the parts, to use the emphatic
language of Mr. Palgrave, are the integers, and the whole the multiple, or
in which the whole is an unit and the parts the fractions. I stated, that on
the decision of this question, I believed, depended not only the liberty and
prosperity of this country, but the place which we are destined to hold in
the intellectual and moral scale of nations. I stated, also, in my remarks on
this point, that there is a striking analogy between this and the great struggle

The United States Senate, February 15 and 16, 1833, on the Revenue Collection
Bill (Force Bill). Except for the omission of introductory references to his speech of
the previous day, this is a complete text of Calhoun's remarks on February 16. *The
Works of John C. Calhoun*, Richard K. Crallé, ed. (New York: D. Appleton and
Company, 1853), II, pp. 197–262. See also *Register of Debates in Congress*, 22nd Cong.,
2nd Sess., pp. 519–533. Crallé took the liberty of casting the reporter's version into
the first person.

between Persia and Greece, which was decided by the battles of Marathon, Platea, and Salamis, and which immortalized the names of Miltiades and Themistocles. I illustrated this analogy by showing that centralism or consolidation, with the exception of a few nations along the eastern borders of the Mediterranean, has been the pervading principle in the Asiatic governments, while the federal system, or, what is the same in principle, that system which organizes a community in reference to its parts, has prevailed in Europe.

Among the few exceptions in the Asiatic nations, the government of the twelve tribes of Israel, in its early period, is the most striking. Their government, at first, was a mere confederation without any central power, till a military chieftain, with the title of king, was placed at its head, without, however, merging the original organization of the twelve distinct tribes. This was the commencement of that central action among that peculiar people which, in three generations, terminated in a permanent division of their tribes. It is impossible even for a careless reader to peruse the history of that event without being forcibly struck with the analogy in the causes which led to their separation, and those which now threaten us with a similar calamity. With the establishment of the central power in the king commenced a system of taxation, which, under King Solomon, was greatly increased, to defray the expenses of rearing the temple, of enlarging and embellishing Jerusalem, the seat of the central government, and the other profuse expenditures of his magnificent reign. Increased taxation was followed by its natural consequences—discontent and complaint, which, before his death, began to excite resistance. On the succession of his son, Rehoboam, the ten tribes, headed by Jeroboam, demanded a reduction of the taxes; the temple being finished, and the embellishment of Jerusalem completed, and the money which had been raised for that purpose being no longer required, or, in other words, the debt being paid, they demanded a reduction of the duties —a repeal of the tariff. The demand was taken under consideration, and after consulting the old men, the counsellors of '98, who advised a reduction, he then took the opinion of the younger politicians, who had since grown up, and knew not the doctrines of their father; he hearkened unto their counsel, and refused to make the reduction, and the secession of the ten tribes under Jeroboam followed. The tribes of Judah and Benjamin, which had received the disbursements, alone remained to the house of David.

But to return to the point immediately under consideration. I know that it is not only the opinion of a large majority of our country, but it may be said to be the opinion of the age, that the very beau ideal of a perfect government is the government of a majority, acting through a representative body, without check or limitation on its power; yet, if we may test this theory by experience and reason, we shall find that, so far from being perfect, the necessary tendency of all governments, based upon the will of an absolute majority, without constitutional check or limitation of power, is to faction, corruption, anarchy, and despotism; and this, whether the will of the majority be expressed directly through an assembly of the people themselves, or by their representatives. I know that, in venturing this assertion, I utter what is unpopular both within and without these walls; but where truth and liberty are concerned, such considerations should not be regarded. I will place the decision of this point on the fact that no government of the kind, among the many attempts which have been made, has ever endured for a single generation, but, on the contrary has invariably experienced the fate which I have assigned to it. Let a single instance be pointed out, and I will surrender my opinion. But, if we had not the aid of experience to direct our judgment, reason itself would be a certain guide. The view which considers the community as an unit, and all its parts as having a similar interest, is radically erroneous. However small the community may be, and however homogeneous its interests, the moment that government is put into operation—as soon as it begins to collect taxes and to make appropriations—the different portions of the community must, of necessity, bear different and opposing relations in reference to the action of the government. There must inevitably spring up two interests—a direction and a stockholder interest—an interest profiting by the action of the government, and interested in increasing its powers and action; and another, at whose expense the political machine is kept in motion. I know how difficult it is to communicate distinct ideas on such a subject, through the medium of general propositions, without particular illustration; and in order that I may be distinctly understood, though at the hazard of being tedious, I will illustrate the important principle which I have ventured to advance, by examples.

Let us, then, suppose a small community of five persons, separated from the rest of the world; and, to make the example strong, let us suppose them all to be engaged in the same pursuit, and to be of equal wealth. Let us further suppose that they determine to govern the community by the will of a majority; and, to make the case as strong as possible, let us suppose that the majority, in order to meet the expenses of the government, lay an equal tax, say of one hundred dollars on each individual of this little community. Their treasury would contain five hundred dollars. Three are a majority; and they, by supposition, have contributed three hundred as their portion, and the other two (the minority), two hundred. The three have the right to make the appropriations as they may think proper. The question is, How would the principle of the absolute and unchecked majority operate, under these circumstances, in this little community? If the three be governed by a sense of justice—if they should appropriate the money to the objects for which it was raised, the common and equal benefit of the five, then the object of the association would be fairly and honestly effected, and each would have a common interest in the government. But, should the majority pursue an opposite course—should they appropriate the money in a manner to benefit their own particular interest, without regard to the interest of the two (and that they will so act, unless there be some efficient check, he who best knows human nature will least doubt), who does not see that the three and the two would have directly opposite interests in reference to the action of the government? The three who contribute to the common treasury but three hundred dollars, could, in fact, by appropriating the five hundred to their own use, convert the action of the government into the means of making money, and, of consequence, would have a direct interest in increasing the taxes. They put in three hundred and take out five; that is, they take back to themselves all that they put in, and, in addition, that which was put in by their associates; or, in other words, taking taxation and appropriation together, they have gained, and their associates have lost, two hundred dollars by the fiscal action of the government. Opposite interests, in reference to the action of the government, are thus created between them: the one having an interest in favor, and the other against the taxes; the one to increase, and the other to decrease the taxes; the one to retain the taxes when the money is no longer wanted, and the other to repeal them when the objects for which they were levied have been secured.

Let us now suppose this community of five to be raised to twenty-four individuals, to be governed, in like manner, by the will of a majority: it is obvious that the same principle would divide them into two interests—into a majority and a minority, thirteen against eleven, or in some other proportion; and that all the consequences which I have shown to be applicable to the small community of five would be applicable to the greater, the cause not depending upon the number, but resulting necessarily from the action of the government itself. Let us now suppose that, instead of governing themselves directly in an assembly of the whole, without the intervention of agents, they should adopt the representative principle; and that, instead of being governed by a majority of themselves, they should be governed by a majority of their representatives. It is obvious that the operation of the system would not be affected by the change: the representatives being responsible to those who chose them, would conform to the will of their constitutents, and would act as they would do were they present and acting for themselves; and the same conflict of interest, which we have shown would exist in one case, would equally exist in the other. In either case, the inevitable result would be a system of hostile legislation on the part of the majority, or the stronger interest, against the minority, or the weaker interest; the object of which, on the part of the former, would be to exact as much as possible from the latter, which would necessarily be resisted by all the means in their power. Warfare, by legislation, would thus be commenced between the parties, with the same object, and not less hostile than that which is carried on between distinct and rival nations—the only distinction would be in the instruments and the mode. Enactments, in the one case, would supply what could only be effected by arms in the other; and the inevitable operation would be to engender the most hostile feelings between the parties, which would merge every feeling of patriotism—that feeling which embraces the whole—and substitute in its place the most violent party attachment; and instead of having one common centre of attachment, around which the affections of the community might rally, there would in fact be two—the interests of the majority, to which those who constitute that majority would be more attached than they would be to the whole,—and that of the minority, to which they, in like manner, would also be more attached than to the interests of the whole. Faction would thus take the place of patriotism; and, with the loss of patriotism, corruption must necessarily follow, and in its train, anarchy, and, finally, despotism, or the establishment of absolute power in a single individual, as a means of arresting the conflict of hostile interests; on the principle that it is better to submit to the will of a single individual, who by being made lord and master of the whole community, would have an equal interest in the protection of all the parts.

Let us next suppose that, in order to avert the calamitous train of consequences, this little community should adopt a written constitution, with limitations restricting the will of the majority, in order to protect the minority against the oppression which I have shown would necessarily result without such restrictions. It is obvious that the case would not be in the slightest degree varied, if the majority be left in possession of the right of judging exclusively of the extent of its powers, without any right on the part of the minority to enforce the restrictions imposed by the constitution on the will of the majority. The point is almost too clear for illustration. Nothing can be more certain than that, when a constitution grants power, and imposes limitations on the exercise of that power, whatever interests may obtain possession of the government, will be in favor of extending the power at the expense of the limitation; and that, unless those in whose behalf the limitations were imposed have, in some form or mode, the right of enforcing them, the power will ultimately supersede the limitation, and the government must operate precisely in the same manner as if the will of the majority governed without constitution or limitation of power.

I have thus presented all possible modes in which a government founded upon the will of an absolute majority will be modified; and have demonstrated that, in all its forms, whether in a majority of the people, as in a mere Democracy, or in a majority of their representatives, without a constitution or with a constitution, to be interpreted as the will of the majority, the result will be the same: two hostile interests will inevitably be created by the action of the government, to be followed by hostile legislation, and that by faction, corruption, anarchy, and despotism.

The great and solemn question here presents itself, Is there any remedy for these evils? on the decision of which depends the question, whether the people can govern themselves, which has been so often asked with so much skepticism and doubt. There is a remedy, and but one,—the effect of which, whatever may be the form, is to organize society in reference to this conflict of interests, which springs out of the action of government; and which can only be done by giving to each part the right of self-protection; which, in a word, instead of considering the community of twenty-four a single community, having a common interest, and to be governed by the single will of an entire majority, shall upon all questions tending to bring the parts into conflict, the thirteen against the eleven, take the will, not of the twenty-four as a unit, but of the thirteen and of the eleven separately,—the majority of each governing the parts, and where they concur, governing the whole,—and where they disagree, arresting the action of the government. This I will call the concurring, as distinct from the absolute majority. In either way the number would be the same, whether taken as the absolute or as the concurring majority. Thus, the majority of the thirteen is seven, and of the eleven six; and the two together make thirteen, which is the majority of twenty-four. But, though the number is the same, the mode of counting is essentially different: the one representing the strongest interest, and the other, the entire interests of the community. The first mistake is, in supposing that the government of the absolute majority is the government of the people —that beau ideal of a perfect government which has been so enthusiastically entertained in every age by the generous and patriotic, where civilization and liberty have made the smallest progress. There can be no greater error: the government of the people is the government of the whole community—of the twenty-four—the self-government of all the parts—too perfect to be reduced to practice in the present, or any past stage of human society. The government of the absolute majority, instead of being the government of the people, is but the government of the strongest interests, and, when not efficiently checked, is the most tyrannical and oppressive that can be devised. Between this ideal perfection on the one side, and despotism on the other, no other system can be devised but that which considers society in reference to its parts, as differently affected by the action of the government, and which takes the sense of each part separately, and thereby the sense of the whole, in the manner already illustrated.

These principles, as I have already stated, are not affected by the number of which the community may be composed, but are just as applicable to one of thirteen millions—the number which composes ours—as of the small community of twenty-four, which I have supposed for the purpose of illustration; and are not less applicable to the twenty-four States united in one community, than to the case of the twenty-four individuals. There is, indeed, a distinction between a large and a small community, not affecting the principle, but the violence of the action. In the former, the similarity of the interests of all the parts will limit the oppression from the hostile action of the parts, in a great degree, to the fiscal action of the government merely; but in the large community, spreading over a country of great extent, and having a great diversity of interests, with different kinds of labor, capital, and production, the conflict and oppression will extend, not only to a monopoly of the appropriations on the part of the stronger interests, but will end in unequal taxes, and a general conflict between the entire interests of conflicting sections, which, if not arrested by the most powerful checks, will terminate in the most oppressive tyranny that can be conceived, or in the destruction of the community itself.

If we turn our attention from these supposed cases, and direct it to our government and its actual operation, we shall find a practical confirmation of the truth of what has been stated, not only of the oppressive operation of the system of an absolute majority, but also a striking and beautiful illustration, in the formation of our system, of the principle of the concurring majority, as distinct from the absolute, which I have asserted to be the only means of efficiently checking the abuse of power, and, of course, the only solid foundation of constitutional liberty. That our government, for many years, has been gradually verging to consolidation; that the constitution has gradually become a dead letter; and that all restrictions upon the power of government have been virtually removed, so as practically to convert the General Government into a government of an absolute majority, without check or limitation, cannot be denied by any one who has impartially observed its operation.

It is not necessary to trace the commencement and gradual progress of the causes which have produced this change in our system; it is sufficient to state that the change has taken place within the last few years. What has been the result? Precisely that which might have been anticipated: the growth of faction, corruption, anarchy, and, if not despotism itself, its near approach, as witnessed in the provisions of this bill. And from what have these consequences sprung? We have been involved in no war. We have been at peace with all the world. We have been visited with no national calamity. Our people have been advancing in general intelligence, and, I will add, as great and alarming as has been the advance of political corruption among the mercenary corps who look to Government for support, the morals and virtue of the community at large have been advancing in improvement. What, I again repeat, is the cause? No other can be assigned but a departure from the fundamental principles of the constitution, which has converted the Government into the will of an absolute and irresponsible majority, and which, by the laws that must inevitably govern in all such majorities, has placed in conflict the great interests of the country, by a system of hostile legislation, by an oppressive and unequal imposition of taxes, by unequal and profuse appropriations, and by rendering the entire labor and capital of the weaker interest subordinate to the stronger.

This is the cause, and these the fruits, which have converted the Government into a mere instrument of taking money from one portion of the community, to be given to another; and which has rallied around it a great, a powerful, and mercenary corps of office-holders, office-seekers, and expectants, destitute of principle and patriotism, and who have no standard of morals or politics but the will of the Executive—the will of him who has the distribution of the loaves and the fishes. I hold it impossible for any one to look at the theoretical illustration of the principle of the absolute majority in the cases which I have supposed, and not be struck with the practical illustration in the actual operation of our Government. Under every circumstance, the absolute majority will ever have its American system (I mean nothing offensive to any Senator); but the real meaning of the American system is, that system of plunder which the strongest interest has ever waged, and will ever wage, against the weaker, where the latter is not armed with some efficient and constitutional check to arrest its action. Nothing but such check on the part of the weaker interest can arrest it: mere constitutional limitations are wholly insufficient. Whatever interest obtains possession of the Government, will, from the nature of things, be in favor of the powers, and against the limitations imposed by the constitution, and will resort to every device that can be imagined to remove those restraints. On the contrary, the opposite interest, that which I have designated as the stockholding interest, the tax-payers, those on whom the system operates, will resist the abuse of powers, and contend for the limitations. And it is on this point, then, that the contest between the delegated and the reserved powers will be waged; but in this contest, as the interests in possession of the Government are organized and armed by all its powers and patronage, the opposite interest, if not in like manner organized and possessed of a power to protect themselves under the provisions of the constitution, will be as inevitably crushed as would be a band of unorganized militia when opposed by a veteran and trained corps of regulars. Let it never be forgotten, that power can only be opposed by power, organization by organization; and on this theory stands our beautiful federal system of Government. No free system was ever further removed from the principle that the absolute majority, without check or limitation, ought to govern. To understand what our Government is, we must look to the constitution, which is the basis of the system. I do not intend to enter into any minute examination of the origin and the source of its powers: it is sufficient for my purpose to state, what I do fearlessly, that it derived its power from the people of the separate States, each ratifying by itself, each binding itself by its own separate majority, through its separate convention,—the concurrence of the majorities of the several States forming the constitution;—thus taking the sense of the whole by that of the several parts, representing the various interests of the entire community. It was this concurring and perfect majority which formed the constitution, and not that majority which would consider the American people as a single community, and which, instead of representing fairly and fully the interests of the whole, would but represent, as has been stated, the interests of the stronger section. No candid man can dispute that I have given a correct description of the constitution-making power: that power which created and organized the Government, which delegated to it, as a common agent, certain powers, in trust for the common good of all the States, and which imposed strict limitations and checks against abuses and usurpations. In administering the delegated powers, the constitution provides, very properly, in order to give promptitude and efficiency, that the Government shall be organized upon the principle of the absolute majority, or, rather, of two absolute majorities combined: a majority of the States considered as bodies politic, which prevails in this body; and a majority of the people of the States, estimated in federal numbers, in the other House of Congress. A combination of the two prevails in the choice of the President, and, of course, in the appointment of Judges, they being nominated by the President and confirmed by the Senate. It is thus that the concurring and the absolute majorities are combined in one complex system: the one in forming the constitution, and the other in making and executing the laws; thus beautifully blending the moderation, justice, and equity of the former, and more perfect majority, with the promptness and energy of the latter, but less perfect.

To maintain the ascendency of the constitution over the law-making majority is the great and essential point, on which the success of the system must depend. Unless that ascendency can be preserved, the necessary consequence must be, that the laws will supersede the constitution; and, finally, the will of the Executive, by the influence of his patronage, will supersede the laws—indications of which are already perceptible. This ascendency can only be preserved through the action of the States as organized bodies, having their own separate governments, and possessed of the right, under the structure of our system, of judging of the extent of their separate powers, and of interposing their authority to arrest the unauthorized enactments of the General Government within their respective limits. I will not enter, at this time, into the discussion of this important point, as it has been ably and fully presented by the Senator from Kentucky (Mr. Bibb), and others who preceded him in this debate on the same side, whose arguments not only remain unanswered, but are unanswerable. It is only by this power of interposition that the reserved rights of the States can be peacefully and efficiently protected against the encroachments of the General Government—that the limitations imposed upon its authority can be enforced, and its movements confined to the orbit allotted to it by the constitution.

It has, indeed, been said in debate, that this can be effected by the organization of the General Government itself, particularly by the action of this body, which represents the States—and that the States themselves must look to the General Government for the preservation of many of the most important of their reserved rights. I do not underrate the value to be attached to the organic arrangement of the General Government, and the wise distribution of its powers between the several departments, and, in particular, the structure and the important functions of this body; but to suppose that the Senate, or any department of this Government, was intended to be the only guardian of the reserved rights, is a great and fundamental mistake. The Government, through all its departments, represents the delegated, and not the reserved powers; and it is a violation of the fundamental principle of free institutions to suppose that any but the responsible representative of any interest can be its guardian. The distribution of the powers of the General Government, and its organization, were arranged to prevent the abuse of power in fulfilling the important trusts confided to it, and not, as preposterously supposed, to protect the reserved powers, which are confided wholly to the guardianship of the several States.

Against the view of our system which I have presented, and the right of the States to interpose, it is objected that it would lead to anarchy and dissolution. I consider the objection as without the slightest foundation; and that, so far from tending to weakness or disunion, it is the source of the highest power and the strongest cement. Nor is its tendency in this respect difficult of explanation. The government of an absolute majority, unchecked by efficient constitutional restraints, though apparently strong is, in reality, an exceedingly feeble government. That tendency to conflict between the parts, which I have shown to be inevitable in such governments, wastes the powers of the state in the hostile action of contending factions, which leaves very little more power than the excess of the strength of the majority over the minority. But a government based upon the principle of the concurring majority, where each great interest possesses within itself the means of self-protection, which ultimately requires the mutual consent of all the parts, necessarily causes that unanimity in council, and ardent attachment of all the parts to the whole, which give an irresistible energy to a government so constituted. I might appeal to history for the truth of these remarks, of which the Roman furnishes the most familiar and striking proofs. It is a well-known fact, that, from the expulsion of the Tarquins to the time of the establishment of the tribunitian power, the government fell into a state of the greatest disorder and distraction, and, I may add, corruption. How did this happen? The explanation will throw important light on the subject under consideration. The community was divided into two parts—the Patricians and the Plebeians; with the power of the state principally in the hands of the former, without adequate checks to protect the rights of the latter. The result was as might be expected. The patricians converted the powers of the government into the means of making money, to enrich themselves and their dependents. They, in a word, had their American system, growing out of the peculiar character of the government and condition of the country. This requires explanation. At that period, according to the laws of nations, when one nation conquered another, the lands of the vanquished belonged to the victor; and, according to the Roman law, the lands thus acquired were divided into two parts—one allotted to the poorer class of the people, and the other assigned to the use of the treasury,—of which the patricians had the distribution and administration. The patricians abused their power by withholding from the plebeians that which ought to have been allotted to them, and by converting to their own use that which ought to have gone to the treasury. In a word, they took to themselves the entire spoils of victory,—and had thus the most powerful motive to keep the state perpetually involved in war, to the utter impoverishment and oppression of the plebeians. After resisting the abuse of power by all peaceable means, and the oppression becoming intolerable, the plebeians, at last, withdrew from the city—they, in a word, seceded; and to induce them to reunite, the patricians conceded to them, as the means of protecting their separate interests, the very power, which I contend is necessary to protect the rights of the States, but which is now represented as necessarily leading to disunion. They granted to them the right of choosing three tribunes from among themselves, whose persons should be sacred, and who should have the right of interposing their veto, not only against the passage of laws, but even against their execution—a power which those, who take a shallow insight into human nature, would pronounce inconsistent with the strength and unity of the state, if not utterly impracticable; yet so far from this being the effect, from that day the genius of Rome became ascendant, and victory followed her steps till she had established an almost universal dominion. How can a result so contrary to all anticipation be explained? The explanation appears to me to be simple. No measure or movement could be adopted without the concurring assent of both the patricians and plebeians, and each thus became dependent on the other; and, of consequence, the desire and objects of neither could be effected without the concurrence of the other. To obtain this concurrence, each was compelled to consult the goodwill of the other, and to elevate to office, not those only who might have the confidence of the order to which they belonged, but also that of the other. The result was, that men possessing those qualities which would naturally command confidence—moderation, wisdom, justice, and patriotism—were elevated to office; and the weight of their authority and the prudence of their counsel, combined with that spirit of unanimity necessarily resulting from the concurring assent of the two orders, furnish the real explanation of the power of the Roman State, and of that extraordinary wisdom, moderation, and firmness which in so remarkable a degree characterized her public men. I might illustrate the truth of the position which I have laid down by a reference to the history of all free states ancient and modern, distinguished for their power and patriotism, and conclusively show, not only that there was not one which had not some contrivance, under some form, by which the concurring assent of the different portions of the community was made necessary in the action of government, but also that the virtue, patriotism, and strength of the state were in direct proportion to the perfection of the means of securing such assent.

In estimating the operation of this principle in our system, which depends, as I have stated, on the right of interposition on the part of a State, we must not omit to take into consideration the amending power, by which new powers may be granted, or any derangement of the system corrected, by the concurring assent of three-fourths of the States; and thus, in the same degree, strengthening the power of repairing any derangement occasioned by the eccentric action of a State. In fact, the power of interposition, fairly understood, may be considered in the light of an appeal against the usurpations of the General Government, the joint agent of all the States, to the States themselves,—to be decided under the amending power, by the voice of three-fourths of the States, as the highest power known under the system. I know the difficulty, in our country, of establishing the truth of the principle for which I contend, though resting upon the clearest reason, and tested by the universal experience of free nations. I know that the governments of the several States, which, for the most part, are constructed on the principle of the absolute majority, will be cited as an argument against the conclusion to which I have arrived; but, in my opinion, the satisfactory answer can be given,—that the objects of expenditure which fall within the sphere of a State Government are few and inconsiderable, so that be their action ever so irregular, it can occasion but little derangement. If, instead of being members of this great confederacy, they formed distinct communities, and were compelled to raise armies, and incur other expenses necessary to their defence, the laws which I have laid down as necessarily controlling the action of a State where the will of an absolute and unchecked majority prevailed, would speedily disclose themselves in faction, anarchy, and corruption. Even as the case is, the operation of the causes to which I have referred is perceptible in some of the larger and more populous members of the Union, whose governments have a powerful central action, and which already show a strong moneyed tendency, the invariable forerunner of corruption and convulsion.

But, to return to the General Government. We have now sufficient experience to ascertain that the tendency to conflict in its action is between the southern and other sections. The latter having a decided majority, must habitually be possessed of the powers of the Government, both in this and in the other House; and, being governed by that instinctive love of power so natural to the human breast, they must become the advocates of the power of Government, and in the same degree opposed to the limitations; while the other and weaker section is as necessarily thrown on the side of the limitations. One section is the natural guardian of the delegated powers, and the other of the reserved; and the struggle on the side of the former will be to enlarge the powers, while that on the opposite side will be to restrain them within their constitutional limits. The contest will, in fact, be a contest between power and liberty, and such I consider the present—a contest in which the weaker section, with its peculiar labor, productions, and institutions, has at stake all that can be dear to freemen. Should we be able to maintain in their full vigor our reserved rights, liberty and prosperity will be our portion; but if we yield, and permit the stronger interest to concentrate within itself all the powers of the Government, then will our fate be more wretched than that of the aborigines whom we have expelled. In this great struggle between the delegated and reserved powers, so far from repining that my lot, and that of those whom I represent, is cast on the side of the latter, I rejoice that such is the fact; for, though we participate in but few of the advantages of the Government, we are compensated, and more than compensated, in not being so much exposed to its corruptions. Nor do I repine that the duty, so difficult to be discharged, of defending the reserved powers against apparently such fearful odds, has been assigned to us. To discharge it successfully requires the highest qualities, moral and intellectual; and should we perform it with a zeal and ability proportioned to its magnitude, instead of mere planters, our section will become distinguished for its patriots and statesmen. But, on the other hand, if we prove unworthy of the trust—if we yield to the steady encroachments of power, the severest calamity and most debasing corruption will overspread the land. Every Southern man, true to the interests of his section, and faithful to the duties which Providence has allotted him, will be for ever excluded from the honors and emoluments of this Government, which will be reserved for those only who have qualified themselves, by political prostitution, for admission into the *Magdalen* Asylum.[1]

[1] An English institution of refuge and reformation for prostitutes, founded 1766 [Eds.].

The Constitution Not a Compact Between Sovereign States

DANIEL WEBSTER
(For biographical sketch, see p. 54.)

Mr. President: The gentleman from South Carolina has admonished us to be mindful of the opinions of those who shall come after us. We must take our chance, Sir, as to the light in which posterity will regard us. I do not decline its judgment, nor withhold myself from its scrutiny. Feeling that I am performing my public duty with singleness of heart and to the best of my ability, I fearlessly trust myself to the country, now and hereafter, and leave both my motives and my character to its decision.

The gentleman has terminated his speech in a tone of threat and defiance towards this bill, even should it become a law of the land, altogether unusual in the halls of Congress. But I shall not suffer myself to be excited into warmth by his denunciation of the measure which I support. Among the feelings which at this moment fill my breast, not the least is that of regret at the position in which the gentleman has placed himself. Sir, he does himself no justice. The cause which he has espoused finds no basis in the Constitution, no succor from public sympathy, no cheering from a patriotic community. He has no foothold on which to stand while he might display the powers of his acknowledged talents. Every thing beneath his feet is hollow and treacherous. He is like a strong man struggling in a morass: every effort to extricate himself only sinks him deeper and deeper. And I fear the resemblance may be carried still farther; I fear that no friend can safely come to his relief, that no one can approach near enough to hold out a helping hand, without danger of going down himself, also, into the bottomless depths of this Serbonian bog.

The United States Senate, February 16, 1833, in reply to Calhoun's resolutions and speech. *The Works of Daniel Webster*, 13th ed. (Boston: Little, Brown and Company, 1864), III, pp. 448–505. See also *Register of Debates in Congress*, 22nd Cong., 2nd Sess., pp. 553–587.

The honorable gentleman has declared, that on the decision of the question now in debate may depend the cause of liberty itself. I am of the same opinion; but then, Sir, the liberty which I think is staked on the contest is not political liberty, in any general and undefined character, but our own well-understood and long-enjoyed *American* liberty.

Sir, I love Liberty no less ardently than the gentleman himself, in whatever form she may have appeared in the progress of human history. As exhibited in the master states of antiquity, as breaking out again from amidst the darkness of the Middle Ages, and beaming on the formation of new communities in modern Europe, she has, always and everywhere, charms for me. Yet, Sir, it is our own liberty, guarded by constitutions and secured by union, it is that liberty which is our paternal inheritance, it is our established, dear-bought, peculiar American liberty, to which I am chiefly devoted, and the cause of which I now mean, to the utmost of my power, to maintain and defend.

Mr. President, if I considered the constitutional question now before us as doubtful as it is important, and if I supposed that its decision, either in the Senate or by the country, was likely to be in any degree influenced by the manner in which I might now discuss it, this would be to me a moment of deep solicitude. Such a moment has once existed. There has been a time, when, rising in this place, on the same question, I felt, I must confess, that something for good or evil to the Constitution of the country might depend on an effort of mine. But circumstances are changed. Since that day, Sir, the public opinion has become awakened to this great question; it has grasped it; it has reasoned upon it, as becomes an intelligent and patriotic community, and has settled it, or now seems in the progress of settling it, by an authority which none can disobey, the authority of the people themselves.

I shall not, Mr. President, follow the gentleman, step by step, through the course of his speech. Much of what he has said he has deemed necessary to the just explanation and defence of his own political character and conduct. On this I shall offer no comment. Much, too, has consisted of philosophical remark upon the general nature of political liberty, and the history of free institutions; and upon other topics, so general in their nature as to possess, in my opinion, only a remote bearing on the immediate subject of this debate.

But the gentleman's speech made some days ago, upon introducing his resolutions, those resolutions themselves, and parts of the speech now just concluded, may, I presume, be justly regarded as containing the whole South Carolina doctrine. That doctrine it is my purpose now to examine, and to compare it with the Constitution of the United States. I shall not consent, Sir, to make any new constitution, or to establish another form of government. I will not undertake to say what a constitution for these United States ought to be. That question the people have decided for themselves; and I shall take the instrument as they have established it, and shall endeavor to maintain it, in its plain sense and meaning, against opinions and notions which, in my judgment, threaten its subversion.

The resolutions introduced by the gentleman were apparently drawn up with care, and brought forward upon deliberation. I shall not be in danger, therefore, of misunderstanding him, or those who agree with him, if I proceed at once to these resolutions, and consider them as an authentic statement of those opinions upon the great constitutional question, by which the recent proceedings in South Carolina are attempted to be justified.

These resolutions are three in number.

The third seems intended to enumerate, and to deny, the several opinions expressed in the President's proclamation, respecting the nature and powers of this government. Of this third resolution, I purpose, at present, to take no particular notice.

The first two resolutions of the honorable member affirm these propositions, viz.: —

1. That the political system under which we live, and under which Congress is now assembled, is a *compact*, to which the people of the several States, as separate and sovereign communities are *the parties*.

2. That these sovereign parties have a right to judge, each for itself, of any alleged violation of the Constitution by Congress; and, in case of such violation, to choose, each for itself, its own mode and measure of redress.

It is true, Sir, that the honorable member calls this a "constitutional" compact; but still he affirms it to be a compact between sovereign States. What precise meaning, then, does he attach to the term *constitutional*? When applied to compacts between sovereign States, the term *constitutional* affixes to the word *compact* no definite idea. Were we to hear of a constitutional league or treaty between England and France, or a constitutional convention between Austria and Russia, we should not understand what could be intended by such a league, such a treaty, or such a convention. In these connections, the word is void of all meaning; and yet, Sir, it is easy, quite easy, to see why the honorable gentleman has used it in these resolutions. He cannot open the book, and look upon our written frame of government, without seeing that it is called a *constitution*. This may well be appalling to him. It threatens his whole doctrine of compact, and its darling derivatives, nullification and secession, with instant confutation. Because, if he admits our instrument of government to be a *constitution*, then, for that very reason, it is not a compact between sovereigns; a constitution of government and a compact between sovereign powers being things essentially unlike in their very natures, and incapable of ever being the same. Yet the word *constitution* is on the very front of the instrument. He cannot overlook it. He seeks, therefore, to compromise the matter, and to sink all the substantial sense of the word, while he retains a resemblance of its sound. He introduces a new word of his own, viz. *compact,* as importing the principal idea, and designed to play the principal part, and degrades *constitution* into an insignificant, idle epithet, attached to *compact.* The whole then stands as a *"constitutional compact"!* And in this way he hopes to pass off a plausible gloss, as satisfying the words of the instrument. But he will find himself disappointed. Sir, I must say to the honorable gentleman, that, in our American political grammar, CONSTITU-TION is a noun substantive; it imports a distinct and clear idea of itself; and it is not to lose its importance and dignity, it is not to be turned into a poor, ambiguous, senseless, unmeaning adjective, for the purpose of accommodating any new set of political notions. Sir, we reject his new rules of syntax alto-gether. We will not give up our forms of political speech to the grammarians of the school of nullification. By the Constitution, we mean, not a "constitu-tional compact," but, simply and directly, the Constitution, the fundamental law; and if there be one word in the language which the people of the United States understand, this is that word. We know no more of a constitu-tional compact between sovereign powers, than we know of a *constitutional* indenture of copartnership, a *constitutional* deed of conveyance, or a *constitu-tional* bill of exchange. But we know what the *Constitution* is; we know what the plainly written, fundamental law is; we know what the bond of our Union and the security of our liberties is; and we mean to maintain and to defend it, in its plain sense and unsophisticated meaning.

The sense of the gentleman's proposition, therefore, is not at all affected, one way or the other, by the use of this word. That proposition still is, that our system of government is but a *compact* between the people of separate and sovereign States.

Was it Mirabeau, Mr. President, or some other master of the human pas-sions, who has told us that words are things? They are indeed things, and things of mighty influence, not only in addresses to the passions and high-wrought feelings of mankind, but in the discussion of legal and political ques-tions also; because a just conclusion is often avoided, or a false one reached, by the adroit substitution of one phrase, or one word, for another. Of this we have, I think, another example in the resolutions before us.

The first resolution declares that the people of the several States *"acceded"* to the Constitution, or to the constitutional compact, as it is called. This word "accede," not found either in the Constitution itself, or in the ratification of it by any one of the States, has been chosen for use here, doubtless, not without a well-considered purpose.

The natural converse of *accession* is *secession;* and, therefore, when it is stated that the people of the States acceded to the Union, it may be more plausibly argued that they may secede from it. If, in adopting the Constitu-tion, nothing was done but acceding to a compact, nothing would seem neces-sary, in order to break it up, but to secede from the same compact. But the term is wholly out of place. *Accession,* as a word applied to political associations, implies coming into a league, treaty, or confederacy, by one hitherto a stranger to it; and *secession* implies departing from such league or confederacy. The people of the United States have used no such form of expression in establishing the present government. They do not say that they *accede* to a league, but they declare that they *ordain* and *establish* a Constitution. Such are the very words of the instrument itself; and in all the States, without an exception, the language used by their conventions was, that they *"ratified the Constitution"*; some of them employing the additional words "assented to" and "adopted," but all of them "ratifying."

There is more importance than may, at first sight, appear, in the introduction of this new word by the honorable mover of these resolutions. Its adoption and use are indispensable to maintain those premises, from which his main conclusion is to be afterwards drawn. But before showing that, allow me to remark, that this phraseology tends to keep out of sight the just view of a previous political history, as well as to suggest wrong ideas as to what was actually done when the present Constitution was agreed to. In 1789, and before this Constitution was adopted, the United States had already been in a union, more or less close, for fifteen years. At least as far back as the meeting of the first Congress, in 1774, they had been in some measure, and for some national purposes, united together. Before the Confederation of 1781, they had declared independence jointly, and had carried on the war jointly, both by sea and land; and this not as separate States, but as one people. When, therefore, they formed that Confederation, and adopted its articles as articles of perpetual union, they did not come together for the first time; and therefore they did not speak of the States as *acceding* to the Confederation, although it was a league, and nothing but a league, and rested on nothing but plighted faith for its performance. Yet, even then, the States were not strangers to each other; there was a bond of union already subsisting between them; they were associated, united States; and the object of the Confederation was to make a stronger and better bond of union. Their representatives deliberated together on these proposed Articles of Confederation, and, being authorized by their respective States, finally *"ratified and confirmed"* them. Inasmuch as they were already in union, they did not speak of *acceding* to the new Articles of Confederation, but of *ratifying and confirming* them; and this language was not used inadvertently, because, in the same instrument, *accession* is used in its proper sense, when applied to Canada, which was altogether a stranger to the existing union. "Canada," says the eleventh article, *"acceding* to this Confederation, and joining in the measures of the United States, shall be admitted into the Union."

Having thus used the terms *ratify* and *confirm,* even in regard to the old Confederation, it would have been strange indeed, if the people of the United States, after its formation, and when they came to establish the present

Constitution, had spoken of the States, or the people of the States, as *acceding* to this Constitution. Such language would have been ill-suited to the occasion. It would have implied an existing separation or disunion among the States, such as never has existed since 1774. No such language, therefore, was used. The language actually employed is, *adopt, ratify, ordain, establish.*

Therefore, Sir, since any State, before she can prove her right to dissolve the Union, must show her authority to undo what has been done, no State is at liberty to *secede,* on the ground that she and other States have done nothing but *accede.* She must show that she has a right to *reverse* what has been *ordained,* to *unsettle* and *overthrow* what has been *established,* to *reject* what the people have *adopted,* and to *break up* what they have *ratified;* because these are the terms which express the transactions which have actually taken place. In other words, she must show her right to make a revolution.

If, Mr. President, in drawing these resolutions, the honorable member had confined himself to the use of constitutional language, there would have been a wide and awful *hiatus* between his premises and his conclusion. Leaving out the two words *compact* and *accession,* which are not constitutional modes of expression, and stating the matter precisely as the truth is, his first resolution would have affirmed that *the people of the several States ratified this Constitution, or form of government.* These are the very words of South Carolina herself, in her act of ratification. Let, then, his first resolution tell the exact truth; let it state the fact precisely as it exists; let it say that the people of the several States ratified a constitution, or form of government; and then, Sir, what will become of his inference in his second resolution, which is in these words, viz. "that, as in all other cases of compact among sovereign parties, each has an equal right to judge for itself, as well of the infraction as of the mode and measure of redress"? It is obvious, is it not, Sir? that this conclusion requires for its support quite other premises; it requires premises which speak of *accession* and of *compact* between sovereign powers; and, without such premises, it is altogether unmeaning.

Mr. President, if the honorable member will truly state what the people did in forming this Constitution, and then state what they must do if they would now undo what they then did, he will unavoidably state a case of revolution. Let us see if it be not so. He must state, in the first place, that the people of the several States adopted and ratified this Constitution, or form of government; and, in the next place, he must state that they have a right to undo this; that is to say, that they have a right to discard the form of government which they have adopted, and to break up the Constitution which they have ratified. Now, Sir, this is neither more nor less than saying that they have a right to make a revolution. To reject an established government, to break up a political constitution, is revolution.

I deny that any man can state accurately what was done by the people, in establishing the present Constitution, and then state accurately what the people, or any part of them, must now do to get rid of its obligations, without stating an undeniable case of the overthrow of government. I admit, of course, that the people may, if they choose, overthrow the government. But, then, that is revolution. The doctrine now contended for is, that, by *nullification* or *secession,* the obligations and authority of the government may be set aside or rejected, without revolution. But that is what I deny; and what I say is, that no man can state the case with historical accuracy, and in constitutional language, without showing that the honorable gentleman's right, as asserted in his conclusion, is a revolutionary right merely; that it does not and cannot exist under the Constitution, or agreeably to the Constitution, but can come into existence only when the Constitution is overthrown. This is the reason, Sir, which makes it necessary to abandon the use of constitutional language for a new vocabulary, and to substitute, in the place of plain historical facts, a series of assumptions. This is the reason why it is necessary to give new names to things, to speak of the Constitution, not as a constitution, but as a compact, and of the ratifications by the people, not as ratifications, but as acts of accession.

Sir, I intend to hold the gentleman to the written record. In the discussion of a constitutional question, I intend to impose upon him the restraints of constitutional language. The people have ordained a Constitution; can they reject it without revolution? They have established a form of government; can they overthrow it without revolution? These are the true questions.

Allow me now, Mr. President, to inquire further into the extent of the propositions contained in the resolutions, and their necessary consequences.

Where sovereign communities are parties, there is no essential difference between a compact, a confederation, and a league. They all equally rest on the plighted faith of the sovereign party. A league, or confederacy, is but a subsisting or continuing treaty.

The gentleman's resolutions, then, affirm, in effect, that these twenty-four United States are held together only by a subsisting treaty, resting for its fulfilment and continuance on no inherent power of its own, but on the plighted faith of each State; or, in other words, that our Union is but a league; and, as a consequence from this proposition, they further affirm that, as sovereigns are subject to no superior power, the States must judge, each for itself, of any alleged violation of the league; and if such violation be supposed to have occurred, each may adopt any mode or measure of redress which it shall think proper.

Other consequences naturally follow, too, from the main proposition. If a league between sovereign powers have no limitation as to the time of its duration, and contain nothing making it perpetual, it subsists only during the good pleasure of the parties, although no violation be complained of. If, in the opinion of either party, it be violated, such party may say that he will no longer fulfil its obligations on his part, but will consider the whole league or compact at an end, although it might be one of its stipulations that it should be perpetual. Upon this principle, the Congress of the United States, in 1798, declared null and void the treaty of alliance between the United States and France, though it professed to be a perpetual alliance.

If the violation of the league be accompanied with serious injuries, the suffering party, being sole judge of his own mode and measure of redress, has a right to indemnify himself by reprisals on the offending members of the league; and reprisals, if the circumstances of the case require it, may be followed by direct, avowed, and public war.

The necessary import of the resolution, therefore, is, that the United States are connected only by a league; that it is in the good pleasure of every State to decide how long she will choose to remain a member of this league; that any State may determine the extent of her own obligations under it, and accept or reject what shall be decided by the whole; that she may also determine whether her rights have been violated, what is the extent of the injury done her, and what mode and measure of redress her wrongs may make it fit and expedient for her to adopt. The result of the whole is, that any State may secede at pleasure; that any State may resist a law which she herself may choose to say exceeds the power of Congress; and that, as a sovereign power, she may redress her own grievances, by her own arm, at her own discretion. She may make reprisals; she may cruise against the property of other members of the league; she may authorize captures, and make open war.

If, Sir, this be our political condition, it is time the people of the United States understood it. Let us look for a moment to the practical consequences of these opinions. One State, holding an embargo law unconstitutional, may declare her opinion, and withdraw from the Union. *She* secedes. Another, forming and expressing the same judgment on a law laying duties on imports, may withdraw also. *She* secedes. And as, in her opinion, money has been taken out of the pockets of her citizens illegally, under pretence of this law, and as she has power to redress their wrongs, she may demand satisfaction; and, if refused, she may take it with a strong hand. The gentleman has himself pronounced the collection of duties, under existing laws, to be nothing but robbery. Robbers, of course, may be rightfully dispossessed of the fruits of their flagitious crimes; and, therefore, reprisals, impositions on the commerce of other States, foreign alliances against them, or open war, are all modes of redress justly open to the discretion and choice of South Carolina; for she is to judge of her own rights, and to seek satisfaction for her own wrongs, in her own way.

But, Sir, a *third* State is of opinion, not only that these laws of imposts are constitutional, but that it is the absolute duty of Congress to pass and to maintain such laws; and that, by omitting to pass and maintain them, its constitutional obligations would be grossly disregarded. She herself relinquished the power of protection, she might allege, and allege truly, and gave it up to Congress, on the faith that Congress would exercise it. If Congress now refuse to exercise it, Congress does, as she may insist, break the condition of the grant, and thus manifestly violate the Constitution; and for this violation of the Constitution, *she* may threaten to secede also. Virginia may secede, and hold the fortresses in the Chesapeake. The Western States may secede, and take to their own use the public lands. Louisiana may secede, if she choose, form a foreign alliance, and hold the mouth of the Mississippi. If one State may secede, ten may do so, twenty may do so, twenty-three may do so. Sir, as these secessions go on, one after another, what is to constitute the United States? Whose will be the army? Whose the navy? Who will pay the debts? Who fulfill the public treaties? Who perform the constitutional guaranties? Who govern this District and the Territories? Who retain the public property?

Mr. President, every man must see that these are all questions which can arise only *after a revolution*. They presuppose the breaking up of the government. While the Constitution lasts, they are repressed; they spring up to annoy and startle us only from its grave.

The Constitution does not provide for events which must be preceded by its own destruction. SECESSION, therefore, since it must bring these consequences with it, is REVOLUTIONARY, and NULLIFICATION is equally REVOLUTIONARY. What is revolution? Why, Sir, that is revolution which overturns, or controls, or successfully resists, the existing public authority; that which arrests the exercise of the supreme power; that which introduces a new paramount authority into the rule of the State. Now, Sir, this is the precise object of nullification. It attempts to supersede the supreme legislative authority. It arrests the arm of the executive magistrate. It interrupts the exercise of the accustomed judicial power. Under the name of an ordinance, it declares null and void, within the State, all the revenue laws of the United States. Is not this revolutionary? Sir, so soon as this ordinance shall be carried into effect, *a revolution* will have commenced in South Carolina. She will have thrown off the authority to which her citizens have heretofore been subject. She will have declared her own opinions and her own will to be above the laws and above the power of those who are intrusted with their administration. If she makes good these declarations, she is revolutionized. As to her, it is as distinctly a change of the supreme power as the American Revolution of 1776. That revolution did not subvert government in all its forms. It did not subvert local laws and municipal administrations. It only threw off the dominion of a power claiming to be superior, and to have a right, in many important respects, to exercise legislative authority. Thinking this authority to have been usurped or abused, the American Colonies, now the United States, bade it defiance, and freed themselves from it by means of a revolution. But that revolution left them with their own municipal laws still, and the forms of local government. If Carolina now shall effectually resist the laws of Congress; if she shall be her own judge, take her remedy into her own hands, obey the laws of the Union when she pleases and disobey them when she pleases, she will relieve herself from a paramount power as distinctly as the American Colonies did the same thing in 1776. In other words, she will achieve, as to herself, a revolution.

But, Sir, while practical nullification in South Carolina would be, as to herself, actual and distinct revolution, its necessary tendency must also be to spread revolution, and to break up the Constitution, as to all the other States. It strikes a deadly blow at the vital principle of the whole Union. To allow State resistance to the laws of Congress to be rightful and proper, to admit nullification in some States, and yet not expect to see a dismemberment of the entire government, appears to me the wildest illusion, and the most extravagant folly. The gentleman seems not conscious of the direction or the rapidity of his own course. The current of his opinions sweeps him along, he knows not whither. To begin with nullification, with the avowed intent, nevertheless, not to proceed to secession, dismemberment, and general revolution, is as if one were to take the plunge of Niagara, and cry out that he would stop half way down. In the one case, as in the other, the rash adventurer must go to the bottom of the dark abyss below, were it not that that abyss has no discovered bottom.

Nullification, if successful, arrests the power of the law, absolves citizens from their duty, subverts the foundation both of protection and obedience, dispenses with oaths and obligations of allegiance, and elevates another authority to supreme command. Is not this revolution? And it raises to supreme command four-and-twenty distinct powers, each professing to be under a general government, and yet each setting its laws at defiance at pleasure. Is not this anarchy, as well as revolution? Sir, the Constitution of the United States was received as a whole, and for the whole country. If it cannot stand altogether, it cannot stand in parts; and if the laws cannot be executed everywhere, they cannot long be executed anywhere. The gentleman very well knows that all duties and imposts must be uniform throughout the country. He knows that we cannot have one rule or one law for South Carolina, and another for other States. He must see, therefore, and does see, and every man sees, that the only alternative is a repeal of the laws throughout the whole Union, or their execution in Carolina as well as elsewhere. And this repeal is demanded because a single State interposes her veto, and threatens resistance! The result of the gentleman's opinion, or rather the very text of his doctrine, is, that no act of Congress can bind all the States, the constitutionality of which is not admitted by all; or, in other words, that no single State is bound, against its own dissent, by a law of imposts. This is precisely the evil experienced under the old Confederation, and for remedy of which this Constitution was adopted. The leading object in establishing this government, an object forced on the country by the condition of the times and the absolute necessity of the law, was to give to Congress power to lay and collect imposts *without the consent of particular States*. The Revolutionary debt remained unpaid; the national treasury was bankrupt; the country was destitute of credit; Congress issued its requisitions on the States, and the States neglected them; there was no power of coercion but war; Congress could not lay imposts, or other taxes, by its own authority; the whole general government, therefore, was little more than a name. The Articles of Confederation, as to purposes of revenue and finance, were nearly a dead letter. The country sought to escape from this condition, at once feeble and disgraceful, by constituting a government which should have power, of itself, to lay duties and taxes, and to pay the public debt, and provide for the general welfare; and to lay these duties and taxes in all the States, without asking the consent of the State governments. This was the very power on which the new Constitution was to depend for all its ability to do good; and without it, it can be no government, now or at any time. Yet, Sir, it is precisely against this power, so absolutely indispensable to the very being of the government, that South Carolina directs her ordinance. She attacks the government in its authority to raise revenue, the very mainspring of the whole system; and if she succeed, every movement of that system must inevitably cease. It is of no avail that she declares that she does not resist the law as a revenue law, but as a law for protecting manufactures. It is a revenue law; it is the very law by force of which the revenue is collected; if it be arrested in any State, the revenue ceases in that State; it is, in a word, the sole reliance of the government for the means of maintaining itself and performing its duties.

Mr. President, the alleged right of a State to decide constitutional questions for herself necessarily leads to force, because other States must have the same right, and because different States will decide differently; and when these questions arise between States, if there be no superior power, they can be decided only by the law of force. On entering into the Union, the people of each State gave up a part of their own power to make laws for themselves, in consideration that, as to common objects, they should have a part in making laws for other States. In other words, the people of all the States agreed to create a common government, to be conducted by common counsels. Pennsylvania, for example, yielded the right of laying imposts in her own ports, in consideration that the new government, in which she was to have a share, should possess the power of laying imposts on all the States. If South Carolina now refuses to submit to this power, she breaks the condition on

which other States entered into the Union. She partakes of the common counsels, and therein assists to bind others, while she refuses to be bound herself.
It makes no difference in the case, whether she does all this without reason
or pretext, or whether she sets up as a reason, that, in her judgment, the acts
complained of are unconstitutional. In the judgment of other States, they are
not so. It is nothing to them that she offers some reason or some apology for
her conduct, if it be one which they do not admit. It is not to be expected
that any State will violate her duty without some plausible pretext. That
would be too rash a defiance of the opinion of mankind. But if it be a pretext
which lies in her own breast; if it be no more than an opinion which she says
she has formed, how can other States be satisfied with this? How can they
allow her to be judge of her own obligations? Or, if she may judge of her
obligations, may they not judge of their rights also? May not the twenty-three
entertain an opinion as well as the twenty-fourth? And if it be their right, in
their own opinion, as expressed in the common council, to enforce the law
against her, how is she to say that her right and her opinion are to be every
thing, and their right and their opinion nothing?

Mr. President, if we are to receive the Constitution as the text, and then
to lay down in its margin the contradictory commentaries which have been,
and which may be, made by different States, the whole page would be a
polyglot indeed. It would speak with as many tongues as the builders of
Babel, and in dialects as much confused, and mutually as unintelligible. The
very instance now before us presents a practical illustration. The law of the
last session is declared unconstitutional in South Carolina, and obedience to
it is refused. In other States, it is admitted to be strictly constitutional. You
walk over the limit of its authority, therefore, when you pass a State line.
On one side it is law, on the other side a nullity; and yet it is passed by a
common government, having the same authority in all the States.

Such, Sir, are the inevitable results of this doctrine. Beginning with the
original error, that the Constitution of the United States is nothing but a
compact between sovereign States; asserting, in the next step, that each State
has a right to be its own sole judge of the extent of its own obligations, and
consequently of the constitutionality of laws of Congress; and, in the next,
that it may oppose whatever it sees fit to declare unconstitutional, and that it
decides for itself on the mode and measure of redress,—the argument arrives
at once at the conclusion, that what a State dissents from, it may nullify;
what it opposes, it may oppose by force; what it decides for itself, it may
execute by its own power; and that, in short, it is itself supreme over the legislation of Congress, and supreme over the decisions of the national judicature;
supreme over the constitution of the country, supreme over the supreme law
of the land. However it seeks to protect itself against these plain inferences,
by saying that an unconstitutional law is no law, and that it only opposes

such laws as are unconstitutional, yet this does not in the slightest degree vary the result; since it insists on deciding this question for itself; and, in opposition to reason and argument, in opposition to practice and experience, in opposition to the judgment of others, having an equal right to judge, it says, only, "Such is my opinion, and my opinion shall be my law, and I will support it by my own strong hand. I denounce the law; I declare it unconstitutional; that is enough; it shall not be executed. Men in arms are ready to resist its execution. An attempt to enforce it shall cover the land with blood. Elsewhere it may be binding; but here it is trampled under foot."

This, Sir, is practical nullification.

And now, Sir, against all these theories and opinions, I maintain,—

1. That the Constitution of the United States is not a league, confederacy, or compact between the people of the several States in their sovereign capacities; but a government proper, founded on the adoption of the people, and creating direct relations between itself and individuals.

2. That no State authority has power to dissolve these relations; that nothing can dissolve them but revolution; and that, consequently, there can be no such thing as secession without revolution.

3. That there is a supreme law, consisting of the Constitution of the United States, and acts of Congress passed in pursuance of it, and treaties; and that, in cases not capable of assuming the character of a suit in law or equity, Congress must judge of, and finally interpret, this supreme law so often as it has occasion to pass acts of legislation; and in cases capable of assuming, and actually assuming, the character of a suit, the Supreme Court of the United States is the final interpreter.

4. That an attempt by a State to abrogate, annul, or nullify an act of Congress, or to arrest its operation within her limits, on the ground that, in her opinion, such law is unconstitutional, is a direct usurpation on the just powers of the general government, and on the equal rights of other States; a plain violation of the Constitution, and a proceeding essentially revolutionary in its character and tendency.

[Webster enters into an extended legal interpretation of the four propositions, in the course of which he offers direct refutation of Calhoun's theories of concurrent majorities.]

. . . .

Sir, those who espouse the doctrines of nullification reject, as it seems to me, the first great principle of all republican liberty; that is, that the majority *must* govern. In matters of common concern, the judgment of a majority *must* stand as the judgment of the whole. This is a law imposed on us by the absolute necessity of the case; and if we do not act upon it, there is no possibility of maintaining any government but despotism. We hear loud and repeated denunciations against what is called *majority government*. It is declared, with much warmth, that a majority government cannot be maintained in the United States. What, then, do gentlemen wish? Do they wish to establish a *minority* government? Do they wish to subject the will of the many to the will of the few? The honorable gentleman from South Carolina has spoken of absolute majorities and majorities concurrent; language wholly unknown to our Constitution, and to which it is not easy to affix definite ideas. As far as I understand it, it would teach us that the absolute majority may be found in Congress, but the majority concurrent must be looked for in the States; that is to say, Sir, stripping the matter of this novelty of phrase, that the dissent of one or more States, as States, renders void the decision of a majority of Congress, so far as that State is concerned. And so this doctrine, running but a short career, like other dogmas of the day, terminates in nullification.

If this vehement invective against *majorities* meant no more than that, in the construction of government, it is wise to provide checks and balances, so that there should be various limitations on the power of the mere majority, it would only mean what the Constitution of the United States has already abundantly provided. It is full of such checks and balances. In its very organization, it adopts a broad and most effective principle in restraint of the power of mere majorities. A majority of the people elects the House of Representatives, but it does not elect the Senate. The Senate is elected by the States, each State having, in this respect, an equal power. No law, therefore, can pass, without the assent of the representatives of the people, and a majority of the representatives of the States also. A majority of the representatives of the people must concur, and a majority of the States must concur, in every act of Congress; and the President is elected on a plan compounded of both these principles. But having composed one house of representatives chosen by the people in each State, according to their numbers, and the other of an equal number of members from every State, whether larger or smaller, the Constitution gives to majorities in these houses thus constituted the full and entire power of passing laws, subject always to the constitutional restrictions and to the approval of the President. To subject them to any other power is clear usurpation. The majority of one house may be controlled by the majority of the other; and both may be restrained by the President's negative. These are checks and balances provided by the Constitution, existing in the government itself, and wisely intended to secure deliberation and caution in legislative proceedings. But to resist the will of the majority in both houses, thus constitutionally exercised; to insist on the lawfulness of interposition by an extraneous power; to claim the right of defeating the will of Congress, by setting up against it the will of a single State,—is neither more nor less, as its strikes me, than a plain attempt to overthrow the government. The constituted authorities of the United States are no longer a government, if they be not masters of their own will; they are no longer a government, if an external power may arrest their proceedings; they are no longer a government, if acts passed by both houses, and approved by the President, may be nullified by State vetoes or State ordinances. Does any one suppose it could make any difference, as to the binding authority of an act of Congress, and of the duty of a State to respect it, whether it passed by a mere majority of both houses, or by three fourths of each, or the unanimous vote of each? Within the limits and restrictions of the Constitution, the government of the United States, like all other popular governments, acts by majorities. It can act no otherwise. Whoever, therefore, denounces the government of majorities, denounces the government of his own country, and denounces all free governments. And whoever would restrain these majorities, while acting within their constitutional limits, by an external power, whatever he may intend, asserts principles which, if adopted, can lead to nothing else than the destruction of the government itself.

Does not the gentleman perceive, Sir, how his argument against majorities might here be retorted upon him? Does he not see how cogently he might be asked, whether it be the character of nullification to practise what it preaches? Look to South Carolina, at the present moment. How far are the rights of minorities there respected? I confess, Sir, I have not known, in peaceable times, the power of the majority carried with a higher hand, or upheld with more relentless disregard of the rights, feelings, and principles of the minority;—a minority embracing, as the gentleman himself will admit, a large portion of the worth and respectability of the State; a minority comprehending in its numbers men who have been associated with him, and with us, in these halls of legislation; men who have served their country at home and honored it abroad; men who would cheerfully lay down their lives for their native State, in any cause which they could regard as the cause of honor and duty; men above fear, and above reproach; whose deepest grief and distress spring from the conviction, that the present proceedings of the State must ultimately reflect discredit upon her. How is this minority, how are these men, regarded? They are enthralled and disfranchised by ordinances and acts of legislation; subjected to tests and oaths, incompatible, as they conscientiously think, with oaths already taken, and obligations already assumed, they are proscribed and denounced, as recreants to duty and patriotism, and slaves to a foreign power. Both the spirit which pursues them, and the positive measures which emanate from that spirit, are harsh and proscriptive beyond all precedent within my knowledge, except in periods of professed revolution.

It is not, Sir, one would think, for those who approve these proceedings to complain of the power of majorities.

Mr. President, all popular governments rest on two principles, or two assumptions:—

First, That there is so far a common interest among those over whom the government extends, as that it may provide for the defence, protection, and good government of the whole, without injustice or oppression to parts; and

Secondly, That the representatives of the people, and especially the people themselves, are secure against general corruption, and may be trusted, therefore, with the exercise of power.

Whoever argues against these principles argues against the practicability of all free governments. And whoever admits these, must admit, or cannot deny, that power is as safe in the hands of Congress as in those of other representative bodies. Congress is not irresponsible. Its members are agents of the people, elected by them, answerable to them, and liable to be displaced or superseded, at their pleasure; and they possess as fair a claim to the confidence of the people, while they continue to deserve it, as any other public political agents.

If, then, Sir, the manifest intention of the Convention, and the contemporary admission of both friends and foes, prove any thing; if the plain text of the instrument itself, as well as the necessary implication from other provisions, prove any thing; if the early legislation of Congress, the course of judicial decisions, acquiesced in by all the States for forty years, prove any thing,—then it is proved that there is a supreme law, and a final interpreter.

. . . .

Mr. President, if the friends of nullification should be able to propagate their opinions, and give them practical effect, they would, in my judgment, prove themselves the most skillful "architects of ruin," the most effectual extinguishers of high-raised expectation, the greatest blasters of human hopes, that any age has produced. They would stand up to proclaim, in tones which would pierce the ears of half the human race, that the last great experiment of representative government had failed. They would send forth sounds, at the hearing of which the doctrine of the divine right of kings would feel, even in its grave, a returning sensation of vitality and resuscitation. Millions of eyes, of those who now feed their inherent love of liberty on the success of the American example, would turn away from beholding our dismemberment, and find no place on earth whereon to rest their gratified sight. Amidst the incantations and orgies of nullification, secession, disunion, and revolution would be celebrated the funeral rites of constitutional and republican liberty.

But, Sir, if the government do its duty, if it act with firmness and with moderation, these opinions cannot prevail. Be assured, Sir, be assured, that, among the political sentiments of this people, the love of union is still uppermost. They will stand fast by the Constitution, and by those who defend it. I rely on no temporary expedients, on no political combination; but I rely on the true American feeling, the genuine patriotism of the people, and the imperative decision of the public voice. Disorder and confusion, indeed, may arise; scenes of commotion and contest are threatened, and perhaps may come. With my whole heart, I pray for the continuance of the domestic peace and quiet of the country. I desire, most ardently, the restoration of affection and harmony to all its parts. I desire that every citizen of the whole country may look to this government with no other sentiments than those of grateful respect and attachment. But I cannot yield even to kind feelings the cause of the Constitution, the true glory of the country, and the great trust which we hold in our hands for succeeding ages. If the Constitution cannot be maintained without meeting these scenes of commotion and contest, however unwelcome, they must come. We cannot, we must not, we dare not, omit to do that which, in our judgment, the safety of the Union requires. Not regardless of consequences, we must yet meet consequences; seeing the hazards which surround the discharge of public duty, it must yet be discharged. For myself, Sir, I shun no responsibility justly devolving on me, here or elsewhere, in attempting to maintain the cause. I am bound to it by indissoluble ties of affection and duty, and I shall cheerfully partake in its fortunes and its fate. I am ready to perform my own appropriate part, whenever and wherever the occasion may call on me, and to take my chance among those upon whom blows may fall first and fall thickest. I shall exert every faculty I possess in aiding to prevent the Constitution from being nullified, destroyed, or impaired; and even should I see it fall, I will still, with a voice feeble, perhaps, but earnest as ever issued from human lips, and with fidelity and zeal which nothing shall extinguish, call on the PEOPLE to come to its rescue.

A HOUSE DIVIDED

THE SLAVERY *controversy in America was muted until the fourth decade of the nineteenth century. On January 1, 1831, William Lloyd Garrison issued a strident challenge in his* Liberator:

I will be *as harsh as truth, and as uncompromising as justice. On this subject, I do not wish to think, or write with moderation. . . . I am in earnest—I will not equivocate —I will not excuse—I will not retreat a single inch—*AND I WILL BE HEARD.

Proslavery apologists have contended that Garrison and other abolitionists were primarily if not exclusively responsible for creating a solid South on the slavery issue. This is part of the mythology of the controversy. For two decades before Garrison's outburst, the dark shadow of slavery insinuated itself into speeches on major public questions given by such statesmen as John Randolph, William Pinkney, and Robert Hayne. By 1830, the South had acquired the psychology of an aggressively defensive, self-conscious minority group.

Two cultures were coming into conflict. The North became increasingly pluralistic and democratic; it experimented with movements that fostered ideals of humanitarianism, liberalism, and perfectionism. Conversely, the South fashioned its ideals of a static society upon a cotton culture and a slave-labor system. George Washington,

*Thomas Jefferson, and George Mason—representatives of
Southern leaders who had been nurtured in the Age of
Enlightenment—had looked upon slavery as morally
wrong and necessarily evanescent. Theirs was a vanish-
ing spirit. When Governor Miller of South Carolina, in
a speech to the legislature in 1829, pronounced slavery
to be "a positive good," he simply made explicit a view
that already commanded widespread assent. Indeed, the
South's instantaneous and volatile reaction to abolitionist
propaganda betrayed their defensive posture. What abolitionist propaganda did do was to intensify Southern feelings and provoke a massive counterattack.*

*Southerners knew they were sitting on top of a com-
bustible society, despite their tableaus of contented
negroes. Slave insurrections were few, but they were
gruesome. Rumors of new outbreaks were always afloat.
Apprehension and fear mounted as abolitionists showered
inflammatory words on the Southland. State legislatures
responded by enacting restrictive slave codes. Gangs forcibly entered United States Post Offices and seized abolitionist tracts. Emancipation societies and individual
abolitionists were hounded out of the region. Liberally
minded Southerners were forced to conform to the pro-
slave line through laws, personal intimidation, and mob
violence. The repression of civil liberties ended self-
criticism and social experimentation.*

*At the national level influential Southerners encour-
aged conservatives in the North to quash abolitionism for
the sake of the Union. Southern congressmen demanded
"gag rules" that had the effect of tabling all petitions sent
by abolitionists to the Congress. New territorial outlets
and guarantees were sought for slavery. Finally the South
seceded from the Union, convinced that their slave-based
culture was doomed within it.*

*Under attack, Southerners took stock of their regional
culture in relation to the rest of the nation. As they*

looked upon a turbulent North, they took to glorifying their settled way of life. What emerged was a creed of self-justification for both home consumption and export purposes. The main article was a prescriptive doctrine that slavery is a positive good. This doctrine furnished the materials for countless editorials, books, pamphlets, sermons, and speeches. Robert Toombs was but one in a galaxy of orators who took up the cause.

Toombs was a full-bodied orator, urbane and witty. He was a lawyer by profession, a wealthy Georgia plantation owner, a national political figure, and a spokesman of consequence. For most of his political life he was a moderate and a Whig. His interests were nation-wide, but as the storms of sectionalism mounted in fury, he trimmed his sails to prevailing winds from the South.

Like other apologists for slavery, Toombs had to dispose of the "self-evident" truths of Jefferson's Natural Rights philosophy. In one way or another these advocates of the new doctrine effaced bothersome words such as liberty and equality—flatly denying their universality, dismissing them as mere abstractions, or emasculating them through logic chopping. The ground cleared, their argument boldly extolled inequality, invoking the Bible, history, sociology, science, and common observation. The argument unfolded in a panoply of claims: Slavery ennobles the barbarian; it is the foundation for true democracy in the classical sense; it is the condition for social stability and progressive civilization.

On January 7, 1861, Toombs made his farewell speech to the Senate of the United States. He held in substance that property in slaves must be protected under constitutional guarantees by all appropriate agencies of the government as the condition for restoring the Union. Thus Toombs laid bare, if ever there were doubts on the score, a major premise that had guided the South through three decades of labyrinthine argument.

It was precisely this idea of property in mankind, sanctioned by the Constitution, that revolted abolitionists. Not all of one temper or mind on tactics and timing, they were deeply convinced that slavery was the monstrous immorality of the age. "The conviction that slavery is a sin," cried Wendell Phillips, their finest orator, "is the Gibraltar of our cause." While essentially theological in their thinking, they drew their secular philosophy from the Declaration of Independence. Hence slavery was a crime against God, nature, and political creed. Abolitionists were under a moral imperative to cleanse the American conscience; for this they submitted to heckling and stoning, and even risked their lives.

Although abolitionists were loosely banded together into the American Anti-Slavery Society, squabbles among factions seriously impaired the effectiveness of the organization. They worked most successfully through local societies. The Garrison wing was totally uncompromising on the moral issue. Garrison demanded immediate emancipation. Nothing must stand in the way, not even the Union. He invoked a higher law than the Constitution of the United States. He denounced the Constitution as "a covenant with death and an agreement with hell," and he flamboyantly enforced his anathema by publicly burning a copy.

More practical-minded abolitionists modified Garrison's doctrine of immediatism and preached "immediate abolition, gradually accomplished." The goal was not to be compromised, but their methods were to take account of possibilities and consequences. Whereas Garrison believed single-mindedly in ideas as weapons with which to assault the hardened conscience, practical-minded crusaders exploited political opportunities to advance their cause. They sent petitions to Congress, and when their petitions came under the gag rules, they won converts from among those who were outraged by this violation of a citizen's

*constitutional right to petition Congress. When the South
moved to open new and old territories to slavery, they
made common cause with free-soilers, first in splinter
parties, then in the Republican party. In the final analysis, abolitionism succeeded to the extent that it linked
moral sentiment to political action.*

*But to the public at large, particularly in the South,
Garrisonism and abolitionism were interchangeable terms.
There were plenty of people who regarded Garrison as a
hair-shirted monomaniac who deserved manhandling.
Though he had fanatical followers, he was also a stormy
petrel within the ranks of abolitionists. Withal, his voice
and pen were mighty instruments in stirring moral frenzy.
Like a Hebrew prophet he showered maledictions upon
the land, and left troubled consciences in his wake. "For
one, I cannot say I ever positively enjoyed one of his
speeches," observed Thomas Wentworth Higginson, "or
that I ever failed to listen with a sense of deference or
moral leadership."*

*Out in Illinois a lawyer-politician brooded on what he
heard and read. Abraham Lincoln knew in his bones that
slavery was immoral and that sometime, somehow, it must
end. But he didn't know how. He did know that the
Union must be preserved, and so he bit his lips and kept
quiet when, in 1850, the Fugitive Slave Act was passed.
Four years later he broke his silence when the Congress
repealed the Missouri Compromise, foreshadowing the
extension of slavery into the Kansas-Nebraska territory.
In 1854 Lincoln ran for the United States Senate on the
single proposition that slavery must be contained within
areas where it already existed. He lost the election, but in
1858 he was nominated for the Senate by the infant
Republican party. This time he ran against Stephen A.
Douglas, an influential Democrat and accomplished orator. Their contest turned out to be the most celebrated
senatorial campaign in our history.*

The background of the campaign kept intruding itself into the foreground. The Northwest Ordinance of 1787 excluded slavery from this domain. The Missouri Compromise of 1820 prohibited it in the Louisiana Territory north of the parallel of 36 degrees, 30 minutes. There things stood until over 500,000 square miles of Mexican territory were added in 1848 by the Treaty of Guadalupe Hidalgo. The South, no longer in a mood to accept either exclusion or containment of slavery, challenged the Federal Government's authority to legislate on the matter in newly acquired lands. Eager to save the Union, elder statesmen such as Clay and Webster engineered the Compromise of 1850. Why insist upon legislative exclusion, they asked, when climate and geography will render slavery uneconomical anyway? Having jettisoned the principle of legislative exclusion, southern politicians soon moved to repeal the Missouri Compromise itself. They succeeded in 1854 when, after angry debate, Congress passed the Kansas-Nebraska Act. Stephen A. Douglas, Chairman of the Senate's Committee on Territories, was the central figure in the drama.

The Kansas-Nebraska Act called for the organization of two territories, and following Douglas' theory of popular sovereignty, left it up to the residents of the territories to admit or exclude slavery. The Act also repealed the Missouri Compromise. Douglas figured it would raise a "hell of a storm," but he thought it would blow over. It didn't. It shattered the Democratic party in the North and smashed the Whig party, which was replaced by the Republican party founded on the free-soil principle. Event followed event. Slaveholders and free-soilers locked in a bloody struggle for control of Kansas. The Supreme Court, in pronouncing on the Dred Scott case in 1857, declared that the Missouri Compromise had always been unconstitutional. The effect of the decision was to deprive Congress of power to exclude slavery in the territories. By implication it also deprived territorial legislatures of this power since they existed by congressional authorization.

As Lincoln reasoned, Douglas' popular sovereignty was a palpable fraud. It would not surprise him, Lincoln stated, if in some future decision the Supreme Court denied to states the right to exclude slavery. That would do it. Then slavery would be national and perpetual. On June 16, 1858, when he accepted the Republican nomination for the Senate, Lincoln outlined "the plot" by which friends of slavery hoped to make it national. Clearly, a showdown was at hand. The nation will become all one thing or the other. It must choose, for "A house divided against itself cannot stand."

In Washington Douglas studied Lincoln's speech, then returned to Illinois to open his campaign. On July 9 Douglas addressed a huge public audience in Chicago. He spoke to vindicate his doctrine of popular sovereignty and his Senatorial record. He charged that Lincoln's "house divided" doctrine would impose uniformity upon the states, subvert the Constitution, and provoke fratricidal war. Lincoln heard Douglas that night and answered him the next. The campaign was on. Down state they went, both speaking in Springfield on July 17. Between August 21 and October 15 they debated jointly at Ottawa, Freeport, Jonesboro, Charleston, Galesburg, Quincy, and Alton. Between times and after the joint debates each cross-hatched the state independently.

They were an ill-assorted pair—the tall, lanky Lincoln pitted against the stubby Little Giant. Each had taken the other's measure many times before. They were friendly rivals, not mortal enemies. They pommeled each other with argument and riposte; they jockeyed for audience favor. But they were deadly serious about the prize and the issues. Both wanted to preserve the Union. Both regarded slavery as a disruptive factor in national life and *a threat to the Union. Douglas contended that the only way to preserve the Union was to make slavery a matter of local option and to stop agitating the question at the national level, as Lincoln and the Republicans were doing. Lincoln insisted that slavery was incongruent with the principles of a free society. The public mind will not remain at rest, he argued, until slavery is placed in the course of its ultimate extinction.*

The practical question on which Lincoln and Douglas differed was, how should slavery be dealt with in the territories? But before the campaign was over, the speakers had plumbed fundamental questions of political life— the nature of the Union, democracy, human rights, public morality, and personal ambition. As Sandburg put it, they gave the nation a book.

Although Lincoln won the popular vote, he lost the election because of an obsolete system of apportionment. But the 1858 campaign "forged the link in a chain of events" that lifted Lincoln to the Presidency, where he presided over the Civil War and the destruction of slavery. "I have been only an instrument," said Lincoln the President. "The logic and moral power of Garrison and the anti-slavery people of the country and the army have done all."

Slavery in the United States; Its Consistency with Republican Institutions, and Its Effect upon the Slave and Society

ROBERT TOOMBS

Born, near Washington, Georgia, July 2, 1810; died, Washington, Georgia, December 15, 1885. Graduated from Union College (New York), 1828; attended University of Virginia Law School; admitted to Georgia bar, 1830. Member of Georgia legislature, 1838, 1840–1841, 1843–1844; of United States House of Representatives, 1845–1853; of United States Senate, 1853–1861. A stanch Whig and Unionist until the middle of the 1850's. Served briefly as Secretary of State in Jefferson Davis' cabinet, then became an officer in the Confederate army. Was in exile for two years after the war, then returned to Georgia.

*P*ublic opinion has always been a recognised element in directing the affairs of the world, and many causes have combined in our day to increase its strength and power. The more general diffusion of education, the increased facilities of personal intercourse, the rapidity with which ideas and intelligence may be transmitted, and a more general agreement among mankind, as to the standard by which man and all of his acts ought to be tried, have made this power formidable beyond

An Oration Delivered Before the Few and Phi Gamma Societies of Emory College, at Oxford, Ga., July, 1853 (Augusta, Georgia: Steam Power Press of Chronicle and Sentinel, 1853).

all former precedent in the world's history. Its jurisdiction seems to be universal, circumscribed by no limits, bounded by no recognised land marks; it invades the sanctuaries of the Most High and questions his oracles—enters the palaces of kings and rulers, and the homes of the people, and summons all to answer at its bar. Being but the judgment of fallible man, it can claim no exemption from his errors, his frailties, his ignorance, or passions, yet being mischievous even in its errors, it is not wise or safe to disregard it.

Before this tribunal our social and political system is arraigned, and we are summoned to answer. It is my purpose, to-day, to respond to the summons. I consider the occasion not inappropriate. The investigative discussion and decision of social questions are no longer confined to legislative halls and political assemblies of the people. The secluded halls of science already resound with the notes of controversy on the subject.

Professors of some of the most ancient and eminent literary institutions in the Northern States have recently entered this arena against us, and their theological seminaries are animating the zeal, if not increasing the knowledge of the combatants. One of the professors of the theological college of New England is now traversing old England, traducing his countrymen and her institutions, and is appropriately remunerated in the pence and plaudits of her aristocracy. The British reviews and periodical literature have entered with zeal into the contest. The Muses have abandoned Arcadian groves and Elysian fields, and have taken up their abode in waving cane and blooming cotton fields. Romance revels in this literary El Dorado, and transmutes unreal woes into substantial coin.

That the British government should second these assaults both at home and abroad, excites no surprise in those who have marked her policy or studied her history. She joins in this crusade under the cry of Religion, Humanity and Liberty, while her whole history proves that she has never, in her public policy, had the slightest regard for either. Her career, from William the Norman to this hour, has been but a continual warfare against the liberties and rights of the whole human race. Every continent of the earth, and every isle of the sea has been the theatre of her violence, inhumanity and injustice; no race, not even her own, has escaped her terrible energy in crime.

[Here Toombs continues his censure of Great Britain.]

. . . .

For nearly twenty years our domestic enemies have struggled by pen and speech to excite discontent among the white race, and insurrection among the black; their efforts have shaken the national government to its deep foundation, and bursted the bonds of Christian unity in our land. Yet the objects of their attacks—the slaveholding states—reposing in the confidence of their strength, have scarcely felt the shock. In glancing over the civilized world, the eye rests upon not a single spot where all classes of society are so well content with their social system, or have greater reason to be so, than in the slaveholding states of the American Union. Stability, progress, order, peace, content and prosperity, reign throughout our borders. Not a single soldier is to be found in our widely extended domain, to overawe or protect society. The desire for organic change nowhere manifests itself. These great social and political blessings are not the results of accident, but the results of a wise, just and humane republican system. It is my purpose to vindicate the wisdom, humanity, and justice of this system, to show that the position of the African race in it is consistent with its principles, advantageous to that race and society.

African slavery existed in all the colonies at the commencement of the revolution. The paramount authority of the crown, with or without the consent of the colonies, had introduced and legalised it; it was inextricably interwoven with the very frame work of society, especially in the Southern States. The question was not presented to us whether it was just or beneficial to the African, or advantageous to us to tear him away by force or fraud from bondage in his own country, and place him in a like condition in ours. England and the Christian world had long since settled that question for us. At the final overthrow of British authority in these states, our ancestors found seven hundred thousand of the African race among them in bondage, concentrated, from the nature of our climate and production, chiefly in the present slaveholding states. It became their duty to establish governments over the country from which their valour had driven out British authority. They entered upon this great work, profoundly impressed with the truth, that that government was best which secured the greatest happiness possible to the whole society, and adopted constitutional Republics as the best mode to secure that great end of human society. They incorporated no Utopian theories in their system. Starting from the point that each state was sovereign, and embodied the collective will and power of its whole people, they affirmed its right and duty to define and fix, as well as protect and defend the rights of each individual member of the state, and to hold all individual rights as subordinate to the great interests of the whole society. This last proposition is the corner stone of Republican government, which must be stricken out before the legal status of the African race among us can be shown to be inconsistent with its principles. The question with the builders up of our system of government, was not what rights man might have in a state of nature, but what rights he ought to have in a state of society; they dealt with rights as things of compact and not of birthright, in the concrete and not in the abstract. A very slight examination of our state constitutions will show how little they regarded vague notions of abstract liberty or natural equality in fixing the rights of the white race, as well as the black. The elective franchise, the cardinal feature of our system, was granted, withheld, or limited, according to their ideas of public policy. It was withheld by all of them from females, not because they were deemed less competent to exercise it than many to whom it was granted, but because it was adjudged that their own and the public happiness would be promoted by the exclusion.

All of them excluded minors because they were adjudged, as a class, incompetent to exercise it wisely. They all excluded the African race, free as well as bond, because as a race they were considered unfit to be trusted with it. All of them excluded the Indian tribes from that right, or any other in the social compact. The constitutions of some of the states excluded from the right of suffrage all persons except the owners of the soil, and all of them, it is believed, originally imposed some condition or restraint upon its exercise, applicable to all persons. The same great principle is no less happily illustrated in the numerous restraints placed by both our state and national constitutions, upon the supposed abstract right of a mere numerical majority to govern society in all cases. Thus our institutions every where affirm the subordination of individual rights to the interest and safety of the whole society.

The slave holders acting upon these principles, finding the Africans already among them in slavery, unfit to be intrusted with political power, and incapable as freemen of either securing their own happiness, or promoting the public prosperity, recognised their condition as slaves, and subjected it to legal control. The justice and policy of this decision have both been greatly questioned, and both must depend upon the soundness of the assumptions upon which it was based. I hold that they were sound and true, and that the African is unfit to be intrusted with political power, and incapable as a freeman of securing his own happiness or contributing to the public prosperity, and that whenever the two races co-exist, a state of slavery is best for him and for society. And under it, in our country, he is in a better condition than any he has ever attained in any other age and country, either in bondage or freedom.

. . . .

Very soon after the discovery and settlement of America, the policy of the Christian world bought large numbers of their people of their savage masters and countrymen, and imported them into the Western World. Here we are enabled to view them under different and far more favorable conditions. In Hayti, by the encouragement of the French government, after a long probation of slavery, they became free; and, led on by the valour and conduct of the mixed breeds, aided by overpowering numbers, they massacred the small number of whites who inhabited the Island, and succeeded to the undisputed sway of the finest island in the West Indies under the highest state of cultivation. Their condition in Hayti left nothing to be desired for the most favorable experiment of the capacity of the race for self-government and civilization. This experiment has now been tested for sixty years, and its results are before the world. A war of races began the moment the fear of foreign invasion ceased, and resulted in the extermination of the greater number of the mulattoes who had rescued them from the dominion of the whites. Revolutions, tumults and disorders have been the ordinary pastimes of the emancipated blacks; production has almost ceased, and their stock of civilization acquired in slavery has become already exhausted, and they are now scarcely distinguishable from the tribes from which they were torn in their native land.

More recently the same experiment has been tried in Jamaica, under the auspices of England. The Island of Jamaica was one of the most beautiful, productive, and prosperous of the British colonial possessions. England, deceived by the theories of her speculative philanthropists into the opinion that free blacks would be more productive laborers than slaves, in 1838 proclaimed total emancipation of the black race in Jamaica. Her arms and her power have watched over and protected them; not only the interest but the absolute necessities of the white proprietors of the land compelled them to offer every inducement and stimulant to industry, yet the experiment stands before the world a confessed failure. Ruin has overwhelmed the proprietors; and the negro, true to his nationality, buries himself in filth, and sloth and crime. In the United States, too, we have peculiar opportunities for studying the African race under different conditions. Here we find him in slavery; here we find him also a freeman in the slaveholding and in the non-slaveholding states. The best specimen of the free blacks to be found are in the Southern States, in the closest contact with slavery and subject to many of its restraints. Upon the theory of the abolitionists the most favorable condition in which you can view the free negro is in the non-slaveholding states of the Union; there we ought to expect to find him displaying all the capability of his race for improvement, in a temperate climate, among an active, industrious, and ingenious people, surrounded by sympathising friends, and mild, and just, and equal institutions; if he fails here, surely it can be chargeable to nothing but himself. He has had seventy years to cleanse himself and his race from the leprosy of slavery, yet what is his condition to-day? He is lord of himself, but he finds it "a heritage of woe." After seventy years of probation among themselves, the Northern States, acting upon the same principles of self-protection which had marked our policy, declare him unfit to enjoy the rights and perform the duties of citizenship. Denied social equality by an irreversible law of nature, and political rights by municipal law, incapable of maintaining an unequal struggle with a superior race, the melancholy history of his career of freedom is here most usually found recorded in criminal courts, jails, poor houses, and penitentiaries. The authentic statistics of crime and poverty show an amount of misery and crime among the free blacks out of all proportion to their numbers, when compared to any class of the white race. This fact has had itself recognised in the most decisive manner throughout the Northern States. No town, or city, or state, encourages their immigration; many of them discourage it by political legislation; and some of the non-slaveholding States have absolutely prohibited their entry into their borders, under any circumstances whatever. If the Northern States which adopt this policy, deny the truth of the principles upon which our policy is built and maintained, they are guilty of a most cruel injury to an unhappy race. They do admit it, and expel them from their borders and drive them out as wanderers and outcasts. The result of this policy is every where apparent. The statistics of population supply the evidence of their condition. In the non-slaveholding states their annual increase, during the last ten years, has been but little over one per cent., even with the additions of fugitives from labor and emancipated slaves from the South, clearly showing that in this their most favored condition when left to themselves they are barely capable of maintaining their existence, and with the prospect of a denser population and greater competition in labor for employment consequent thereon, they are in danger of becoming extinct. The Southern States, acting upon the same admitted fact, keep them in the condition in which we found them, protect them against themselves and compel them to contribute to their own and the public interests and welfare. That our system does promote the well-being of the African race subject to it, and the public interest I shall now proceed to show by facts which are open to all men and can be neither controverted or denied. We submit our slave institutions to the same tests by which we try the labor of other countries, and which are admitted to be sound by the common consent of mankind, and we say that under them we have not only elevated the African above his own race in any other country, but that his condition is superior to that of millions of laborers in England, who neglects her own to look after the condition of our operatives.

Our political system gives the slave great and valuable rights. His life is equally protected with that of his master, his person is secure from assault against all others except his master, and his power in this respect is placed under salutary restraints. He is entitled by law to ample food and clothing, and exempted from excessive labor, and when no longer capable of labor, in old age or disease, his comfortable maintenance is a legal charge upon his master. We know that these rights are, in the main, faithfully secured to him. . . . But these legal rights of the slave embrace but a small portion of the privileges actually enjoyed by him. The nature of the relation of

master and slave begets kindnesses, imposes duties (and secures their performance), which exist in no other relation of capital and labor. Interest and
humanity co-operate in harmony for the well-being of our laborer. A striking
evidence of this fact is found in our religious statistics. While religious instruction is not enjoined by law in all the states, the number of slaves who
are in communion with the different churches, abundantly proves the universality of their enjoyment of religious privileges. And a learned clergyman
in New York has recently shown, from the records of our evangelical
churches, that a greater number of African slaves in the United States have
enjoyed, and are enjoying, the consolations of religion than the combined
efforts of all the Christian churches have been able to redeem from the
heathen world, since the introduction of slavery among us. . . .

It is objected that our slaves are debarred educational advantages. The
objection is well taken, but is without great force; their station in society
makes education neither necessary nor useful. . . .

We are reproached that the marriage relation is neither recognised nor
protected by law. This reproach is not wholly unjust, this is an evil not yet
remedied by law, but marriage is not inconsistent with the institution of
slavery as it exists among us, and the objection, therefore, lies rather to an
incident than to the essence of the system. But even in this we have deprived
the slave of no pre-existing right. We found the race without any knowledge
of, or regard for the institution of marriage, and we are reproached for not
having, as yet, secured that and all other blessings of civilization. The
separation of families is much relied on by the abolitionists in Europe and
America. Some of the slaveholding states have already made partial provision against this evil, and all of them may do so; but the objection is far
more formidable in theory than practice, even without legislative interposition.

The tendency of slave labor is to aggregation—of free labor to dispersion.
The accidents of life, the desire to better one's condition, and the pressure
of want (the proud man's contumely and oppressor's wrong) produce infinitely a greater amount of separation in families of the white races than that
which ever happened to the slave. This is true every where, even in the
United States, where the general condition of the people is prosperous. But
it is still more marked in Europe. The injustice and despotism of England
to Ireland has produced more separation of Irish families, and sundered more
domestic ties within the last ten years, than slavery has effected since its
introduction into the United States. The twenty millions of freemen in the
United States are living witnesses to the dispersive injustice of the old
world. And to-day England is purchasing coolies in India, and apprentices in
Africa, to redeem her West India possessions from the folly of emancipation.
What securities has she thrown around the family altars of these miserable

savages? It is in vain to call this separation voluntary—if it were true, that fact mitigates none of its evils. But it is the result of a necessity as stern, inexorable and irresistible, as the physical force which brings the slave from Virginia to Georgia.

But the monster objection to our institution of slavery in the estimation of its opponents is, that wages are withheld from labor—the force of the objection is lost in its want of truth. An examination of the true theory of wages will expose its fallacy. Under the system of free labor, wages are paid in money, the representative of products, in ours in products themselves. If we pay, in the comforts of life, more than the free laborer's pecuniary wages will buy, then our laborer is paid higher wages than the free laborer. The Parliamentary Reports in England show that the wages of agricultural and unskilled labor in Great Britain not only fails to furnish the laborer with the comforts of the slave, but even with the necessaries of life, and no slave holder in Georgia could escape a conviction for cruelty to his slaves who exacted from them the same amount of labor, for the same compensation in the necessaries of life, which noblemen and gentlemen of England pay their free laborers. Under their system man has become less valuable and less cared for than their domestic animals; and noble Dukes will depopulate whole districts of men to supply their places with sheep, and then with intrepid audacity lecture and denounce American slaveholders.

The great conflict between labor and capital under free competition has ever been how the earnings of labor shall be divided between it and capital. In new and sparsely settled countries, where land is cheap, and food is easily produced, and education and intelligence approximate equality, labor can struggle successfully in this warfare with capital. But this is an exceptional and temporary condition of society. In the old world this state of things has long since passed away, and the conflict with the lower grades of labor has long since ceased. There the compensation of unskilled labor, which first succumbs to capital, is reduced to a point scarcely adequate to the continuance of the race. . . . Here the portion due the slave is a charge upon the whole product of capital and upon the capital itself. It is neither dependent upon seasons nor subject to accidents, and survives his own capacity for labor and even the ruin of his master. The general happiness, cheerfulness, and contentment of the slaves, compare favorably with that of laborers in any other age or country. They require no standing armies to enforce their obedience, while the evidences of discontent, and the appliance of force to repress it, are every where visible among the toiling millions of the earth. Even in the northern states of this Union, strikes and mobs, and labor unions, and combinations against employers, attest at once the misery and discontent of labor among them. . . .

That the condition of the slave offers great opportunities for abuse is true, that these opportunities are frequently used to violate justice and humanity, is also true. But our laws restrain these abuses and punish these crimes, in this, as well as in all the other relations of life. They who assume it as a fundamental principle in the constitution of man, that abuse is the unvarying concomitant of power and crime of opportunity, subvert the foundations of all private morals and of every social system. No where does this principle find a nobler refutation than in the treatment of the African race by southern slaveholders. And we may, with hope and confidence, safely leave to them the removal of the existing abuses under which it now labors and such further ameliorations of its condition as may be demanded by justice and humanity. His condition is not permanent among us and we may find his exodus in the unvarying laws of population. Under the conditions of labor in England, and the continent of Europe, slavery could not exist here or anywhere else. The moment wages descend to a point barely sufficient to support the laborer and his family, capital cannot afford to own labor, and slavery instantly ceases. Slavery ceased in England in obedience to this law, and not from any regard to liberty or humanity. The increase of population will produce the same result in this country, and American slavery, like that of England, will find its euthanasy in the general prostration of all labor.

The next aspect in which I propose to view this question, is its effects upon the interests of the slaveholding states themselves. The great argument by which slavery was formerly assailed was that it was a dear, unprofitable and unproductive labor; it was held that the slave himself would be a more productive member of society as a freeman than in bondage. The results of emancipation in the British and French West India Islands has not only disproven but annihilated this theory. And an inquiry into the wealth and production of our slaveholding states will demonstrate that slave labor can be more economically and productively applied, at least to agriculture, than any other. The same truth will be made manifest by a comparison of the products of Cuba and Brazil, not only with these Islands and Hayti, but with those of the free races occupying the same latitudes and engaged in the same, or similar productions, in any part of the world. The slaveholding states with about one-half of the white population, and three millions of slaves, furnish four-fifths of the whole exports of the Republic containing twenty-three millions of inhabitants, and their entire products, including every branch of industry, exceed those of the more populous northern states. And a distinguished statesman of our own state has recently conclusively shown, by an accurate examination of our statistics, that Georgia with less than half of the population, about equals, in her productions of industry, the State of Ohio, one of the most prosperous of the northern states. The difference in realised wealth in proportion to population is not less remarkable and equally favorable to the slaveholding states.

I may safely leave the question of the fitness of slave labor for the production of wealth, to the authentic facts disclosed in the late census. But the fact needs some explanation, as it seems to be a profound mystery to the opponents of slavery, how the system is capable at the same time of increasing the comforts of the slave, the profits of the master, and do no violence to humanity. Yet its solution rests upon the soundest principles of political economy. Here the labor of the country is united with and protected by its capital, directed by the educated and intelligent, secured against its own weakness, waste and folly, associated in such form, as to give the greatest efficiency in production, and the least cost of maintenance. Each individual laborer of the North is the victim not only of his folly and extravagance, but of his ignorance, misfortunes and necessities. His isolation enlarges his expenses without increasing his comforts, his want of capital increases the price of everything he buys, disables him from supplying his wants at favorable times, or on advantageous terms, and throws him in the hands of retailers and extortioners. But labor united with capital, directed by skill, forecast and intelligence, while it is capable of its highest production, is freed from these evils, leaves a margin both for increased comforts to the laborer and additional profits to capital. This is the explanation of the seeming paradox.

The opponents of slavery, true to their monomania that it is the sum of all evils and crimes, in spite of all history, sacred and profane, ancient or modern, all facts and all truth, insist that its effect on the commonwealth is to enervate it, demoralise it, and render it incapable of advancement and a high civilization, and upon the citizen to debase him morally, physically and intellectually. Such is neither the truth of history, sacred or profane, nor the experience of our own past or present. To the Hebrew race were committed the oracles of the Most High, slaveholding priests administered at his altar, and slaveholding patriarchs and prophets received his revelations, taught them to their own, and transmitted them to all generations of men. Letters, and arts, and science, and power, and wealth, and dominion, first arose from the dark night of the past in slaveholding Egypt. The highest forms of ancient civilization, and the noblest development of the individual man, are to be found in the ancient commonwealths of Greece and Rome. In Greece, liberty, in the midst of domestic slavery, first erected legal barriers against political despotism, and maintained them with a heroism which has excited the admiration of all subsequent ages.

In great achievements in arms, in science and arts, she stands preeminent among the nations of the earth. Statesmen study her institutions, and learn lessons of political wisdom, and the highest intellects of every age have delighted in her literature, notwithstanding the boasted advancement of our age. Homer, Demosthenes, Aristotle, Thucydides, and Xenophon, are yet text books in our schools and colleges; and in eloquence, in rhetoric, in poetry, in painting, in sculpture and architecture, you must still go and search amid the wreck and ruins of her genius for "the pride of every model and the perfection of every master."

Public liberty and domestic slavery were cradled together and marked the civil polity of the commonwealth of ancient Rome. Her hardy sons, distinguished for personal prowess, for frugality and simplicity of manners, for public and private virtue, and the intensity of their patriotism, carried her victorious eagles in triumph over the then known world. She overran Greece, appropriated her civilization, studied her literature, and rivalled her glory in letters. She carried her civilization with her conquests over western Europe, and time has not yet been able to efface the footprints of her language, her literature, or her liberty; and her jurisprudence, surviving her nationality, has incorporated itself in that of all the civilized nations of Europe and America. The language and literature of both, stamped with immortality, passes on to mingle itself in the thought and speech of all lands and all countries. But it is needless to multiply illustrations. That domestic slavery neither enfeebles or deteriorates our race, that it is not inconsistent with the highest advancement of man or society, is the lesson taught by all ancient and confirmed by all modern history.

Its effects in strengthening rather than weakening the attachment of the dominant race to liberty was clearly perceived and eloquently expressed in the British Parliament by Edmund Burke, one of the most accomplished and philosophical statesmen England ever produced. Mr. Burke, in his speech on conciliation with America, uses the following language:

Where this is the case, those who are free, are by far the most proud and jealous of their freedom. . . . I can not alter the nature of man. The fact is so, and these people of the southern colonies are much more strongly, and with a higher and more stubborn spirit, attached to liberty than those to the northward. Such were all the ancient commonwealths, such were our Gothic ancestors, and such in our day were the Poles; and such will be all masters of slaves who are not slaves themselves. In such a people the haughtiness of domination combines itself with the spirit of freedom, fortifies it, and renders it invincible.

[Toombs goes on to discuss the historic contributions of Southerners to the spirit of American liberty.]

. . . .

Such is our social system and such our condition under it. Its political wisdom is vindicated in its effects on society, its morality by the practices of the Patriarchs and the teachings of the Apostles; we submit it to the judgment of the civilized world with the firm conviction that the adoption of no other system under our circumstances would have exhibited the individual man (bond or free) in a higher development, or society in a happier civilization.

No Compromise with Slavery

WILLIAM LLOYD GARRISON

*Born, Newburyport, Massachusetts, December 10, 1805;
died, New York City, May 24, 1879. Largely self-educated. Entered newspaper work as an apprentice and
became editor successively of several reform papers.
Founded the Liberator, 1830. Helped found the New
England Anti-Slavery Society, 1831, and the American
Anti-Slavery Society, 1833. Espoused various reforms but
is best known as a militant crusader for abolitionism.*

An earnest espousal of the Anti-Slavery cause for a
quarter of a century, under circumstances which have
served in a special manner to identify my name and labours with it, will
shield me from the charge of egotism, in assuming to be its exponent—at least
for myself—on this occasion. All that I can compress within the limits of a
single lecture, by way of its elucidation, it shall be my aim to accomplish. I
will make a clean breast of it. You shall know all that is in my heart per-
taining to Slavery, its supporters, and apologists.

Of necessity, as well as of choice, I am a "Garrisonian" Abolitionist—the
most unpopular appellation that any man can have applied to him, in the
present state of public sentiment; yet, I am more than confident, destined
ultimately to be honourably regarded by the wise and good. For though I
have never assumed to be a leader—have never sought conspicuity of position,
or notoriety of name—have desired to follow, if others, better qualified, would
go before, and to be lost sight of in the throng of Liberty's adherents, as a
drop is merged in the ocean; yet, as the appellation alluded to is applied, not
with any reference to myself invidiously, but to excite prejudice against

*An Address Delivered in the Broadway Tabernacle, New York, February 14, 1854,
By William Lloyd Garrison* (New York: American Anti-Slavery Society, 1854).

the noblest movement of the age, in order that the most frightful system of oppression ever devised by human ingenuity and wickedness may be left to grow and expand to the latest generation—I accept it as the synonym of absolute trust in God, and utter disregard of "that fear of man which bringeth a snare"—and so deem it alike honourable and praiseworthy.

Representing, then, that phase of Abolitionism which is the most contemned—to the suppression of which, the means and forces of the Church and the State are most actively directed—I am here to defend it against all its assailants as the highest expediency, the soundest philosophy, the noblest patriotism, the broadest philanthropy, and the best religion extant. To denounce it as fanatical, disorganizing, reckless of consequences, bitter and irreverent in spirit, infidel in heart, deaf alike to the suggestions of reason and the warnings of history, is to call good evil, and evil good; to put darkness for light, and light for darkness; to insist that Barabbas is better than Jesus; to cover with infamy the memories of patriarchs and prophets, apostles and martyrs; and to inaugurate Satan as the God of the universe. If, like the sun, it is not wholly spotless, still, like the sun, without it there is no light. If murky clouds obscure its brightness, still it shines in its strength. If, at any time, it seems to wane to its final setting, it is only to reveal itself in the splendour of a new ascension, unquenchable, glorious, sublime.

Let me define my positions, and at the same time challenge any one to show wherein they are untenable.

I. I am a believer in that portion of the Declaration of American Independence in which it is set forth, as among self-evident truths, "that all men are created equal; that they are endowed by their Creator with certain inalienable rights; that among these are life, liberty, and the pursuit of happiness." Hence, I am an Abolitionist. Hence, I cannot but regard oppression in every form—and most of all, that which turns a man into a thing—with indignation and adhorrence. Not to cherish these feelings would be recreancy to principle. They who desire me to be dumb on the subject of Slavery, unless I will open my mouth in its defence, ask me to give the lie to my professions, to degrade my manhood, and to stain my soul. I will not be a liar, a poltroon, or a hypocrite, to accommodate any party, to gratify any sect, to escape any odium or peril, to save any interest, to preserve any institution, or to promote any object. Convince me that one man may rightfully make another man his slave, and I will no longer subscribe to the Declaration of Independence. Convince me that liberty is not the inalienable birthright of every human being, of whatever complexion or clime, and I will give that instrument to the consuming fire. I do not know how to espouse freedom and slavery together. I do not know how to worship God and Mammon at the same time. If other men choose to go upon all-fours, I choose to stand erect, as God designed every man to stand. If, practically falsifying its heaven-attested principles, this nation denounces me for refusing to imitate its example, then, adhering all the more tenaciously to those principles, I will not cease to rebuke it for its guilty inconsistency. Numerically, the contest may be an unequal one, for the time being; but the Author of liberty and the Source of justice, the adorable God, is more than multitudinous, and he will defend the right. My crime is, that I will not go with the multitude to do evil. My singularity is, that when I say that Freedom is of God, and Slavery is of the devil, I mean just what I say. My fanaticism is, that I insist on the American people abolishing Slavery, or ceasing to prate of the rights of man. . . .

II. Notwithstanding the lessons taught us by Pilgrim Fathers and Revolutionary Sires, at Plymouth Rock, on Bunker Hill, at Lexington, Concord and Yorktown; notwithstanding our Fourth of July celebrations, and ostentatious displays of patriotism; in what European nation is personal liberty held in such contempt as in our own? Where are there such unbelievers in the natural equality and freedom of mankind? Our slaves outnumber the entire population of the country at the time of our revolutionary struggle. In vain do they clank their chains, and fill the air with their shrieks, and make their supplications for mercy. In vain are their sufferings portrayed, their wrongs rehearsed, their rights defended. As Nero fiddled while Rome was burning, so the slaveholding spirit of this nation rejoices, as one barrier of liberty after another is destroyed, and fresh victims are multiplied for the cotton-field and the auction-block. For one impeachment of the slave system, a thousand defences are made. For one rebuke of the man-stealer, a thousand denunciations of the Abolitionists are heard. For one press that bears a faithful testimony against Slavery, a score are ready to be prostituted to its service. For one pulpit that is not "recreant to its trust," there are ten that openly defend slaveholding as compatible with Christianity, and scores that are dumb. For one church that excludes the human enslaver from its communion table, multitudes extend to him the right hand of religious fellowship. The wealth, the enterprise, the literature, the politics, the religion of the land, are all combined to give extension and perpetuity to the Slave Power. Everywhere to do homage to it, to avoid collision with it, to propitiate its favour, is deemed essential—nay, *is* essential to political preferment and ecclesiastical advancement. Nothing is so unpopular as impartial liberty. The two great parties which absorb nearly the whole voting strength of the Republic are pledged to be deaf, dumb and blind to whatever outrages the Slave Power may attempt to perpetrate. Cotton is in their ears—blinds are over their eyes—padlocks are upon their lips. They are as clay in the hands of the potter, and already moulded into vessels of dishonour, to be used for the vilest purposes. The tremendous power of the Government is actively wielded to "crush out" the little Anti-Slavery life that remains in individual hearts, and to open new and boundless domains for the expansion of the Slave system. No man known or suspected to be hostile to "the Compromise Measures, including the Fugitive Slave Law," is allowed to hope for any office under the present Administration. The ship of State is labouring in the trough of the sea—her engine powerless, her bulwarks swept away, her masts gone, her lifeboats destroyed, her pumps choked, and the leak gaining rapidly upon her; and as wave after wave dashes over her, all that might otherwise serve to keep her afloat is swallowed by the remorseless deep. God of heaven! if the ship is destined to go down "full many a fathom deep," is every soul on board to perish? Ho! a sail! a sail! The weather-beaten, but staunch ship Abolition, commanded by the Genius of Liberty, is bearing towards the wreck, with the cheering motto, inscribed in legible capitals, "WE WILL NOT FORSAKE YOU!" Let us hope, even against hope, that rescue is not wholly impossible.

To drop what is figurative for the actual. I have expressed the belief that, so lost to all self-respect and all ideas of justice have we become by the corrupting presence of Slavery, in no European nation is personal liberty held at such discount, as a matter of principle, as in our own. See how clearly this is demonstrated. The reasons adduced among us in justification of slaveholding, and therefore against personal liberty, are multitudinous. I will enumerate only a dozen of these: 1. "The victims are black." 2. "The slaves belong to an inferior race." 3. "Many of them have been fairly purchased." 4. "Others have been honestly inherited." 5. "Their emancipation would impoverish their owners." 6. "They are better off as slaves than they would be as freemen." 7. "They could not take care of themselves if set free." 8. "Their simultaneous liberation would be attended with great danger." 9. "Any interference in their behalf will excite the ill-will of the South, and thus seriously affect Northern trade and commerce." 10. "The Union can be preserved only by letting Slavery alone, and that is of paramount importance." 11. "Slavery is a lawful and constitutional system, and therefore not a crime." 12. "Slavery is sanctioned by the Bible; the Bible is the word of God; therefore God sanctions Slavery, and the Abolitionists are wise above what is written."

Here, then, are twelve reasons which are popularly urged in all parts of the country, as conclusive against the right of a man to himself. If they are valid, in any instance, what becomes of the Declaration of Independence? On what ground can the revolutionary war, can any struggle for liberty, be justified? Nay, cannot all the despotisms of the earth take shelter under them? If they are valid, then why is not the jesuitical doctrine, that the end sanctifies the means, and that it is right to do evil that good may come, morally sound? If they are valid, then how does it appear that God is no respecter of persons? or how can he say, "All souls are mine"? or what is to be done with Christ's injunction, "Call no man master"? or with what justice can the same duties and the same obligations (such as are embodied in the Decalogue and the gospel of Christ) be exacted of chattels as of men?

But they are not valid. They are the logic of Bedlam, the morality of the pirate ship, the diabolism of the pit. They insult the common sense and shock the moral nature of mankind.

[He quotes from a variety of foreign writers and statesmen to prove that "in regard to personal liberty . . . even Italy, Austria, and Tunis are in advance of this boasted Republic."]

. . . .

III. The Abolitionism which I advocate is as absolute as the law of God, and as unyielding as His throne. It admits of no compromise. Every slave is a stolen man; every slaveholder is a man-stealer. By no precedent, no example, no law, no compact, no purchase, no bequest, no inheritance, no combination of circumstances, is slaveholding right or justifiable. While a slave remains in his fetters, the land must have no rest. Whatever sanctions his doom must be pronounced accursed. The law that makes him a chattel is to be trampled under foot; the compact that is formed at his expense, and cemented with his blood, is null and void; the church that consents to his enslavement is horribly atheistical; the religion that receives to its communion the enslaver is the embodiment of all criminality. Such, at least, is the verdict of my own soul, on the supposition that I am to be the slave; that my wife is to be sold from me for the vilest purposes; that my children are to be torn from my arms, and disposed of to the highest bidder, like sheep in the market. And who am I but a man? What right have I to be free, that another man cannot prove himself to possess by nature? Who or what are my wife and children, that they should not be herded with four-footed beasts, as well as others thus sacredly related? If I am white, and another is black, complexionally, what follows?

> Does, then, th' immortal principle within
> Change with the casual colour of the skin?
> Does matter govern spirit? or is mind
> Degraded by the form to which 'tis joined?

What if I am rich, and another is poor—strong, and he is weak—intelligent, and he is benighted—elevated, and he is depraved? "Have we not one Father? Hath not one God created us?"

> How rich, how poor, how abject, how august,
> How complicate, how wonderful is man!
> Distinguished link in being's endless chain,

> Midway from nothing to the Deity!
> A beam ethereal, sullied and absorpt;
> Though sullied and dishonoured, still divine!

Such is man, in every clime—above all compacts, greater than all institutions, sacred against every outrage, priceless, immortal!

By this sure test, every institution, every party, every form of government, every kind of religion, is to be tried. God never made a human being either for destruction or degradation. It is plain, therefore, that whatever cannot flourish except at the sacrifice of that being, ought not to exist. Show me the party that can obtain supremacy only by trampling upon human individuality and personal sovereignty, and you will thereby pronounce sentence of death upon it. Show me the government which can be maintained only by destroying the rights of a portion of the people, and you will indicate the duty of openly revolting against it. Show me the religion which sanctions the ownership of one man by another, and you will demonstrate it to be purely infernal in its origin and spirit.

No man is to be injured in his person, mind, or estate. He cannot be with benefit to any other man, or to any state of society. Whoever would sacrifice him for any purpose is both morally and politically insane. Every man is equivalent to every other man. Destroy the equivalent, and what is left? "So God created man in his own image—male and female created he them." This is a death-blow to all claims of superiority, to all charges of inferiority, to all usurpation, to all oppressive dominion.

But all these declarations are truisms. Most certainly; and they are all that is stigmatized as "Garrisonian Abolitionism." I have not, at any time, advanced an ultra sentiment, or made an extravagant demand. I have avoided fanaticism on the one hand, and folly on the other. No man can show that I have taken one step beyond the line of justice, or forgotten the welfare of the master in my anxiety to free the slave. . . . If the slaves are not men; if they do not possess human instincts, passions, faculties and powers; if they are below accountability, and devoid of reason; if for them there is no hope of immortality, no God, no heaven, no hell; if, in short, they are, what the Slave Code declares them to be, rightly "deemed, sold, taken, reputed and adjudged in law to be chattels personal in the hands of their owners and possessors, and their executors, administrators and assigns, to all intents, constructions, and purposes whatsoever;" then, undeniably, I am mad, and can no longer discriminate between a man and a beast. But, in that case, away with the horrible incongruity of giving them oral instruction, of teaching them the catechism, of recognising them as suitably qualified to be members of Christian churches, of extending to them the ordinance of baptism, and admitting them to the communion table, and enumerating many of them as belonging to the household of faith! Let them be no more included in our religious sympathies or denominational statistics than are the dogs in our streets, the swine in our pens, or the utensils in our dwellings. It is right to own, to buy, to sell, to inherit, to breed, and to control them, in the most absolute sense. All constitutions and laws which forbid their possession ought to be so far modified or repealed as to concede the right.

But, if they are men; if they are to run the same career of immortality with ourselves; if the same law of God is over them as over all others; if they have souls to be saved or lost; if Jesus included them among those for whom he laid down his life; if Christ is within many of them "the hope of glory"; then, when I claim for them all that we claim for ourselves, because we are created in the image of God, I am guilty of no extravagance, but am bound, by every principle of honour, by all the claims of human nature, by obedience to Almighty God, to "remember them that are in bonds as bound with them," and to demand their immediate and unconditional emancipation.

[Garrison defends himself against charges of fanaticism, and goes on to lay the blame for the growth and extension of slavery on both North and South.]

. . . .

Some men are still talking of preventing the spread of the cancer, but leaving it just where it is. They admit that, constitutionally, it has now a right to ravage two-thirds of the body politic—but they protest against its extension. This is moral quackery. Even some, whose zeal in the Anti-Slavery cause is fervent, are so infatuated as to propose no other remedy for Slavery but its non-extension. Give it no more room, they say, and it may be safely left to its fate. Yes, but who shall "bell the cat"? Besides, with fifteen Slave States, and more than three millions of Slaves, how can we make any moral issue with the Slave Power against its further extension? Why should there not be twenty, thirty, fifty Slave States, as well as fifteen? Why should not the star-spangled banner wave over ten, as well as over three millions of Slaves? Why should not Nebraska be cultivated by Slave labour, as well as Florida or Texas? If men, under the American Constitution, may hold slaves at discretion and without dishonour in one-half of the country, why not in the whole of it? If it would be a damning sin for us to admit another Slave State into the Union, why is it not a damning sin to permit a Slave State to remain in the Union? Would it not be the acme of effrontery for a man, in amicable alliance with fifteen pickpockets, to profess scruples of conscience in regard to admitting another pilfering rogue to the fraternity? "Thou that sayest, A man should not steal, dost thou steal," or consent, in any instance, to stealing? "If the Lord be God, serve Him; but if Baal, then serve him." The South may well laugh to scorn the affected moral sensibility of the North against the extension of her slave system. It is nothing, in the present relations of the States, but sentimental hypocrisy. It has no stamina—no backbone. The argument for non-extension is an argument for the dissolution of the Union. With a glow of moral indignation, I protest against the promise and the pledge, by whomsoever made, that if the Slave Power will seek no more to lengthen its cords and strengthen its stakes, it may go unmolested and unchallenged, and survive as long as it can within its present limits. I would as soon turn pirate on the high seas as to give my consent to any such arrangement. I do not understand the moral code of those who, screaming in agony at the thought of Nebraska becoming a Slave Territory, virtually say to the South: "Only desist from your present designs, and we will leave you to flog, and lacerate, and plunder, and destroy the millions of hapless wretches already within your grasp. If you will no longer agitate the subject, we will not." There is no sense, no principle, no force in such an issue. Not a solitary slaveholder will I allow to enjoy repose on any other condition than instantly ceasing to be one. Not a single slave will I leave in his chains, on any conditions, or under any circumstances. I will not try to make as good a bargain for the Lord as the Devil will let me, and plead the necessity of a compromise, and regret that I cannot do any better, and be thankful that I can do so much. The Scriptural injunction is to be obeyed: "Resist the devil, and he will flee from you." My motto is, "No union with slaveholders, religiously or politically." Their motto is "Slavery forever! No alliance with Abolitionists, either in Church or State!" The issue is clear, explicit, determinate. The parties understand each other, and are drawn in battle array. They can never be reconciled—never walk together—never consent to a truce— never deal in honeyed phrases—never worship at the same altar—never acknowledge the same God. Between them there is an impassable gulf. In manners, in morals, in philosophy, in religion, in ideas of justice, in notions of law, in theories of government, in valuations of men, they are totally dissimilar.

I would to God that we might be, what we have never been—a united people; but God renders this possible only by "proclaiming liberty throughout all the land, unto all the inhabitants thereof." By what miracle can Freedom and Slavery be made amicably to strike hands? How can they administer the same Government, or legislate for the same interests? How can they receive the same baptism, be admitted to the same communion-table, believe in the same Gospel, and obtain the same heavenly inheritance? . . . The present American Union, therefore, is only one in form, not in reality. It is, and it always has been, the absolute supremacy of the Slave Power over the whole country—nothing more. What sectional heart-burnings or conflictive interests exist between the several Free States? None. They are homogeneous, animated by the same spirit, harmonious in their action as the movement of the spheres. It is only when we come to the dividing line between the Free States and the Slave States that shoals, breakers and whirlpools beset the ship of State, and threaten to engulf or strand it. Then the storm rages loud and long, and the ocean of popular feeling is lashed into fury.

While the present Union exists, I pronounce it hopeless to expect any repose, or that any barrier can be effectually raised against the extension of Slavery. With two thousand million dollars' worth of property in human flesh in its hands, to be watched and wielded as one vast interest for all the South—with forces never divided, and purposes never conflictive—with a spurious, negro-hating religion universally diffused, and everywhere ready to shield it from harm—with a selfish, sordid, divided North, long since bereft of its manhood, to cajole, bribe and intimidate—with its foot planted on two-thirds of our vast national domains, and there unquestioned, absolute and bloody in its sway—with the terrible strength and boundless resources of the whole country at its command—it cannot be otherwise than that the Slave Power will consummate its diabolical purposes to the uttermost. The North-west Territory, Nebraska, Mexico, Cuba, Hayti, the Sandwich Islands, and colonial possessions in the tropics—to seize and subjugate these to its accursed reign, and ultimately to re-establish the foreign Slave Trade as a lawful commerce, are among its settled designs. It is not a question of probabilities, but of time. And whom will a just God hold responsible for all these results? All who despise and persecute men on account of their complexion; all who endorse a slave-holding religion as genuine; all who give the right hand of Christian fellowship to men whose hands are stained with the blood of the slave; all who regard material prosperity as paramount to moral integrity, and the law of the land as above the law of God; all who are either hostile or indifferent to the Anti-Slavery movement; and all who advocate the necessity of making compromises with the Slave Power, in order that the Union may receive no detriment.

In itself, Slavery has no resources and no strength. Isolated and alone, it could not stand an hour; and, therefore, further aggression and conquest would be impossible.

Says the Editor of the Marysville (Tenn.) *Intelligencer*, in an article on the character and condition of the slave population:

We of the South are emphatically surrounded by a dangerous class of beings —degraded, stupid savages—who, if they could but once entertain the idea that immediate and unconditional death would not be their portion, would re-enact the St. Domingo tragedy. But the consciousness, with all their stupidity, that a ten-fold force, superior in discipline, if not in barbarity, would gather from the four corners of the United States and slaughter them, keeps them in subjection. *But, to the non-slaveholding States, particularly, we are indebted for a permanent safeguard against insurrection.* Without their assistance, the white population of the South would be too weak to quiet that insane desire for liberty which is ever ready to act itself out with every rational creature.

In the debate in Congress on the resolution to censure John Quincy Adams, for presenting a petition for the dissolution of the Union, Mr. Underwood, of Kentucky, said:

They (the South) were the weaker portion, were in the minority. *The North could do what they pleased with them;* they could adopt their own measures. All he asked was, that they would let the South know what those measures were. One thing he knew well; that State, which he in part represented, had perhaps a deeper interest in this subject than any other, except Maryland and a small portion of Virginia. And why? Because he knew that to dissolve the Union, and separate the different States composing the confederacy, making the Ohio River and the Mason and Dixon's line the boundary line, *he knew as soon as that was done, Slavery was done* in Kentucky, Maryland and a large portion of Virginia, and it would extend to all the States South of this line. *The dissolution of the Union was the dissolution of Slavery.* It has been the common practice for Southern men to get up on this floor, and say, "Touch this subject, and we will dissolve this Union as a remedy." *Their remedy was the destruction of the thing which they wished to save,* and any sensible man could see it. If the Union was dissolved into two parts, the slave would cross the line, and then turn round and curse the master from the other shore.

. . . .

These witnesses can neither be impeached nor ruled out of Court, and their testimony is true. While, therefore, the Union is preserved, I see no end to the extension or perpetuity of Chattel Slavery—no hope for peaceful deliverance of the millions who are clanking their chains on our blood-red soil. Yet I know that God reigns, and that the slave system contains within itself the elements of destruction. But how long it is to curse the earth, and desecrate his image, he alone foresees. It is frightful to think of the capacity of a nation like this to commit sin, before the measure of its iniquities be filled, and the exterminating judgments of God overtake it. . . .

These are solemn times. It is not a struggle for national salvation; for the nation, as such, seems doomed beyond recovery. The reason why the South rules, and the North falls prostrate in servile terror, is simply this: With the South, the preservation of Slavery is paramount to all other considerations—above party success, denominational unity, pecuniary interest, legal integrity, and constitutional obligation. With the North, the preservation of the Union is placed above all other things—above honour, justice, freedom, integrity of soul, the Decalogue and the Golden Rule—the Infinite God himself. All these she is ready to discard for the Union. Her devotion to it is the latest and the most terrible form of idolatry. She has given to the Slave Power a *carte blanche,* to be filled as it may dictate—and if, at any time, she grows restive under the yoke, and shrinks back aghast at the new atrocity contemplated, it is only necessary for that Power to crack the whip of Disunion over her head, as it has done again and again, and she will cower and obey like a plantation slave—for has she not sworn that she will sacrifice everything in heaven and on earth, rather than the Union?

What then is to be done? Friends of the slave, the question is not whether by our efforts we can abolish Slavery, speedily or remotely—for duty is ours, the result is with God; but whether we will go with the multitude to do evil, sell our birthright for a mess of pottage, cease to cry aloud and spare not, and remain in Babylon when the command of God is, "Come out of her, my people, that ye be not partakers of her sins, and that ye receive not of her plagues." Let us stand in our lot, "and having done all, to stand." At least, a remnant shall be saved. Living or dying, defeated or victorious, be it ours to exclaim, "No compromise with Slavery! Liberty for each, for all, forever! Man above all institutions! The supremacy of God over the whole earth!"

A House Divided

ABRAHAM LINCOLN

*Born near Hodgenville, Kentucky, February 12, 1809;
died, Washington, D.C., April 15, 1865. Largely self-
educated. Worked as farm-hand, clerk in a store, surveyor,
postmaster. Admitted to Illinois bar, 1836. Member of
Illinois legislature, 1834-1842; of United States House
of Representatives, 1847-1849. Unsuccessful as candidate
for United States Senate in 1855 and 1858. As the candidate of the Republican party, was elected President of
the United States in 1860 and 1864.*

*M*r. President and Gentlemen of the Convention: If
we could first know *where* we are, and *whither* we
are tending, we could then better judge *what* to do, and *how* to do it.

We are now far into the *fifth* year, since a policy was initiated, with the
avowed object, and *confident* promise, of putting an end to slavery agitation.

Under the operation of that policy, that agitation has not only, *not ceased,*
but has *constantly augmented.*

In *my* opinion, it *will* not cease, until a *crisis* shall have been reached, and
passed.

"A house divided against itself cannot stand."

I believe this government cannot endure, permanently half *slave* and
half *free.*

I do not expect the Union to be *dissolved*—I do not expect the house to
fall—but I *do* expect it will cease to be divided.

It will become *all* one thing, or *all* the other.

Republican State Convention, Springfield, Illinois, June 16, 1858. Paul M. Angle, ed.,
Created Equal? (Chicago: University of Chicago Press, 1958), pp. 1-9. Reprinted by
permission.

Either the *opponents* of slavery will arrest the further spread of it, and place it where the public mind shall rest in the belief that it is in course of ultimate extinction; or its *advocates* will push it forward, till it shall become alike lawful in *all* the states, *old* as well as *new—North* as well as *South*.

Have we no *tendency* to the latter condition?

Let any one who doubts, carefully contemplate that now almost complete legal combination—piece of *machinery* so to speak—compounded of the Nebraska doctrine, and the Dred Scott decision. Let him consider not only *what work* the machinery is adapted to do, and *how well* adapted; but also, let him study the *history* of its construction, and trace, if he can, or rather *fail,* if he can, to trace the evidences of design, and concert of action, among its chief bosses, from the beginning.

But, so far, *Congress* only had acted; and an *indorsement* by the people, *real* or apparent, was indispensable, to *save* the point already gained, and give chance for more.

The new year of 1854 found slavery excluded from more than half the states by state constitutions, and from most of the national territory by congressional prohibition.

Four days later, commenced the struggle, which ended in repealing that congressional prohibition.

This opened all the national territory to slavery; and was the first point gained.

This necessity had not been overlooked; but had been provided for, as well as might be, in the notable argument of *"squatter sovereignty,"* otherwise called *"sacred right of self government,"* which latter phrase, though expressive of the only rightful basis of any government, was so perverted in this attempted use of it as to amount to just this: That if any *one* man choose to enslave *another,* no *third* man shall be allowed to object.

That argument was incorporated into the Nebraska Bill itself, in the language which follows: *"It being the true intent and meaning of this act not to legislate slavery into any territory or state, nor exclude it therefrom; but to leave the people thereof perfectly free to form and regulate their domestic institutions in their own way, subject only to the Constitution of the United States."*

Then opened the roar of loose declamation in favor of "Squatter Sovereignty," and "Sacred right of self government."

"But," said opposition members, "let us be more *specific*—let us *amend* the bill so as to expressly declare that the people of the territory *may* exclude slavery." "Not we," said the friends of the measure; and down they voted the amendment.

While the Nebraska Bill was passing through Congress, a *law* case, involving the question of a negro's freedom, by reason of his owner having voluntarily taken him first into a free state and then a territory covered by the congressional prohibition, and held him as a slave, for a long time in each, was passing through the U. S. Circuit Court for the District of Missouri; and both Nebraska Bill and law suit were brought to a decision in the same month of May, 1854. The negro's name was "Dred Scott," which name now designates the decision finally made in the case.

Before the *then* next presidential election, the law case came *to*, and was argued *in* the Supreme Court of the United States; but the *decision* of it was deferred until *after* the election. Still, *before* the election, Senator Trumbull, on the floor of the Senate, requests the leading advocate of the Nebraska Bill to state *his opinion* whether the people of the territory can constitutionally exclude slavery from their limits; and the latter answers, "That is a question for the Supreme Court."

The election came. Mr. Buchanan was elected, and the *indorsement,* such as it was, secured. That was the *second* point gained. The indorsement, however, fell short of a clear popular majority by nearly four hundred thousand votes, and so, perhaps, was not overwhelmingly reliable and satisfactory.

The *outgoing* President, in his last annual message, as impressively as possible *echoed back* upon the people the *weight* and *authority* of the indorsement.

The Supreme Court met again; *did not* announce their decision, but ordered a reargument.

The presidential inauguration came, and still no decision of the court; but the *incoming* President, in his inaugural address, fervently exhorted the people to abide by the forthcoming decision, *whatever it might be.*

Then, in a few days, came the decision.

The reputed author of the Nebraska Bill finds an early occasion to make a speech at this capitol indorsing the Dred Scott decision, and vehemently denouncing all opposition to it.

The new President, too, seizes the early occasion of the Silliman letter to *indorse* and strongly *construe* that decision, and to express his *astonishment* that any different view had ever been entertained.

At length a squabble springs up between the President and the author of the Nebraska Bill, on the *mere* question of *fact,* whether the Lecompton constitution was or was not, in any just sense, made by the people of Kansas; and in that squabble the latter declares that all he wants is a fair vote for the people, and that he *cares* not whether slavery be voted *down* or voted *up.* I do not understand his declaration that he cares not whether slavery be voted down or voted up, to be intended by him other than as an *apt definition* of the *policy* he would impress upon the public mind—the *principle* for which he declares he has suffered much, and is ready to suffer to the end.

And well may he cling to that principle. If he has any parental feeling, well may he cling to it. That principle is the only *shred* left of his original Nebraska doctrine. Under the Dred Scott decision, "squatter sovereignty" squatted out of existence, tumbled down like temporary scaffolding—like the mould at the foundry served through one blast and fell back into loose sand— helped to carry an election, and then was kicked to the winds. His late *joint* struggle with the Republicans, against the Lecompton constitution involves nothing of the original Nebraska doctrine. That struggle was made on a point, the right of a people to make their own constitution, upon which he and the Republicans have never differed.

The several points of the Dred Scott decision, in connection with Senator Douglas' "care not" policy, constitute the piece of machinery, in its *present* state of advancement. This was the third point gained.

The *working* points of that machinery are:

First, that no negro slave, imported as such from Africa, and no descendant of such slave can ever be a *citizen* of any state, in the sense of that term as used in the Constitution of the United States.

This point is made in order to deprive the negro, in every possible event, of the benefit of this provision of the United States Constitution, which declares that—

"The citizens of each state shall be entitled to all privileges and immunities of citizens in the several states."

Secondly, that "subject to the Constitution of the United States," neither *Congress* nor a *territorial legislature* can exclude slavery from any United States territory.

This point is made in order that individual men may *fill up* the territories with slaves, without danger of losing them as property, and thus to enhance the chances of *permanency* to the institution through all the future.

Thirdly, that whether the holding a negro in actual slavery in a free state, makes him free, as against the holder, the United States courts will not decide, but will leave to be decided by the courts of any slave state the negro may be forced into by the master.

This point is made, not to be pressed *immediately;* but, if acquiesced in for a while, and apparently *indorsed* by the people at an election, *then* to sustain the logical conclusion that what Dred Scott's master might lawfully do with Dred Scott, in the free state of Illinois, every other master may lawfully do with any other *one,* or one *thousand* slaves, in Illinois, or in any other free state.

Auxiliary to all this, and working hand in hand with it, the Nebraska doctrine, or what is left of it, is to *educate* and *mould* public opinion, at least *Northern* public opinion, to not *care* whether slavery is voted *down* or voted *up.*

This shows exactly where we now *are;* and *partially* also, whither we are tending.

It will throw additional light on the latter, to go back, and run the mind over the string of historical facts already stated. Several things will *now* appear less *dark* and *mysterious* than they did *when* they were transpiring. The people were to be left "perfectly free" "subject only to the Constitution." What the *Constitution* had to do with it, outsiders could not *then* see. Plainly enough *now,* it was an exactly fitted *niche,* for the Dred Scott decision to afterwards come in, and declare the *perfect freedom* of the people to be just no freedom at all.

Why was the amendment, expressly declaring the right of the people to exclude slavery, voted down? Plainly enough *now,* the adoption of it would have spoiled the niche for the Dred Scott decision.

Why was the court decision held up? Why even a Senator's individual opinion withheld, till *after* the presidential election? Plainly enough *now,* the speaking out *then* would have damaged the *"perfectly free"* argument upon which the election was to be carried.

Why the *outgoing* President's felicitation on the indorsement? Why the delay of a reargument? Why the incoming President's *advance* exhortation in favor of the decision?

These things *look* like the cautious *patting* and *petting* a spirited horse, preparatory to mounting him, when it is dreaded that he may give the rider a fall.

And why the hasty after-indorsements of the decision by the President and others?

We can not absolutely *know* that all these exact adaptations are the result of preconcert. But when we see a lot of framed timbers, different portions of which we know have been gotten out at different times and places and by different workmen—Stephen, Franklin, Roger and James,* for instance—and when we see these timbers joined together, and see they exactly make the frame of a house or a mill, all the tenons and mortices exactly fitting, and all the lengths and proportions of the different pieces exactly adapted to their respective places, and not a piece too many or too few—not omitting even scaffolding—or, if a single piece be lacking, we can see the place in the frame exactly fitted and prepared to yet bring such piece in—in *such* a case, we find it impossible to not *believe* that Stephen and Franklin and Roger and James all understood one another from the beginning, and all worked upon a common *plan* or *draft* drawn up before the first lick was struck.

It should not be overlooked that, by the Nebraska Bill, the people of a *state* as well as *territory,* were to be left *"perfectly free" "subject only to the Constitution."*

* Stephen A. Douglas, Franklin Pierce, Roger B. Taney, James Buchanan.

Why mention a *state?* They were legislating for *territories,* and not *for* or *about* states. Certainly the people of a state *are* and *ought to be* subject to the Constitution of the United States; but why is mention of this *lugged* into this merely *territorial* law? Why are the people of a *territory* and the people of a *state* therein *lumped* together, and their relation to the Constitution therein treated as being *precisely* the same?

While the opinion of the *Court,* by Chief Justice Taney, in the Dred Scott case, and the separate opinions of all the concurring judges, expressly declare that the Constitution of the United States neither permits Congress nor a territorial legislature to exclude slavery from any United States territory, they all *omit* to declare whether or not the same constitution permits a *state,* or the people of a state, to exclude it.

Possibly, this was a mere *omission;* but who can be *quite* sure, if McLean or Curtis* had sought to get into the opinion a declaration of unlimited power in the people of a *state* to exclude slavery from their limits, just as Chase and Macy† sought to get such declaration, in behalf of the people of a territory, into the Nebraska Bill—I ask, who can be quite *sure* that it would not have been voted down, in the one case, as it had been in the other.

The nearest approach to the point of declaring the power of a state over slavery, is made by Judge Nelson.‡ He approaches it more than once, using the precise idea, and *almost* the language too, of the Nebraska Act. On one occasion his exact language is, "except in cases where the power is restrained by the Constitution of the United States, the law of the state is supreme over the subject of slavery within its jurisdiction."

In what *cases* the power of the *states* is so restrained by the U. S. Constitution, is left an *open* question, precisely as the same question, as to the restraint on the power of the *territories* was left open in the Nebraska Act. Put *that* and *that* together, and we have another nice little niche, which we may, ere long, see filled with another Supreme Court decision, declaring that the Constitution of the United States does not permit a *state* to exclude slavery from its limits.

And this may especially be expected if the doctrine of "care not whether slavery be voted *down* or voted *up,*" shall gain upon the public mind sufficiently to give promise that such a decision can be maintained when made.

Such a decision is all that slavery now lacks of being alike lawful in all the states.

Welcome or unwelcome, such decision *is* probably coming, and will soon be upon us, unless the power of the present political dynasty shall be met and overthrown.

We shall *lie down* pleasantly dreaming that the people of *Missouri* are

* Justices John McLean and Benjamin R. Curtis, who filed dissenting opinions.
† Senator Salmon P. Chase of Ohio and Representative Daniel Macy of Indiana.
‡ Justice Samuel Nelson.

on the verge of making their state *free;* and we shall *awake* to the *reality,* instead, that the *Supreme* Court has made *Illinois* a *slave* state.

To meet and overthrow the power of that dynasty, is the work now before all those who would prevent that consummation.

That is *what* we have to do.

But *how* can we best do it?

There are those who denounce us *openly* to their *own* friends, and yet whisper *us softly,* that *Senator Douglas* is the *aptest* instrument there is, with which to effect that object. *They* do *not* tell us, nor has *he* told us, that he *wishes* any such object to be effected. They wish us to *infer* all, from the facts, that he now has a little quarrel with the present head of the dynasty; and that he has regularly voted with us, on a single point, upon which he and we have never differed.

They remind us that *he* is a very *great man,* and that the largest of *us* are very small ones. Let this be granted. But "a *living dog* is better than a *dead lion.*" Judge Douglas, if not a *dead* lion *for this work,* is at least a *caged* and *toothless* one. How can he oppose the advances of slavery? He don't *care* anything about it. His avowed *mission is impressing* the "public heart" to *care* nothing about it.

A leading Douglas Democratic newspaper thinks Douglas' superior talent will be needed to resist the revival of the African slave trade.

Does Douglas believe an effort to revive that trade is approaching? He has not said so. Does he *really* think so? But if it is, how can he resist it? For years he has labored to prove it a *sacred right* of white men to take negro slaves into the new territories. Can he possibly show that it is *less* a sacred right to *buy* them where they can be bought cheapest? And, unquestionably they can be bought *cheaper in Africa* than in *Virginia.*

He has done all in his power to reduce the whole question of slavery to one of a mere *right of property;* and as such, how can *he* oppose the foreign slave trade—how can he refuse that trade in that "property" shall be "perfectly free"—unless he does it as a *protection* to the home production? And as the home *producers* will probably not *ask* the protection, he will be wholly without a ground of opposition.

Senator Douglas holds, we know, that a man may rightfully be *wiser to-day* than he was *yesterday*—that he may rightfully *change* when he finds himself wrong.

But, can we for that reason, run ahead, and *infer* that he *will* make any particular change, of which he, himself, has given no intimation? Can we *safely* base *our* action upon any such *vague* inference?

Now, as ever, I wish to not *misrepresent* Judge Douglas' *position,* question his *motives,* or do aught that can be personally offensive to him.

Whenever, *if ever,* he and we can come together on *principle* so that *our great cause* may have assistance from *his great ability,* I hope to have inter-posed no adventitious obstacle.

But clearly, he is not *now* with us—he does not *pretend* to be—he does not *promise* to *ever* be.

Our cause, then, must be intrusted to, and conducted by its own undoubted friends—those whose hands are free, whose hearts are in the work—who *do care* for the result.

Two years ago the Republicans of the nation mustered over thirteen hundred thousand strong.

We did this under the single impulse of resistance to a common danger, with every external circumstance against us.

Of *strange, discordant,* and even, *hostile* elements, we gathered from the four winds, and *formed* and fought the battle through, under the constant hot fire of a disciplined, proud, and pampered enemy.

Did we brave all *then,* to *falter* now?—*now*—when that same enemy is *wavering,* dissevered and belligerent?

The result is not doubtful. We shall not fail—if we stand firm, we shall not fail.

Wise councils may *accelerate* or *mistakes delay* it, but, sooner or later the victory is sure to come.

Popular Sovereignty

STEPHEN A. DOUGLAS

Born, Brandon, Vermont, April 23, 1813; died, Chicago, Illinois, June 3, 1861. Attended schools at Brandon, and at Canandaigua, New York. Admitted to Illinois bar, 1834; state's attorney, 1835; judge of Illinois Supreme Court, 1841–1843. Member of Illinois legislature, 1835–1837. Secretary of State for Illinois, 1840. Member of United States House of Representatives, 1843–1847; of United States Senate, 1847–1861. Sought unsuccessfully the nomination for the Presidency in 1852 and 1856. Nominated by Democrats in 1860 for President of the United States, whereupon the Southern wing of the party withdrew and nominated John C. Breckinridge. Split in the Democratic party gave Lincoln his victory. Vigorously supported Lincoln's efforts to preserve the Union.

*M*r. Chairman and Fellow-Citizens: I can find no language which can adequately express my profound gratitude for the magnificent welcome which you have extended to me on this occasion. This vast sea of human faces indicates how deep an interest is felt by our people in the great questions which agitate the public mind, and which underlie the foundations of our free institutions. A reception like this, so great in numbers that no human voice can be heard to its countless thousands—so enthusiastic that no one individual can be the object of such enthusiasm—clearly shows that there is some great principle which sinks deep in the heart of the masses, and involves the rights and the liberties of a whole people, that has brought you together with a unanimity and a

Chicago, Illinois, July 9, 1858. Paul M. Angle, ed., *Created Equal?* (Chicago: University of Chicago Press, 1958), pp. 12–24. Reprinted by permission.

cordiality never before excelled, if, indeed, equalled on any occasion. I have not the vanity to believe that it is any personal compliment to me.

It is an expression of your devotion to that great principle of self-government, to which my life for many years past has been, and in the future will be devoted. If there is any one principle dearer and more sacred than all others in free governments, it is that which asserts the exclusive right of a free people to form and adopt their own fundamental law, and to manage and regulate their own internal affairs and domestic institutions.

When I found an effort being made during the recent session of Congress to force a constitution upon the people of Kansas against their will, and to force that state into the Union with a constitution which her people had rejected by more than 10,000, I felt bound as a man of honor and a representative of Illinois, bound by every consideration of duty, of fidelity, and of patriotism, to resist to the utmost of my power the consummation of that fraud. With others I did resist it, and resisted it successfully until the attempt was abandoned. We forced them to refer that constitution back to the people of Kansas, to be accepted or rejected as they shall decide at an election, which is fixed for the first Monday of August next. It is true that the mode of reference, and the form of the submission was not such as I could sanction with my vote, for the reason that it discriminated between free states and slave states; providing that if Kansas consented to come in under the Lecompton constitution it should be received with a population of 35,000; but that if she demanded another constitution, more consistent with the sentiments of her people and their feelings, that it should not be received into the Union until she has 93,420 inhabitants. I did not consider that mode of submission fair, for the reason that any election is a mockery which is not free—that any election is a fraud upon the right of the people which holds out inducements for affirmative votes, and threatens penalties for negative votes. But whilst I was not satisfied with the mode of submission, whilst I resisted it to the last, demanding a fair, a just, a free mode of submission, still, when the law passed placing it within the power of the people of Kansas at that election to reject the Lecompton constitution, and then make another in harmony with their principles and their opinions, I did not believe that either the penalties on the one hand, or the inducements on the other, would force that people to accept a constitution to which they are irreconcilably opposed. All I can say is, that if their votes can be controlled by such considerations, all the sympathy which has been expended upon them has been misplaced, and all the efforts that have been made in defence of their right to self-government have been made in an unworthy cause.

Hence, my friends, I regard the Lecompton battle as having been fought and the victory won, because the arrogant demand for the admission of Kansas under the Lecompton constitution unconditionally, whether her people wanted it or not, has been abandoned, and the principle which recognizes the right of the people to decide for themselves has been submitted to its place.

. . . .

The great principle is the right of every community to judge and decide for itself, whether a thing is right or wrong, whether it would be good or evil for them to adopt it; and the right of free action, the right of free thought, the right of free judgment upon the question is dearer to every true American than any other under a free government. My objection to the Lecompton contrivance was that it undertook to put a constitution on the people of Kansas against their will, in opposition to their wishes, and thus violated the great principle upon which all our institutions rest. It is no answer to this argument to say that slavery is an evil and hence should not be tolerated. You must allow the people to decide for themselves whether it is a good or an evil. You allow them to decide for themselves whether they desire a Maine liquor law or not; you allow them to decide for themselves what kind of common schools they will have; what system of banking they will adopt, or whether they will adopt any at all; you allow them to decide for themselves the relations between husband and wife, parent and child, the guardian and ward; in fact, you allow them to decide for themselves all other questions, and why not upon this question? Whenever you put a limitation upon the right of any people to decide what laws they want, you have destroyed the fundamental principle of self-government.

In connection with this subject, perhaps, it will not be improper for me on this occasion to allude to the position of those who have chosen to arraign my conduct on this same subject. I have observed from the public prints that but a few days ago the Republican party of the state of Illinois assembled in convention at Springfield, and not only laid down their platform, but nominated a candidate for the United States Senate as my successor. I take great pleasure in saying that I have known, personally and intimately, for about a quarter of a century, the worthy gentleman who has been nominated for my place, and I will say that I regard him as a kind, amiable, and intelligent gentleman, a good citizen and an honorable opponent; and whatever issue I may have with him will be of principle, and not involving personalities.—Mr. Lincoln made a speech before that Republican Convention which unanimously nominated him for the Senate—a speech evidently well prepared and carefully written— in which he states the basis upon which he proposes to carry on the campaign during this summer. In it he lays down two distinct propositions which I shall notice, and upon which I shall take a direct and bold issue with him.

His first and main proposition I will give in his own language, scripture quotations and all, (laughter) I give his exact language—" 'A house divided against itself cannot stand.' I believe this government cannot endure, permanently, half *slave* and half *free*. I do not expect the Union to be *dissolved*. I do not expect the house to *fall;* but I do expect it to cease to be divided. It will become *all* one thing or *all* the other."

In other words, Mr. Lincoln asserts as a fundamental principle of this government, that there must be uniformity in the local laws and domestic institutions of each and all the states of the Union; and he therefore invites all the non-slaveholding states to band together, organize as one body, and make war upon slavery in Kentucky, upon slavery in Virginia, upon the Carolinas, upon slavery in all of the slave-holding states in this Union, and to persevere in that war until it shall be exterminated. He then notifies the slaveholding states to stand together as a unit and make an aggressive war upon the free states of this Union with a view of establishing slavery in them all; of forcing it upon Illinois, of forcing it upon New York, upon New England, and upon every other free state, and that they shall keep up the warfare until it has been formally established in them all. In other words, Mr. Lincoln advocates boldly and clearly a war of sections, a war of the North against the South, of the free states against the slave states—a war of extermination—to be continued relentlessly until the one or the other shall be subdued and all the states shall either become free or become slave.

Now, my friends, I must say to you frankly, that I take bold, unqualified issue with him upon that principle. I assert that it is neither desirable nor possible that there should be uniformity in the local institutions and domestic regulations of the different states of this Union. The framers of our government never contemplated uniformity in its internal concerns. The fathers of the Revolution, and the sages who made the Constitution well understood that the laws and domestic institutions which would suit the granite hills of New Hampshire would be totally unfit for the rice plantations of South Carolina; they well understood that the laws which would suit the agricultural districts of Pennsylvania and New York would be totally unfit for the large mining regions of the Pacific, or the lumber regions of Maine. They well understood that the great varieties of soil, of production and of interests, in a republic as large as this, required different local and domestic regulations in each locality, adapted to the wants and interests of each separate state, and for that reason it was provided in the federal Constitution that the thirteen original states should remain sovereign and supreme within their own limits in regard to all that was local, and internal, and domestic, while the federal government should have certain specified powers which were general and national, and could be exercised only by the federal authority.

The framers of the Constitution well understood that each locality, having separate and distinct interests, required separate and distinct laws, domestic institutions, and police regulations adapted to its own wants and its own condition; and they acted on the presumption, also, that these laws and institutions would be as diversified and as dissimilar as the states would be numerous, and that no two would be precisely alike, because the interests of the two would [not] be precisely the same. Hence, I assert, that the great fundamental principle which underlies our complex system of state and federal governments, contemplated diversity and dissimilarity in the local institutions and domestic affairs of each and every state then in the Union, or thereafter to be admitted into the confederacy. I therefore conceive that my friend, Mr. Lincoln, has totally misapprehended the great principles upon which our government rests. Uniformity in local and domestic affairs would be destructive of state rights, of state sovereignty, of personal liberty and personal freedom. Uniformity is the parent of despotism the world over, not only in politics, but in religion. Wherever the doctrine of uniformity is proclaimed, that all the states must be free or all slave, that all labor must be white or all black, that all the citizens of the different states must have the same privileges or be governed by the same regulations, you have destroyed the greatest safeguard which our institutions have thrown around the rights of the citizen.

How could this uniformity be accomplished, if it was desirable and possible? There is but one mode in which it could be obtained, and that must be by abolishing the state legislatures, blotting out state sovereignty, merging the rights and sovereignty of the states in one consolidated empire, and vesting Congress with the plenary power to make all the police regulations, domestic and local laws, uniform throughout the limits of the Republic. When you shall have done this you will have uniformity. Then the states will all be slave or all be free; then negroes will vote everywhere or nowhere; then you will have a Maine liquor law in every state or none; then you will have uniformity in all things local and domestic by the authority of the federal government. But when you attain that uniformity, you will have converted these thirty-two sovereign, independent states into one consolidated empire, with the uniformity of despotism reigning triumphant throughout the length and breadth of the land.

From this view of the case, my friends, I am driven irresistibly to the conclusion that diversity, dissimilarity, variety in all our local and domestic institutions, is the great safeguard of our liberties; and that the framers of our institutions were wise, sagacious, and patriotic when they made this government a confederation of sovereign states with a legislature for each, and conferred upon each legislature the power to make all local and domestic institutions to suit the people it represented, without interference from any other state or from the general Congress of the Union. If we expect to maintain our liberties we must preserve the rights and sovereignty of the states, we must maintain and carry out that great principle of self-government incorporated in the compromise measures of 1850: endorsed by the Illinois legislature in 1851; emphatically embodied and carried out in the Kansas-Nebraska Bill, and vindicated this year by the refusal to bring Kansas into the Union with a constitution distasteful to her people.

The other proposition discussed by Mr. Lincoln in his speech consists in a crusade against the Supreme Court of the United States on account of the Dred Scott decision. On this question, also, I desire to say to you unequivocally, that I take direct and distinct issue with him. I have no warfare to make on the Supreme Court of the United States, either on account of that or any other decision which they have pronounced from that bench. The Constitution of the United States has provided that the powers of government (and the constitution of each state has the same provision) shall be divided into three departments, executive, legislative, and judicial. The right and the province of expounding the Constitution, and construing the law, is vested in the judiciary established by the Constitution.—As a lawyer, I feel at liberty to appear before the Court and controvert any principle of law while the question is pending before the tribunal; but when the decision is made, my private opinion, your opinion, all other opinions must yield to the majesty of that authoritative adjudication. I wish you to bear in mind that this involves a great principle, upon which our rights, our liberty and our property all depend. What security have you for your property, for your reputation, and for your personal rights, if the courts are not upheld, and their decisions respected when once firmly rendered by the highest tribunal known to the Constitution? I do not choose, therefore, to go into any argument with Mr. Lincoln in reviewing the various decisions which the Supreme Court has made, either upon the Dred Scott case, or any other. I have no idea of appealing from the decision of the Supreme Court upon a constitutional question to the decisions of a tumultuous town meeting. I am aware that once an eminent lawyer of this city, now no more, said that the state of Illinois had the most perfect judicial system in the world, subject to but one exception, which could be cured by a slight amendment, and that amendment was to so change the law as to allow an appeal from the decisions of the Supreme Court of Illinois, on all constitutional questions, to Justice of the Peace.

My friend, Mr. Lincoln, who sits behind me, reminds me that that proposition was made when I was Judge of the Supreme Court. Be that as it may, I do not think that fact adds any greater weight or authority to the suggestion. It matters not with me who was on the bench, whether Mr. Lincoln or myself, whether a Lockwood or a Smith, a Taney or a Marshall; the decision of the highest tribunal known to the Constitution of the country must be final till it has been reversed by an equally high authority. Hence, I am opposed to this doctrine of Mr. Lincoln, by which he proposes to take an appeal from the decision of the Supreme Court of the United States, upon this high constitutional question to a Republican caucus sitting in the country. Yes, or any other caucus or town meeting, whether it be Republican, American, or Democratic. I respect the decisions of that august tribunal; I shall always bow in deference to them. I am a law-abiding man. I will sustain the Constitution of my country as our fathers have made it. I will yield obedience to the laws, whether I like them or not, as I find them on the statute book. I will sustain the judicial tribunals and constituted authorities in all matters within the pale of their jurisdiction as defined by the Constitution.

But I am equally free to say that the reason assigned by Mr. Lincoln for resisting the decision of the Supreme Court in the Dred Scott case does not in itself meet my approbation. He objects to it because that decision declared that a negro descended from African parents who were brought here and sold as slaves is not, and cannot be a citizen of the United States. He says it is wrong, because it deprives the negro of the benefits of that clause of the Constitution which says that citizens of one state shall enjoy all the privileges and immunities of citizens of the several states; in other words, he thinks it wrong because it deprives the negro of the privileges, immunities, and rights of citizenship, which pertain, according to that decision, only to the white man. I am free to say to you that in my opinion this government of ours is founded on the white basis. It was made by the white man, for the benefit of the white man, to be administered by white men, in such manner as they should determine. It is also true that a negro, an Indian, or any other man of an inferior race to a white man, should be permitted to enjoy, and humanity requires that he should have all the rights, privileges and immunities which he is capable of exercising consistent with the safety of society. I would give him every right and every privilege which his capacity would enable him to enjoy, consistent with the good of the society in which he lived. But you may ask me what are these rights and these privileges. My answer is that each state must decide for itself the nature and extent of these rights. Illinois has decided for herself. We have decided that the negro shall not be a slave, and we have at the same time decided that he shall not vote, or serve on juries, or enjoy political privileges. I am content with that system of policy which we have adopted for ourselves. I deny the right of any other State to complain of our policy in that respect, or to interfere with it, or to attempt to change it. On the other hand, the state of Maine has decided that in that state a negro man may vote on an equality with the white man. The sovereign power of Maine had the right to prescribe that rule for herself. Illinois has no right to complain of Maine for conferring the right of negro suffrage, nor has Maine any right to interfere with, or complain of Illinois because she has denied negro suffrage.

The state of New York has decided by her constitution that a negro may vote, provided that he own $250 worth of property, but not otherwise. The rich negro can vote, but the poor one cannot. Although that distinction does not commend itself to my judgment, yet I assert that the sovereign power of

New York had a right to prescribe that form of the elective franchise. Kentucky, Virginia, and other states have provided that negroes, or a certain class of them in those states, shall be slaves, having neither civil or political rights. Without endorsing the wisdom of that decision, I assert that Virginia has the same power by virtue of her sovereignty to protect slavery within her limits, as Illinois has to banish it forever from our own borders. I assert the right of each state to decide for itself on all these questions and I do not subscribe to the doctrine of my friend, Mr. Lincoln, that uniformity is either desirable or possible. I do not acknowledge that the states must all be free or must all be slave.

I do not acknowledge that the negro must have civil and political rights everywhere or nowhere. I do not acknowledge that the Chinese must have the same rights in California that we would confer upon him here. I do not acknowledge that the coolie imported into this country must necessarily be put upon an equality with the white race. I do not acknowledge any of these doctrines of uniformity in the local and domestic regulations in the different states.

Thus you see, my fellow-citizens, that the issues between Mr. Lincoln and myself, as respective candidates for the U.S. Senate, as made up, are direct, unequivocal, and irreconcilable. He goes for uniformity in our domestic institutions, for a war of sections, until one or the other shall be subdued. I go for the great principle of the Kansas-Nebraska Bill, the right of the people to decide for themselves.

On the other point, Mr. Lincoln goes for a warfare upon the Supreme Court of the United States, because of their judicial decision in the Dred Scott case. I yield obedience to the decisions of that Court—to the final determination of the highest judicial tribunal known to our Constitution. He objects to the Dred Scott decision because it does not put the negro in the possession of the rights of citizenship on an equality with the white man. I am opposed to negro equality. I repeat that this nation is a white people—a people composed of European descendants—a people that have established this government for themselves and their posterity, and I am in favor of preserving not only the purity of the blood, but the purity of the government from any mixture or amalgamation with inferior races. I have seen the effects of this mixture of superior and inferior races—this amalgamation of white men and Indians and negroes; we have seen it in Mexico, in Central America, in South America, and in all the Spanish-American states, and its result has been degeneration, demoralization, and degradation below the capacity for self-government.

I am opposed to taking any step that recognizes the negro man or the Indian as the equal of the white man. I am opposed to giving him a voice in the administration of the government. I would extend to the negro, and the

Indian, and to all dependent races every right, every privilege, and every immunity consistent with the safety and welfare of the white races; but equality they never should have, either political or social, or in any other respect whatever.

My friends, you see that the issues are distinctly drawn. I stand by the same platform that I have so often proclaimed to you and to the people of Illinois heretofore. I stand by the Democratic organization, yield obedience to its usages, and support its regular nominations. I endorse and approve the Cincinnati platform, and I adhere to and intend to carry out as part of that platform, the great principle of self-government, which recognizes the right of the people in each state and territory to decide for themselves their domestic institutions. In other words, if the Lecompton issue shall arise again, you have only to turn back and see where you have found me during the last six months, and then rest assured that you will find me in the same position, battling for the same principle, and vindicating it from assault from whatever quarter it may come, so long as I have the power to do it.

Fellow-citizens, you now have before you the outlines of the propositions which I intend to discuss before the people of Illinois during the pending campaign. I have spoken without preparation and in a very desultory manner, and may have omitted some points which I desired to discuss, and may have been less explicit on others than I could have wished. I have made up my mind to appeal to the people against the combination which has been made against me. The Republican leaders have formed an alliance, an unholy, unnatural alliance with a portion of the unscrupulous federal office-holders. I intend to fight that allied army wherever I meet them. I know they deny the alliance while avowing the common purpose, but yet these men who are trying to divide the Democratic party for the purpose of electing a Republican Senator in my place, are just as much the agents, the tools, the supporters of Mr. Lincoln as if they were avowed Republicans, and expect their reward for their services when the Republicans come into power. I shall deal with these allied forces just as the Russians dealt with the allies at Sebastopol. The Russians when they fired a broadside at the common enemy did not stop to inquire whether it hit a Frenchman, an Englishman or a Turk, nor will I stop to inquire, nor shall I hesitate, whether my blows hit the Republican leaders or their allies, who are holding the federal offices and yet acting in concert with the Republicans to defeat the Democratic party and its nominees. I do not include all of the federal office holders in this remark. Such of them as are Democrats and show their Democracy by remaining inside of the Democratic organization and supporting its nominees, I recognize as Democrats, but those who, having been defeated inside of the organization, go outside and attempt to divide and destroy the party in concert with the Republican leaders, have ceased to be Democrats, and belong to the allied army whose avowed object is to elect the Republican ticket by dividing and destroying the Democratic party.

My friends, I have exhausted myself, and I certainly have fatigued you, in the long and desultory remarks which I have made. It is now two nights since I have been in bed, and I think I have a right to a little sleep. I will, however, have an opportunity of meeting you face to face, and addressing you on more than one occasion before the November election. In conclusion, I must again say to you, justice to my own feelings demands it, that my gratitude for the welcome you have extended to me on this occasion knows no bounds, and can be described by no language which I can command. I see that I am literally at home when among my constituents. This welcome has amply repaid me for every effort that I have made in the public service during nearly twenty-five years that I have held office at your hands. It not only compensates me for the past, but it furnishes an inducement and incentive for future effort which no man, no matter how patriotic, can feel who has not witnessed the magnificent reception you have extended to me to-night on my return.

RECONSTRUCTION OF THE
FEDERAL UNION

ABRAHAM LINCOLN, *in his Second Inaugural Address delivered March 4, 1865, clearly and movingly expressed the spirit in which he proposed to deal with the problems of postwar reconstruction:*

With malice toward none; with charity for all; with firmness in the right, as God gives us to see the right, let us strive on to finish the work we are in; to bind up the nation's wounds . . . to do all which may achieve and cherish a just and lasting peace, among ourselves, and with all nations.

A month later "the work we are in" was finished; Lee surrendered to Grant at Appomattox, and the Civil War was over. In another week President Lincoln was dead.

While the war was still in progress, Lincoln had laid down the provisions of his plan for restoring the Union. Remarkably generous in its terms, it offered full amnesty and pardon for those taking a loyalty oath (excepted from the oath were certain groups, such as high civil and military officers of the Confederacy). When ten percent of the voters of 1860 should have taken this oath of allegiance, they might then proceed to form a state government, after which they would be recognized as having resumed proper relations with the Union. It was hoped through this "Ten Per Cent Plan" to establish in each state a nucleus of loyal citizens which would grow as others were drawn to it.

These magnanimous conditions for restoration were, however, completely unacceptable to Republican leaders of Congress, who favored much more stringent measures, and who believed that they, and not the President, should have charge of reconstruction. In order to set aside Lincoln's efforts and establish a Congressional plan, the Wade-Davis bill was passed in June, 1864. On July 4, Congress being adjourned, the President disposed of this bill by a pocket veto. The administrative branch had for the moment gained the upper hand; but the debate on the bill, the President's veto message, and the angry response it evoked, all revealed the extent of the difference between the executive and Congress with respect to reconstruction policies.

At the time of Lincoln's death no plan of reconstruction had actually been adopted. Republican Congressional leaders welcomed the accession of Andrew Johnson to the Presidency, feeling that he would prove more tractable than his predecessor, and inferring from his vigorous denunciation of secession that he was inclined to their point of view. One of the chief points of controversy continued to be the political status of the states which had constituted the Confederacy. This question, of course, had an important bearing on the steps necessary to effect a restoration or reconstruction of the Union. President Lincoln had taken the line that the Southern states had not, in fact, seceded—that they were, therefore, never actually out of the Union, but "out of proper relation to the Union." He reasoned, therefore, that it was up to the President to decide when a state was sufficiently repentant to be adjudged once more in proper relation to the Union, although the admission of individual Senators and Representatives remained the right of Congress alone. Senator Charles Sumner's theory of "state suicide" held that the states had by seceding abandoned their Constitutional rights and had been reduced to the status of mere terri-

tories; they were, consequently, under the jurisdiction of Congress. Representative Thaddeus Stevens went still farther. The Southern states, he maintained, had indeed seceded; they had left the Union. They had subsequently been defeated in a war. They were, therefore, conquered provinces, at the complete mercy of their conquerors.

The "Radical Republicans," as Congressional advocates of a harsh reconstruction policy were called, were impelled by a variety of motives. Their leaders, Sumner in the Senate and Stevens in the House, both had long championed Negro emancipation; both were filled with animus toward the slavocracy. But there was a practical political motivation as well. The Radicals sought to provide for the continued ascendency of the Republican party by avoiding an alliance of Southern and Northern Democrats against the industrial interests of the North. This they hoped to accomplish by disfranchising and ultimately destroying the great planter class, making Republican voters of the Negroes, and placing political control in the hands of loyal whites. Thaddeus Stevens made no attempt to conceal this political motivation. He candidly offered as an argument in favor of the First Reconstruction Act that "it would insure the ascendency of the Union [Republican] party." He went on to assert his belief "that on the continued ascendency of that party depends the safety of this nation. If impartial suffrage is excluded in the rebel States, then every one of them is sure to send a solid rebel representative delegation to Congress, and cast a solid rebel electoral vote."

The hopes of men like Sumner and Stevens that the new President would coöperate with them in imposing their vindictive, iron-fisted policies upon the South soon proved mistaken. After an initial period of vacillation, Johnson accepted the main features of Lincoln's plan and, even more infuriating to the Congressional leaders, he followed Lincoln in his insistence that reconstruction *was an executive and not a legislative function. His amnesty proclamation issued six weeks after Lincoln's death, and subsequent proclamations appointing provisional governors instructed to call conventions of delegates who had taken the oath of allegiance, were interpreted as indications that Johnson would adhere to Lincoln's policies, and as a virtual declaration of war against the vengeful Radical Republicans.*

By the time the Thirty-ninth Congress convened in December, 1865, all the Southern states but Texas had formed governments under the Presidential plan of recognition, and many had begun to draft repressive legislation against the freedmen. The Radicals, wishing not only to block the admission of these states, but also to bring about the creation of entirely new governments based on universal Negro suffrage, cast about for delaying tactics. On the very first day of the new Congress, Thaddeus Stevens offered a resolution establishing a Joint Committee of Fifteen on Reconstruction, nine from the House and six from the Senate, to study the condition of the Southern states and report on their readiness for admission. The following day, December 5, 1865, President Johnson's message, prepared with the aid of historian George Bancroft, was read to Congress. This moderate, judicious message, conveying much of the spirit of Lincoln's Second Inaugural, was well received throughout the nation, though as might have been expected, its very moderation antagonized the Radicals. On December 18, Stevens, in his answer to the President, fired the opening gun in the Radical attack. Stevens adduced evidence in support of his "conquered provinces" theory, bluntly denied presidential authority to determine the conditions of readmission, and closed with a passionate defense of the rights of the freedmen in the South.

Administration forces, not wishing Stevens' speech to go unanswered during the Christmas recess scheduled to

*begin on December 21, chose Mr. Henry J. Raymond, a
newcomer to Congress, but nationally known as a gifted
speaker and writer, to make the reply.[1] Unfortunately
for administration supporters on the Republican side, Mr.
Raymond was preceded on December 21 by a Democratic
spokesman, Mr. Finck of Ohio, whose endorsement of
President Johnson's position was regarded at the moment
as being more of a liability than an asset. Raymond, seeking Republican support, and embarrassed by this unwelcome assistance from the opposition party, directed his
opening remarks to Finck, noting caustically that such
support had been a little late in coming and observing
that had it come earlier the nation "might have been
spared some years of war, some millions of money and
rivers of blood and tears." Having delivered this sharp
rebuke to the Democrats, Raymond proceeded to rebut
Stevens' argument and to defend the policies of the
administration. He closed his speech with a moving appeal for allaying, rather than stimulating, existent hatreds
and animosities.*

*Thus began the Congressional debate on reconstruc-
tion, which proved to be one of the longest and bitterest
in American political history. The advocates of moderation soon found themselves fighting a losing battle. In
1866 the Radicals won the Congressional elections and
gained control of reconstruction, despite the strenuous
speaking tour of President Johnson in behalf of his
policies. Henry Raymond, Johnson's champion in the
House, admitting his personal failure to rally administration support, refused renomination and retired after one
term. On March 2, 1867, the First Reconstruction Act,
placing the former Confederate states under military rule,
was passed over the President's veto. The effect of this
act was to declare "provisional" all state governments set*

[1] James G. Blaine, *Twenty Years of Congress* (Norwich, Connecticut: Henry Bill Publishing Company, 1886), II, pp. 130-
132.

up under the presidential plan and ultimately to replace them with new governments established on the basis of universal Negro suffrage. Only after Congressional approval of these newly organized governments were the military governments to be removed, the states' Senators and Representatives to be admitted to Congress, and the states themselves to be readmitted to the Union. Not satisfied with this victory, the Radicals sought to destroy the President himself. In February, 1868, Johnson was charged with violating the Tenure of Office Act which had been passed expressly to tie his hands, and impeachment proceedings were brought against him. In the ensuing trial, in which the members of the Senate sat as his jury, the President was saved by a single vote from being removed from office, and was allowed to serve the few remaining months of his term.

By 1870 all ten states placed under military control in 1867 had adopted new constitutions in conventions dominated by carpetbaggers, Negroes, and scalawags. The Radicals had succeeded in wiping out the old Southern planter class, although Southern whites soon managed to overthrow carpetbag government and regain control over the Negro. The Radicals also managed to establish Republican domination over national politics, and were not seriously challenged until 1872, when insurgents in Republican ranks joined with Democrats in protesting political corruption and punitive reconstruction measures. Not until 1885 were the Democrats able again to place a candidate in the White House.

Radical Republican Theory

THADDEUS STEVENS

Born, Danville, Vermont, April 4, 1792; died, Washington, D.C., August 11, 1868. Graduated from Dartmouth, 1814. Studied law, took bar examination in Maryland, and moved to Gettysburg, Pennsylvania to begin practice. Entered politics as an anti-Mason. Member of Pennsylvania legislature, 1833–1841. Here, as a strong and able advocate of free public schools, he made what was probably the outstanding contribution of his long political career. In 1842 he moved to Lancaster, Pennsylvania. Defended fugitive slaves without fee. Member of United States House of Representatives, 1849–1853, 1858–1868. Chairman of Ways and Means Committee. A leader of the Radical Republicans during Reconstruction, he introduced a resolution for the impeachment of President Johnson and served as one of the impeachment managers. Stevens is recognized as one of our most brilliant parliamentarians. Intelligent, well-read, a master of language, wielder of a merciless sarcasm, he was almost invincible in debate.

A candid examination of the power and proper principles of reconstruction can be offensive to no one, and may possibly be profitable by exciting inquiry. One of the suggestions of the message which we are now considering has special reference to this. Perhaps it is the principle most interesting to the people at this time. The President assumes, what no one doubts, that the late rebel States have lost their

United States House of Representatives, December 18, 1865. *Congressional Globe,* 39th Cong., 1st Sess., pt. I, pp. 72–75.

constitutional relations to the Union, and are incapable of representation in Congress, except by permission of the Government. It matters but little, with this admission, whether you call them States out of the Union, and now conquered territories, or assert that because the Constitution forbids them to do what they did do, that they are therefore only dead as to all national and political action, and will remain so until the Government shall breathe into them the breath of life anew and permit them to occupy their former position. In other words, that they are not out of the Union, but are only dead carcasses lying within the Union. In either case, it is very plain that it requires the action of Congress to enable them to form a State government and send representatives to Congress. Nobody, I believe, pretends that with their old constitutions and frames of government they can be permitted to claim their old rights under the Constitution. They have torn their constitutional States into atoms, and built on their foundations fabrics of a totally different character. Dead men cannot raise themselves. Dead States cannot restore their own existence "as it was." Whose especial duty is it to do it? In whom does the Constitution place the power? Not in the judicial branch of Government, for it only adjudicates and does not prescribe laws. Not in the Executive, for he only executes and cannot make laws. Not in the Commander-in-Chief of the armies, for he can only hold them under military rule until the sovereign legislative power of the conqueror shall give them law.

There is fortunately no difficulty in solving the question. There are two provisions in the Constitution, under one of which the case must fall. The fourth article says:

"New States may be admitted by the Congress into this Union."

In my judgment this is the controlling provision in this case. Unless the law of nations is a dead letter, the late war between two acknowledged belligerents severed their original compacts, and broke all the ties that bound them together. The future condition of the conquered power depends on the will of the conqueror. They must come in as new States or remain as conquered provinces. Congress—the Senate and House of Representatives, with the concurrence of the President—is the only power that can act in the matter. But suppose, as some dreaming theorists imagine, that these States have never been out of the Union, but have only destroyed their State governments so as to be incapable of political action; then the fourth section of the fourth article applies, which says:

"The United States shall guaranty to every State in this Union a republican form of government."

Who is the United States? Not the judiciary; not the President; but the sovereign power of the people, exercised through their representatives in Congress, with the concurrence of the Executive. It means the political Government—the concurrent action of both branches of Congress and the Executive. The separate action of each amounts to nothing, either in admitting new States or guarantying republican governments to lapsed or outlawed States. Whence springs the preposterous idea that either the President, or the Senate, or the House of Representatives, acting separately, can determine the right of States to send members or Senators to the Congress of the Union?

To prove that they are and for four years have been out of the Union for all legal purposes, and being now conquered, subject to the absolute disposal of Congress, I will suggest a few ideas and adduce a few authorities. If the so called "confederate States of America" were an independent belligerent, and were so acknowledged by the United States and by Europe, or had assumed and maintained an attitude which entitled them to be considered and treated as a belligerent, then, during such time, they were precisely in the condition of a foreign nation with whom we were at war; nor need their independence as a nation be acknowledged by us to produce that effect. . . .

[Mr. Stevens quotes several legal authorities to support his position that all legal bonds between the Federal Government and the seceding states were broken by the act of war and the recognition of these states as belligerents.]

After such clear and repeated decisions it is something worse than ridiculous to hear men of respectable standing attempting to nullify the law of nations, and declare the Supreme Court of the United States in error, because, as the Constitution forbids it, the States could not go out of the Union in fact. A respectable gentleman was lately reciting this argument, when he suddenly stopped and said, "Did you hear of that atrocious murder committed in our town? A rebel deliberately murdered a Government official." The person addressed said, "I think you are mistaken." "How so? I saw it myself." "You are wrong, no murder was or could be committed, for the law forbids it."

The theory that the rebel States, for four years a separate power and without representation in Congress, were all the time here in the Union, is a good deal less ingenious and respectable than the metaphysics of Berkeley, which proved that neither the world nor any human being was in existence. If this theory were simply ridiculous it could be forgiven; but its effect is deeply injurious to the stability of the nation. I cannot doubt that the late confederate States are out of the Union to all intents and purposes for which the conqueror may choose so to consider them.

But on the ground of estoppel, the United States have the clear right to elect to adjudge them out of the Union. They are estopped both by matter of record and matter *in pais*. One of the first resolutions passed by seceded South Carolina in January, 1861, is as follows:

Resolved, unanimously, That the separation of South Carolina from the Federal Union is final, and she has no further interest in the Constitution of the United States; and that the only appropriate negotiations between her and the Federal Government are as to their mutual relations as foreign States.

Similar resolutions appear upon all their State and confederate government records. The speeches of their members of congress, their generals and executive officers, and the answers of their government to our shameful sueings for peace, went upon the defiant ground that no terms would be offered or received except upon the prior acknowledgment of the entire and permanent independence of the confederate States. After this, to deny that we have a right to treat them as a conquered belligerent, severed from the Union in fact, is not argument but mockery. Whether it be our interest to do so is the only question hereafter and more deliberately to be considered.

But suppose these powerful but now subdued belligerents, instead of being out of the Union, are merely destroyed, and are now lying about, a dead corpse, or with animation so suspended as to be incapable of action, and wholly unable to heal themselves by any unaided movements of their own. Then they may fall under the provision of the Constitution which says "the United States shall guaranty to every State in the Union a republican form of government." Under that power can the judiciary, or the President, or the Commander-in-Chief of the Army, or the Senate or House of Representatives, acting separately, restore them to life and readmit them into the Union? I insist that if each acted separately, though the action of each was identical with all the others, it would amount to nothing. Nothing but the joint action of the two Houses of Congress and the concurrence of the President could do it. If the Senate admitted their Senators, and the House their members, it would have no effect on the future action of Congress. The Fortieth Congress might reject both. Such is the ragged record of Congress for the last four years. . . .

Congress alone can do it. But Congress does not mean the Senate or the House of Representatives, and President, all acting severally. Their joint action constitutes Congress. Hence a law of Congress must be passed before any new State can be admitted; or any dead ones revived. Until then no member can be lawfully admitted into either House. Hence it appears with how little knowledge of constitutional law each branch is urged to admit members separately from these destroyed States. The provision that "each House shall be the judge of the elections, returns, and qualifications of its own members," has not the most distant bearing on this question. Congress must create States and declare when they are entitled to be represented. Then each House must judge whether the members presenting themselves from a recognized State possess the requisite qualifications of age, residence, and citizenship; and whether the election and returns are according to law. The Houses, separately, can judge of nothing else. It seems amazing that any man of legal education could give it any larger meaning.

It is obvious from all this that the first duty of Congress is to pass a law declaring the condition of these outside or defunct States, and providing proper civil governments for them. Since the conquest they have been governed by martial law. Military rule is necessarily despotic, and ought not to exist longer than is absolutely necessary. As there are no symptoms that the people of these provinces will be prepared to participate in constitutional government for some years, I know of no arrangement so proper for them as territorial governments. There they can learn the principles of freedom and eat the fruit of foul rebellion. Under such governments, while electing members to the Territorial Legislatures, they will necessarily mingle with those to whom Congress shall extend the right of suffrage. In Territories Congress fixes the qualifications of electors; and I know of no better place nor better occasion for the conquered rebels and the conqueror to practice justice to all men, and accustom themselves to make and to obey equal laws.

As these fallen rebels cannot at their option reënter the heaven which they have disturbed, the garden of Eden which they have deserted, and flaming swords are set at the gates to secure their exclusion, it becomes important to the welfare of the nation to inquire when the doors shall be reopened for their admission.

According to my judgment they ought never to be recognized as capable of acting in the Union, or of being counted as valid States, until the Constitution shall have been so amended as to make it what its framers intended; and so as to secure perpetual ascendency to the party of the Union; and so as to render our republican Government firm and stable forever. The first of those amendments is to change the basis of representation among the States from Federal numbers to actual voters. Now all the colored freemen in the slave States, and three-fifths of the slaves, are represented, though none of them have votes. The States have nineteen representatives of colored slaves. If the slaves are now free then they can add, for the other two-fifths, thirteen more, making the slave representation thirty-two. I suppose the free blacks in those States will give at least five more, making the representation of non-voting people of color about thirty-seven. The whole number of representatives now from the slave States is seventy. Add the other two-fifths and it will be eighty-three.

If the amendment prevails, and those States withhold the right of suffrage from persons of color, it will deduct about thirty-seven, leaving them but forty-six. With the basis unchanged, the eighty-three southern members, with the Democrats that will in the best times be elected from the North, will always give them a majority in Congress and in the Electoral College. They will at the very first election take possession of the White House and the halls of Congress. I need not depict the ruin that would follow. Assumption of the rebel debt or repudiation of the Federal debt would be sure to follow. The oppression of the freedmen; the reamendment of their State constitutions, and the reëstablishment of slavery would be the inevitable result. That they would scorn and disregard their present constitutions, forced upon them in the midst of martial law, would be both natural and just. No one who has any regard for freedom of elections can look upon those governments, forced upon them in duress, with any favor. If they should grant the right of suffrage to persons of color, I think there would always be Union white men enough in the South, aided by the blacks, to divide the representation, and thus continue the Republican ascendency. If they should refuse to thus alter their election laws it would reduce the representatives of the late slave States to about forty-five and render them powerless for evil.

It is plain that this amendment must be consummated before the defunct States are admitted to be capable of State action, or it never can be.

The proposed amendment to allow Congress to lay a duty on exports is precisely in the same situation. Its importance cannot well be overstated. It is very obvious that for many years the South will not pay much under our internal revenue laws. The only article on which we can raise any considerable amount is cotton. It will be grown largely at once. With ten cents a pound export duty it would be furnished cheaper to foreign markets than they could obtain it from any other part of the world. The late war has shown that. Two million bales exported, at five hundred pounds to the bale, would yield $100,000,000. This seems to be the chief revenue we shall ever derive from the South. Besides, it would be a protection to that amount to our domestic manufactures. Other proposed amendments—to make all laws uniform; to prohibit the assumption of the rebel debt—are of vital importance, and the only thing that can prevent the combined forces of copperheads and secessionists from legislating against the interests of the Union whenever they may obtain an accidental majority.

But this is not all that we ought to do before these inveterate rebels are invited to participate in our legislation. We have turned, or are about to turn, loose four million slaves without a hut to shelter them or a cent in their pockets. The infernal laws of slavery have prevented them from acquiring an education, understanding the commonest laws of contract, or of managing the ordinary business of life. This Congress is bound to provide for them until they can take care of themselves. If we do not furnish them with homesteads, and hedge them around with protective laws; if we leave them to the legislation of their late masters, we had better have left them in bondage. Their condition would be worse than that of our prisoners at Andersonville. If we fail in this great duty now, when we have the power, we shall deserve and receive the execration of history and of all future ages.

Two things are of vital importance.

1. So to establish a principle that none of the rebel States shall be counted in any of the amendments of the Constitution until they are duly admitted into the family of States by the law-making power of their conqueror. For more than six months the amendment of the Constitution abolishing slavery has been ratified by the Legislatures of three-fourths of the States that acted on its passage by Congress, and which had Legislatures, or which were States capable of acting, or required to act, on the question.

I take no account of the aggregation of whitewashed rebels, who without any legal authority have assembled in the capitals of the late rebel States and simulated legislative bodies. Nor do I regard with any respect the cunning byplay into which they deluded the Secretary of State by frequent telegraphic announcements that "South Carolina had adopted the amendment;" "Alabama has adopted the amendment, being the twenty-seventh State," &c. This was intended to delude the people, and accustom Congress to hear repeated the names of these extinct States as if they were alive; when, in truth, they have now no more existence than the revolted cities of Latium, two-thirds of whose people were colonized and their property confiscated, and their right of citizenship withdrawn by conquering and avenging Rome.

2. It is equally important to the stability of this Republic that it should now be solemnly decided what power can revive, recreate, and reinstate these provinces into the family of States, and invest them with the rights of American citizens. It is time that Congress should assert its sovereignty, and assume something of the dignity of a Roman senate. It is fortunate that the President invites Congress to take this manly attitude. After stating with great frankness in his able message his theory, which, however, is found to be impracticable, and which I believe very few now consider tenable, he refers the whole matter to the judgment of Congress. If Congress should fail firmly and wisely to discharge that high duty it is not the fault of the President.

This Congress owes it to its own character to set the seal of reprobation upon a doctrine which is becoming too fashionable, and unless rebuked will be the recognized principle of our Government. Governor Perry and other provisional governors and orators proclaim that "this is the white man's Government." The whole copperhead party, pandering to the lowest prejudices of the ignorant, repeat the cuckoo cry, "This is the white man's Government." Demagogues of all parties, even some high in authority, gravely shout, "This is the white man's Government." What is implied by this? That one race of men are to have the exclusive right forever to rule this nation, and to exercise all acts of sovereignty, while all other races and nations and colors are to be their subjects, and have no voice in making the laws and choosing the rulers by whom they are to be governed. Wherein does this differ from slavery except in degree? Does not this contradict all the distinctive principles of the Declaration of Independence? When the great and good men promulgated that instrument, and pledged their lives and sacred honors to defend it, it was supposed to form an epoch in civil government. Before that time it was held that the right to rule was vested in families, dynasties, or races, not because of superior intelligence or virtue, but because of a divine right to enjoy exclusive privileges.

Our fathers repudiated the whole doctrine of the legal superiority of families or races, and proclaimed the equality of men before the law. Upon that they created a revolution and built the Republic. They were prevented by slavery from perfecting the superstructure whose foundation they had thus broadly laid. For the sake of the Union they consented to wait, but never relinquished the idea of its final completion. The time to which they looked forward with anxiety has come. It is our duty to complete their work. If this Republic is not now made to stand on their great principles, it has no honest foundation, and the Father of all men will still shake it to its center. If we have not yet been sufficiently scourged for our national sin to teach us to do justice to all God's creatures, without distinction of race or color, we must expect the still more heavy vengeance of an offended Father, still increasing his inflictions as he increased the severity of the plagues of Egypt until the tyrant consented to do justice. And when that tyrant repented of his reluctant consent, and attempted to reënslave the people, as our southern tyrants are attempting to do now, he filled the Red sea with broken chariots and drowned horses, and strewed the shores with dead carcasses.

Mr. Chairman, I trust the Republican party will not be alarmed at what I am saying. I do not profess to speak their sentiments, nor must they be held responsible for them. I speak for myself, and take the responsibility, and will settle with my intelligent constituents.

This is not a "white man's Government," in the exclusive sense in which it is used. To say so is political blasphemy, for it violates the fundamental principles of our gospel of liberty. This is man's Government; the Government of all men alike; not that all men will have equal power and sway within it. Accidental circumstances, natural and acquired endowment and ability, will vary their fortunes. But equal rights to all the privileges of the Government is innate in every immortal being, no matter what the shape or color of the tabernacle which it inhabits.

If equal privileges were granted to all, I should not expect any but white men to be elected to office for long ages to come. The prejudice engendered by slavery would not soon permit merit to be preferred to color. But it would still be beneficial to the weaker races. In a country where political divisions will always exist, their power, joined with just white men, would greatly modify, if it did not entirely prevent, the injustice of majorities. Without the right of suffrage in the late slave States, (I do not speak of the free States,) I believe the slaves had far better been left in bondage. I see it stated that very distinguished advocates of the right of suffrage lately declared in this city that they do not expect to obtain it by congressional legislation, but only by administrative action, because, as one gallant gentleman said, the States had not been out of the Union. Then they will never get it. The President is far sounder than they. He sees that administrative action has nothing to do with it. If it ever is to come, it must be constitutional amendments or congressional action in the Territories, and in enabling acts.

How shameful that men of influence should mislead and miseducate the public mind! They proclaim, "This is the white man's Government," and the whole coil of copperheads echo the same sentiment, and upstart, jealous Republicans join the cry. Is it any wonder ignorant foreigners and illiterate natives should learn this doctrine, and be led to despise and maltreat a whole race of their fellow-men?

Sir, this doctrine of a white man's Government is as atrocious as the infamous sentiment that damned the late Chief Justice to everlasting fame; and, I fear, to everlasting fire.

Administration Theory

HENRY JARVIS RAYMOND

> *Born, Lima, New York, January 24, 1820; died, New*
> *York City, June 18, 1869. Graduated from University*
> *of Vermont. Soon gained a wide reputation as a news-*
> *paperman and public speaker. Elected in 1849 to New*
> *York State Assembly; reëlected, became Speaker in 1851.*
> *In this year he and his friend George Jones established*
> *the New York Daily Times. Lieutenant Governor of*
> *New York from 1855 to 1857. In 1856 he participated*
> *in the founding of the Republican party and drafted its*
> *statement of principles. For his efforts in the campaign*
> *of 1864 (he helped write the platform and was instru-*
> *mental in obtaining the Vice-Presidential nomination for*
> *Andrew Johnson) he was rewarded with the Chair-*
> *manship of the Republican National Committee. Elected*
> *to Congress in 1865, he entered the House with unusual*
> *prestige for a newcomer and immediately became spokes-*
> *man for the administration. But he proved no match for*
> *Stevens, and Raymond's career in national politics was*
> *tragic and short. He was expelled from the National*
> *Committee and retired from the House after a single*
> *term. In 1869, apparently only at the beginning of his*
> *career, he died at the age of 49 of a cerebral hemorrhage*
> *brought on by emotional strain and overwork. Charming,*
> *urbane, eloquent, Raymond sought to sound a note of*
> *moderation and conciliation in a time of inflamed pas-*
> *sions. Elmer Davis has said of his political career that*
> *his misfortune was "that he was a temperamental non-*
> *partisan incurably addicted to party politics."*

United States House of Representatives, December 21, 1865. *Congressional Globe*,
39th Cong., 1st Sess., pt. I, pp. 120–125.

*M*r. *Chairman:*   I should be glad, if it meet the sense of those members who are present, to make some remarks upon the general question now before the House; but I do not wish to trespass at all upon their disposition in regard to this matter. I do not know, however, that there will be a better opportunity to say what little I have to say than is now offered; and if the House shall indicate no other wish, I will proceed to say it. . . . I am glad to assume and to believe that there is not a member of this House, nor a man in this country, who does not wish, from the bottom of his heart, to see the day speedily come when we shall have this nation—the great American Republic—again united, more harmonious in its action than it has ever been, and forever one and indivisible. We in this Congress are to devise the means to restore its union and its harmony, to perfect its institutions, and to make it in all its parts and in all its action, through all time to come, too strong, too wise, and too free ever to invite or ever to permit the hand of rebellion again to be raised against it.

Now sir, in devising those ways and means to accomplish that great result, the first thing we have to do is to know the point from which we start, to understand the nature of the material with which we have to work—the condition of the territory and the States with which we are concerned. I had supposed at the outset of this session that it was the purpose of this House to proceed to that work without discussion, and to commit it almost exclusively, if not entirely, to the joint committee raised by the two Houses for the consideration of that subject. But, sir, I must say that I was glad when I perceived the distinguished gentleman from Pennsylvania [Mr. Stevens], himself the chairman on the part of this House of that great committee on reconstruction, lead off in a discussion of this general subject, and thus invite all the rest of us who choose to follow him in the debate. In the remarks which he made in this body a few days since, he laid down, with the clearness and the force which characterize everything he says and does, his point of departure in commencing this great work. I had hoped that the ground he would lay down would be such that we could all of us stand upon it and cooperate with him in our common object. I feel constrained to say, sir—and I do it without the slightest disposition to create or to exaggerate differences—that there were features in his exposition of the condition of the country with which I cannot concur. I cannot for myself start from precisely the point which he assumes.

In his remarks on that occasion he assumed that the States lately in rebellion were and are out of the Union. Throughout his speech—I will not trouble you with reading passages from it—I find him speaking of those States as "outside of the Union," as "dead States," as having forfeited all their rights and terminated their State existence. I find expressions still more definite and distinct; I find him stating that they "are and for four years have been out of the Union for all legal purposes;" as having been for four years a "separate power," and "a separate nation."

His position therefore is that these States, having been in rebellion, are now out of the Union, and are simply within the jurisdiction of the Constitution of the United States as so much territory to be dealt with precisely as the will of the conqueror, to use his own language, may dictate. Now, sir, if that position is correct, it prescribes for us one line of policy to be pursued very different from the one that will be proper if it is not correct. His belief is that what we have to do is to create new States out of this territory at the proper time—many years distant—retaining them meantime in a territorial condition, and subjecting them to precisely such a state of discipline and tutelage as Congress or the Government of the United States may see fit to prescribe. If I believed in the premises which he assumes, possibly, though I do not think probably, I might agree with the conclusion he has reached.

But, sir, I cannot believe that this is our condition. I cannot believe that these States have ever been out of the Union, or that they are now out of the Union. I cannot believe that they ever have been, or are now, in any sense a separate Power. If they were, sir, how and when did they become so? They were once States of this Union—that every one concedes; bound to the Union and made members of the Union by the Constitution of the United States. If they ever went out of the Union it was at some specific time and by some specific act. I regret that the gentleman from Pennsylvania [Mr. Stevens] is not now in his seat. I should have been glad to ask him by what specific act, and at what precise time, any one of those States took itself out of the American Union. Was it by the ordinance of secession? I think we all agree that an ordinance of secession passed by any State of this Union is simply a nullity, because it encounters in its practical operation the Constitution of the United States, which is the supreme law of the land. It could have no legal, actual force or validity. It could not operate to effect any actual change in the relations of the State adopting it to the national Government, still less to accomplish the removal of that State from the sovereign jurisdiction of the Constitution of the United States.

Well, sir, did the resolutions of these States, the declarations of their officials, the speeches of members of their Legislatures, or the utterances of their press accomplish the result? Certainly not. They could not possibly work any change whatever in the relations of these States to the General Government. All their ordinances and all their resolutions were simply declarations of a purpose to secede. Their secession, if it ever took place, certainly could not date from the time when their intention to secede was first announced. After declaring that intention, they proceeded to carry it into effect. How? By war. By sustaining their purpose by arms against the force which the United States brought to bear against it. Did they sustain it? Were their arms victorious? If they were, then their secession was an accomplished fact. If not, it was nothing more than an abortive attempt—a purpose unfulfilled. This, then, is simply a question of fact, and we all know what the fact is. They did not succeed. They failed to maintain their ground by force of arms—in other words, they failed to secede.

But the gentleman from Pennsylvania [Mr. Stevens] insists that they did secede, and that this fact is not in the least affected by the other fact that the Constitution forbids secession. He says that the law forbids murder, but that murders are nevertheless committed. But there is no analogy between the two cases. If secession had been accomplished, if these States had gone out, and overcome the armies that tried to prevent their going out, then the prohibition of the Constitution could not have altered the fact. In the case of murder the man is killed, and murder is thus committed in spite of the law. The fact of killing is essential to the committal of the crime; and the fact of going out is essential to secession. But in this case there was no such fact. I think I need not argue any further the position that the rebel States have never for one moment, by any ordinances of secession, or by any successful war, carried themselves beyond the rightful jurisdiction of the Constitution of the United States. They have interrupted for a time the practical enforcement and exercise of that jurisdiction; they rendered it impossible for a time for this Government to enforce obedience to its laws; but there has never been an hour when this Government, or this Congress, or this House, or the gentleman from Pennsylvania himself, ever conceded that those States were beyond the jurisdiction of the Constitution and laws of the United States.

During all these four years of war Congress has been making laws for the government of those very States, and the gentleman from Pennsylvania has voted for them, and voted to raise armies to enforce them. Why was this done if they were a separate nation? Why, if they were not part of the United States? Those laws were made for them as States. Members have voted for laws imposing upon them direct taxes, which are apportioned, according to the Constitution, only "among the several States" according to their population. In a variety of ways—to some of which the gentleman who preceded me has referred—this Congress has by its action assumed and asserted that they were still States in the Union, though in rebellion, and that it was with the rebellion that we were making war, and not with the States themselves as States, and still less as a separate, as a foreign, Power.

. . . .

The gentleman from Pennylvania [Mr. Stevens] spoke of States forfeiting their State existence by the fact of rebellion. Well, I do not see how there can be any such forfeiture involved or implied. The individual citizens of those States went into the rebellion. They thereby incurred certain penalties under the laws and Constitution of the United States. What the States did was to endeavor to interpose their State authority between the individuals in rebellion and the Government of the United States, which assumed, and which would carry out the assumption, to declare those individuals traitors for their acts. The individuals in the States who were in rebellion, it seems to me, were the only parties who under the Constitution and laws of the United States could incur the penalties of treason. I know of no law, I know of nothing in the Constitution of the United States, I know of nothing in any recognized or established code of international law, which can punish a State as a State for any act it may perform. It is certain that our Constitution assumes nothing of the kind. It does not deal with States, except in one or two instances, such as elections of members of Congress, and the election of electors of President and Vice President.

Indeed, the main feature which distinguishes the Union under the Constitution from the old Confederation is this, that whereas the old Confederation did deal with States directly, making requisitions upon them for supplies and relying upon them for the execution of its laws, the Constitution of the United States, in order to form a more perfect Union, made its laws binding on the individual citizens of the several States, whether living in one State or in another. Congress, as the legislative branch of this Government, enacts a law which shall be operative upon every individual within its jurisdiction. It is binding upon each individual citizen, and if he resists it by force he is guilty of a crime and is punished accordingly, anything in the constitution or laws of his State to the contrary notwithstanding. But the States themselves are not touched by the laws of the United States or by the Constitution of the United States. A State cannot be indicted; a State cannot be tried; a State cannot be hung for treason. The individuals in a State may be so tried and hung, but the State as an organization, as an organic member of the Union, still exists, whether its individual citizens commit treason or not.

. . . .

Mr. Chairman, I am here to act with those who seek to complete the restoration of the Union, as I have acted with those through the last four years who have sought to maintain its integrity and prevent its destruction. I shall say no word and do no act and give no vote to recognize its division, or to postpone or disturb its rapidly-approaching harmony and peace. I have no right and no disposition to lay down rules by which others shall govern and guide their conduct; but for myself I shall endeavor to act upon this whole question in the broad and liberal temper which its importance demands. We are not conducting a controversy in a court of law. We are not seeking to enforce a remedy for private wrongs, nor to revenge or retaliate private griefs. We have great communities of men, permanent interests of great States, to deal with, and we are bound to deal with them in a large and liberal spirit. It may be for the welfare of this nation that we shall cherish toward the millions of our people lately in rebellion feelings of hatred and distrust; that we shall nurse the bitterness their infamous treason has naturally and justly engendered, and make that the basis of our future dealings with them. Possibly we may best teach them the lessons of liberty, by visiting upon them the worst excesses of despotism. Possibly they may best learn to practice justice toward others, to admire and emulate our republican institutions, by suffering at our hands the absolute rule we denounce in others. It may be best for us and for them that we discard, in all our dealings with them, all the obligations and requirements of the Constitution, and assert as the only law for them the unrestrained will of conquerors and masters.

I confess I do not sympathize with the sentiments or the opinions which would dictate such a course. I would exact of them all needed and all just guarantees for their future loyalty to the Constitution and laws of the United States. I would exact from them, or impose upon them through the constitutional legislation of Congress, and by enlarging and extending, if necessary, the scope and powers of the Freedmen's Bureau, proper care and protection for the helpless and friendless freedmen, so lately their slaves. I would exercise a rigid scrutiny into the character and loyalty of the men whom they may send to Congress, before I allowed them to participate in the high prerogative of legislating for the nation. But I would seek to allay rather than stimulate the animosities and hatred, however just they may be, to which the war has given rise. But for our own sake as well as for theirs I would not visit upon them a policy of confiscation which has been discarded in the policy and practical conduct of every civilized nation on the face of the globe.

I believe it important for us as well as for them that we should cultivate friendly relations with them, that we should seek the promotion of their interests as part and parcel of our own. We have been their enemies in war, in peace let us show ourselves their friends. Now that slavery has been destroyed—that prolific source of all our alienations, all our hatreds, and all our disasters—there is nothing longer to make us foes. They have the same interests, the same hopes, the same aspirations that we have. They are one with us; we must share their sufferings and they will share our advancing prosperity. They have been punished as no community was ever punished before for the treason they have committed. I trust, sir, the day will come ere long when all traces of this great conflict will be effaced, except those which mark the blessings that follow in its train.

I hope and believe we shall soon see the day when the people of the southern States will show us, by evidences that we cannot mistake, that they have
returned, in all sincerity and good faith, to their allegiance to the Union; that
they intend to join henceforth with us in promoting its prosperity, in defending the banner of its glory, and in fighting the battles of democratic freedom,
not only here, but wherever the issue may be forced upon our acceptance. I
rejoice with heartfelt satisfaction that we have in these seats of power—in the
executive department and in these halls of Congress—men who will cooperate
for the attainment of these great and beneficent ends. I trust they will act with
wisdom; I know they will act from no other motives than those of patriotism
and love of their fellow-men.

PART TWO

Ferment in an Industrial Age

RUGGED INDIVIDUALISM AND
SOCIAL PROTEST

AFTER the Civil War, America burst its seams with raw energy and desire. Railroads spanned and cross-hatched the continent, carrying settlers westward and returning the produce of their lands to big city markets. Immigrants came in waves to take up the new lands and to swell the labor force in sprawling cities. Smokestacks towering against the sky symbolized economic empires that reached into the Menominee, Gogebic, and Mesabi ranges for ore and into Europe and the Orient for markets. By 1900 America had been transformed from a parochial society into one that was corporate, impersonal, and international.

The American industrial revolution changed the mind as well as the face of the nation. Although the outward changes were impressive, industrial progress was not accompanied by widely shared social and economic gains. Rapacity made a mockery of older political and social values. Plutocratic America revised its inherited credo of life, liberty, and the pursuit of happiness to read life and liberty for the pursuit of wealth. The new loyalty was to "the bitch goddess Success" who presided callously over "the great barbecue." Standards of human worth were fashioned out of economic virtues; to lose out in the economic race was counted a defect in character.

The big change was sanctioned by a book, or more accurately, by its interpreters. In his The Origin of Species (1859), Charles Darwin offered a biological theory of

223

organic evolution based on natural selection. A fellow Englishman, Herbert Spencer, appropriated Darwin's leading ideas to explain conditions under which social progress occurs. Spencer's doctrine of Social Darwinism, coupled with laissez-faire economics, furnished the outlines of the prevailing belief system of his generation. The catchwords "struggle for existence" and "survival of the fittest" fixed in popular imagination a kinship between the natural and social worlds. Above all, Spencer gave sanction to strenuosity and economic ruthlessness. Rewards came legitimately to those who hacked their way through the competitive jungle; laggards and drop-outs were the inevitable price of social progress.

Spencer was lionized when he came to the United States in 1882. Two hundred men of prominence and large affairs threw a banquet in his honor at Delmonico's. Anticipating the speech he must make, Spencer was almost at the point of nervous collapse, and he squirmed painfully under round after round of unrestrained testimonials. Exclaimed Henry Ward Beecher: "To my father and my mother I owe my physical being; to you, sir, I owe my intellectual being. At a critical moment you provided the safe paths through bogs and morasses; you were my teacher."[1] William Graham Sumner was among those present, and while incapable of Beecher's effusions, he did add his "amen." And well he might, for among all of Spencer's disciples, Sumner was America's most vigorous and influential Social Darwinist.

Sumner was a clergyman who shed the cloth to become Professor of Political Economy at Yale University in 1872. He was a productive scholar and, despite his gruffness and arctic exterior, also a stimulating teacher and platform speaker. Sumner's standard text, stated baldly, was that the progress of civilization requires an environment

---

[1] Andrew Carnegie, *Autobiography* (Boston: Houghton, Mifflin Company, 1920), p. 336.

of unrestricted competition wherein the process of natural selection may operate unhindered. He never backed away from conclusions to which his premise led, though he provoked outcries from both right and left. No hireling of moguls, he rebuked businessmen who mouthed clichés about the virtues of competition and then wheedled congressmen into voting for preferential tariffs. He attacked reformers as sentimental quacks who were trying quixotically "to make the world over." Men simply were not equal, and Natural Rights were a chimera. Any system of socialism or semisocialism was doomed and would destroy liberty if attempted.

Sumner prided himself on hard-headed realism and respect for facts. Echoing Malthus, he regarded nature as niggardly. It was "root, hog, or die." If poverty were to be overcome, the struggle must be pursued energetically by self-reliant men who were disciplined to sobriety, prudence, and industry. Sumner's model was his immigrant father, "the forgotten man" in the lecture of that title. This was Sumner's heart-felt exposition of his creed of rugged individualism.

Had Sumner been asked to nominate the improvident man of his generation, he might have chosen Henry George, foremost among free-lance reformers. Sumner looked upon George as a mischievous peddler of nostrums.

Henry George left school at age thirteen and knocked around the world seeking adventure and wealth. Dreams of gold lured him to California, but for years failure and poverty dogged his steps. Then he tried his hand at writing and rapidly won influential posts with newspapers in San Francisco and Oakland. In the presidential campaign of 1876 he stumped the state for Tilden and the Democratic ticket. He was rewarded by the self-discovery of his power in public speaking, and with a political sinecure which enabled him to complete his book, Progress and Poverty, *published in 1879. After a slow start, the book caught on in a big way.* Progress and Poverty *catapulted George to fame and paved the way for his reformist campaigns and speaking tours the world over.*

In his title, Progress and Poverty, *George stated the paradox of the age: As wealth increases, so does poverty and misery. It is irrelevant, said George, to gloss over poverty in America because it does not match the widespread despair in Europe and Asia. Poverty everywhere destroys human personality and produces social convulsions. If poverty is an evil and a palpable threat to liberty, what can be done to abolish it?*

Once George listened to a friend bemoan poverty and political corruption. "What do you intend to do about it?" he asked. "Nothing," sighed the friend. "You and I can do nothing at all. . . . We can only wait for evolution. Perhaps in four or five thousand years evolution may have carried men beyond this state of affairs."[2] George disagreed and made it his life business to dissolve "the steel chain of ideas"[3] that shackled men's minds. Through his writing and speaking he argued that man is not the pawn of immutable laws of nature or economics. Civilization is neither sustained nor urged forward by any slow grinding of impersonal forces in history. As a creature of God, man is endowed with Natural Rights, and he is under a continuing obligation to redress society in the interest of its members. Man must win social justice by thinking afresh on the great problems of the times. Thus George encouraged millions of people to break with fixed assumptions about their world and to think fluidly.

Following his own injunctions, George denied that nature was niggardly, as Malthus and Sumner had stated. Nature has spread a banquet, said George, and modern technology has all but solved the problems of

[2] Quoted by Eric Goldman, *Rendezvous with Destiny* (New York: Vintage Books, 1956), p. 66.

[3] *Ibid.*

production. Poverty is caused by imperfect distribution of wealth. Where, then, is the flaw in our system of distribution? Since wealth is produced by labor and capital applied to land, it follows that in the distribution of wealth, land commands rent, labor commands wages, and capital commands interest. So far so good, but of these components of wealth, land alone is God-given. Moreover, land-value and economic rent are produced by population growth and concentrations, not by productive labor. Land-value and rent, then, constitute unearned increment that is unjustly pocketed by landholders and speculators. Therefore, George proposed public appropriation of rent through what he called the single tax. The net effect of the plan, he insisted, would be to replace other taxes, to augment rewards that belong to labor and capital, and to stimulate civic enterprise. In short, George's single tax was designed to redistribute wealth without jeopardy to individualism, capitalism, or political liberty.

The single-tax movement created a stir, but it never took hold. But George's passionate cry for social justice and for fresh thinking was heeded. He stimulated a helter-skelter of reform movements, and he jogged countless individuals into following some liberal or radical path. George Bernard Shaw, for example, once heard George speak in London and was moved by his social message. Through this door Shaw entered Fabian Socialism. The kind of influence George exercised in America through his speeches is suggested by his two-night stand in Burlington, Iowa. The first night he spoke to the Knights of Labor on "The Crime of Poverty" and on the next night he gave his lecture on "Moses" in the Congregational Church. A close observer estimated that "perhaps a dozen men were now confirmed followers" while "some fifty followed at a greater distance." His biographer concludes that "It seems fair to assume that

Burlington represents the impact of Henry George in many towns." [4]

The speeches of Sumner and George are, in a general sense, touchstones to major thought currents and agitations of the era—rugged individualism and melioristic reform. And each speech faithfully mirrors the style of mind and expression of the man who uttered it.

[4] Charles A. Barker, *Henry George* (New York: Oxford University Press, 1955), pp. 442–443.

The Forgotten Man

WILLIAM GRAHAM SUMNER

Born, Paterson, New Jersey, October 30, 1840; died, Englewood, New Jersey, April 12, 1910. Graduated from Yale, 1863; studied at Geneva and Göttingen, 1863–1866. Ordained Episcopal clergyman, 1869; active in ministry until 1872. Professor of Political Economy at Yale, 1872–1909. Famed as teacher and scholar, as speaker and essayist on controversial subjects. Last important book is Folkways, 1907.

I *propose* in this lecture to discuss one of the most *subtile* and widespread social fallacies. It consists in the impression made on the mind for the time being by a particular fact, or by the interests of a particular group of persons, to which attention is directed while other facts or the interests of other persons are entirely left out of account. I shall give a number of instances and illustrations of this in a moment, and I cannot expect you to understand what is meant from an abstract statement until these illustrations are before you, but just by way of a general illustration I will put one or two cases.

Whenever a pestilence like yellow fever breaks out in any city, our attention is especially attracted towards it, and our sympathies are excited for the sufferers. If contributions are called for, we readily respond. Yet

New Haven, Connecticut, February 8 or 9, 1883. William Graham Sumner, *The Forgotten Man and Other Essays*, A. G. Keller, ed. (New Haven: Yale University Press, 1918), pp. 465–495. Reprinted by permission. Original ms. in Sterling Library, Yale University.

On time and place of first delivery, compare Keller, p. 505, with Maurice R. Davie, ed., *Sumner Today* (New Haven: Yale University Press, 1940), p. 3, footnote: "The original lecture on this subject, delivered January 30, 1883, in the Brooklyn Historical Rooms."

the number of persons who die prematurely from consumption every year greatly exceeds the deaths from yellow fever or any similar disease when it occurs, and the suffering entailed by consumption is very much greater. The suffering from consumption, however, never constitutes a public question or a subject of social discussion. If an inundation takes place anywhere, constituting a public calamity (and an inundation takes place somewhere in the civilized world nearly every year), public attention is attracted and public appeals are made, but the losses by great inundations must be insignificant compared with the losses by runaway horses, which, taken separately, scarcely obtain mention in a local newspaper. In hard times insolvent debtors are a large class. They constitute an interest and are able to attract public attention, so that social philosophers discuss their troubles and legislatures plan measures of relief. Insolvent debtors, however, are an insignificant body compared with the victims of commonplace misfortune, or accident, who are isolated, scattered, ungrouped and ungeneralized, and so are never made the object of discussion or relief. In seasons of ordinary prosperity, persons who become insolvent have to get out of their troubles as they can. They have no hope of relief from the legislature. The number of insolvents during a series of years of general prosperity, and their losses, greatly exceed the number and losses during a special period of distress.

These illustrations bring out only one side of my subject, and that only partially. It is when we come to the proposed measures of relief for the evils which have caught public attention that we reach the real subject which deserves our attention. As soon as A observes something which seems to him to be wrong, from which X is suffering, A talks it over with B, and A and B then propose to get a law passed to remedy the evil and help X. Their law always proposes to determine what C shall do for X or, in the better case, what A, B and C shall do for X. As for A and B, who get a law to make themselves do for X what they are willing to do for him, we have nothing to say except that they might better have done it without any law, but what I want to do is to look up C. I want to show you what manner of man he is. I call him the Forgotten Man. Perhaps the appellation is not strictly correct. He is the man who never is thought of. He is the victim of the reformer, social speculator and philanthropist, and I hope to show you before I get through that he deserves your notice both for his character and for the many burdens which are laid upon him.

No doubt one great reason for the phenomenon which I bring to your attention is the passion for reflection and generalization which marks our period. Since the printing press has come into such wide use, we have all been encouraged to philosophize about things in a way which was unknown to our ancestors. They lived their lives out in positive contact with actual cases as they arose. They had little of this analysis, introspection, reflection and speculation which have passed into a habit and almost into a disease with us. Of all things which tempt to generalization and to philosophizing, social topics stand foremost. Each one of us gets some experience of social forces. Each one has some chance for observation of social phenomena. There is certainly no domain in which generalization is easier. There is nothing about which people dogmatize more freely. Even men of scientific training in some department in which they would not tolerate dogmatism at all will not hesitate to dogmatize in the most reckless manner about social topics. The truth is, however, that science, as yet, has won less control of social phenomena than of any other class of phenomena. The most complex and difficult subject which we now have to study is the constitution of human society, the forces which operate in it, and the laws by which they act, and we know less about these things than about any others which demand our attention. In such a state of things, over-hasty generalization is sure to be extremely mischievous. You cannot take up a magazine or newspaper without being struck by the feverish interest with which social topics and problems are discussed, and if you were a student of social science, you would find in almost all these discussions evidence, not only that the essential preparation for the discussion is wanting, but that the disputants do not even know that there is any preparation to be gained. Consequently we are bewildered by contradictory dogmatizing. We find in all these discussions only the application of pet notions and the clashing of contradictory "views." Remedies are confidently proposed for which there is no guarantee offered except that the person who prescribes the remedy says that he is sure it will work. We hear constantly of "reform," and the reformers turn out to be people who do not like things as they are and wish that they could be made nicer. We hear a great many exhortations to make progress from people who do not know in what direction they want to go. Consequently social reform is the most barren and tiresome subject of discussion amongst us, except aesthetics.

I suppose that the first chemists seemed to be very hardhearted and unpoetical persons when they scouted the glorious dream of the alchemists that there must be some process for turning base metals into gold. I suppose that the men who first said, in plain, cold assertion, there is no fountain of eternal youth, seemed to be the most cruel and cold-hearted adversaries of human happiness. I know that the economists who say that if we could transmute lead into gold, it would certainly do us no good and might do great harm, are still regarded as unworthy of belief. Do not the money articles of the newspapers yet ring with the doctrine that we are getting rich when we give cotton and wheat for gold rather than when we give cotton and wheat for iron?

Let us put down now the cold, hard fact and look at it just as it is. There is no device whatever to be invented for securing happiness without industry, economy, and virtue. We are yet in the empirical stage as regards all our social devices. We have done something in science and art in the domain of production, transportation and exchange. But when you come to the laws of the social order, we know very little about them. Our laws and institutions by which we attempt to regulate our lives under the laws of nature which control society are merely a series of haphazard experiments. We come into collision with the laws and are not intelligent enough to understand wherein we are mistaken and how to correct our errors. We persist in our experiments instead of patiently setting about the study of the laws and facts in order to see where we are wrong. Traditions and formulae have a dominion over us in legislation and social customs which we seem unable to break or even to modify.

For my present purpose I ask your attention for a few moments to the notion of liberty, because the Forgotten Man would no longer be forgotten where there was true liberty. You will say that you know what liberty is. There is no term of more common or prouder use. None is more current, as if it were quite beyond the need of definition. Even as I write, however, I find in a leading review a new definition of civil liberty. Civil liberty the writer declares to be "the result of the restraint exercised by the sovereign people on the more powerful individuals and classes of the community, preventing them from availing themselves of the excess of their power to the detriment of the other classes." You notice here the use of the words "sovereign people" to designate a class of the population, not the nation as a political and civil whole. Wherever "people" is used in such a sense, there is always fallacy. Furthermore, you will recognize in this definition a very superficial and fallacious construction of English constitutional history. The writer goes on to elaborate that construction and he comes out at last with the conclusion that "a government by the people can, in no case, become a paternal government, since its lawmakers are its mandataries and servants carrying out its will, and not its fathers or its masters." This, then, is the point at which he desires to arrive, and he has followed a familiar device in setting up a definition to start with which would produce the desired deduction at the end.

In the definition the word "people" was used for a class or section of the population. It is now asserted that if *that* section rules, there can be no paternal, that is, undue, government. That doctrine, however, is the very opposite of liberty, and contains the most vicious error possible in politics. The truth is that cupidity, selfishness, envy, malice, lust, vindictiveness, are constant vices of human nature. They are not confined to classes or to nations or particular ages of the world. They present themselves in the palace, in the parliament, in the academy, in the church, in the workshop, and in the hovel. They appear in autocracies, theocracies, aristocracies, democracies, and ochlocracies all alike. They change their masks somewhat from age to age and from one form of society to another. All history is only one long story to this effect: men have struggled for power over their fellow-men in order that they might win the joys of earth at the expense of others and might shift the burdens of life from their own shoulders upon those of others. It is true that, until this time, the proletariat, the mass of mankind, have rarely had the power and they have not made such a record as kings and nobles and priests have made of the abuses they would perpetrate against their fellow-men when they could and dared. But what folly it is to think that vice and passion are limited by classes, that liberty consists only in taking power away from nobles and priests and giving it to artisans and peasants and that these latter will never abuse it! They will abuse it just as all others have done unless they are put under checks and guarantees, and there can be no civil liberty anywhere unless rights are guaranteed against all abuses, as well from proletarians as from generals, aristocrats, and ecclesiastics.

Now what has been amiss in all the old arrangements? The evil of the old military and aristocratic governments was that some men enjoyed the fruits of other men's labor; that some persons' lives, rights, interests and happiness were sacrificed to other persons' cupidity and lust. What have our ancestors been striving for, under the name of civil liberty, for the last five hundred years? They have been striving to bring it about that each man and woman might live out his or her life according to his or her own notions of happiness and up to the measure of his or her own virtue and wisdom. How have they sought to accomplish this? They have sought to accomplish it by setting aside all arbitrary personal or class elements and introducing the reign of law and the supremacy of constitutional institutions like the jury, the habeas corpus, the independent judiciary, the separation of church and state, and the ballot. Note right here one point which will be important and valuable when I come more especially to the case of the Forgotten Man: whenever you talk of liberty, you must have *two* men in mind. The sphere of rights of one of these men trenches upon that of the other, and whenever you establish liberty for the one, you repress the other. Whenever absolute sovereigns are subjected to constitutional restraints, you always hear them remonstrate that their liberty is curtailed. So it is, in the sense that their power of determining what shall be done in the state is limited below what it was before and the similar power of other organs in the state is widened. Whenever the privileges of an aristocracy are curtailed, there is heard a similar complaint. The truth is that the line of limit or demarcation between classes as regards civil power has been moved and what has been taken from one class is given to another.

We may now, then, advance a step in our conception of civil liberty. It is the status in which we find the true adjustment of rights between classes and individuals. Historically, the conception of civil liberty has been constantly changing. The notion of rights changes from one generation to another and the conception of civil liberty changes with it. If we try to formulate a true definition of civil liberty as an ideal thing towards which the development of political institutions is all the time tending, it would be this: Civil liberty is the status of the man who is guaranteed by law and civil institutions the exclusive employment of all his own powers for his own welfare.

This definition of liberty or civil liberty, you see, deals only with concrete and actual relations of the civil order. There is some sort of a poetical and metaphysical notion of liberty afloat in men's minds which some people dream about but which nobody can define. In popular language it means that a man may do as he has a mind to. When people get this notion of liberty into their heads and combine with it the notion that they live in a free country and ought to have liberty, they sometimes make strange demands upon the state. If liberty means to be able to do as you have a mind to, there is no such thing in this world. Can the Czar of Russia do as he has a mind to? Can the Pope do as he has a mind to? Can the President of the United States do as he has a mind to? Can Rothschild do as he has a mind to? Could a Humboldt or a Faraday do as he had a mind to? Could a Shakespeare or a Raphael do as he had a mind to? Can a tramp do as he has a mind to? Where is the man, whatever his station, possessions, or talents, who can get any such liberty? There is none. There is a doctrine floating about in our literature that we are born to the inheritance of certain rights. That is another glorious dream, for it would mean that there was something in this world which we got for nothing. But what is the truth? We are born into no right whatever but what has an equivalent and corresponding duty right alongside of it. There is no such thing on this earth as something for nothing. Whatever we inherit of wealth, knowledge, or institutions from the past has been paid for by the labor and sacrifice of preceding generations; and the fact that these gains are carried on, that the race lives and that the race can, at least within some cycle, accumulate its gains, is one of the facts on which civilization rests. The law of the conservation of energy is not simply a law of physics; it is a law of the whole moral universe, and the order and truth of all things conceivable by man depends upon it. If there were any such liberty as that of doing as you have a mind to, the human race would be condemned to everlasting anarchy and war as these erratic wills crossed and clashed against each other. True liberty lies in the equilibrium of rights and duties, producing peace, order, and harmony. As I have defined it, it means that a man's right to take power and wealth out of the social product is measured by the energy and wisdom which he has contributed to the social effort.

Now if I have set this idea before you with any distinctness and success, you see that civil liberty consists of a set of civil institutions and laws which are arranged to act as impersonally as possible. It does not consist in majority rule or in universal suffrage or in elective systems at all. These are devices which are good or better just in the degree in which they secure liberty. The institutions of civil liberty leave each man to run his career in life in his own way, only guaranteeing to him that whatever he does in the way of industry, economy, prudence, sound judgment, etc., shall redound to his own welfare and shall not be diverted to some one else's benefit. Of course it is a necessary corollary that each man shall also bear the penalty of his own vices and his own mistakes. If I want to be free from any other man's dictation, I must understand that I can have no other man under my control.

Now with these definitions and general conceptions in mind, let us turn to the special class of facts to which, as I said at the outset, I invite your attention. We see that under a régime of liberty and equality before the law, we get the highest possible development of independence, self-reliance, individual energy, and enterprise, but we get these high social virtues at the expense of the old sentimental ties which used to unite baron and retainer, master and servant, sage and disciple, comrade and comrade. We are agreed that the son shall not be disgraced even by the crime of the father, much less by the crime of a more distant relative. It is a humane and rational view of things that each life shall stand for itself alone and not be weighted by the faults of another, but it is useless to deny that this view of things is possible only in a society where the ties of kinship have lost nearly all the intensity of poetry and romance which once characterized them. The ties of sentiment and sympathy also have faded out. We have come, under the régime of liberty and equality before the law, to a form of society which is based not on status, but on free contract. Now a society based on status is one in which classes, ranks, interests, industries, guilds, associations, etc., hold men in permanent relations to each other. Custom and prescription create, under status, ties, the strength of which lies in sentiment. Feeble remains of this may be seen in some of our academical societies to-day, and it is unquestionably a great privilege and advantage for any man in our society to win experience of the sentiments which belong to a strong and close association, just because the chances for such experience are nowadays very rare. In a society based on free contract, men come together as free and independent parties to an agreement which is of mutual advantage. The relation is rational, even rationalistic. It is not poetical. It does not exist from use and custom, but for reasons given, and it does not endure by prescription but ceases when the reason for it ceases. There is no sentiment in it at all. The fact is that, under the régime of liberty and equality before the law, there is no place for sentiment in trade or politics as public interests. Sentiment is thrown back into private life, into personal relations, and if ever it comes into a public discussion of an impersonal and general public question it always produces mischief.

Now you know that "the poor and the weak" are continually put forward as objects of public interest and public obligation. In the appeals which are made, the terms "the poor" and "the weak" are used as if they were terms of exact definition. Except the pauper, that is to say, the man who cannot earn his living or pay his way, there is no possible definition of a poor man. Except a man who is incapacitated by vice or by physical infirmity, there is no definition of a weak man. The paupers and the physically incapacitated are an inevitable charge on society. About them no more need be said. But the weak who constantly arouse the pity of humanitarians and philanthopists are the shiftless, the imprudent, the negligent, the impractical, and the inefficient, or they are the idle, the intemperate, the extravagant, and the vicious. Now the troubles of these persons are constantly forced upon public attention, as if they and their interests deserved especial consideration, and a great portion of all organized and unorganized effort for the common welfare consists in attempts to relieve these classes of people. I do not wish to be understood now as saying that nothing ought to be done for these people by those who are stronger and wiser. That is not my point. What I want to do is to point out the thing which is overlooked and the error which is made in all these charitable efforts. The notion is accepted as if it were not open to any question that if you help the inefficient and vicious you may gain something for society or you may not, but that you lose nothing. This is a complete mistake. Whatever capital you divert to the support of a shiftless and good-for-nothing person is so much diverted from some other employment, and that means from somebody else. I would spend any conceivable amount of zeal and eloquence if I possessed it to try to make people grasp this idea. Capital is force. If it goes one way it cannot go another. If you give a loaf to a pauper you cannot give the same loaf to a laborer. Now this other man who would have got it but for the charitable sentiment which bestowed it on a worthless member of society is the Forgotten Man. The philanthropists and humanitarians have their minds all full of the wretched and miserable whose case appeals to compassion, attacks the sympathies, takes possession of the imagination, and excites the emotions. They push on towards the quickest and easiest remedies and they forget the real victim.

Now who is the Forgotten Man? He is the simple, honest laborer, ready to earn his living by productive work. We pass him by because he is independent, self-supporting, and asks no favors. He does not appeal to the emotions or excite the sentiments. He only wants to make a contract and fulfill it, with respect on both sides and favor on neither side. He must get his living out of the capital of the country. The larger the capital is, the better living he can get. Every particle of capital which is wasted on the vicious, the idle, and the shiftless is so much taken from the capital available to reward the independent and productive laborer. But we stand with our backs to the independent and productive laborer all the time. We do not remember him because he makes no clamor; but I appeal to you whether he is not the man who ought to be remembered first of all, and whether, on any sound social theory, we ought not to protect him against the burdens of the good-for-nothing. In these last years I have read hundreds of articles and heard scores of sermons and speeches which were really glorifications of the good-for-nothing, as if these were the charge of society, recommended by right reason to its care and protection. We are addressed all the time as if those who are respectable were to blame because some are not so, and as if there were an obligation on the part of those who have done their duty towards those who have not done their duty. Every man is bound to take care of himself and his family and to do his share of the work of society. It is totally false that one who has done so is bound to bear the care and charge of those who are wretched because they have not done so. The silly popular notion is that the beggars live at the expense of the rich, but the truth is that those who eat and produce not, live at the expense of those who labor and produce. The next time that you are tempted to subscribe a dollar to a charity, I do not tell you not to do it, because after you have fairly considered the matter, you may think it right to do it, but I do ask you to stop and remember the Forgotten Man and understand that if you put your dollar in the savings bank it will go to swell the capital of the country which is available for division amongst those who, while they earn it, will reproduce it with increase.

Let us now go on to another class of cases. There are a great many schemes brought forward for "improving the condition of the working classes." I have shown already that a free man cannot take a favor. One who takes a favor or submits to patronage demeans himself. He falls under obligation. He cannot be free and he cannot assert a station of equality with the man who confers the favor on him. The only exception is where there are exceptional bonds of affection or friendship, that is, where the sentimental relation supersedes the free relation. Therefore, in a country which is a free democracy, all propositions to do something for the working classes have an air of patronage and superiority which is impertinent and out of place. No one can do anything for anybody else unless he has a surplus of energy to dispose of after taking care of himself. In the United States, the working classes, technically so called, are the strongest classes. It is they who have a surplus to dispose of if anybody has. Why should anybody else offer to take care of them or to serve them? They can get whatever they think worth having and, at any rate, if they are free men in a free state, it is ignominious and unbecoming to introduce fashions of patronage and favoritism here. A man who, by superior education and experience of business, is in a position to advise a struggling man of the wages class, is certainly held to do so and will, I believe, always be willing and glad to do so; but this sort of activity lies in the range of private and personal relations.

I now, however, desire to direct attention to the public, general, and impersonal schemes, and I point out the fact that, if you undertake to lift anybody, you must have a fulcrum of point of resistance. All the elevation you give to one must be gained by an equivalent depression on some one else. The question of gain to society depends upon the balance of the account, as regards the position of the persons who undergo the respective operations. But nearly all the schemes for "improving the condition of the working man" involve an elevation of some working men at the expense of other working men. When you expend capital or labor to elevate some persons who come within the sphere of your influence, you interfere in the conditions of competition. The advantage of some is won by an equivalent loss of others. The difference is not brought about by the energy and effort of the persons themselves. If it were, there would be nothing to be said about it, for we constantly see people surpass others in the rivalry of life and carry off the prizes which the others must do without. In the cases I am discussing, the difference is brought about by an interference which must be partial, arbitrary, accidental, controlled by favoritism and personal preference. I do not say, in this case, either, that we ought to do no work of this kind. On the contrary, I believe that the arguments for it quite outweigh, in many cases, the arguments against it. What I desire, again, is to bring out the forgotten element which we always need to remember in order to make a wise decision as to any scheme of this kind. I want to call to mind the Forgotten Man, because, in this case also, if we recall him and go to look for him, we shall find him patiently and perseveringly, manfully and independently struggling against adverse circumstances without complaining or begging. If, then, we are led to heed the groaning and complaining of others and to take measures for helping these others, we shall, before we know it, push down this man who is trying to help himself.

Let us take another class of cases. So far we have said nothing about the abuse of legislation. We all seem to be under the delusion that the rich pay the taxes. Taxes are not thrown upon the consumers with any such directness and completeness as is sometimes assumed; but that, in ordinary states of the market, taxes on houses fall, for the most part, on the tenants and that taxes on commodities fall, for the most part, on the consumers, is beyond question. Now the state and municipality go to great expense to support policemen and sheriffs and judicial officers, to protect people against themselves, that is, against the results of their own folly, vice, and recklessness. Who pays for it? Undoubtedly the people who have not been guilty of folly, vice, or recklessness. Out of nothing comes nothing. We cannot collect taxes from people who produce nothing and save nothing. The people who have something to tax must be those who have produced and saved.

When you see a drunkard in the gutter, you are disgusted, but you pity him. When a policeman comes and picks him up you are satisfied. You say that "society" has interfered to save the drunkard from perishing. Society is a fine word, and it saves us the trouble of thinking to say that society acts. The truth is that the policeman is paid by somebody, and when we talk about society we forget who it is that pays. It is the Forgotten Man again. It is the industrious workman going home from a hard day's work, whom you pass without noticing, who is mulcted of a percentage of his day's earnings to hire a policeman to save the drunkard from himself. All the public expenditure to prevent vice has the same effect. Vice is its own curse. If we let nature alone, she cures vice by the most frightful penalties. It may shock you to hear me say it, but when you get over the shock, it will do you good to think of it: a drunkard in the gutter is just where he ought to be. Nature is working away at him to get him out of the way, just as she sets up her processes of dissolution to remove whatever is a failure in its line. Gambling and less mentionable vices all cure themselves by the ruin and dissolution of their victims. Nine-tenths of our measures for preventing vice are really protective towards it, because they ward off the penalty. "Ward off," I say, and that is the usual way of looking at it; but is the penalty really annihilated? By no means. It is turned into police and court expenses and spread over those who have resisted vice. It is the Forgotten Man again who has been subjected to the penalty while our minds were full of the drunkards, spendthrifts, gamblers, and other victims of dissipation. Who is, then, the Forgotten Man? He is the clean, quiet, virtuous, domestic citizen, who pays his debts and his taxes and is never heard of out of his little circle. Yet who is there in the society of a civilized state who deserves to be remembered and considered by the legislator and statesman before this man?

Another class of cases is closely connected with this last. There is an apparently invincible prejudice in people's minds in favor of state regulation. All experience is against state regulation and in favor of liberty. The freer the civil institutions are, the more weak or mischievous state regulation is. The Prussian bureaucracy can do a score of things for the citizen which no governmental organ in the United States can do; and, conversely, if we want to be taken care of as Prussians and Frenchmen are, we must give up something of our personal liberty.

Now we have a great many well-intentioned people among us who believe that they are serving their country when they discuss plans for regulating the relations of employer and employee, or the sanitary regulations of dwellings, or the construction of factories, or the way to behave on Sunday, or what people ought not to eat or drink or smoke. All this is harmless enough and well enough as a basis of mutual encouragement and missionary enterprise, but it is almost always made a basis of legislation. The reformers want to get a majority, that is, to get the power of the state and so to make other people do what the reformers think it right and wise to do. A and B agree to spend Sunday in a certain way. They get a law passed to make C pass it in their way. They determine to be teetotallers and they get a law passed to make C be a teetotaller for the sake of D who is likely to drink too much. Factory acts for women and children are right because women and children are not on an equal footing with men and cannot, therefore, make contracts properly. Adult men, in a free state, must be left to make their own contracts and defend themselves. It will not do to say that some men are weak and unable to make contracts any better than women. Our civil institutions assume that all men are equal in political capacity and all are given equal measure of political power and right, which is not the case with women and children. If, then, we measure political rights by one theory and social responsibilities by another, we produce an immoral and vicious relation. A and B, however, get factory acts and other acts passed regulating the relation of employers and employee and set armies of commissioners and inspectors traveling about to see to things, instead of using their efforts, if any are needed, to lead the free men to make their own conditions as to what kind of factory buildings they will work in, how many hours they will work, what they will do on Sunday and so on. The consequence is that men lose the true education in freedom which is needed to support free institutions. They are taught to rely on government officers and inspectors. The whole system of government inspectors is corrupting to free institutions. In England, the liberals used always to regard state regulation with suspicion, but since they have come into power, they plainly believe that state regulation is a good thing—if *they* regulate—because, of course, they want to bring about good things. In this country each party takes turns, according as it is in or out, in supporting or denouncing the non-interference theory.

Now, if we have state regulation, what is always forgotten is this: Who pays for it? Who is the victim of it? There always is a victim. The workmen who do not defend themselves have to pay for the inspectors who defend them. The whole system of social regulation by boards, commissioners, and inspectors consists in relieving negligent people of the consequences of their negligence and so leaving them to continue negligent without cor-rection. That system also turns away from the agencies which are close, direct, and germane to the purpose, and seeks others. Now, if you relieve negligent people of the consequences of their negligence, you can only throw those consequences on the people who have not been negligent. If you turn away from the agencies which are direct and cognate to the purpose, you can only employ other agencies. Here, then, you have your Forgotten Man again. The man who has been careful and prudent and who wants to go on and reap his advantages for himself and his children is arrested just at that point, and he is told that he must go and take care of some negligent employees in a factory or on a railroad who have not provided precautions for themselves or have not forced their employers to provide precautions, or negligent tenants who have not taken care of their own sanitary arrangements, or negligent householders who have not pro-vided against fire, or negligent parents who have not sent their children to school. If the Forgotten Man does not go, he must hire an inspector to go. No doubt it is often worth his while to go or send, rather than leave the thing undone, on account of his remoter interest; but what I want to show is that all this is unjust to the Forgotten Man, and that the re-formers and philosophers miss the point entirely when they preach that it is his duty to do all this work. Let them preach to the negligent to learn to take care of themselves. Whenever A and B put their heads together and decide what A, B and C must do for D, there is never any pressure on A and B. They consent to it and like it. There is rarely any pressure on D because he does not like it and contrives to evade it. The pressure all comes on C. Now, who is C? He is always the man who, if let alone, would make a reasonable use of his liberty without abusing it. He would not constitute any social problem at all and would not need any regulation. He is the Forgotten Man again, and as soon as he is brought from his obscurity you see that he is just that one amongst us who is what we all ought to be.

[Through a series of examples, Sumner goes on to decry claims to preferential treatment for various social and economic groups, all of which impose an unjust burden upon the Forgotten Man.]

. . . .

It is plain enough that the Forgotten Man and the Forgotten Woman are the very life and substance of society. They are the ones who ought to be first and always remembered. They are always forgotten by sentimental-

ists, philanthropists, reformers, enthusiasts, and every description of speculator in sociology, political economy, or political science. If a student of
any of these sciences ever comes to understand the position of the Forgotten Man and to appreciate his true value, you will find such student
an uncompromising advocate of the strictest scientific thinking on all social
topics, and a cold and hard-hearted skeptic towards all artificial schemes of
social amelioration. If it is desired to bring about social improvements,
bring us a scheme for relieving the Forgotten Man of some of his burdens.
He is our productive force which we are wasting. Let us stop wasting his
force. Then we shall have a clean and simple gain for the whole society.
The Forgotten Man is weighted down with the cost and burden of the
schemes for making everybody happy, with the cost of public beneficence,
with the support of all the loafers, with the loss of all the economic quackery,
with the cost of all the jobs. Let us remember him a little while. Let us
take some of the burdens off him. Let us turn our pity on him instead of
on the good-for-nothing. It will be only justice to him, and society will
greatly gain by it. Why should we not also have the satisfaction of thinking
and caring for a little while about the clean, honest, industrious, independent,
self-supporting men and women who have not inherited much to make life
luxurious for them, but who are doing what they can to get on in the
world without begging from anybody, especially since all they want is
to be let alone, with good friendship and honest respect? Certainly the
philanthropists and sentimentalists have kept our attention for a long time
on the nasty, shiftless, criminal, whining, crawling, and good-for-nothing
people, as if they alone deserved our attention.

The Forgotten Man is never a pauper. He almost always has a little
capital because it belongs to the character of the man to save something. He
never has more than a little. He is, therefore, poor in the popular sense,
although in the correct sense he is not so. I have said already that if you
learn to look for the Forgotten Man and to care for him, you will be very
skeptical toward all philanthropic and humanitarian schemes. It is clear
now that the interest of the Forgotten Man and the interest of "the poor,"
"the weak," and the other petted classes are in antagonism. In fact, the
warning to you to look for the Forgotten Man comes the minute that
the orator or writer begins to talk about the poor man. That minute the
Forgotten Man is in danger of a new assault, and if you intend to meddle
in the matter at all, then is the minute for you to look about for him and
to give him your aid. Hence, if you care for the Forgotten Man, you will
be sure to be charged with *not* caring for the poor. Whatever you do for
any of the petted classes wastes capital. If you do anything for the Forgotten
Man, you must secure him his earnings and savings, that is, you legislate
for the security of capital and for its free employment; you must oppose

paper money, wildcat banking and usury laws and you must maintain the inviolability of contracts. Hence you must be prepared to be told that you favor the capitalist class, the enemy of the poor man.

What the Forgotten Man really wants is true liberty. Most of his wrongs and woes come from the fact that there are yet mixed together in our institutions the old mediaeval theories of protection and personal dependence and the modern theories of independence and individual liberty. The consequence is that the people who are clever enough to get into positions of control, measure their own rights by the paternal theory and their own duties by the theory of independent liberty. It follows that the Forgotten Man, who is hard at work at home, has to pay both ways. His rights are measured by the theory of liberty, that is, he has only such as he can conquer. His duties are measured by the paternal theory, that is, he must discharge all which are laid upon him, as is always the fortune of parents. People talk about the paternal theory of government as if it were a very simple thing. Analyze it, however, and you see that in every paternal relation there must be two parties, a parent and a child, and when you speak metaphorically, it makes all the difference in the world who is parent and who is child. Now, since we, the people, are the state, whenever there is any work to be done or expense to be paid, and since the petted classes and the criminals and the jobbers cost and do not pay, it is they who are in the position of the child, and it is the Forgotten Man who is the parent. What the Forgotten Man needs, therefore, is that we come to a clearer understanding of liberty and to a more complete realization of it. Every step which we win in liberty will set the Forgotten Man free from some of his burdens and allow him to use his powers for himself and for the commonwealth.

The Crime of Poverty

HENRY GEORGE

Born, Philadelphia, Pennsylvania, September 2, 1839; died, New York City, October 29, 1897. Attended public school in Philadelphia. Went to California, 1858, and ultimately became a newspaperman. Wrote Our Land and Land Policy, *1871, which he expanded into* Progress and Poverty, *1879. Campaigned for single tax, free trade, and assorted causes. Ran unsuccessfully in 1886 as liberal and labor candidate for mayor of New York City. He died while again campaigning for that office in 1897.*

*L*adies and Gentlemen: I propose to talk to you to-night of the Crime of Poverty. I cannot, in a short time, hope to convince you of much; but the thing of things I should like to show you is that poverty is a crime. I do not mean that it is a crime to be poor. Murder is a crime; but it is not a crime to be murdered; and a man who is in poverty, I look upon not as a criminal in himself so much as the victim of a crime for which others, as well, perhaps, as himself, are responsible. That poverty is a curse, the bitterest of curses, we all know. Carlyle was right when he said that the hell of which Englishmen were most afraid was the hell of poverty; and this is true, not of Englishmen alone, but of people all over the civilized world, no matter what their nationality. It is to escape this hell that we strive and strain and struggle; and work on oftentimes in blind habit long after the necessity for work is gone.

The curse born of poverty is not confined to the poor alone; it runs through all classes, even to the very rich. They, too, suffer; they must suffer; for there

Opera House, Burlington, Iowa, April, 1885, under the auspices of Burlington Assembly, No. 3135, Knights of Labor, which afterwards distributed 50,000 copies of the speech. Henry George, *The Crime of Poverty* (Cincinnati: The Joseph Fels Fund of America, n.d.), pp. 5–39. Complete text also in Henry George, *Our Land and Land Policy* (New York: Doubleday, Page & Company, 1904), pp. 187–218.

cannot be suffering in a community from which any class can totally escape. The vice, the crime, the ignorance, the meanness, born of poverty, poison, so to speak, the very air which rich and poor alike must breathe.

I walked down one of your streets this morning, and I saw three men going along with their hands chained together. I knew for certain that those men were not rich men; and, although I do not know the offense for which they were carried in chains through your streets, this, I think, I can safely say, that, if you trace it up you will find it in some way to spring from poverty. Nine-tenths of human misery, I think you will find, if you look, to be due to poverty. If a man chooses to be poor, he commits no crime in being poor, provided his poverty hurts no one but himself. If a man has others dependent upon him; if there are a wife and children whom it is his duty to support, then, if he voluntarily chooses poverty, it is a crime—aye, and I think that, in most cases, the men who have no one to support but themselves are men that are shirking their duty. A woman comes into the world for every man; and for every man who lives a single life, caring only for himself, there is some woman who is deprived of her natural supporter. But while a man who chooses to be poor cannot be charged with crime, it is certainly a crime to force poverty on others. And it seems to me clear that the great majority of those who suffer from poverty are poor not from their own particular faults, but because of conditions imposed by society at large. Therefore, I hold that poverty is a crime—not an individual crime, but a social crime; a crime for which we all, poor as well as rich, are responsible.

Two or three weeks ago I went one Sunday evening to the church of a famous Brooklyn preacher. Mr. Sankey was singing, and something like a revival was going on there. The clergyman told some anecdotes connected with the revival, and recounted some of the reasons why men failed to become Christians. One case he mentioned struck me. He said he had noticed on the outskirts of the congregation, night after night, a man who listened intently, and who gradually moved forward. One night, the clergyman said, he went to him, saying, "My brother, are you not ready to become a Christian?" The man said, no he was not. He said it, not in a defiant tone, but in a sorrowful tone. The clergyman asked him why, whether he did not believe in the truths he had been hearing? Yes, he believed them all. Why, then, wouldn't he become a Christian? "Well," he said, "I can't join the church without giving up my business; and it is necessary for the support of my wife and children. If I give that up, I don't know how in the world I can get along. I had a hard time before I found my present business, and I cannot afford to give it up. Yet, I can't become a Christian without giving it up." The clergyman asked, "Are you a rum-seller?" No, he was not a rum-seller. Well, the clergyman said, he didn't know what in the world the man could be; it seemed to him that a rum-seller was the only man who does a business that would prevent his becoming a Christian; and he finally said, "What is your business?" The man said, "I sell soap." "Soap!" exclaimed the clergyman, "you sell soap? How in the world does that prevent you becoming a Christian?" "Well," the man said, "it is this way; the soap I sell is one of these patent soaps that are extensively advertised as enabling you to clean clothes very quickly; as containing no deleterious compound whatever. Every cake of the soap I sell is wrapped in a paper on which is printed a statement that it contains no injurious chemicals, whereas the truth of the matter is that it does, and that though it will take the dirt out of the clothes pretty quickly, it will, in a little while, rot them completely out. I have to make my living in this way; and I cannot feel that I can become a Christian if I sell that soap." The minister went on, describing how he labored unsuccessfully with that man, and finally wound up by saying, "He stuck to his soap, and lost his soul."

But, if that man lost his soul, was it his fault alone? Whose fault is it that social conditions are such that men have to make that terrible choice between what conscience tells them is right, and the necessity of earning a living? I hold that it is the fault of society; that it is the fault of us all. Pestilence is a curse. The man who would bring cholera to this country, or the man who, having the power to prevent its coming here, would make no effort to do so, would be guilty of a crime. Poverty is worse than cholera; poverty kills more people than pestilence, even in the best of times. Look at the death statistics of our cities; see where the deaths come quickest; see where it is that little children die like flies—it is in the poorer quarters. And the man who looks with careless eyes upon the ravages of this pestilence, the man who does not set himself to stay and eradicate it, he, I say, is guilty of a crime.

If poverty is appointed by the power which is above us all, then it is no crime; but if poverty is unnecessary, then it is a crime for which society is responsible, and for which society must suffer.

I hold, and I think no one who looks at the facts can fail to see, that poverty is utterly unnecessary. It is not by the decree of the Almighty, but it is because of our own injustice, our own selfishness, our own ignorance, that this scourge, worse than any pestilence, ravages our civilization, bringing want and suffering and degradation, destroying souls as well as bodies. Look over the world, in this hey-day of nineteenth century civilization. In every civilized country under the sun you will find men and women whose condition is worse than that of the savage; men and women and little children with whom the veriest savage could not afford to exchange. Even in this new city of yours, with virgin soil around you, you have had this winter to institute a relief society. Your roads have been filled with tramps, fifteen, I am told, at one time taking shelter in a round-house here. As here, so everywhere, and poverty is deepest where wealth most abounds.

What more unnatural than this? There is nothing in nature like this poverty which today curses us. We see rapine in nature; we see one species destoying another; but as a general thing animals do not feed on their own kind; and, wherever we see one kind enjoying plenty, all individuals of that kind share it. No man, I think, ever saw a herd of buffalo, of which a few were fat and the great majority lean. No man ever saw a flock of birds, of which two or three were swimming in grease, and the others all skin and bone. Nor in savage life is there anything like the poverty that festers in our civilization.

In a rude state of society there are seasons of want, seasons when people starve; but they are seasons when the earth has refused to yield her increase, when the rain has not fallen from the heavens, or when the land has been swept by some foe—not when there is plenty; and yet the peculiar character-istic of this modern poverty of ours is, that it is deepest where wealth most abounds.

Why, today, while over the civilized world there is so much distress, so much want? What is the cry that goes up? What is the current explanation of the hard times? Over-production! There are so many clothes that men must go ragged; so much coal that in the bitter winters people have to shiver; such over-filled granaries that people actually die by starvation! Want due to over-production! Was a greater absurdity ever uttered? How can there be over-production till all have enough? It is not over-production; it is unjust distribution.

Poverty necessary! Why, think of the enormous powers that are latent in the human brain! Think how invention enables us to do with the power of one man, what not long ago could not be done by the power of a thousand. Think that in England alone, the steam machinery in operation is said to exert a productive force greater than the physical force of the population of the world, were they all adults. And yet we have only begun to invent and discover. We have not yet utilized all that has already been invented and discovered. And look at the powers of the earth. They have hardly been touched. In every direction as we look, new resources seem to open. Man's ability to produce wealth seems almost infinite—we can set no bounds to it. Look at the power that is flowing by your city in the current of the Mississippi that might be set at work for you. So in every direction energy that we might utilize goes to waste; resources that we might draw upon are untouched. Yet men are delving and straining to satisfy mere animal wants; women are working, working, working their lives away, and too frequently turning in despair from that hard struggle to cast away all that makes the charm of woman.

. . . .

There is a cause for this poverty, and if you trace it down, you will find its root in a primary injustice. Look over the world today—poverty everywhere. The cause must be a common one. You cannot attribute it to the tariff, or to the form of government, or to this thing or to that in which nations differ; because, as deep poverty is common to them all, the cause that produces it must be a common cause. What is that common cause? There is one sufficient cause that is common to all nations; and that is, the appropriation as the property of some, of that natural element on which and from which, all must live.

Take that fact I have spoken of, that appalling fact that, even now, it is harder to live than it was in the ages dark and rude five centuries ago— how do you explain it? There is no difficulty in finding the cause. Whoever reads the history of England, or the history of any other civilized nation (but I speak of the history of England because that is the history with which we are best acquainted) will see the reason. For century after century a Parliament composed of aristocrats and employers passed laws endeavoring to reduce wages, but in vain. Men could not be crowded down to wages that gave a mere living because the bounty of nature was not wholly shut up from them; because some remains of the recognition of the truth that all men have equal rights on the earth still existed; because the land of that country, that which was held in private possession, was only held on a tenure derived from the nation, and for a rent payable back to the nation. The church lands supported the expenses of public worship, of the maintenance of seminaries, and the care of the poor; the crown lands defrayed the expenses of the civil list; and from a third portion of the lands, those held under military tenures, the army was provided for. There was no national debt in England at that time. They carried on wars for hundreds of years, but at the charge of the landowners. And, more important still, there remained everywhere, and you can see in every old English town their traces to this day, the common lands to which any of the neighborhood was free. It was as those lands were enclosed; it was as the commons were gradually monopolized, as the church lands were made the prey of greedy courtiers, as the crown lands were given away as absolute property to the favorites of the king, as the military tenants shirked their rents, and laid the expenses they had agreed to defray upon the nation in taxation, that bore upon industry and upon thrift—it was then that poverty began to deepen, and the tramp appeared in England, just as today he is appearing in our new States.

Now, think of it—is not land monopolization a sufficient reason for poverty? What is man? In the first place, he is an animal, a land animal, who cannot live without land. All that man produces comes from land; all productive labor in the final analysis consists in working up land; or materials are drawn from land into such forms as fit them for the satisfaction of human wants and desires. Why, man's very body is drawn from the land. Children of the soil, we come from the land, and to the land we must return. Take away from man all that belongs to the land, and what have you but a disembodied spirit? Therefore, he who holds the land on which and from which another man must live, is that man's master; and the man is his slave. The man who holds the land on which I must live can command me to life or to death just as absolutely as though I were his chattel. Talk about abolishing slavery—we have not abolished slavery—we have only abolished one rude form of it, chattel slavery. There is a deeper and more insidious form, a more cursed form yet before us to abolish, in this industrial slavery that makes a man a virtual slave, while taunting him and mocking him with the name of freedom. Poverty! want! they will sting as much as the lash. Slavery! God knows there are horrors enough in slavery; but there are deeper horrors in our civilized society today. Bad as chattel slavery was, it did not drive slave mothers to kill their children, yet you may read in official reports that the system of child insurance, which has taken root so strongly in England, and which is now spreading over our Eastern States, has perceptibly and largely increased the rate of child mortality!— What does that mean?

Robinson Crusoe, as you know, when he rescued Friday from the cannibals, made him his slave. Friday had to serve Crusoe. But, supposing Crusoe had said, "Oh, man and brother, I am very glad to see you, and I welcome you to this island, and you shall be a free and independent citizen, with just as much to say as I have—except that this island is mine—and, of course, as I can do as I please with my own property, you must not use it save upon my terms." Friday would have been just as much Crusoe's slave as though he had called him one. Friday was not a fish, he could not swim off through the sea; he was not a bird, and could not fly off through the air; if he lived at all, he had to live on that island. And if that island was Crusoe's, Crusoe was his master through life to death.

. . . .

This land question is the bottom question. Man is a land animal. Suppose you want to build a house; can you build it without a place to put it? What is it built of? Stone, or mortar, or wood, or iron—they all come from the earth. Think of any article of wealth you choose, any of those things which men struggle for, where do they come from? From the land. It is the bottom question.

The land question is simply the labor question; and when some men own that element from which all wealth must be drawn, and upon which all must live, then they have the power of living without work, and, therefore, those who do work get less of the products of work.

Did you ever think of the utter absurdity and strangeness of the fact that, all over the civilized world, the working classes are the poor classes? Go into any city in the world, and get into a cab, and ask the man to drive you to where the working people live; he won't take you to where the fine houses are; he will take you, on the contrary, into the squalid quarters, the poorer quarters. Did you ever think how curious that is? Think for a moment how it would strike a rational being who had never been on the earth before, if such an intelligence could come down, and you were to explain to him how we live on earth, how houses, and food and clothing, and all the many things we need, are all produced by work, would he not think that the working people would be the people who lived in the finest houses and had most of everything that work produces? Yet, whether you took him to London or Paris, or New York, or even to Burlington, he would find that those called working people were the people who lived in the poorest houses.

All this is strange—just think of it. We naturally despise poverty; and it is reasonable that we should. I do not say—I distinctly repudiate it— that the people who are poor are poor always from their own fault, or even in most cases; but it ought to be so. If any good man or woman had the power to create a world, it would be a sort of a world in which no one would be poor unless he was lazy or vicious. But that is just precisely the kind of a world that this is; that is just precisely the kind of a world that the Creator has made. Nature gives to labor, and to labor alone; there must be human work before any article of wealth can be produced; and, in a natural state of things, the man who toiled honestly and well would be the rich man, and he who did not work would be poor. We have so reversed the order of nature, that we are accustomed to think of a workingman as a poor man.

And if you trace it out I believe you will see that the primary cause of this is that we compel those who work to pay others for permission to do so. You buy a coat, a horse, a house; there you are paying the seller for labor exerted, for something that he has produced, or that he has got from the man who did produce it; but when you pay a man for land, what are you paying him for? You pay him for something that no man produced; you pay him for something that was here before man was, or for a value that was created, not by him individually, but by the community of which you are a part. What is the reason that the land here, where we stand tonight, is worth more than it was twenty-five years ago? What is the reason that land in the center of New York, that once could be bought by the mile for a jug of whiskey, is now worth so much that, though you were to cover it with gold, you would not have its value? Is it not because of the increase of population? Take away that population, and where would the value of the land be? Look at it in any way you please.

We talk about over-production. How can there be such a thing as over-production while people want? All these things that are said to be over-produced are desired by many people. Why do they not get them? They do not get them because they have not the means to buy them; not that they do not want them. Why have they not the means to buy them? They earn too little. When great masses of men have to work for an average of $1.40 a day, it is no wonder that great quantities of goods cannot be sold.

Now, why is it that men have to work for such low wages? Because, if they were to demand higher wages, there are plenty of unemployed men ready to step into their places. It is this mass of unemployed men who compel that fierce competition that drives wages down to the point of bare subsistence. Why is it that there are men who cannot get employment? Did you ever think what a strange thing it is that men cannot find employment? Adam had no difficulty in finding employment; neither had Robinson Crusoe; the finding of employment was the last thing that troubled them.

If men cannot find an employer, why can they not employ themselves? Simply because they are shut out from the element on which human labor can alone be exerted; men are compelled to compete with each other for the wages of an employer, because they have been robbed of the natural opportunities of employing themselves; because they cannot find a piece of God's world on which to work without paying some other human creature for the privilege.

I do not mean to say that, even after you had set right this fundamental injustice, there would not be many things to do; but this I do mean to say, that our treatment of land lies at the bottom of all social questions. This I do mean to say, that, do what you please, reform as you may, you never can get rid of widespread poverty so long as the element on which, and from which, all men must live is made the private property of some men. It is utterly impossible. Reform government—get taxes down to the minimum —build railways; institute coöperative stores; divide profits, if you choose, between employers and employed—and what will be the result? The result will be that land will increase in value—that will be the result—that and nothing else. Experience shows this. Do not all improvements simply increase the value of land—the price that some must pay others for the privilege of living?

Consider the matter. I say it with all reverence, and merely say it because I wish to impress a truth upon your minds—it is utterly impossible, so long as His laws are what they are, that God Himself could relieve poverty— utterly impossible. Think of it, and you will see. Men pray to the Almighty to relieve poverty. But poverty comes not from God's laws—it is blasphemy of the worst kind to say that; it comes from man's injustice to his fellows. Supposing the Almighty were to hear the prayer, how could He carry out the request, so long as His laws are what they are? Consider—the Almighty gives us nothing of the things that constitute wealth; He merely gives us the raw material, which must be utilized by man to produce wealth. Does He not give us enough of that now? How could He relieve poverty even if He were to give us more? Supposing, in answer to these prayers, He were to increase the power of the sun, or the virtues of the soil? Supposing He were to make plants more prolific, or animals to produce after their kind more abundantly? Who would get the benefit of it? Take a country where land is completely monopolized, as it is in most of the civilized countries— who would get the benefit of it? Simply the landowners. And even if God, in answer to prayer, were to send down out of the heavens those things that men require, who would get the benefit?

In the Old Testament we are told that, when the Israelites journeyed through the desert, they were hungered, and that God sent down out of the heavens—manna. There was enough for all of them, and they all took it and were relieved. But, supposing that desert had been held as private property, as the soil of Great Britain is held; as the soil even of our new States is being held. Supposing that one of the Israelites had a square mile, and another one had twenty square miles, and another one had a hundred square miles, and the great majority of the Israelites did not have enough to set the soles of their feet upon, which they could call their own—what would become of the manna? What good would it have done to the majority? Not a whit. Though God had sent down manna enough for all, that manna would have been the property of the landholders; they would have employed some of the others, perhaps, to gather it up in heaps for them, and would have sold it to the hungry brethren. Consider it: this purchase and sale of manna might have gone on until the majority of the Israelites had given up all they had, even to the clothes off their backs. What then? Well, then they would not have had anything left with which to buy manna, and the consequence would have been that while they went hungry the manna would be lying in great heaps, and the landowners would be complaining about the over-production of manna. There would have been a great harvest of manna and hungry people, just precisely the phenomenon that we see today.

I cannot go over all the points I would like to; but I wish to call your attention to the utter absurdity of private property in land! Why, consider it—the idea of a man selling the earth—the earth, our common mother. A man selling that which no man produced. A man passing title from one generation to another. Why, it is the most absurd thing in the world. Did you ever think of this? What right has a dead man to land? For whom was this earth created? It was created for the living, certainly not for the dead. Well, now, we treat it as though it was created for the dead. Where do our land titles come from? They come from men who, for the most part, have passed and gone. Here, in this new country, you get a little nearer the original source; but go to the Eastern States, and go over the Atlantic. There you may clearly see the power that comes from land ownership.

. . . .

What is the reason for this overcrowding of cities? There is no natural reason. Take New York, one-half of its area is not built upon. Why, then, must people crowd together as they do there? Simply because of private ownership of land. There is plenty of room to build houses, and plenty of people who want to build houses, but before anybody can build a house a blackmail price must be paid to some dog-in-the-manger. It costs, in many cases, more to get vacant ground upon which to build a house than it does to build the house. And then what happens to the man who pays this blackmail and builds a house? Down comes the tax-gatherer and fines him for building the house.

It is so all over the United States—the men who improve, the men who turn the prairie into farms, and the desert into gardens, the men who beautify your cities, are taxed and fined for having done these things. Now, nothing is clearer than that the people of New York want more houses; and I think that even here in Burlington you could get along with more houses. Why, then, should you fine a man that builds one? Look all over this country—the bulk of the taxation rests upon the improver; the man who puts up a building or establishes a factory, or cultivates a farm, he is taxed for it; and not merely taxed for it, but I think, in nine cases out of ten, the land which he uses, the bare land, is taxed more than the adjoining lot, or the adjoining 160 acres that some speculator is holding as a mere dog-in-the-manger, not using it himself, and not allowing anybody else to use it.

I am talking too long; but let me, in a few words, point out the way of getting rid of land monopoly, securing the right of all to the elements which are necessary for life. We could not divide the land. In a rude state of society, as among the ancient Hebrews, giving each family its lot, and making it inalienable, we might secure something like equality. But in a complex civilization that will not suffice. It is not, however, necessary to divide up the land. All that is necessary is to divide up the income that comes from the land. In that way we can secure absolute equality; nor could the adoption of this principle involve any rude shock or violent change. It can be brought about gradually and easily by abolishing the taxes that now rest upon capital, labor, and improvements, and raising all our public revenues by the taxation of land values; and the longer you think of it the clearer you will see that in every possible way it will be a benefit.

Now, supposing we should abolish all other taxes, direct and indirect, substituting for them a tax upon land values, what would be the effect? In the first place, it would be to kill speculative values. It would be to remove from the newer parts of the country the bulk of the taxation, and put it on the richer parts. It would be to exempt the pioneer from taxation, and make the larger cities pay more of it. It would be to relieve energy and enterprise, capital and labor, from all those burdens that now bear upon them. What a start that would give to production! In the second place, we could, from the value of land, not merely pay all the present expenses of government, but we could do infinitely more. In the city of San Francisco, James Lick left a few blocks of ground to be used for public purposes there, and the rent amounts to so much, that out of it will be built the largest telescope in the world, large public baths, and other public buildings, and various costly monuments. If, instead of these few blocks, the whole value of the land upon which the city is built had accrued to San Francisco, what could she not do?

So in this little town, where land values are very low as compared with such cities as Chicago and San Francisco, you could do many things for mutual benefit and public improvement did you appropriate to public purposes the land values that now go to individuals. You could have a great free library; you could have an art gallery; you could get yourselves a public park, a magnificent public park, too. You have here one of the finest natural sites for a beautiful town that I know of, and I have traveled much. You might make on this site a city that it would be a pleasure to live in. You will not, as you go now—oh! no! Why, the very fact that you have a magnificent view here will cause somebody to hold on all the more tightly to the land that commands this view, and charge higher prices for it. The State of New York wants to buy a strip of land so as to enable the people to see the Niagara, but what a price she must pay for it. Look at all the great cities; in Philadelphia, for instance, in order to build their great city hall they had to block up the only two wide streets they had in the city. Everywhere you go you may see how private property in land prevents public as well as private improvement.

But I have no time to enter further into details. I can only ask you to think upon this thing, and the more you will see its desirability. As an English friend of mine puts it, "No taxes and a pension for everybody;" and why should it not be? To take land values for public purposes is not really to impose a tax, but to take for public purposes a value created by the community. And out of the fund which would thus accrue from the common property, we might, without degradation to anybody, provide enough to actually secure from want all who were deprived of their natural protectors, or met with accident; or any man who should grow so old that he could not work. All prating that is heard from some quarters about its hurting the common people to give them what they do not work for is humbug. The truth is, that anything that injures self-respect, degrades, does harm; but if you give it as a right, as something to which every citizen is entitled, it does not degrade. Charity schools do degrade the children that are sent to them, but public schools do not.

But all such benefits as these, while great, would be incidental. The great thing would be that the reform I propose would tend to open opportunities to labor and enable men to provide employment for themselves. That is the great advantage. We should gain the enormous productive power that is going to waste all over the country, the power of idle hands that would gladly be at work. And that removed, then you would see wages begin to mount. It is not that everyone would turn farmer, or everyone build himself a house if he had an opportunity for doing so, but so many could, and would, as to relieve the pressure on the labor market and provide employment for all others. And as wages mounted to the higher levels then you would see the productive power increased. The country where wages are high is the country of greatest productive power. Where wages are highest there will invention be most active; there will labor be most intelligent; there will be the greatest yield for the expenditure of exertion. The more you think of it the more clearly you will see what I say is true. I cannot hope to convince you in talking for an hour or two, but I shall be content if I shall put you upon inquiry. Think for yourselves; ask yourselves whether this widespread fact of poverty is not a crime, and a crime for which everyone of us, man and woman, who does not do what he or she can do to call attention to it and to do away with it, is responsible.

THE GOSPEL OF WEALTH VS.
THE SOCIAL GOSPEL

IN JUNE, 1889, *the* North American Review *carried an article by Andrew Carnegie called "Wealth." At the promptings of Gladstone it was republished in England by the* Pall Mall Budget *and christened the "Gospel of Wealth."*[1] *In 1900 sundry Carnegie articles were republished in book form under the title* The Gospel of Wealth.

Carnegie, who had risen from bobbin boy to modern Croesus, was one of the most enlightened and certainly the most literate of the capitalist princes. Primitives such as Jim Fiske and Jay Gould were "grab and hold" barons, but Carnegie elevated the pursuit of wealth to the status of a social philosophy by coupling it to a doctrine of stewardship. His own philanthropies lent authority to his injunctions.

Carnegie's doctrine was well-timed. Like the mansions of millionaires, city slums and depressed farm areas were becoming uncomfortably conspicuous. Reformers roamed about, unsettling people with their insistent question as to how it was possible for personal acquisitiveness to result in the common good. In "Wealth" Carnegie acknowledged that the problem of the age was "to bind together the rich and poor in harmonious relationship." His answer, in part, was merely a restatement of folk philosophy composed of commonplace themes: Despite imperfections,

[1] Andrew Carnegie, *Autobiography* (Boston: Houghton Mifflin Company, 1920), footnote, p. 255.

ours is the best world yet; collectivist schemes are but the dreams of drones; the pillars of modern society are "Individualism, Private Property, the Law of Accumulation, and the Law of Competition." Carnegie went on, however, to urge the rich to practice unostentatious living and generous giving for civic purposes. They were to be cautious trustees of the poor, exercising care lest their charities encourage the drunkard in his drunkenness and the slothful in his sloth. A judicious administration of wealth would enable the rich and the poor to live in social harmony.

The metaphor "gospel of wealth" forced into alliance two traditionally alien interests, but its unintended irony escaped mammon-minded children of the Gilded Age. And well it might, for the churches themselves acceded to the established order either by maintaining a rigid posture of otherworldliness or by buttressing the values of middle and upper economic classes with the rationalizations of vulgarized Calvinism. The ultimate endorsement came from Bishop William Lawrence of Massachusetts, who insisted that in the long run wealth comes only to the moral man. "Godliness," he declared, "is in league with riches. . . . Material prosperity is helping to make the national character sweeter, more joyous, more unselfish, more Christlike."[2]

The new gospel's foremost evangelist was Russell Herman Conwell. Conwell was educated at Yale, served in the Union army, was businessman, reporter, and lawyer before he became a minister. While working the Lord's vineyard in Lexington, Massachusetts, he was beseeched to shore up a dwindling Baptist congregation in Philadelphia. The congregation could pay him a salary of only $800, so he made them a sporting proposition. Each time he doubled the membership, they would double his

[2] "The Relation of Wealth to Morals," *World's Work*, I (1901), pp. 286–292.

salary. *Unwittingly the congregation agreed, then cried
for renegotiation when Conwell speedily boosted his
salary to $10,000 annually. People flocked to hear him.
He built a huge modern Baptist Temple. For young men
eager to get ahead, he organized and taught night classes
—the beginnings of Temple University. While making a
dazzling local reputation during the eighties, the inde-
fatigable Conwell was building simultaneously a national
reputation as a lecturer.*

*Conwell was not a single speech man, yet he was best
known to his contemporaries, as he is best remembered
today, for his one lecture, "Acres of Diamonds." He delivered this speech over six thousand times to audiences
in America and abroad. Veterans of the Chautauqua
circuit called the lecture "Old Dependable," and noted
that it "was studied, analyzed, marked off into sections,
and its every element weighed and measured. The philosophy was imitated and its appeal duplicated in countless
orations that rang from coast to coast, from Mexico to
Canada."[3] Its Horatio Alger message of Upward and Onward inspired ambition in hundreds of thousands of
youths. "Acres of Diamonds" became so prized an article
in American life that a celebration was staged in Philadelphia in 1914 to honor Conwell's 5000th presentation.
Nine state governors joined in a national committee to
sponsor the event. Had Conwell chosen to retain his fees,
the lecture would easily have made him a millionaire.
But true to the "gospel," he spent the income subsidizing
the college education of young men.*

*The lecture was always narrative and anecdotal, always
opened with the same exotic master example that set the
theme, which was then amplified by a string of success
stories. Examples varied with the audience, and the
speech could be lengthened or shortened at will. But the*

[3] Victoria and Robert O. Case, *We Called It Culture* (Garden
City, New York: Doubleday & Company, Inc., 1948), pp. 62–63.

message never varied: "I say that you ought to get rich, and it is your duty to get rich." Critics asked Conwell, "Why don't you preach the gospel instead of preaching about man's making money?" He answered forthrightly: "Because to make money honestly is to preach the gospel." Conwell took pains to point out that money must be gained honestly or it would be a withering curse, and like Bishop Lawrence, he reassured his middle-class audiences on the inexorable connection between wealth and moral- ity: ". . . ninety-eight out of one-hundred of the rich men of America are honest. That is why they are rich." It was right to sympathize with the poor, "but the number of poor who are to be sympathized with is very small. To sympathize with a man whom God has punished for his sins, thus to help him when God would still continue a just punishment, is to do wrong. . . ." Having entered his caution, Conwell extolled wealth as power for good. Thus he fired the ambitions of those who still hoped for wealth and conferred the blessings of rectitude on those who possessed it. Although Conwell was not the theologian of the gospel of wealth, he was its most effective and durable circuit-rider.

In the early decades of the industrial revolution, ortho- dox churches gave tacit support to acquisitiveness by single-minded concentration upon rescuing souls from the fiery pits and readying them for eternal bliss. This world was but a prelude to the next, its trials and sorrows a proving ground. Insofar as orthodoxy spoke out on the here and now, it defended the emery wheel of competi- tion for honing character. Yet by the end of the century a counterrevolution called the Social Gospel penetrated almost every denomination and offered vigorous challenge to the gospel of wealth.

The Social Gospel movement was indigenous, largely Protestant, and reformist. As a movement it originated in the eighteen seventies and flourished vigorously in the

Progressive Era. Its American antecedents included the liberal doctrines and preachings of William Ellery Channing, Theodore Parker, Horace Bushnell, and others. It took root first among Unitarians, Congregationalists, and Episcopalians, but as the movement assumed an evangelistic character, it grew among Baptists, Methodists, and other denominations of this heritage.

The Social Gospel was a protest against social blight in an industrial age. It laid bare the growing irrelevance of churches to the life of the masses, and the palpable contradictions between the ethical teachings of Jesus and a society that was ruled by the harsh Spencerian doctrine of fang and claw. In their reconsideration of religion and society, Social Gospelers drew upon scriptural or Higher Criticism, scientific thought, sociology and economics, and the social critiques of secular reformers. Their achievements included an impressive body of criticism on the ethics and practices of unregulated capitalism; a searching critique of conventional Christianity; a revised theology that postulated the immanence of God, corporate as well as personal sin, and salvation as a stage in history rather than a stage beyond history; an active program of propaganda and reform.

Washington Gladden, commonly considered "the father" of the Social Gospel movement, typified widespread partiality among Social Gospelers for moderate and piecemeal reform. A Congregationalist minister in Columbus, Ohio, Gladden championed particularly the cause of labor at a time when conservative church publications were shocked by his theory that a company had an obligation to confer with employees on conditions of labor and wages. Gladden was enormously effective with practical reforms on many fronts while at the same time he pressed upon parishioners and the public the larger goal of a modified capitalism based on brotherhood.

The more radical wing of the Social Gospel movement was represented by George Davis Herron. An obscure

Congregational minister, he was catapulted into prominence by his lecture, "The Message of Jesus to Men of Wealth," given to the Minnesota Congregational Club in 1890. It was a sharp attack upon unlimited individualism and competition, self-interest and acquisitiveness. He challenged his audience to carry the Sermon on the Mount into the transactions of the market-place.

Herron's "Message of Jesus" foreshadowed and stimulated experiments in preaching applied Christianity. Out in Topeka, Kansas, the Reverend Charles M. Sheldon was groping for a means of heightening the impact of the Social Gospel message. In 1891 he began to experiment with serialized sermon stories that depicted the hopeless struggles of the disinherited. Departing from customary abstractions on social injustice, he dramatized its consequences in the lives of individuals. After delivering his sermon stories, Sheldon sought a wider audience by publishing them. His most successful work, In His Steps (1896), enjoyed a sensational sale. In it Sheldon urged each parishioner, when faced with a difficult decision between choices, to ask himself, "What would Jesus do?" The book recounts the revolutionary consequences in the lives of those who asked the question and then followed in His steps. In similar vein, though dealing in fact instead of fiction, William T. Stead, an English journalist, organized and spoke to a mass meeting on the question, "If Christ came to Chicago today, what would He think of it?" Stead made a shattering exposé of crime, poverty, drunkenness, prostitution, black lists, tax-dodging—a veritable decalogue of evil. He proposed that "a living faith in Citizen Christ would lead directly to the civic and social regeneration of Chicago."[4]

In addition to inspiring a pulpit, platform, and literary

---

[4] Ralph Gabriel, *The Course of American Democratic Thought* (New York: The Ronald Press Company, 1940), pp. 308–330; Charles H. Hopkins, *The Rise of the Social Gospel in American Protestantism* (New Haven: Yale University Press, 1940), pp. 140–148.

genre, Herron was swept up in a speaking campaign for social regeneration and reconstruction. During the eighteen-nineties, invitations poured in from everywhere. As he talked on, his views became more radical, controversy gathered around him, and many of his engagements ended in stormy encounters. Ultimately Herron rejected capitalism and espoused socialism as the Christian answer to the ills of the age, and in so doing isolated himself from the mainstream of Social Gospel thought and action.

Henry George, himself a religious man, charged that churches were in alliance with social injustice. Had he lived on into the twentieth centry, undoubtedly he would have withdrawn his stricture. In 1912 the Federal Council of Churches, an outgrowth of the Social Gospel, adopted a sixteen-point platform that exhibited social consciousness in every point.[5] Not only had Protestantism regained its relevance to the modern world, but the ideals and goals of Social Gospelers were fostered by Theodore Roosevelt, Woodrow Wilson, and a host of lesser liberals in the Progressive Era.

[5] *Ibid.,* pp. 316–317.

Acres of Diamonds

RUSSELL HERMAN CONWELL

Born, South Worthington, Massachusetts, February 15, 1843; died, Philadelphia, Pennsylvania, December 6, 1925. Educated at Wilbraham Academy and Yale. Officer in Union Army. Admitted to bar, 1865. Practiced law in Minneapolis and Boston. Served Minnesota as immigration agent in Germany. Founded the Daily Chronicle in Minneapolis. Ordained as Baptist minister, 1879. Held pastorates in Lexington, Massachusetts, and Philadelphia. Founder and first president of Temple University. Popular lecturer, preacher, essayist, and biographer.

W hen going down the Tigris and Euphrates rivers many years ago with a party of English travelers I found myself under the direction of an old Arab guide whom we hired up at Bagdad, and I have often thought how that guide resembled our barbers in certain mental characteristics. He thought that it was not only his duty to guide us down those rivers, and do what he was paid for doing, but also to entertain us with stories curious and weird, ancient and modern, strange and familiar. Many of them I have forgotten, and I am glad I have, but there is one I shall never forget.

The old guide was leading my camel by its halter along the banks of those ancient rivers, and he told me story after story until I grew weary of his story-telling and ceased to listen. I have never been irritated with that guide

Probably first delivered at Springfield, Massachusetts, 1870, at a reunion of Conwell's regiment. Condensed version first published as a text in Conwell's *Gleams of Grace* (1887), based on a presentation at the Amphitheatre, Chautauqua, New York, August 3, 1886. Text reproduced here (approximately the first half of the lecture) is from Russell H. Conwell, *Acres of Diamonds*, with biography by Robert Shackleton (New York: Harper & Brothers, 1915), pp. 3–59.

when he lost his temper as I ceased listening. But I remember that he took off his Turkish cap and swung it in a circle to get my attention. I could see it through the corner of my eye, but I determined not to look straight at him for fear he would tell another story. But although I am not a woman, I did finally look, and as soon as I did he went right into another story.

Said he, "I will tell you a story now which I reserve for my particular friends." When he emphasized the words "particular friends," I listened, and I have ever been glad I did. I really feel devoutly thankful, that there are 1,674 young men who have been carried through college by this lecture who are also glad that I did listen. The old guide told me that there once lived not far from the River Indus an ancient Persian by the name of Ali Hafed. He said that Ali Hafed owned a very large farm, that he had orchards, grain-fields, and gardens; that he had money at interest, and was a wealthy and contented man. He was contented because he was wealthy, and wealthy because he was contented. One day there visited that old Persian farmer one of those ancient Buddhist priests, one of the wise men of the East. He sat down by the fire and told the old farmer how this world of ours was made. He said that this world was once a mere bank of fog, and that the Almighty thrust His finger into this bank of fog, and began slowly to move His finger around, increasing the speed until at last He whirled this bank of fog into a solid ball of fire. Then it went rolling through the universe, burning its way through other banks of fog, and condensed the moisture without, until it fell in floods of rain upon its hot surface, and cooled the outward crust. Then the internal fires bursting outward through the crust threw up the mountains and hills, the valleys, the plains and prairies of this wonderful world of ours. If this internal molten mass came bursting out and cooled very quickly it became granite; less quickly cooper, less quickly silver, less quickly gold, and, after gold, diamonds were made.

Said the old priest, "A diamond is a congealed drop of sunlight." Now that is literally scientifically true, that a diamond is an actual deposit of carbon from the sun. The old priest told Ali Hafed that if he had one diamond the size of his thumb he could purchase the country, and if he had a mine of diamonds he could place his children upon thrones through the influence of their great wealth.

Ali Hafed heard all about diamonds, how much they were worth, and went to his bed that night a poor man. He had not lost anything, but he was poor because he was discontented, and discontented because he feared he was poor. He said, "I want a mine of diamonds," and he lay awake all night.

Early in the morning he sought out the priest. I know by experience that a priest is very cross when awakened early in the morning, and when he shook that old priest out of his dreams, Ali Hafed said to him:

"Will you tell me where I can find diamonds?"

"Diamonds! What do you want with diamonds?" "Why, I wish to be immensely rich." "Well, then, go along and find them. That is all you have to do; go and find them, and then you have them." "But I don't know where to go." "Well, if you will find a river that runs through white sands, between high mountains, in those white sands you will always find diamonds." "I don't believe there is any such river." "Oh yes, there are plenty of them. All you have to do is to go and find them, and then you have them." Said Ali Hafed, "I will go."

So he sold his farm, collected his money, left his family in charge of a neighbor, and away he went in search of diamonds. He began his search, very properly to my mind, at the Mountains of the Moon. Afterward he came around into Palestine, then wandered on into Europe, and at last when his money was all spent and he was in rags, wretchedness, and poverty, he stood on the shore of that bay at Barcelona, in Spain, when a great tidal wave came rolling in between the pillars of Hercules, and the poor, afflicted, suffering, dying man could not resist the awful temptation to cast himself into that incoming tide, and he sank beneath its foaming crest, never to rise in this life again.

When that old guide had told me that awfully sad story he stopped the camel I was riding on and went back to fix the baggage that was coming off another camel, and I had an opportunity to muse over his story while he was gone. I remember saying to myself, "Why did he reserve that story for his 'particular friends'?" There seemed to be no beginning, no middle, no end, nothing to it. That was the first story I had ever heard told in my life, and would be the first one I ever read, in which the hero was killed in the first chapter. I had but one chapter of that story, and the hero was dead.

When the guide came back and took up the halter of my camel, he went right ahead with the story, into the second chapter, just as though there had been no break. The man who purchased Ali Hafed's farm one day led his camel into the garden to drink, and as that camel put its nose into the shallow water of that garden brook, Ali Hafed's successor noticed a curious flash of light from the white sands of the stream. He pulled out a black stone having an eye of light reflecting all the hues of the rainbow. He took the pebble into the house and put it on the mantel which covers the central fires, and forgot all about it.

A few days later this same old priest came in to visit Ali Hafed's successor, and the moment he opened that drawing-room door he saw that flash of light on the mantel, and he rushed up to it, and shouted: "Here is a diamond! Has Ali Hafed returned?" "Oh no, Ali Hafed has not returned, and that is not a diamond. That is nothing but a stone we found right out here in our own garden." "But," said the priest, "I tell you I know a diamond when I see it. I know positively that is a diamond."

Then together they rushed out into that old garden and stirred up the white sands with their fingers, and lo! there came up other more beautiful and valuable gems than the first. "Thus," said the guide to me, and, friends, it is historically true, "was discovered the diamond-mine of Golconda, the most magnificent diamond-mine in all the history of mankind, excelling the Kimberly itself. The Kohinoor, and the Orloff of the crown jewels of England and Russia, the largest on earth, came from that mine."

When that old Arab guide told me the second chapter of his story, he then took off his Turkish cap and swung it around in the air again to get my attention to the moral. Those Arab guides have morals to their stories, although they are not always moral. As he swung his hat, he said to me, "Had Ali Hafed remained at home and dug in his own cellar, or underneath his own wheat-fields, or in his own garden, instead of wretchedness, starvation, and death by suicide in a strange land, he would have had 'acres of diamonds.' For every acre of that old farm, yes, every shovelful, afterward revealed gems which since have decorated the crowns of monarchs."

When he had added the moral to his story I saw why he reserved it for "his particular friends." But I did not tell him I could see it. It was that mean old Arab's way of going around a thing like a lawyer, to say indirectly what he did not dare say directly, that "in his private opinion there was a certain young man then traveling down the Tigris River that might better be at home in America." I did not tell him I could see that, but I told him his story reminded me of one, and I told it to him quick, and I think I will tell it to you.

I told him of a man out in California in 1847, who owned a ranch. He heard they had discovered gold in southern California, and so with a passion for gold he sold his ranch to Colonel Sutter, and away he went, never to come back. Colonel Sutter put a mill upon a stream that ran through that ranch, and one day his little girl brought some wet sand from the raceway into their home and sifted it through her fingers before the fire, and in that falling sand a visitor saw the first shining scales of real gold that were ever discovered in California. The man who had owned that ranch wanted gold, and he could have secured it for the mere taking. Indeed, thirty-eight millions of dollars has been taken out of a very few acres since then. About eight years ago I delivered this lecture in a city that stands on that farm, and they told me that a one-third owner for years and years had been getting one hundred and twenty dollars in gold every fifteen minutes, sleeping or waking, without taxation. You and I would enjoy an income like that—if we didn't have to pay an income tax.

But a better illustration really than that occurred here in our own Pennsylvania. If there is anything I enjoy above another on the platform, it is to get one of these German audiences in Pennsylvania before me, and fire that at them, and I enjoy it to-night. There was a man living in Pennsylvania, not unlike some Pennsylvanians you have seen, who owned a farm, and he did with that farm just what I should do with a farm if I owned one in Pennsylvania—he sold it. But before he sold it he decided to secure employment collecting coal-oil for his cousin, who was in the business in Canada, where they first discovered oil on this continent. They dipped it from the running streams at that early time. So this Pennsylvania farmer wrote to his cousin asking for employment. You see, friends, this farmer was not altogether a foolish man. No, he was not. He did not leave his farm until he had something else to do. *Of all the simpletons the stars shine on I don't know of a worse one than the man who leaves one job before he has gotten another.* That has especial reference to my profession, and has no reference whatever to a man seeking a divorce. When he wrote to his cousin for employment, his cousin replied, "I cannot engage you because you know nothing about the oil business."

Well, then the old farmer said, "I will know," and with most commendable zeal (characteristic of the students of Temple University) he set himself at the study of the whole subject. He began away back at the second day of God's creation when this world was covered thick and deep with that rich vegetation which since has turned to the primitive beds of coal. He studied the subject until he found that the drainings really of those rich beds of coal furnished the coal-oil that was worth pumping, and then he found how it came up with the living springs. He studied until he knew what it looked like, smelled like, tasted like, and how to refine it. Now said he in his letter to his cousin, "I understand the oil business." His cousin anwered, "All right, come on."

So he sold his farm, according to the county record, for $833 (even money, "no cents"). He had scarcely gone from that place before the man who purchased the spot went out to arrange for the watering of the cattle. He found the previous owner had gone out years before and put a plank across the brook back of the barn, edgewise into the surface of the water just a few inches. The purpose of that plank at that sharp angle across the brook was to throw over to the other bank a dreadful-looking scum through which the cattle would not put their noses. But with that plank there to throw it all over to one side, the cattle would drink below, and thus that man who had gone to Canada had been himself damming back for twenty-three years a flood of coal-oil which the state geologists of Pennsylvania declared to us ten years later was even then worth a hundred millions of dollars to our state, and four years ago our geologist declared the discovery to be worth to our state a thousand millions of dollars. The man who owned that territory on which the city of Titusville now stands, and those Pleasantville valleys, had studied the subject from the second day of God's creation clear down to the present time. He studied it until he knew all about it, and yet he is said to have sold the whole of it for $833, and again I say, "no sense."

But I need another illustration. I found it in Massachusetts, and I am sorry I did because that is the state I came from. This young man in Massachusetts furnishes just another phase of my thought. He went to Yale College and studied mines and mining, and became such an adept as a mining engineer that he was employed by the authorities of the university to train students who were behind their classes. During his senior year he earned $15 a week for doing that work. When he graduated they raised his pay from $15 to $45 a week, and offered him a professorship, and as soon as they did he went right home to his mother. *If they had raised that boy's pay from $15 to $15.60 he would have stayed and been proud of the place, but when they put it up to $45 at one leap, he said, "Mother, I won't work for $45 a week. The idea of a man with a brain like mine working for $45 a week!* Let's go out in California and stake out gold-mines and silver-mines, and be immensely rich."

Said his mother, "Now, Charlie, it is just as well to be happy as it is to be rich."

"Yes," said Charlie, "but it is just as well to be rich and happy, too." And they were both right about it. As he was an only son and she a widow, of course he had his way. They always do.

They sold out in Massachusetts, and instead of going to California they went to Wisconsin, where he went into the employ of the Superior Copper Mining Company at $15 a week again, but with the proviso in his contract that he should have an interest in any mines he should discover for the company. I don't believe he ever discovered a mine, and if I am looking in the face of any stockholder of that copper company you wish he had discovered something or other. I have friends who are not here because they could not afford a ticket, who did have stock in that company at the time this young man was employed there. This young man went out there, and I have not heard a word from him. I don't know what became of him, and I don't know whether he found any mines or not, but I don't believe he ever did.

But I do know the other end of the line. He had scarcely gotten out of the old homestead before the succeeding owner went out to dig potatoes. The potatoes were already growing in the ground when he bought the farm, and as the old farmer was bringing in a basket of potatoes it hugged very tight between the ends of the stone fence. You know in Massachusetts our farms are nearly all stone wall. There you are obliged to be very economical of front gateways in order to have some place to put the stone. When that basket hugged so tight he set it down on the ground, and then dragged on one side, and pulled on the other side, and as he was dragging that basket through this farmer noticed in the upper and outer corner of that stone wall, right next the gate, a block of native silver eight inches square. That professor of mines, mining, and mineralogy who knew so much about the subject that he would not work for $45 a week, when he sold that homestead in Massachusetts sat right on that silver to make the bargain. He was born on that homestead, was brought up there, and had gone back and forth rubbing the stone with his sleeve until it reflected his countenance, and seemed to say, "Here is a hundred thousand dollars right down here just for the taking." But he would not take it. It was in a home in Newburyport, Massachusetts, and there was no silver there, all away off—well, I don't know where, and he did not, but somewhere else, and he was a professor of mineralogy.

My friends, that mistake is very universally made, and why should we even smile at him. I often wonder what has become of him. I do not know at all, but I will tell you what I "guess" as a Yankee. I guess that he sits out there by his fireside to-night with his friends gathered around him, and he is saying to them something like this: "Do you know that man Conwell who lives in Philadelphia?" "Oh yes, I have heard of him." "Do you know that man Jones that lives in Philadelphia?" "Yes, I have heard of him, too."

Then he begins to laugh, and shakes his sides, and says to his friends, "Well, they have done just the same thing I did, precisely"—and that spoils the whole joke, for you and I have done the same thing he did, and while we sit here and laugh at him he has a better right to sit out there and laugh at us. I know I have made the same mistakes, but, of course, that does not make any difference, because we don't expect the same man to preach and practise, too.

As I come here to-night and look around this audience I am seeing again what through these fifty years I have continually seen—men that are making precisely that same mistake. I often wish I could see the younger people, and would that the Academy had been filled to-night with our high-school scholars and our grammar-school scholars, that I could have them to talk to. While I would have preferred such an audience as that, because they are most susceptible, as they have not grown up into their prejudices as we have, they have not gotten into any custom that they cannot break, they have not met with any failures as we have; and while I could perhaps do such an audience as that more good than I can do grown-up people, yet I will do the best I can with the material I have. I say to you that you have "acres of diamonds" in Philadelphia right where you now live. "Oh," but you will say, "you cannot know much about your city if you think there are any 'acres of diamonds' here."

I was greatly interested in that account in the newspaper of the young man who found that diamond in North Carolina. It was one of the purest diamonds that has ever been discovered, and it has several predecessors near the same locality. I went to a distinguished professor in mineralogy and asked him where he thought those diamonds came from. The professor secured the map of the geologic formations of our continent, and traced it. He said it went either through the underlying carboniferous strata adapted for such production, westward through Ohio and the Mississippi, or in more probability came eastward through Virginia and up the shore of the Atlantic Ocean. It is a fact that the diamonds were there, for they have been discovered and sold; and that they were carried down there during the drift period, from some northern locality. Now who can say but some person going down with his drill in Philadelphia will find some trace of a diamond-mine yet down here? Oh, friends! you cannot say that you are not over one of the greatest diamond-mines in the world, for such a diamond as that only comes from the most profitable mines that are found on earth.

But it serves simply to illustrate my thought, which I emphasize by saying if you do not have the actual diamond-mines literally you have all that they would be good for to you. Because now that the Queen of England has given the greatest compliment ever conferred upon American woman for her attire because she did not appear with any jewels at all at the late reception in England, it has almost done away with the use of diamonds anyhow. All you would care for would be the few you would wear if you wish to be modest, and the rest you would sell for money.

Now then, I say again that the opportunity to get rich, to attain unto great wealth, is here in Philadelphia now, within the reach of almost every man and woman who hears me speak to-night, and I mean just what I say. I have not come to this platform even under these circumstances to recite something to you. I have come to tell you what in God's sight I believe to be the truth, and if the years of life have been of any value to me in the attainment of common sense, I know I am right; that the men and women sitting here, who found it difficult perhaps to buy a ticket to this lecture or gathering to-night, have within their reach "acres of diamonds," opportunities to get largely wealthy. There never was a place on earth more adapted than the city of Philadelphia to-day, and never in the history of the world did a poor man without capital have such an opportunity to get rich quickly and honestly as he has now in our city. I say it is the truth, and I want you to accept it as such; for if you think I have come to simply recite something, then I would better not be here. I have no time to waste in any such talk, but to say the things I believe, and unless some of you get richer for what I am saying to-night my time is wasted.

I say that you ought to get rich, and it is your duty to get rich. How many of my pious brethren say to me, "Do you, a Christian minister, spend your time going up and down the country advising young people to get rich, to get money?" "Yes, of course I do." They say, "Isn't that awful! Why don't you preach the gospel instead of preaching about man's making money?"

"Because to make money honestly is to preach the gospel." That is the reason. The men who get rich may be the most honest men you find in the community.

"Oh," but says some young man here to-night, "I have been told all my life that if a person has money he is very dishonest and dishonorable and mean and contemptible." My friend, that is the reason why you have none, because you have that idea of people. The foundation of your faith is altogether false. Let me say here clearly, and say it briefly, though subject to discussion which I have not time for here, ninety-eight out of one hundred of the rich men of America are honest. That is why they are rich. That is why they are trusted with money. That is why they carry on great enterprises and find plenty of people to work with them. It is because they are honest men.

Says another young man, "I hear sometimes of men that get millions of dollars dishonestly." Yes, of course you do, and so do I. But they are so rare a thing in fact that the newspapers talk about them all the time as a matter of news until you get the idea that all the other rich men got rich dishonestly.

My friend, you take and drive me—if you furnish the auto—out into the suburbs of Philadelphia, and introduce me to the people who own their homes around this great city, those beautiful homes with gardens and flowers, those magnificent homes so lovely in their art, and I will introduce you to the very best people in character as well as in enterprise in our city, and you know I will. A man is not really a true man until he owns his own home, and they that own their homes are made more honorable and honest and pure, and true and economical and careful, by owning the home.

For a man to have money, even in large sums, is not an inconsistent thing. We preach against covetousness, and you know we do, in the pulpit, and oftentimes preach against it so long and use the terms about "filthy lucre" so extremely that Christians get the idea that when we stand in the pulpit we believe it is wicked for any man to have money—until the collection-basket goes around, and then we almost swear at the people because they don't give more money. Oh, the inconsistency of such doctrines as that!

Money is power, and you ought to be reasonably ambitious to have it. You ought because you can do more good with it than you could without it. Money printed your Bible, money builds your churches, money sends your missionaries, and money pays your preachers, and you would not have many of them, either, if you did not pay them. I am always willing that my church should raise my salary, because the church that pays the largest salary always raises it the easiest. You never knew an exception to it in your life. The man who gets the largest salary can do the most good with the power that is furnished to him. Of course he can if his spirit be right to use it for what it is given to him.

I say, then, you ought to have money. If you can honestly attain unto riches in Philadelphia, it is your Christian and godly duty to do so. It is an awful mistake of these pious people to think you must be awfully poor in order to be pious.

Some men say, "Don't you sympathize with the poor people?" Of course I do, or else I would not have been lecturing these years. I won't give in but what I sympathize with the poor, but the number of poor who are to be sympathized with is very small. To sympathize with a man whom God has punished for his sins, thus to help him when God would still continue a just punishment, is to do wrong, no doubt about it, and we do that more than we help those who are deserving. While we should sympathize with God's poor—that is, those who cannot help themselves—let us remember there is not a poor person in the United States who was not made poor by his own shortcomings, or by the shortcomings of some one else. It is all wrong to be poor, anyhow. Let us give in to that argument and pass that to one side.

A gentleman gets up back there, and says, "Don't you think there are some things in this world that are better than money?" Of course I do, but I am talking about money now. Of course there are some things higher than money. Oh yes, I know by the grave that has left me standing alone that there are some things in this world that are higher and sweeter and purer than money. Well do I know there are some things higher and grander than gold. Love is the grandest thing on God's earth, but fortunate the lover who has plenty of money. Money is power, money is force, money will do good as well as harm. In the hands of good men and women it could accomplish, and it has accomplished, good.

I hate to leave that behind me. I heard a man get up in a prayer-meeting in our city and thank the Lord he was "one of God's poor." Well, I wonder what his wife thinks about that? She earns all the money that comes into that house, and he smokes a part of that on the veranda. I don't want to see any more of the Lord's poor of that kind, and I don't believe the Lord does. And yet there are some people who think in order to be pious you must be awfully poor and awfully dirty. That does not follow at all. While we sympathize with the poor, let us not teach a doctrine like that.

Yet the age is prejudiced against advising a Christian man (or, as a Jew would say, a godly man) from attaining unto wealth. The prejudice is so universal and the years are far enough back, I think, for me to safely mention that years ago up at Temple University there was a young man in our theological school who thought he was the only pious student in that department. He came into my office one evening and sat down by my desk, and said to me: "Mr. President, I think it is my duty sir, to come in and labor with you." "What has happened now?" Said he, "I heard you say at the Academy, at the Peirce School commencement, that you thought it was an honorable ambition for a young man to desire to have wealth, and that you thought it made him temperate, made him anxious to have a good name, and made him industrious. You spoke about man's ambition to have money helping to make him a good man. Sir, I have come to tell you the Holy Bible says that 'money is the root of all evil.'"

I told him I had never seen it in the Bible, and advised him to go out into the chapel and get the Bible, and show me the place. So out he went for the Bible, and soon he stalked into my office with the Bible open, with all the bigoted pride of the narrow sectarian, or of one who founds his Christianity on some misinterpretation of Scripture. He flung the Bible down on my desk, and fairly squealed into my ear: "There it is, Mr. President; you can read it for yourself." I said to him: "Well, young man, you will learn when you get a little older that you cannot trust another denomination to read the Bible for you. You belong to another denomination. You are taught in the theological school, however, that emphasis is exegesis. Now, will you take that Bible and read it yourself, and give the proper emphasis to it?"

He took the Bible, and proudly read, " 'The love of money is the root of all evil.' "

Then he had it right, and when one does quote aright from that same old Book he quotes the absolute truth. I have lived through fifty years of the mightiest battle that old Book has ever fought, and I have lived to see its banners flying free; for never in the history of this world did the great minds of earth so universally agree that the Bible is true—all true—as they do at this very hour.

So I say that when he quoted right, of course he quoted the absolute truth. "The love of money is the root of all evil." He who tries to attain unto it too quickly, or dishonestly, will fall into many snares, no doubt about that. The love of money. What is that? It is making an idol of money, and idolatry pure and simple everywhere is condemned by the Holy Scriptures and by man's common sense. The man that worships the dollar instead of thinking of the purposes for which it ought to be used, the man who idolizes simply money, the miser that hoards his money in the cellar, or hides it in his stocking, or refuses to invest it where it will do the world good, that man who hugs the dollar until the eagle squeals has in him the root of all evil.

I think I will leave that behind me now and answer the question of nearly all of you who are asking, "Is there opportunity to get rich in Philadelphia?" Well, now, how simple a thing it is to see where it is, and the instant you see where it is it is yours. Some old gentleman gets up back there and says, "Mr. Conwell, have you lived in Philadelphia for thirty-one years and don't know that the time has gone by when you can make anything in this city?" "No, I don't think it is." "Yes, it is; I have tried it." "What business are you in?"

"I kept a store here for twenty years, and never made over a thousand dollars in the whole twenty years."

"Well, then, you can measure the good you have been to this city by what this city has paid you, because a man can judge very well what he is worth by what he receives; that is, in what he is to the world at this time. If you have not made over a thousand dollars in twenty years in Philadelphia, it would have been better for Philadelphia if they had kicked you out of the city nineteen years and nine months ago. A man has no right to keep a store in Philadelphia twenty years and not make at least five hundred thousand dollars, even though it be a corner grocery up-town." You say, "You cannot make five thousand dollars in a store now." Oh, my friends, if you will just take only four blocks around you, and find out what the people want and what you ought to supply and set them down with your pencil, and figure up the profits you would make if you did supply them, you would very soon see it. There is wealth right within the sound of your voice.

Some one says: "You don't know anything about business. A preacher never knows a thing about business." Well, then, I will have to prove that I am an expert. I don't like to do this, but I have to do it because my testimony will not be taken if I am not an expert. My father kept a country store, and if there is any place under the stars where a man gets all sorts of experience in every kind of mercantile transactions, it is in the country store. I am not proud of my experience, but sometimes when my father was away he would leave me in charge of the store, though fortunately for him that was not very often. But this did occur many times, friends: A man would come in the store, and say to me, "Do you keep jack-knives?" "No, we don't keep jack-knives," and I went off whistling a tune. What did I care about that man, anyhow? Then another farmer would come in and say, "Do you keep jack-knives?" "No, we don't keep jack-knives." Then I went away and whistled another tune. Then a third man came right in the same door and said, "Do you keep jack-knives?" "No. Why is every one around here asking for jack-knives? Do you suppose we are keeping this store to supply the whole neighborhood with jack-knives?" Do you carry on your store like that in Philadelphia? The difficulty was I had not then learned that the foundation of godliness and the foundation principle of success in business are both the same precisely. The man who says, "I cannot carry my religion into business" advertises himself either as being an imbecile in business, or on the road to bankruptcy, or a thief, one of the three, sure. He will fail within a very few years. He certainly will if he doesn't carry his religion into business. If I had been carrying on my father's store on a Christian plan, godly plan, I would have had a jack-knife for the third man when he called for it. Then I would have actually done him a kindness, and I would have received a reward myself, which it would have been my duty to take.

There are some over-pious Christian people who think if you take any profit on anything you sell that you are an unrighteous man. On the contrary, you would be a criminal to sell goods for less than they cost. You have no right to do that. You cannot trust a man with your money who cannot take care of his own. You cannot trust a man in your family that is not true to his own wife. You cannot trust a man in the world that does not begin with his own heart, his own character, and his own life. It would have been my duty to have furnished a jack-knife to the third man, or the second, and to have sold it to him and actually profited myself. I have no more right to sell goods without making a profit on them than I have to overcharge him dishonestly beyond what they are worth. But I should so sell each bill of goods that the person to whom I sell shall make as much as I make.

To live and let live is the principle of the gospel, and the principle of every-day common sense. Oh, young man, hear me; live as you go along. Do not wait until you have reached my years before you begin to enjoy anything of this life. If I had the millions back, or fifty cents of it, which I have tried to earn in these years, it would not do me anything like the good that it does me now in this almost sacred presence to-night. Oh, yes, I am paid over and over a hundredfold to-night for dividing as I have tried to do in some measure as I went along through the years. I ought not speak that way, it sounds egotistic, but I am old enough now to be excused for that. I should have helped my fellow-men, which I have tried to do, and every one should try to do, and get the happiness of it. The man who goes home with the sense that he has stolen a dollar that day, that he has robbed a man of what was his honest due, is not going to sweet rest. He arises tired in the morning, and goes with an unclean conscience to his work the next day. He is not a successful man at all, although he may have laid up millions. But the man who has gone through life dividing always with his fellow-men, making and demanding his own rights and his own profits, and giving to every other man his rights and profits, lives every day, and not only that, but it is the royal road to great wealth. The history of the thousands of millionaires shows that to be the case.

The Message of Jesus to Men of Wealth

GEORGE DAVIS HERRON

Born, Montezuma, Indiana, January 21, 1862; died, Munich, Bavaria, October 9, 1925. Attended preparatory department, Ripon College (Wisconsin), 1879–1882. Entered ministry, 1883, holding successive pastorates at Lake City, Minnesota and Burlington, Iowa. Professor of Applied Christianity, Iowa College (later Grinnell), 1893–1899. Deposed from Iowa Congregational Council because of his divorce and unorthodox views toward marriage. Embraced left-wing Utopian thought and movements. Helped found Rand School of Social Science, New York City. Resided in Italy for most of his life in twentieth century. Served as emissary for Wilson in peace negotiations after World War I.

I am appointed to present to you, this evening, what I understand to be the message of Jesus to men of wealth, and to apply that message to the problems of society which the best thought and truest sympathy of our times are reaching out to solve. I assume, in what I shall say, that I am addressing an audience of Christ's disciples.

In their essence, the social problems of to-day are not different from those of yesterday; they are as old as society itself. They date back to the infancy of the race, when sin couched at the door of Adam's eldest son, to spring up

Plymouth Church, Minneapolis, Minnesota, September 22, 1890, at the annual meeting of the Minnesota Congregational Club. George D. Herron, *The Message of Jesus to Men of Wealth* (New York and Chicago: Fleming H. Revell Company, 1891), pp. 5–32. Full text also in *The Christian Union*, 42 (December 11, 1890), pp. 804–805.

276

within his heart as hatred for his younger brother. Ever since Cain—whom President Hitchcock calls "that first godless political economist"—killed his brother Abel, the associability of human beings for good and common ends has been a problem: a problem, be it kept in mind, born in a heart of covetousness, and set by the hand of hate for the race to solve. Cain's murder of his brother Abel was the first bald, brutal assertion of self-interest as the law of human life—an assertion always potential with murder: an assertion whose acceptance involves the triumph of the brute man over the God-imaged man: an assertion which the divine heart of humanity has always denied: a theory of society which will be remembered as a frightful dream of the past when the race recovers its moral sanity. Cain's hands were the first to grasp and wield competition as the weapon of progress; a weapon from which no economic theorists have ever been able to wash the blood of human suffering. When Cain replied to God, "Am I my brother's keeper?" he stated the question to which all past and present problems of man's earthly existence are reducible. The search for the final and comprehensive answer to Cain's question has been the race's sacred sorrow; and obedience to such an answer would carry in it the perfect solvent of all the problems that perplex the minds and hearts of men.

The Dream of the Ages

History and prophecy have always pointed toward a time of industrial peace and social brotherhood. The most unselfish aspirations of the noblest men have been along the line of the social unity of the race. About this hope statesmen and philosophers have woven their sublimest theories of society and government. It has been the highest inspiration of poetry. It is the end toward which Moses and Plato looked. It is the lofty strain borne along from prophet to prophet through Israel's glory and shame. Outside of Biblical prophecy there is no purer expression of this ancient hope than in John Stuart Mill's autobiography: "I yet looked forward," he says, "to a time . . . when the division of the produce of labor, instead of depending, as in so great a degree it now does, on the accident of birth, will be made by an acknowledged principle of justice; and when it will no longer be, or be thought to be, impossible for human beings to exert themselves strenuously in procuring benefits which are not to be exclusively their own, but to be shared by society to which they belong."

And yet, with all the history and prophecy, the schools and temples, the philosophy and poetry, the governments and civilizations, the day of brotherhood seems no nearer than generations ago. The hope grows faint with age. The problems of society are still unsolved.

The question of Cain is the master question of our age. It has grown articulate with the greed and cruelty of history. It threatens our American day and nation with the crisis of the centuries. It must be answered; and answered with justice and righteousness. The blood of Abel cries out through toiling millions. The expectation of the poor shall not forever perish in hopeless toiling and longing for better days. As John Ruskin says, "There are voices of battle and famine through all the earth, which must be heard some day, whoever keeps silence." No arrogant reply as to the historic and legal rights of private and corporate property will silence these voices.

CIVILIZATION CANNOT FULFILL THE DREAM OF SOCIAL JUSTICE

The natural development of our civilization will not unfold the solution of our industrial problems. When we watch the mammoth enginery of this modern civilization through the assurances of a partisan press, or the mercenary declamation of the politician who estimates the moral stupidity of the people by his own, the movements of its great wheels seem wonderfully safe and perfect; but when we, in our sober, honest, thoughtful moments, view it through the sympathies and purposes of the divine Man of Sorrows, we see torn, bleeding, mangled, sorrowing, famishing multitudes beneath the wheels of its remorseless enginery; we see that greed and not love is the power that moves our civilization; we see politics, commerce, and the social club moving on the economic assumption that selfishness is the only considerable social force, and assuming that civilization can advance only through the equal balancing of warring, selfish interests; we see men valuing brute cunning and the low instinct of shrewdness more than whiteness of soul.

A civilization based on self-interest, and securing itself through competition, has no power within itself to secure justice. We speak to pitiless forces when we appeal to its processes to right the wrongs and inequalities of society. The world is not to be saved by civilization. It is civilization that needs saving. A civilization basing itself upon self-interest has a more dangerous foundation than dynamite. It is built upon falsehood. It carries in it the elements of anarchy because it has no ground in moral realities. It is atheistic because it treats God and his righteousness as external to itself. It is nihilistic because it thrives on destruction. It is a civilization which Bishop Huntington declares "leads by a sure course to barbarism." It is a civilization under whose procession John Stuart Mill affirms the very idea of "justice, or any proportionality between success and merit, or between success and exertion," to be "so chimerical as to be relegated to the region of romance." The end to which the civilization of the present tends is material, and not moral; it tends to the enslavement of society and the smothering of its highest life. Civilization is the flower of the character of the dominant classes; it is an effect more than a cause; its forces originate in character; its activities are the expression of the people's being. No civilization can be made righteous, or can make itself righteous, by any restraints or regulations external to itself. A righteous civilization can have no other source than the inward righteousness of those who originate and control its forces.

The Impotency of Abstract Truth

There is no power in abstract truth, either economic, ethical, or theological, to cure our social ills. Economic laws naturally deal with things external to man's being; with principles which will be accepted or rejected according to inward forces of character which they can obey, but cannot control. Ethical truth taught to an unspiritualized race, or generation, or civilization, is a childish waste of time and strength. There is no ethics apart from religion. The springs of human virtue are all in God. There is no ethical truth other than the expression of the will of God. Socrates, Plato and Shakespeare seem to have understood this better than some of us who teach our fellow-men to-day. Nearly all the warnings of the Old and New Testament, which we so self-assuringly address to so-called unbelievers, were addressed in the first place to those who presumed themselves to be already in the kingdom of God; to those in the temple services and the churches. The ethical instructions of Jesus and the apostles were all based upon and developed from the cross. Theological truth has repeatedly shown its barrenness of the fruit of righteousness. The darkest crimes of history have been committed by the conservators of religion. A jealousy for theological truth often accompanies a hatred of duty. The Pharisees were so orthodox that they crucified Christ for heresy. They possessed the oracles of God. Yet the truth did not save them from greedy, heartless, malignant, hypocritical lives. A slavish and enslaving conservatism has always joined hands with an indifferent worldlyism for the crucifixion of God's perennial revelations of incarnate truth. I suspect the devil knows more truth than any of us; and he is all the more devilish for knowing it. Truth that does not strike its roots in love is a curse; and the truer the truth the more accursed its results. There is a pregnant thought, which the Church has yet to learn, in a saying of Mozoomdar's in his "Oriental Christ": "Unless our creeds fertilize the world, and our lives furnish meat and drink to mankind, the curse uttered on barrenness will descend on us."

Hope, Not in the State

We cannot look to the State to solve our social woes and grant our social hopes. All the great political prophets, from Moses to Milton, and from Milton to Sumner and Mulford, recognize that the people are the makers of the State rather than the State the makers of the people. The State is the expression of the highest common thought of the people; it is the work of the people's faith. Hegel says "the State is the realization of the moral idea" of the people. The people must be righteous before the State can be righteous. If we agree with Milton that the State "ought to be but as one huge Christian personage, one mighty growth or stature of an honest man," then the Christian State must be the offspring of a Christian people. If we regard the State, with Sumner, as a grand moral institution, it must be moral because the people build it with their moral thought and purpose. The best and strongest institutions have been powerless to restrain people whose moral conceptions they did not embody. The Mosaic legislation was never fully enforced. Roman law could find no expression in the thought and life of later Rome. Alfred the Great incorporated the Ten Commandments and Golden Rule in the early English constitution, but they are yet far from being the laws of English industrial and social life. Laws written on tables of stone and printed in statute books are but the playthings of politicians if they are not written in people's hearts. Laws cannot make men unselfish. They can restrain; but all legal righteousness is but temporary. Police righteousness is not divine righteousness. Force-justice is unreal justice. The State cannot, by any possible process, make the rich man unselfish, or the poor man thrifty. The State cannot establish justice and righteousness on the earth; but justice and righteousness must establish the State. Except the State be born again, it cannot see the Kingdom of God.

The Heart Disease of Society

The heart of all our social disputes is what Mulford calls "the crude assertion of an enlightened self-interest as a law of human activity." This assertion is the essence of the gospel which Professor Sumner proclaims from his chair in a great Christian university. Social classes, he decides, owe each other nothing; benevolence is simply barter, and "the yearning after equality the offspring of envy and covetousness." This is a gospel which would have caused the proclaimer to be mobbed in the streets of Athens in the days of Pericles; a gospel which would have astounded Moses, and seemed ancient and barbarous to Abraham. The supremacy of the law of self-interest is the conclusion of Herbert Spencer's materialistic philosophy; and of the wretched pessimism of Hartmann and Schopenhauer. It is the principle upon which Cain slew his brother. It was the seductive whisper of the serpent in Eve's ear. It is the principle upon which crime is committed. It is the principle upon which the capitalist acts who treats labor as no more than a commodity subject to the lowest market rate and the law of supply and demand. It is the principle upon which railroads are bonded and bankrupted for private ends. It is the law by which the New England deacon chattels his money upon the Dakota farmer's meager possessions at a usurious and impoverishing rate of interest—a deed which will not be obscured from the eyes of a just God by the endowment of a chair in a denominational college. It is the principle upon which a Chicago financier proceeds, with no more moral justification than the highwayman's robbery of an express train, to "corner" the pork market, and thus force from the hungry mouths of toiling families a million and a half of dollars into his private treasury—a deed for which the giving of some thousands to found city missions and orphans' homes will be no atonement in the reckoning of the God who judges the world in righteousness and not by the ethics of the stock exchange. The law of self-interest is the eternal falsehood which mothers all social and private woes; for sin is pure individualism—the assertion of self against God and humanity.

The Divine Remedy

God's answer to Cain's question, God's solvent of the social problems of our day, is the cross. And the cross is more than an historic event. It is the law by which God acts, and expects men to act. It is the creed of God which will never be revised. It is the principle upon which creation and history proceed. It was the assertion intensified which God has been making through all history, of self-sacrifice as the law of human development and achievement. Self-sacrifice is the law which God asserts in Christ over against the law of self-interest which Satan asserts in Cain. The trial in progress is Christ *versus* Cain. The decision to which the times are hastening us is, Shall Christ or Cain reign in our American civilization? And well may the heavens await our decision in silent and awful wonder; for we are deciding the destiny of the earth!

. . . .

The Kingdom Is at Hand

The whole question of labor and capital, and all the problems of our day, can be restated in this form: Is the Gospel of Jesus livable? God is calling to-day for able men who are willing to be financially crucified in order to establish the world's market on a Golden Rule basis. He is calling for noble women who are willing to be socially crucified to make society the agency for uplifting instead of crushing the poor and ignorant and weak. "Whoever," says Benjamin Franklin, "introduces into the public affairs the principles of primitive Christianity will change the face of the world." It is for this work that God would anoint you, O Christian business men of America! History has never presented to man an opportunity richer than yours. You can make the market as sacred as the church. You can make the whirl of industrial wheels like the joyous music of worship. You can be the knights of the noblest chivalry the world has ever seen; not going forth "to recover the tomb of a buried god," as Ruskin said of the crusaders of Richard Lionheart, but to fulfill the commands of the eternal Christ. And where you go, flowers of hope will spring in your footprints. You can bear the weak in your arms, and set the captives of poverty free. You can cause the deserts of human despair to blossom with the gladness of fulfilled prophecy, and hush the voices of discontent in the sweetness of fruitful toil. You can give work to the wageless; teach the thriftless and ignorant; seat the poor in the best pews of your churches. You need not strive nor cry, nor wear plumes and flaunt banners; but you can be the heralds of a new civilization, the creators of a Christian industry whose peaceful procession will reach around the globe. You need carry no crosses of wood or gold or silver; but you can bury the cross of your Christ deep within your hearts and stretch forth consecrated hands to realize the life of humanity by upraising it into the idealism of Jesus. You can draw the world's trades and traffics within the onsweep of Christ's redemptive purpose. You can plant everlasting peace underneath the feet of men, so that there shall be no more strife; and light earth's night of toil with skies of love, so that there shall be no more night. You can be the makers of the new earth wherein dwelleth righteousness; in which the race will be at last human because it is divine, and divine because it is human.

God's new day of judgment is surely and swiftly dawning. Voices from out the future are crying repentance unto this mammon-worshiping generation. The axe is laid at the root of the trees. New John Baptists are arising who will speak truth and justice to the Herods of finance, though their ecclesiastical heads be the price of the message.

In the lead of human progress I see the matchless figure of the Son of God—

> Toiling up new Calvaries ever with the cross that
> turns not back.

Behold the Lamb of God that beareth away the sin of the world! Let us close about him, O brother men, and keep step with the march of the cross!

> Till upon earth's grateful sod
> Rests the city of our God!

REVEALED RELIGION VS. THE
RELIGION OF HUMANITY

SOCIAL GOSPELERS *sought to harmonize man's life in his worldly setting with eschatological doctrine. Clergymen such as Washington Gladden and Henry Ward Beecher, son of the redoubtable Lyman Beecher, applauded science both for its contributions to man's lot on earth and for the light it shed on God's cosmic plan. Religious liberals dissolved the latest tensions between naturalism and supernaturalism—tensions stimulated by developments in biological science—through recourse to doctrines of "design" and "secondary causes," ideas derived from efforts in earlier centuries to reconcile emergent physical science with God.*

"Design" postulated that every scientific discovery testified to "God's all-wise purpose"; and "secondary causes," as Curti puts it, "divided the fiat functions of the Creator in the first instance with the detailed and subsequent working out, by scientific law, of His ultimate intentions." Thus Beecher could relax comfortably and designate himself a "cordial Christian evolutionist." Although "design" and "secondary causes" helped liberals out of their intellectual dilemma, these devices also had the effect of depersonalizing God, and of eroding popular faith in the doctrine of supernaturalism.

Orthodox religionists, of course, had no truck with these innovations and compromises. They perceived the latent perils to supernaturalism that resided in revisionist theories. As heretofore, they maintained that God is not only the Author of nature, but He "directly intervenes in natural events and the affairs of men through miracles and the granting of grace."[1] These defenders of the old faith had strength in depth. They drew upon various wings of Protestant orthodoxy, supported by the resurgent revivalism of Dwight L. Moody and others, and their ranks were steadily swelled by immigrant Roman Catholics. Protestants stood upon Holy Writ, and Roman Catholics looked as ever to the church as their custodian of revealed truth. Whichever authority was invoked, the claims of revealed truth were stoutly maintained against compromisers and downright infidels.

But the challenges to supernaturalism kept coming, and from all sides. Scholarly investigations of the Scriptures, called Higher Criticism, cast doubt on the Bible as a stenographic report of God's word. The comparative study of religions undermined confidence in the Bible as a reliable authority on which to base claims for the uniqueness of Christianity among religions. Darwin's theory of organic evolution seemed to contest the very basis of revealed truth. And secularists generally, however they reached their conclusion, were prone to accept man as a creature who is quite adequate to his purposes.

Orthodox Christians stood at Armageddon. They contested painstaking textual and anthropological studies as best they could, or ingenuously brushed criticism aside, as did Dwight L. Moody when he declared that "the Bible was not made to understand." They recoiled from the thought that man had ascended by stages from primeval ooze, and contended for the Biblical account of man as a special creation of God. Self-styled emancipated Christians who turned to the "religion of humanity" were

[1] Merle Curti, *The Growth of American Thought* (New York: Harper & Brothers, 1943), p. 532.

reminded that man is impotent unless sustained by the grace of God. So the arguments ran.

The publication of Darwin's The Origin of Species in 1859 triggered a hot war of words. The ink was hardly dry before challenges were flying. In June, 1860, Thomas Huxley, Darwin's bulldog, debated Samuel Wilberforce, Bishop of Oxford, on the theory of organic evolution. Wilberforce asked Huxley if it was through his grandfather or grandmother that he claimed to have descended from a monkey. In high dudgeon, Huxley said he preferred having an ape for his ancestor to an intellectual prostitute like Bishop Wilberforce. Wilberforce's diatribe and Huxley's heated rejoinder exposed the inflammatory possibilities of the issue.

A decade after the Huxley-Wilberforce fracas, an American, Robert Green Ingersoll, set out on a one-man mission to rescue mankind from religious captivity. He was an avowed agnostic, a word Huxley claimed to have invented. Ingersoll was not just another peripatetic freethinker who appealed to misfits drawn from the marginal fringes of society. He had credentials. His father was a respected clergyman. Though the son rejected his father's religion, he inclined toward his father's reformist bent. He had been a soldier in the Civil War. He was the Republican party's greatest orator and turned up regularly during campaigns to wave the bloody shirt. He acquired national fame through a single speech when, in 1876, he nominated James Blaine for President and named him the "Plumed Knight." He was one of the great trial lawyers of his age. In short, Ingersoll had access to the middling and influential classes, for he could pass the tests of respectability, religion excepted. And to spike canards that he drew his audiences from under the rocks, he always charged an admission fee for his lectures on religion.

Ingersoll was largely self-educated. He read voraciously

and readily assimilated what he read. Early in life he concluded that belief in supernaturalism was founded on ignorance and superstition, that through the ages churches had "picked the pockets and brains of the world." Ingersoll regarded his unremitting lecture tours as demolition activity. The job of the demolitionist was to blast illusions and open the way for exact science. Ingersoll relished his work.

In an early lecture, "The Gods" (1872), Ingersoll defined his role and world view. He opened with a paraphrase on Alexander Pope, "An honest God is the noblest work of man." The god-market, he continued, is glutted with phantoms that bespeak men's fears and ignorance.

For the vagaries of the clouds the infidels propose to substitute the realities of earth; for superstition, the splendid demonstrations and achievements of science; and for theological tyranny, the chainless liberty of thought.

The demolition of gods and supernaturalism was not an end in itself.

It is a means to an end: the real end being the happiness of man. . . . We are laying the foundation of the grand temple of the future—not the temple of all the gods, but of all the people—wherein, with appropriate rites, will be celebrated the religion of humanity.

But it was not Ingersoll's doctrine alone that threatened to accelerate creeping secularism and infidelity. It was also the speaker, his drawing power, and those pamphlets of his based on speeches that boys smuggled into the haymows. Few speakers had Ingersoll's energy, joie de vivre, mental agility, or felicity in language. None equaled his devastating wit in speech, not even Mark Twain, though some assailed it as profane laughter.

The heretically inclined Henry Ward Beecher rejoiced in his friendship with Ingersoll and even introduced the infidel with glowing words at a public meeting. Another

*and a more orthodox Brooklyn clergyman, the Reverend
T. DeWitt Talmage, proceeded to exorcise this latest
Satanic scourge. Talmage was only one of a host of outraged Christians who took out after Ingersoll, but Talmage's great following made his thwackings resound
through the land. Like Beecher, Talmage had a flair for
experimental preaching. Both Talmage and Beecher did
away with the pulpit—an obstacle to muscular Christianity; both favored wide, open platforms for energetic
roaming. Both preferred the topical homiletic method to
the expository; both were pictorial in style. Both drew
huge audiences, and both were internationally reported
in the press. But whereas Beecher espoused evolution and
sponsored Ingersoll, Talmage donned the armor of St.
George to destroy the dragons of infidelity and blasphemy.*

*Between January 15 and February 26, 1882, Talmage
delivered six sermons on Ingersoll in his Brooklyn Tabernacle. He opened the series with "Mr. Ingersoll, the
Champion Blasphemer of America, Answered," and closed
with "Victory for God." Talmage simulated a courtroom
setting and invited his audience to render their verdict
at the end of the series in the case of "Infidelity, the plaintiff, versus Christianity, the defendant." Though Talmage
protested there was nothing personal about it all, he left
no doubts as to who was the villain in the piece. He took
up Ingersoll's allegations point by point—the Bible is a
false book, the Bible is a cruel book, the Bible is an impure book, and so on. He scoffed at "infidel scientists who
have fifty different theories about the origin of life," and
concluded that "The only exact science is Christianity—
the only thing under which you can appropriately write:
'Quod erat demonstrandum.'" Thus Talmage the prose-
cutor concluded his case, disregarding his initial invitation
to his congregation by turning himself into judge and
jury as well.*

His case stated, tried, and adjudicated by the theo-

logian, Ingersoll the lawyer lost no time in repaying the compliments. He gave long interviews on Talmage and Talmagian theology which, in published form, run to approximately 450 pages in the Dresden Edition of his Works. He singled out Talmage for special treatment in a number of public addresses in New York and Chicago because "He is the only Presbyterian minister in the United States who can draw an audience. He stands at the head of the denomination, and I answer him."

On Sunday afternoon, November 12, 1882, when a paying audience of three thousand people packed Mc-Vicker's Theatre in Chicago to watch Ingersoll dissect the anatomy of Talmagian theology, they were fully confident that blood would be spilled. Ingersoll did not disappoint them. The next day, Monday, some troubled souls gathered in Chicago's Lower Farwell Hall to deprecate Ingersoll's lecture and to placate Jehovah, lest in His wrath He destroy Chicago as He did Jerusalem after the crucifixion of Christ.[2]

Public hassles over religion and agnosticism subsided after Ingersoll's death in 1899. Then, following a decade of quiescence, Biblical literalists took to raking over old coals. After World War I many of the old issues flared up again, aided by William Jennings Bryan's vigorous stoking. Speaking under such provocative titles as "Brute or Brother," Bryan became the principal figure in stirring up the controversy between Fundamentalists and Modernists in the nineteen twenties.

---

[2] The Chicago Tribune, November 14, 1882, p. 8.

Victory for God

T. DEWITT TALMAGE

Born, Middlebrook, New Jersey, January 7, 1832; died, Washington, D.C., April 12, 1902. Educated at the University of the City of New York and the New Brunswick Seminary of the Dutch Reformed Church. Held pastorates successively at Belleville, New Jersey; Syracuse; Philadelphia; Brooklyn; and Washington, D.C. Internationally popular as preacher and lecturer. His weekly sermons are said to have been carried in as many as 3500 newspapers.

Behold the days come, saith the Lord, that the ploughman shall overtake the reaper. Amos 9:13.

*P*icture a tropical clime with a season so prosperous that the harvest reaches clear over to the planting time, and the swarthy husbandman swinging the sickle in the thick grain almost feels the breath of the horses on his shoulders, the horses hitched to the plough preparing for a new crop. "Behold, the days come, saith the Lord, that the ploughman shall overtake the reaper." When is that? That is now. That is this day when hardly have you done reaping one harvest than the ploughman is getting ready for another.

I know that Mr. Ingersoll and coadjutors say in their lectures and in their interviews, and in phraseology charged with all venom and abuse and caricature, that Christianity has collapsed, that the Bible is an obsolete book, that the Christian Church is on the retreat. I shall answer that wholesale charge this morning, in this my last sermon on infidelity, because I must

The Brooklyn Tabernacle, February 26, 1882. T. DeWitt Talmage, *The Brooklyn Tabernacle* (New York: Funk & Wagnalls, 1884), pp. 115-120.

enter into the pentecostal blessing which is coming upon us, and turn your attention to other subjects. But I now here declare what I declare for the first time, what has been the chief motive in the delivery of these discourses against infidelity. It was merely a preparation for what we are now to begin in the way of evangelistic services. I know, as you know, that thorough belief in the Bible as the Word of God is the best influence to waken people up to act in regard to their present and everlasting welfare. Vast multitudes, I believe, during these sermons have been persuaded that the Bible is a commonsensical book, that it is a reasonable book, that it is an authentic book. Men have told me that while they had been accustomed to receive the New Testament they had disbelieved the Old Testament, until by the blessing of God upon this exposition they have come to believe that the Old Testament is just as true as the New Testament, and I have had so many encouragements to go on that I have kept on to this time with these discourses. A man said to me last Saturday night in Cleveland, Ohio, as he tapped me on the shoulder: "I want to tell you that my son who was at college and who was a confirmed infidel, wrote me in a letter which I got this morning, saying that through the arguments you have presented in behalf of the truth of the Bible, he has given up his scepticism and surrendered his heart to God. I thought you would like to hear it." I said, "God bless you, that is the best thing I have heard to-night." And so I believe the people are all going to be persuaded that this is God's word.

An Arab guide was leading a French infidel across a desert, and ever and anon the Arab guide would get down in the sand and pray to the Lord. It disgusted the French infidel, and after a while as the Arab got up from one of his prayers the infidel said: "How do you know there is any God?" and the Arab guide said: "How do I know that a man and a camel passed along our tent last night? I know it by the footprint in the sand. And you want to know how I know whether there is any God. Look at that sunset. Is that the footstep of a man?" And by the same process you and I have come to understand that this is the footstep of a God.

But now let us see whether the Bible is a last year's almanac. Let us see whether the Church of God is in a Bull Run retreat, muskets, canteens, and haversacks strewing all the way. The great English historian, Sharon Turner, a man of vast learning and of great accuracy, not a clergyman, but an attorney, as well as a historian, gives this overwhelming statistic in regard to Christianity and in regard to the number of Christians in the different centuries. In the first century 500,000 Christians; in the second century, 2,000,000 Christians; in the third century, 5,000,000 Christians; in the fourth century, 10,000,000 Christians; in the fifth century, 15,000,000 Christians; in the sixth century, 20,000,000 Christians; in the seventh century, 24,000,000 Christians; in the eighth century, 30,000,000 Christians; in the ninth century, 40,000,000 Christians; in the tenth century, 50,000,000 Christians; in the eleventh century, 70,000,000 Christians; in the twelfth century, 80,000,000 Christians; in the thirteenth century, 75,000,000 Christians; in the fourteenth century, 80,000,000 Christians; in the fifteenth century, 100,000,000 Christians; in the sixteenth century, 125,000,000 Christians; in the seventeenth century, 155,000,000 Christians; in the eighteenth century, 200,000,000 Christians—a decadence, as you observe, in only one century, and more than made up in the following centuries, while it is the usual computation that there will be, when the record of the nineteenth century is made up, at least 300,000,000 Christians. Poor Christianity! what a pity it has no friends. How lonesome it must be. Who will take it out of the poorhouse? Poor Christianity! Three hundred millions in one century. In a few weeks of last year 2,500,000 copies of the New Testament distributed. Why, the earth is like an old castle with twenty gates and a park of artillery ready to thunder down every gate. Lay aside all Christendom and see how heathendom is being surrounded and honey-combed and attacked by this all-conquering Gospel. At the beginning of this century there were only 150 missionaries; now there are 25,000 missionaries and native helpers and evangelists. At the beginning of this century there were only 50,000 heathen converts; now there are 1,650,000 converts from heathendom. There is not a sea-coast on the planet but the battery of the Gospel is planted and ready to march on, north, south, east, west. You all know that the chief work of an army is to plant the batteries. It may take many days to plant the batteries, and they may do all the work in ten minutes. These batteries are being planted all along the sea-coasts and in all nations. It may take a good while to plant them, and they may do all their work in one day. They will. Nations are to be born in a day. But just come back to Christendom and recognize the fact that during the last ten years as many people have connected themselves with evangelical churches as connected themselves with the churches in the first fifty years of this century.

So Christianity is falling back, and the Bible, they say, is becoming an obsolete book. I go into a court, and wherever I find a judge's bench or a clerk's desk, I find a Bible. Upon what book could there be uttered the solemnity of an oath? What book is apt to be put in the trunk of the young man as he leaves for city life? The Bible. What shall I find in nine out of every ten homes in Brooklyn? The Bible. In nine out of every ten homes in Christendom? The Bible. Voltaire wrote the prophecy that the Bible in the nineteenth century would become extinct. The century is gone all except eighteen years, and as there have been more Bibles published in the latter part of the century than in the former part of the century, do you think the Bible will become extinct in the next eighteen years? I have to tell you that the room in which Voltaire wrote that prophecy, not long ago was crowded from floor to ceiling with Bibles from Switzerland. Suppose the Congress of the United States should pass a law that there should be no more Bibles printed in America, and no more Bibles read. If there are thirty million grown people in the United States there would be thirty million people in an army to put down such a law and defend their right to read the Bible. But suppose the Congress of the United States should make a law against the reading or the publication of any other book, how many people would go out in such a crusade? Could you get thirty million people to go out and risk their lives in the defence of Shakespeare's tragedies or Gladstone's tracts, or Macaulay's History of England? You know that there are a thousand men who would die in the defence of this book, where there is not more than one man who would die in defence of any other book. You try to insult my common-sense by telling me the Bible is fading out from the world. It is the most popular book of the century. How do I know it? I know it just as I know in regard to other books. How many volumes of that book are published? Well, you say, five thousand. How many copies of that book are published? A hundred thousand. Which is the more popular? Why of course the one that has a hundred thousand circulation. And if this book has more copies abroad in the world, if there are five times as many Bibles abroad as any other book, does that show you that the most popular book on the planet to-day is the Word of God?

"Oh," say people, "the church is a collection of hypocrites, and it is losing its power and it is fading out from the world." Is it? A bishop of the Methodist Church told me that that denomination averages a new church every day of the year. In other words, they build three hundred and sixty-five churches in that denomination in a year, and there are at least one thousand new Christian churches built in America every year. Does that look as though the church were fading out, as though it were a defunct institution? Which institution stands nearest the hearts of the people of America today? I do not care in what village or in what city, or what neighborhood you go. Which institution is it? Is it the post-office? Is it the hotel? Is it the lecturing hall? Ah, you know it is not. You know that the institution which stands nearest to the hearts of the American people is the Christian church. If you have ever seen a church burn down, you have seen thousands of people standing and looking at it—people who never go into a church—the tears raining down their cheeks. The whole story is told.

You may talk about the church being a collection of hypocrites, but when the diphtheria sweeps your children off, whom do you send for? The postmaster? the attorney-general? the hotel keeper? alderman? No, you send for a minister of this Bible religion. And if you have not a room in your house for the obsequies, what building do you solicit? Do you say: "Give me the finest room in the hotel?" Do you say: "Give me that theatre?" Do you say: "Give me a place in that public building where I can lay my dead for a little while until we say a prayer over it?" No; you say: "Give us the house of God." And if there is a song to be sung at the obsequies what do you want? What does anybody want? The Marseillaise Hymn? God Save the Queen? Our own grand national air? No. They want the hymn with which they sang their old Christian mother into her last sleep, or they want sung the Sabbath-school hymn which their little girl sang the last Sabbath afternoon she was out before she got that awful sickness which broke your heart. I appeal to your common-sense. You know the most endearing institution on earth, the most popular institution on earth to-day, is the church of the Lord Jesus Christ. A man is a fool that does not recognize it.

The infidels say: "There is great liberty now for infidels; we never had such freedom of platform; infidelity shows its power from the fact that it is everywhere accepted, and it can say what it will." Why, my friends, infidelity is not half so blatant in our day as it was in the days of our fathers. Do you know that in the days of our fathers there were pronounced infidels in public authority and they could get any political position? Let a man to-day declare himself antagonistic to the Christian religion, and what city wants him for mayor, what State wants him for governor, what nation wants him for president or for king? Let a man openly proclaim himself the enemy of our glorious Christianity, and he cannot get a majority of votes in any State, in any city, in any country, in any ward of America.

Mr. Ingersoll, years ago, riding in a rail-car in Illinois, said: "What has Christianity ever done?" An old Christian woman said: "It has done one thing, anyhow; it has kept Mr. Ingersoll from being Governor of Illinois!" As I stood in the side room of the opera house at Peoria, Illinois, a prominent gentleman of that city said: "I can tell you the secret of that tremendous bitterness against Christianity." Said I: "What was it?" "Why," said he, "in this very house there was a great convention to nominate a governor, and there were three or four candidates. At the same time, there was in a church in this city a Sabbath-school convention, and it happened that one of the men who was in the Sabbath-school convention was also a member of the political convention. In the political convention, the name highest on the roll at that time and about to be nominated was the name of the great champion infidel. There was an adjournment between ballots, and in the afternoon, when the nominations were being made, a plain farmer got up and said: "Mr. Chairman, that nomination must not be made;

the Sunday-schools of Illinois will defeat him." That ended all prospect of his nomination. The Christian religion is mightier to-day than it ever was.

Do you think that such a scene could be enacted now as was enacted in the days of Robespierre, when a shameless woman was elevated to a goddess, and was carried in a golden chair to a cathedral where incense was burned to her and people bowed down before her as a divine being, she taking the place of the Bible and God Almighty, while in the corridors of that cathedral were enacted such scenes of drunkenness and debauchery and obscenity as have never been witnessed? Do you believe such a thing could possibly occur in Christendom to-day? No, sir. The police, whether of Paris or New York, would swoop on it. I know infidelity makes a good deal of talk in our day. One infidel can make great excitement, but I will tell you on what principle it is. It is on the principle that if a man jump overboard from a Cunard steamer he makes more excitement than all the five hundred people that stay on the decks. But the fact that he jumps overboard—does that stop the ship? Does that wreck the five hundred passengers? It makes great excitement when a man jumps from the lecturing platform, or from the pulpit, into infidelity; but does that keep the Bible and the Church from carrying their millions of passengers into the skies?

They say, these men, that science is overcoming religion in our day. They look through the spectacles of the infidel scientists, and they say, "It is impossible that this book be true; people are finding it out; the Bible has got to go overboard; science is going to throw it overboard." Do you believe that the Bible account of the origin of life will be overthrown by infidel scientists who have fifty different theories about the origin of life? If they should come up in solid phalanx, all agreeing on one sentiment and one theory, perhaps Christianity might be damaged; but there are not so many differences of opinion inside the church as outside the church. People used to say, "there are so many different denominations of Christians—that shows there is nothing in religion." I have to tell you that all denominations agree on the two or three or four radical doctrines of the Christian religion. They are unanimous in regard to Jesus Christ, and they are unanimous in regard to the divinity of the Scriptures. How is it on the other side? All split up, you cannot find two of them alike. Oh, it makes me sick to see these literary fops going along with a copy of Darwin under one arm and a case of transfixed grasshoppers and butterflies under the other arm, telling about the "survival of the fittest," and Huxley's protoplasm, and the nebular hypothesis. The fact is, that some naturalists just as soon as they find out the difference between the feelers of a wasp and the horns of a beetle, they begin to patronize the Almighty; while Agassiz, glorious Agassiz, who never made any pretension to being a Christian, puts both his feet on the doctrine of evolution, and says: "I see that many of the naturalists of our day are adopting facts which do not bear observation, or have not passed under observation." These men warring with each other—Darwin warring against Lamarck, Wallace warring against Cope, even Herschel denouncing Ferguson. They do not agree about anything. They do not agree on embryology, do not agree on the gradation of the species. What do they agree on? Herschel writes a whole chapter on the errors of astronomy. La Place declares that the moon was not put in the right place. He says if it had been put four times further from the earth than it is now, there would be more harmony in the universe; but Lionville comes up just in time to prove that the moon was put in the right place. How many colors woven into the light? Seven, says Isaac Newton. Three, says David Brewster. How high is the Aurora Borealis? Two and a half miles, says Lias. One hundred and sixty-eight miles, says Twining. How far is the sun from the earth? Seventy-six million miles, says Lacalle. Eighty-two million miles, says Humboldt. Ninety million miles, says Henderson. One hundred and four million miles, says Mayer. Only a little difference of twenty-eight million miles! All split up among themselves—not agreeing on anything. They come and say that the churches of Jesus Christ are divided on the great doctrines. All united they are, in Jesus Christ, in the divinity of the Scriptures; while they come up and propose to render their verdict, and no two of them agree on that verdict. "Gentlemen of the jury, have you agreed on a verdict?" asks the court or the clerk of the jury as they come in after having spent the whole night in deliberating. If the jury say "Yes, we have agreed," the verdict is recorded; but suppose one of the jurymen says, "I think the man was guilty of murder," and another says, "I think he was guilty of manslaughter in the second degree," and another man says, "I think he was guilty of assault and battery with intent to kill," the judge would say, "Go back to your room and bring in a verdict; agree on something; that is no verdict."

Here these infidel scientists have empanelled themselves as a jury to decide this trial between Infidelity, the plaintiff, and Christianity, the defendant, and after being out for centuries they come in to render their verdict. Gentlemen of the jury, have you agreed on a verdict? No, no. Then go back for another five hundred years and deliberate and agree on something. There is not a poor miserable wretch in the Tombs court to-morrow that could be condemned by a jury that did not agree on the verdict, and yet you expect us to give up our glorious Christianity to please these men who cannot agree on anything.

Ah! my friends, the church of Jesus Christ instead of falling back is on the advance. I am certain it is on the advance. I see the glittering of swords, I hear the tramping of the troops, I hear the thunderings of parks of artillery. Oh my God and Saviour, I thank Thee that I have been permitted to see this day—this day of Thy triumph, this day of the confusion of Thine enemies. O Lord God, take Thy sword from Thy thigh and ride forth to the victory.

I am mightily encouraged because I find among other things that while this Christianity has been bombarded for centuries, infidelity has not destroyed one church, or crippled one minister, or uprooted one verse of one chapter of all the Bible. If that has been their magnificent record for the centuries that are past, what may we expect for the future? The church all the time getting the victory, and their shot and shell all gone. I have been examining their ammunition lately, I have looked all through their cartridge-boxes. They have not in the last twenty years advanced one new idea. They have utterly exhausted their ammunition in the battle against the church and against the Scriptures, while the sword of the Lord Almighty is as keen as it ever was. We are just getting our troops into line; they are coming up in companies and in regiments and in battalions, and you will hear a shout after a while that will make the earth quake and the heavens ring with Alleluia. It will be this: "Forward, the whole line."

And then I find another most encouraging thought in the fact that the secular printing-press and the pulpit seem harnessed in the same team for the proclamation of the Gospel. Every Wall Street banker to-morrow in New York, every State Street banker to-morrow in Boston, every Third Street banker to-morrow in Philadelphia, every banker in the United States, and every merchant will have in his pocket a treatise on Christianity, a call to repentance, ten, twenty, or thirty passages of Scripture in the reports of sermons preached throughout these cities and throughout the land to-day. It will be so in Chicago, so in New Orleans, so in Charleston, so in Boston, so in Philadelphia, so everywhere. I know the tract societies are doing a grand and glorious work, but I tell you there is no power on earth to-day equal to the fact that the American printing-press is taking up the sermons which are preached to a few hundred or a few thousand people, on Monday morning and Monday evening, in the morning and evening papers, scattering that truth to the millions. What a thought it is! What an encouragement for every Christian man.

Beside that, have you noticed that during the past few years every one of the doctrines of the Bible came under discussion in the secular press? Do you not remember a few years ago—I think not more than six or seven years ago—when every paper in the United States had an editorial on the subject: "Is there such a thing as future punishment?" It was the strangest thing that there should be a discussion in the secular papers on that subject, but every paper in the United States and in Christendom discussed: "Is there such a thing as retribution?" I know there were small wits who made sport of the discussion, but there was not an intelligent man on earth who as the result of that discussion did not ask himself the question: "What is going to be my eternal destiny?" So it was in regard to Tyndall's prayer gauge. Some seven or nine years ago you remember the secular papers discussed that, and with just as much earnestness as the religious papers, and there was not a man in Christendom who did not ask himself the question: "Is there anything in prayer? May the creature impress the Creator?" Oh, what a mighty fact, what a glorious fact, the secular printing-press and the pulpit of the Church of Jesus Christ harnessed in the same team.

Then look at the International Series of Sunday-school lessons. Do you know that this afternoon, I suppose between three and five o'clock, there will be five million children studying the same lesson, a lesson prepared by the leading minds of the country, and printed in the papers, and then these subjects are discussed and given over to the teachers, who give them over to the children; so whereas once—and within our memory—the children nibbled here and there at a story of the Bible, now they are taken through from Genesis to Revelation, and we shall have five million children forestalled for Christianity. My soul is full of exultation. I feel as if I could shout—I will shout, "Alleluia, the Lord God omnipotent reigneth!"

Then you notice a more significant fact still further—you have noticed if you have talked with people on the subject, that they are getting dissatisfied with philosophy and science as a matter of comfort. They say it does not amount to anything when you have a dead child in the house. They tell you when they were sick and the door of the future seemed opening, the only comfort they could find was in the Gospel. People are having demonstrated all over the land that science and philosophy cannot solace the trouble and woes of the world, and they want some other religion, and they are taking Christianity, the only sympathetic religion that ever came into the world. You just take your scientific consolation into that room where a mother has lost her child. Try in that case your splendid doctrine of the "survival of the fittest." Tell her that child died because it was not worth as much as the other children. That is your "survival of the fittest." Go to that dying man and tell him to pluck up courage for the future. Use your transcendental phraseology upon him. Tell him he ought to be confident in "the great to be," and the "everlasting now," and the "eternal what-is-it." Just try your transcendentalism and your philosophy and your science on him. Go to that widowed soul, and tell her it was a geological necessity that her companion should be taken away from her, just as in the course of the world's history the megatherium had to pass out of existence; and then you go on in your scientific consolation until you get to the sublime fact that fifty million years from now we ourselves may be scientific specimens on a geological shelf, petrified specimens of an extinct human race. And after you have got all through with your consolation, if the poor afflicted soul is not crazed by it, I will send forth from this church the plainest Christian we have, and with one half hour of prayer and reading of Scripture promises, the tears will be wiped away, and the house from floor to cupola will be flooded with the calmness of an Indian summer sunset. There is where I see the triumph of Christianity. People are dissatisfied with everything else. They want God. They want Jesus Christ.

Talk about the exact sciences, there is only one exact science. It is not mathematics. Taylor's logarithms have many imperfections. The French metric system has many imperfections. The only exact science is Christianity —the only thing under which you can appropriately write: *"Quod erat demonstrandum."* You tell me that two and two make four. I do not dispute it, but it is not so plain that two and two make four as that the Lord God Almighty made this world. And for man, the sinner, He sent His only begotten Son to die.

In this trial that has been going on between Infidelity and Christianity, we have only called one witness, and that was Robert G. Ingersoll. He testified in behalf of Infidelity. We have put one witness on the stand. We have shown that his testimony was not worthy of being received. We showed it was founded on ignorance geological, ignorance chemical, ignorance astronomical, ignorance geographical, and if he would misrepresent in one case he would misrepresent in all cases. We had one witness on the stand. I put others on the stand this morning. I put on the church on earth and all the church in heaven. Not fifty, not a thousand, not a million, but all the church on earth and all the redeemed in heaven. Whose testimony is worth the most?

You tell me James A. Garfield was inaugurated President of the United States on the fourth of March last. How do I know it? You tell me there were twenty thousand persons who distinctly heard his inaugural address. I deny both. I deny that he was inaugurated. I deny that his inaugural address was delivered. You ask why? I did not see it. I did not hear it. But you say that there were twenty thousand persons who did see and hear him. I say I cannot take it anyhow; I did not see and hear him. Whose testimony will you take? You will not take my testimony. You say, "You know nothing about it, you were not there; let us have the testimony of the twenty thousand persons who stood before the capitol and heard that magnificent inaugural." Why, of course, that is as your common-sense dictates.

Now, here are some men who say they have never seen Christ crowned in the heart and they do not believe it is ever done. There is a group of men who say they have never heard the voice of Christ, they have never heard the voice of God. They do not believe it ever transpired, or was ever heard—that anything like it ever occurred. I point to twenty, a hundred thousand or a million people who say: "Christ was crowned in our heart's affections, we have seen Him and felt Him in our soul, and we have heard His voice; we have heard it in storm and darkness; we have heard it again and again." Whose testimony will you take? These men, the Ingersolls of earth, who say they have not heard the voice of Christ, have not seen the coronation; or will you take the thousands and tens of thousands of Christians who testify of what they saw with their own eyes and heard with their own ears?

Father Pierson, after fifty years' experience of the power of godliness in his soul, put his testimony against Robert G. Ingersoll's. Ask this man whether, when he buried his dead, the religion of Jesus Christ was not a consolation. Ask him if through the long years of his pilgrimage the Lord ever forsook him. Ask him when he looks forward to the future, if he has not a peace and a joy and a consolation the world cannot take away. Put his testimony of what he has seen and what he has felt opposite to the testimony of a man who says he has not seen anything on the subject or felt anything on the subject—confesses he has not tried it. Will you take the testimony of people who have not seen, or people who have seen?

You say morphia puts one to sleep. You say in time of sickness it is very useful. I deny it. Morphia never puts anybody to sleep, it never alleviates pain. You ask why I say that. I have never tried it, I never took it. I deny that morphia is any soothing to the nerves, or any quiet in times of sickness. I deny that morphia ever put anybody to sleep; but here are twenty persons who say they have all felt the soothing effects of a physician's prescribing morphine. Whose testimony will you take? Those who took the medicine, or my testimony, I never having taken the medicine? Here is the Gospel of Jesus Christ, an anodyne for all trouble, the mightiest medicine that ever came down to earth. Here is a man who says: "I don't believe in it; there is no power in it." Here are other people who say, "We have found out its power, and know its soothing influence; it has cured us." Whose testimony will you take in regard to this healing medicine?

I feel that I have convinced every man in this house that it is utter folly to take the testimony of those who have never tried the Gospel of Jesus Christ in their own heart and life. We have tens of thousands of witnesses. I believe you are ready to take their testimony.

Young man, do not be ashamed to be a friend of the Bible. Do not put your thumb in your vest, as young men sometimes do, and swagger about, talking of the glorious light of the nineteenth century, and of there being no need of a Bible. They have the light of nature in India and China and in all the dark places of the earth. Did you ever hear that the light of nature gave them comfort for their trouble? They have lancets to cut and juggernauts to crush, but no comfort. Ah! my friends, you had better stop your scepticism. Suppose you are put in this crisis. O father! Your child is dying. What are you going to say to her?

Colonel Ethan Allen was a famous infidel in his day. His wife was a very consecrated woman. The mother instructed the daughter in the truths of Christianity. The daughter sickened and was about to die, and she said to her father: "Father, shall I take your instruction? or shall I take mother's instruction? I am going to die now; I must have this matter decided." That man, who had been loud in his infidelity, said to his dying daughter: "My dear, you had better take your mother's religion." My advice is the same to you, O young man, you had better take your mother's religion. You know how it comforted her. You know what she said to you when she was dying. You had better take your mother's religion.

Victory for Man

ROBERT GREEN INGERSOLL

> *Born, Dresden, New York, August 11, 1833; died, Dobbs*
> *Ferry, New York, July 21, 1899. Meager formal school-*
> *ing. Taught school briefly, studied law, was admitted to*
> *the Illinois bar, 1854. Raised and commanded a cavalry*
> *regiment for the Union army. Attorney-general of Illinois,*
> *1867–1869. Nationally known as lawyer, political cam-*
> *paigner for Republican party, and public lecturer.*

*L**adies and Gentlemen:* Nothing can be more certain than that no human being can by any possibility control his thought. We are in this world—we see, we hear, we feel, we taste; and everything in Nature makes an impression upon the brain, and that wonderful something, enthroned there with these materials, weaves what we call thought, and the brain can no more help thinking than the heart can help beating. The blood pursues its old accustomed round without our will. The heart beats without asking leave of us, and the brain thinks in spite of all that we can do. This being true, no human being can justly be held responsible for his thought any more than for the beating of his heart, any more than for the course pursued by the blood, any more than for breathing air. And yet for thousands of years thought has been thought to be a crime, and thousands and millions have threatened us with eternal fire if we give the product of that brain. Each brain, in my judgment, is a field where Nature sows the seeds of thought, and thought is the crop that man reaps, and it certainly cannot be a crime to gather it; it certainly cannot be a crime to tell it, which simply amounts to the right to sell your

McVicker's Theatre, Chicago, Illinois, Sunday, November 12, 1882. *The Chicago Tribune*, November 13, 1882, p. 6. (The title of this speech has been supplied by the editors.)

crop or to exchange your product for the product of some other man's brain. That is all it is. Most brains—at least some—are rather poor fields, and the orthodox worst of all. That field produces mostly sorrel and mullein, while there are fields which, like the tropic world, are filled with growth, and where you find the vine and the palm, royal children of the sun and brain. I then stand simply for absolute freedom of thought—absolute, and I don't believe, if there is a God, that it will be or can be pleasing to Him to see one of His children afraid to express what he thinks. And, if I were God, I never would cease making men until I succeeded in making one grand enough to tell his honest opinion.

Now there has been a struggle, you know, a long time between the believers in the natural and the supernatural—between gentlemen who are going to reward us in another world and those who propose to make life worth living here and now. In all ages the priest, the medicine man, the magician, the astrologer, in other words, gentlemen who have traded upon the fear and ignorance of their fellow-man in all countries, they have sought to make their living out of others. There was a time when a God presided over every department of human interest, when a man about to take a voyage bribed the priest of Neptune so that he might have a safe journey, and, when he came back, he paid more, telling the priest that he was infinitely obliged to him that he had kept waves from the sea and storms in their caves. And so, when one was sick he went to a priest; when one was about to take a journey he visited the priest of Mercury; if he were going to war he consulted the representative of Mars. We have gone along. When the poor agriculturist plowed his ground and put in the seed he went to the priest of some god and paid him to keep off the frost. And the priest said he would do it; "but," added the priest, "you must have faith." If the frost came early he said, "You didn't have faith." And besides all that he says to him: "Anything that has happened badly, after all, was for your good." Well, we found out, day by day, that a good boat for the purposes of navigating the sea was better than prayers, better than the influence of priests; and you had better have a good Captain attending to business than thousands of priests ashore praying.

We also found that we could cure some diseases, and just as soon as we found that we could cure diseases we dismissed the priest. We have left him out now of all of them except, it may be, cholera and smallpox. When visited by a plague some people get frightened enough to go back to the old idea—go back to the priest, and the priest says, "It has been sent as a punishment." Well, sensible people began to look about; they saw that the good died as readily as the bad; they saw that this disease would attack the dimpled child in the cradle and allow the murderer to go unpunished; and so they began to think in time that it was not sent as a punishment; that it was a natural result; and so the priest stepped out of medicine.

In agriculture we need him no longer; he has nothing to do with the crops. All the clergymen in this world can never get one drop of rain out of the sky; and all the clergymen in the civilized world could not save one human life if they tried it.

"Oh, but," they say, "we do not expect a direct answer to prayer; it is the reflex action we are after." It is like a man endeavoring to lift himself up by the straps of his boots; he will never do it, but he will get a great deal of useful exercise.

The missionary goes to some pagan land, and there finds a man praying to a god of stone, and it excites the wrath of the missionary. I ask you tonight, Does not that stone god answer prayer just as well as ours? Does he not cause rain? Does he not delay frost? Does he not snatch the ones that we love from the grasp of death, precisely the same as ours? Yet we have ministers that are still engaged in that business. They tell us that they have been "called"; that they do not go at their professions as other people do, but they are "called"; that God, looking over the world, carefully selects his priests, his ministers, and his exhorters.

I don't know. They say their calling is sacred. I say to you tonight that every kind of business that is honest, that a man engages in for the purpose of feeding his wife and children, for the purpose of building up his home, and for the purpose of feeding and clothing the ones he loves—that business is sacred. They tell me that statesmen and poets, philosophers, heroes, and scientists, and inventors come by chance; that all other departments depend entirely upon luck; but when God wants exhorters He selects.

They also tell me that it is infinitely wicked to attack the Christian religion, and when I speak of the Christian religion I do not refer especially to the Christianity of the New Testament; I refer to the Christianity of the orthodox church, and when I refer to the clergy I refer to the clergy of the orthodox church. There was a time when men of genius were in the pulpits of the orthodox church; that time is past. When you find a man with brains now occupying an orthodox pulpit you will find him touched with heresy— every one of them.

How do they get most of these ministers? There will be a man in the neighborhood not very well—not having constitution enough to be wicked; and it instantly suggests itself to everybody who sees him he would make an excellent minister. There are so many other professions, so many cities to be built, so many railways to be constructed, so many poems to be sung, so much music to be composed, so many papers to edit, so many books to read, so many splendid things, so many avenues to distinction and glory, so many things beckoning from the horizon of the future to every great and splendid man that the pulpit has to put up with the leavings, ravelings, selvages.

These preachers say, "How can any man be wicked enough and infamous enough to attack our religion and to take from the world the solace of orthodox Christianity?" What is that solace? Let us be honest. What is it? If the Christian religion be true, the grandest, greatest, noblest of the world are now in Hell, and the narrowest and meanest are now in Heaven. Humboldt, the Shakespeare of science, the most learned man of the most learned nation, with a mind grand enough to grasp not simply this globe, but this constellation—a man who shed light upon the whole earth—a man who honored human nature, and who won all his victories on the fields of thought —that man, pure and upright, noble beyond description, if Christianity be true, is in Hell this moment. That is what they call "solace"; "tidings of great joy." La Place, who read the heavens like an open book, who enlarged the horizon of human thought, is there too. Beethoven, master of melody and harmony, who added to the joy of human life, and who has borne upon the wings of harmony and melody millions of spirits to the height of joy, with his heart still filled with melody—he is in Hell today. Robert Burns, poet of love and liberty, and from his heart, like a spring gurgling and running down the highways, his poems have filled the world with music. They have added lustre to human love. That man who, in four lines, gave all the philosophy of life—

> To make a happy fireside clime
> For weans and wife
> Is the true pathos and sublime
> Of human life.

—he is there with the rest. Charles Dickens, whose genius will be a perpetual shield, saving thousands and millions of children from blows, who did more to make us tender with children than any other writer that ever touched a pen—he is there with the rest, according to our Christian religion. A little while ago there died in this country a philosopher—Ralph Waldo Emerson— a man of the loftiest ideal, a perfect model of integrity, whose mind was like a placid lake and reflected truths like stars. If the Christian religion be true, he is in perdition today. And yet he sowed the seeds of thought, and raised the whole world intellectually. And Longfellow, whose poems, tender as the dawn, have gone into millions of homes, not an impure, not a stained word in them all; but he was not a Christian. He did not believe in the "tidings of great joy." He didn't believe that God so loved the world that He intended to damn most everybody. And now he has gone to his reward. And Charles Darwin—a child of Nature—one who knew more about his mother than any other child she had. What is philosophy? It is to account for phenomena by which we are surrounded—that is to find the hidden cord that unites everything. Charles Darwin threw more light upon the problem of human existence than all the priests who ever lived from Melchisedek to the last exhorter. He would have traversed this globe on foot had it been possible to have found one new fact or to have corrected one error that he had made. No nobler man has lived—no man who has studied with more reverence (and by reverence I mean simply one who lives and studies for the truth)—no man who studied with more reverence than he. And yet, according to orthodox religion, Charles Darwin is in Hell. Consolation! So, if Christianity be true, Shakespeare, the greatest man who ever touched this planet, within whose brain were the fruits of all thought past, the seeds of all to be— Shakespeare, who was an intellectual ocean toward which all rivers ran, and from which now the isles and continents of thought receive their dew and rain—that man who has added more to the intelligence of the world than any other who ever lived—that man, whose creations will live as long as man has imagination, and who has given more happiness upon the stage and more instruction than has flown from all the pulpits of this earth—that man is in Hell, too. And Harriet Martineau, who did as much for English liberty as any man, brave and free—she is there. "George Eliot," the greatest woman the English-speaking people ever produced—she is with the rest. And this is called "Tidings of Great Joy."

Who are in heaven? How could there be much of a Heaven without the men I have mentioned—the great men that have endeavored to make the world grander—such men as Voltaire, such men as Diderot, such men as the Encyclopedists, such men as Hume, such men as Bruno, such men as Thomas Paine? If Christianity is true, that man who spent his life in breaking chains is now wearing the chains of God; that man who wished to break down the prison walls of tyranny is now in the prison of the most merciful Christ. It will not do. I can hardly express to you today my contempt for such a doctrine; and if it be true, I make my choice today, and I prefer Hell.

Who is in Heaven? John Calvin! John Knox! Jonathan Edwards! Torquemada—the builders of dungeons, the men who have obstructed the march of the human race. These are the men who are in Heaven; and who else? Those who never had brain enough to harbor a doubt. And they ask me: "How can you be wicked enough to attack the Christian religion?"

"Oh," but they say, "God will never forgive you if you attack the orthodox religion." Now, when I read the history of this world, and when I think of the experience of my fellow-men, when I think of the millions living in poverty and when I know that in the very air we breathe and in the sunlight that visits our homes there lurks an assassin ready to take our lives, and even when we believe we are in the fullness of health and joy, they are undermining us with their contagion—when I know that we are surrounded by all these evils, and when I think of what man has suffered, I do not wonder if God can forgive man, but I often ask myself, "Can man forgive God?"

There is another thing. Some of these ministers have talked about me, and have made it their business to say unpleasant things. Among others the Rev. Mr. Talmage, of Brooklyn—a man of not much imagination, but of most excellent judgment—charges that I am a "blasphemer." A frightful charge! Terrible, if true!

What is blasphemy? It is a sin, as I understand, against God. Is God infinite? He is, so they say; He is infinite; absolutely conditionless. Can I injure the conditionless? No. Can I sin against anything that I cannot injure? No. That is a perfectly plain proposition. I can injure my fellow-man, because he is a conditioned being, and I can help to change those conditions. He must have air; he must have food; he must have clothing; he must have shelter; but God is conditionless, and I cannot by any possibility affect Him. Consequently I cannot sin against Him. But I can sin against my fellow-man, so that I ought to be a thousand times more fearful of doing injustice than of uttering blasphemy. There is no blasphemy but injustice, and there is no worship except the practice of justice. It is a thousand times more important that we should love our fellow-men than that we should love God. It is better to love wife and children than to love Jesus Christ. He is dead; they are alive. I can make their lives happy and fill all their hours with the fullness of joy. That is my religion; and the holiest temple ever erected beneath the stars is the home: the holiest altar is the fireside.

What is this blasphemy? First, it is a geographical question. There was a time when it was blasphemy in Jerusalem to say that Christ was God. In this country it is now blasphemy to say that He was not. It is blasphemy in Constantinople to deny that Mohamet was the prophet of God; it is blasphemy here to say that he was. It is a geographical question; you cannot tell whether it is blasphemy or not without looking at the map. What is blasphemy? It is what the mistake says about the fact. It is what the last year's leaf says about this year's bud. It is the last cry of the defeated priest. Blasphemy is the little breastwork behind which hypocrisy hides; behind which mental impotency feels safe. There is no blasphemy but the avowal of thought, and he who speaks what he thinks blasphemes.

What is the next thing? That I have had the hardihood—it doesn't take much—to attack the sacred Scriptures. I have simply given my opinion; and yet they tell me that that book is holy—that you can take rags, make pulp, put ink on it, bind it in leather, and make something holy. The Catholics have a man for a Pope; the Protestants have a book. The Catholics have the best of it. If they elect an idiot he will not live forever, and it is impossible for us to get rid of the barbarisms in our book. The Catholics said, "We will not let the common people read the Bible." That was right. If it is necessary to believe it in order to get to Heaven no man should run the risk of reading it. To allow a man to read the Bible on such conditions is to set a trap for his soul. The right way is never to open it, and when you get to the day of

judgment, and they ask you if you believe it say, "Yes, I have never read it."
The Protestant gives the book to a poor man and says, "Read it. You are at
liberty to read it." "Well, suppose I don't believe it, when I get through?"
"Then you will be damned." No man should be allowed to read it on those
conditions. And yet Protestants have done that infinitely cruel thing. If I
thought it was necessary to believe it I would say never read another line in
it but just believe it and stick to it. And yet these people really think that
there is something miraculous about that book. They regard it as a fetish—a
kind of amulet—a something charmed, that will keep off evil spirits, or bad
luck, stop bullets, and do a thousand handy things for the preservation of life.

I heard a story upon that subject. You know that thousands of them are
printed in the Sunday-school books. Here is one they don't print. There was
a poor man who had belonged to the church, but he got cold, and he rather
neglected it, and he had bad luck in his business, and he went down and
down and down until he hadn't a dollar—not a thing to eat; and his wife said
to him, "John, this comes of your having abandoned the church. This comes
of your having done away with family worship. Now, I beg of you, let's go
back." Well, John said it wouldn't do any harm to try. So he took down the
Bible, blew the dust off it, read a little from a chapter, and had family worship. As he was putting it up he opened it again, and there was a $10 bill
between the leaves. He rushed out to the butcher's and bought meat, to the
grocer's and bought tea and bread, and butter and eggs, and rushed back
home and got them cooked, and the house was filled with the perfume of
food; and he sat down at the table, tears in every eye and a smile on every
face. She said, "What did I tell you?" Just then there was a knock on the
door, and in came a constable who arrested him for passing a $10 counterfeit
bill.

They tell me that I ought not to attack the Bible—that I have misrepresented it, and among other things that I have said that, according to the Bible,
the world was made of nothing. Well, what was it made of? They say God
created everything. Consequently, there must have been nothing when He
commenced. If He didn't make it of nothing what did He make it of? Where
there was nothing, He made something. Yes; out of what? I don't know.
This doctor of divinity, and I should think such a divinity would need a
doctor, says that God made the universe out of His omnipotence. Why not
out of His omniscience, or His omnipresence? Omnipotence is not a raw
material. It is the something to work raw material with. Omnipotence is simply all powerful, and what good would strength do with nothing? The weak-
est man ever born could lift as much nothing as God. And he could do as
much with it after he got it lifted. And yet a doctor of divinity tells me that
this world was made of omnipotence. And right here let me say I find even
in the mind of the clergyman the seeds of infidelity. He is trying to explain

things. That is a bad symptom. The greater the miracle the greater the reward for believing it. God cannot afford to reward a man for believing anything reasonable. Why, even the Scribes and Pharisees would believe a reasonable thing. Do you suppose God is to crown you with eternal joy and give you a musical instrument for believing something where the evidence is clear? No, sir. The larger the miracle the more grace. And let me advise the ministers of Chicago and of this country, never to explain a miracle; it cannot be explained. If you succeed in explaining it, the miracle is gone. If you fail you are gone. My advice to the clergy is use assertion, just say "it is so," and the larger the miracle the greater the glory reaped by the eternal. And yet this man is trying to explain, pretending that He had some raw material of some kind on hand.

And then I objected to the fact that He didn't make the sun until the fourth day, and that, consequently, the grass could not have grown—could not have thrown its mantle of green over the shoulders of the hill—and that the trees would not blossom and cast their shade upon the sod without some sunshine; and what does this man say? Why, that the rocks, when they crystallized, emitted light, even enough to raise a crop by. And he says "vegetation might have depended on the glare of volcanoes in the moon." What do you think would be the fate of agriculture depending on "the glare of volcanoes in the moon?" Then he says, "the aurora borealis." Why, you couldn't raise cucumbers by the aurora borealis. And he says "liquid rivers of molten granite." I would like to have had a farm on that stream. He guesses everything of the kind except lightning-bugs and foxfire. Now, think of that explanation in the last half of the nineteenth century by a minister. The truth is, the gentleman who wrote the account knew nothing of astronomy— knew as little as the modern preacher does—just about the same; and if they don't know more about the next world than they do about this, it is hardly worth while talking with them on the subject. There was a time, you know, when the minister was the educated man in the country, and when, if you wanted to know anything, you asked him. Now you do if you don't. So I find this man expounding the flood, and he says it was not very wet. He begins to doubt whether God had water enough to cover the whole earth. Why not stand by his book? He says that some of the animals got in there to keep out of the wet. I believe that is the way the Democrats got to the polls last Tuesday.

Another divine says that God would have drowned them all, but it was purely for the sake of economy that He saved any of them. Just think of that! According to this Christian religion all the people in the world were totally depraved through the fall, and God found He could not do anything with them, so He drowned them. Now, if God wanted to get up a flood big enough to drown sin, why did He not get up a flood big enough to drown the snake? That was His mistake. Now, these people say that if Jonah had walked rapidly up and down the whale's belly he would have avoided the action of its gastric-juice. Imagine Jonah sitting in the whale's mouth, on the back of a molar-tooth; and yet this doctor of divinity would have us believe that the infinite God of the universe was sitting under his gourd and made the worm that was at the foot of Jonah's vine. Great business.

David is said to have been a man after God's own heart, and if you will read the twenty-eighth chapter of Chronicles you will find that David died full of years and honors. So I find in the great book of prophecy, concerning Solomon, "He shall reign in peace and quietness, he shall be my son, and I shall be his father, and I will preserve his Kingdom." Was that true?

It won't do. But they say God couldn't do away with slavery suddenly, nor with polygamy all at once—that He had to do it gradually—that if He had told this man you mustn't have slaves, and one man that he must have one wife, and one wife that she must have one husband, He would have lost the control over them, notwithstanding all the miraculous power. Is it not wonderful that, when they did all these miracles, nobody paid any attention to them? Isn't it wonderful that, in Egypt, when they performed these wonders—when the waters were turned into blood, when the people were smitten with disease and covered with horrible animals—isn't it wonderful that it had no influence on them? Do you know why all these miracles didn't effect the Egyptians? They were there at the time. Isn't it wonderful, too, that the Jews who had been brought from bondage—had followed a cloud by day and a pillar of fire by night—who had been miraculously fed, and for whose benefit water had leaked from the rocks and followed them up and down hill through all their journeying—isn't it wonderful, when they had seen the earth open and their companions swallowed, when they had seen God Himself write in robes of flames from Sinai's crags, when they had seen Him talking face to face with Moses—isn't it a little wonderful that He had no more influence over them? They were there at the time. And that is the reason they didn't mind it—they were there. And yet, with all these miracles, this God could not prevent polygamy and slavery. Was there no room on the two tables of stone to put two more commandments? Better have written them on the back, then. Better have left the others all off and put these two on. Man shall not enslave his brother, you shall not live on unpaid labor, and the one man shall have the one wife. If these two had been written and the other ten left off, it would have been a thousand times better for this world.

But they say, God works gradually. No hurry about it. He is not gradual about keeping Sunday, because, if he met a man picking up sticks, He killed him; but in other things He is gradual. Suppose we wanted now to break certain cannibals of eating missionaries—wanted to stop them from eating them raw? Of course we would not tell them, in the first place, it was wrong. That would not do. We would induce them to cook them. That would be the first step toward civilization. We would have them stew them. We would not say it is wrong to eat missionary but it is wrong to eat missionary raw. Then, after they began stewing them, we would put in a little mutton—not enough to excite suspicion but just a little, and so, day by day, we would put in a little more mutton and a little less missionary until, in about what the Bible calls "the fullness of time," we would have clear mutton and no missionary. That is God's way.

The next great charge against me is that I have disgraced my parents by expressing my honest thoughts. No man can disgrace his parents that way. I want my children to express their real opinions, whether they agree with mine or not. I want my children to find out more than I have found, and I would be gratified to have *them* discover the errors I have made. And if my father and mother are still alive I feel and know that I am pursuing a course of which they would approve. I am true to my manhood. But think of it! Suppose the father of Dr. Talmage had been a Methodist and his mother an infidel. Then what? Would he have to disgrace them both to be a Presbyterian? The disciples of Christ, according to this doctrine, disgraced their parents. The founder of every new religion, according to this doctrine, was a disgrace to his father and mother. Now there must have been a time when a Talmage was not a Presbyterian, and the one that left something else to join that church disgraced his father and mother. Why, if this doctrine be true why do you send missionaries to other lands and ask those people to disgrace their parents? If this doctrine be true nobody has religious liberty except foundlings; and it should be written over every Foundling Hospital: "Home for Religious Liberty." It won't do.

. . . .

The next argument in favor of the "sacred Scriptures" is the argument of numbers; and this minister congratulates himself that the infidels could not carry a precinct, or a county, or a State in the United States. Well, I tell you, they can come proportionately near it—just in proportion that that part of the country is educated. The whole world doesn't move together in one life. There has to be some man to take a step forward and the people follow; and when they get where that man was, some other Titan has taken another step, and you can see him there on the great mountain of progress. That is why the world moves. There must be pioneers, and if nobody is right except he who is with the majority, then we must turn and walk toward the setting sun. He says "We will settle this by suffrage." The Christian religion was submitted to a popular vote in Jerusalem, and what was the result? "Crucify Him!" An infamous result, showing that you can't depend on the vote of barbarians. But I am told that there are 300,000,000 of Christians in the world. Well, what of it? There are more Buddhists. And they say, what a number of Bibles are printed!—more Bibles than any other book. Does this prove anything? True, because more of them. Suppose you should find published in the New York *Herald* something about you, and you should go to the editor and tell him: "That is a lie," and he should say: "That can't be; the *Herald* has the largest circulation of any paper in the world." Three hundred millions of Christians, and here are the nations that prove the truth of Christianity: Russia, 80,000,000 of Christians. I am willing to admit it; a country without freedom of speech, without freedom of press—a country in which every mouth is a bastile and every tongue a prisoner for life—a country in which assassins are the best men in it. They call that Christian. Girls sixteen years of age for having spoken of human liberty are now working in Siberian mines. That is a Christian country. Only a little while ago a man shot at the Emperor twice. The Emperor was protected by his armor. The man was convicted, and they asked him if he wished religious consolation. "No." "Do you believe in a God?" "No; if there was a God there would be no Russia." Sixteen millions of Christians in Spain—Spain that never touched a shore except as a robber—Spain that took the gold and silver of the New World and used it as an engine of oppression in the Old—a country in which cruelty was worship, in which murder was prayer—a country where flourished the inquisition—I admit Spain is a Christian country. If you don't believe it I do. Read the history of Holland, read the history of South America, read the history of Mexico—a chapter of cruelty beyond the power of language to express. I admit that Spain is orthodox. If you will go there you will find the man who robs you and asks God to forgive you—a country where infidelity hasn't made much headway, but, thank God, where there are such men as Castelar and others, who begin to see that one school house is equal to three cathedrals and one teacher worth all the priests. Italy is another Christian nation, with 28,000,000 of Christians. In Italy lives the only authorized agent of God, the Pope. For hundreds of years Italy was the beggar of the earth, and held out both hands. Gold and silver flowed from every land into her palms, and she became covered with nunneries, monasteries, and the pilgrims of the world.

Italy was sacred dust. Her soil was a perpetual blessing, her sky was an eternal smile. Italy was guilty not simply of the death of the Catholic Church, but Italy was dead and buried and would have been in her grave still had it not been for Mazzini, Garibaldi, and Cavour. When the prophecy of Garibaldi shall be fulfilled, when the priests, with spades in their hands, shall dig ditches to drain the Pontine marshes, when the monasteries shall be factories, when the whirling wheels of industry shall drown the drowsy and hypocritical prayers, then, and not till then, will Italy be great and free. Italy is the only instance in our history and in the history of the world, so far as we know, of the resurrection of a nation. She is the first fruits of them that sleep. Portugal is another Christian country. She made her living in the slave trade for centuries. I admit that all the blessings that that country enjoyed flowed naturally from Catholicism, and we believe in the same Scriptures. If you don't believe it, read the history of the persecution of the Jewish people. I admit that Germany is a Christian nation; that is, Christians are in power. When the bill was introduced for the purpose of ameliorating the condition of the Jews, Bismarck spoke against it, and said, "Germany is a Christian nation, and therefore we cannot pass the bill." Austria is another Christian nation. If you don't believe it, read the history of Hungary, and, if you still have doubts, read the history of the partition of Poland. But there is one good thing in that country. They believe in education, and education is the enemy of ecclesiasticism. Every thoroughly educated man is his own church, and his own Pope, and his own priest. They tell me that the United States—our country—is Christian. I deny it. It is neither Christian or pagan; it is human. Our fathers retired all the gods from politics. Our fathers laid down the doctrine that the right to govern comes from the consent of the governed, and not from the clouds. Our fathers knew that if they put an infinite God in the Constitution there would be no room left for the people. Our fathers used the language of Lincoln, and they made a Government for the people by the people. This is not a Christian country.

. . . .

The Bible is not inspired, and ministers know nothing about another world. They don't know. I am satisfied there is no world of eternal pain. If there is a world of joy, so much the better. I have never put out the faintest star of human hope that ever trembled in the night of life. There was a time when I was not; after that I was; now I am. And it is just as probable that I will live again as it was that I could have lived before I did. Let it go. Ah! but what will life be? The world will be here. Men and women will be here. The page of history will be open. The walls of the world will be adorned with art, the niches with sculpture; music will be here, and all there is of life and joy. And there will be homes here, and the fireside, and there will be a common hope without a common fear. Love will be here, and love is the only bow on life's dark cloud. Love was the first to dream of immortality. Love is morning and the evening star. It shines upon the child; it sheds its radiance upon the peaceful tomb. Love is the mother of beauty—the mother of melody, for music is its voice. Love is the builder of every hope, the kindler of every fire on every hearth. Love is the enchanter, the magician that changes worthless things to joy, and makes right royal Kings and Queens out of common clay. Love is the perfume of that wondrous flower, the heart. Without that divine passion, without that divine sway, we are less than beasts, and with it earth is heaven and we are gods.

CRUSADE FOR THE BALLOT

In *1881, thirty-three years after the inception of the movement, and thirty-nine years before the achievement of its goal, the first volume of* History of Woman Suffrage *was published. The authors of this work, Elizabeth Stanton, Susan Anthony, and Matilda Gage, closed their Introduction with these words:*

> *That equal rights for woman have not long ago been secured, is due to causes beyond the control of the actors in this reform. "The success of a movement," says Lecky, "depends much less upon the force of its arguments, or upon the ability of its advocates, than the predisposition of society to receive it."*

The suffrage movement, during its more than seventy years upon the American scene, lacked neither able advocates nor forceful arguments, but it was not until after all three of these ladies were in their graves that society, through its elected representatives, was disposed to amend the Federal Constitution to permit women to vote.

The organized campaign for woman's rights had its beginnings in 1848 in Seneca Falls, N.Y., home of Elizabeth Cady Stanton, with the calling of the first Woman's Rights Convention in history. The idea of such a convention had originated several years before, when in 1840 a group of women delegates to a World's Anti-Slavery Convention in London had been barred from taking their seats. Lucretia Mott and Elizabeth Stanton, indignant at this discrimination against properly accredited delegates solely because of their sex, decided then and there that woman, as well as the Negro, stood in need of outspoken champions of her rights.

The Declaration of Woman's Rights drawn up and adopted at Seneca Falls, and adopted again two weeks later by a similar convention in Rochester, proved an effective rallying cry. Local suffrage societies sprang up in many parts of the country. The first National Woman's Rights Convention was held in Worcester, Massachusetts, in October, 1850, with delegates from eleven states attending. National conventions were held annually during the next decade, and the battle for woman's rights made remarkable progress until interrupted by the outbreak of the Civil War. When, after the war, the fourteenth and fifteenth amendments enacted for the Negro were so drawn as to exclude women, the leaders of the movement were bitterly disappointed. But a precedent had been set in extending the franchise by federal amendment; the advocates of woman suffrage, who at first had attempted to change state constitutions, now saw the way to their goal. In 1869 they formed the National Woman Suffrage Association, dedicated to securing a sixteenth amendment for the enfranchisement of women. This organization (which in 1890 merged with Lucy Stone's American Woman Suffrage Association to form the National American Woman Suffrage Association) held a convention every year for fifty years, and subjected the Congress and the state legislatures to an incessant barrage of lobbying activity.

Despite these persistent efforts, it was not until 1887 that the woman suffrage amendment was first brought to a vote on the floor of the Senate of the United States. On January 25 of that year Senator Henry W. Blair of New Hampshire called attention to the delay in con-

sidering this amendment which, as he said, "has been pending in this body and in Congress for twenty or twenty-five years without ever having reached a vote at all." On the motion of Senator Blair the Senate proceeded to consider a joint resolution (S.R. 5) providing that: "The right of citizens of the United States to vote shall not be denied or abridged by the United States or by any state on account of sex." Speaking for the bill were Senators Joseph N. Dolph (Ore.), George Hoar (Mass.), and Blair; leading the opposition were Senators Joseph E. Brown (Ga.) and George G. Vest (Mo.). Senator Brown began the debate with a speech which according to the authors of History of Woman Suffrage *"embodied the stock objections to woman suffrage, practically all in fact which are ever made."[1] Incredible as some of these arguments seem today, examination of the speeches and writings of the period reveals that they are typical of those raised by both women and men—in many cases persons of great prominence and learning.*

Both Brown and Blair had been members of the seven-man Senate Committee on Woman Suffrage before whom a group of women led by Susan B. Anthony had presented their case March 7, 1884. This committee had submitted a favorable recommendation to the Senate, with Senators Brown and Cockrell dissenting. Brown's speech to the Senate on January 25, 1887 reiterated the points made in this dissenting report. At the completion of Brown's remarks, Senator Dolph spoke in favor of the amendment. He assured his colleagues that since women had been enfranchised in Washington Territory, the sun had continued to rise and set, the seasons had come and gone, marriages had been just as frequent and divorces no more so, and that women had not lost their influence for good, while men had been elevated and refined.

[1] Susan B. Anthony and Ida H. Harper, *History of Woman Suffrage* (Rochester, N.Y.: Susan B. Anthony, c. 1902), IV, p. 93.

In his speech against the amendment Senator Vest of Missouri read into the Record a list of eminent men, including the President of Harvard and numerous clergymen, who opposed woman suffrage. He quoted extensively from the anti-suffrage arguments of a Mrs. Clara T. Leonard and asked permission to print in full a pamphlet, "The Law of Woman Life," by Adeline D. T. Whitney. Senator Blair then requested permission to have printed in the Record the arguments that Miss Anthony and her associates had originally presented on March 7, 1884 before the Senate committee. "I think it only just," he said, "that woman, who is most interested, should be heard, at least under the circumstances when she has herself been heard on the other side through printed matter."² Senator Hoar closed the debate with a few brief remarks in which he referred pointedly to Senator Vest's address. He observed that Vest, a brilliant man, a lawyer and a logician, had furnished "the gush and the emotion and the eloquence," but had called on two women for the argument. He ventured the opinion that if women had to argue for Mr. Vest, it might be reasonable to give them seats in the Senate to make their own arguments. The Senate then voted on the amendment, defeating it 34 to 16.

This was the first and only occasion in the nineteenth century on which the woman suffrage amendment was brought to a vote in the United States Senate. No further vote was taken in the Senate until 1914 (with the vote 35 for, 34 against), and none at all in the House until 1915. Meanwhile the fight for the vote continued unabated. Miss Anthony and Mrs. Stanton were succeeded

---

² Since authentic versions of Miss Anthony's speeches are so rare, this stenographic report of her remarks before a Congressional committee provides one of the few opportunities to hear her "as she really was." "Miss Anthony never wrote her addresses and no stenographic reports were made. Brief and inadequate newspaper accounts are all that remain." Anthony and Harper, *History of Woman Suffrage,* IV, p. 28, footnote.

in the twentieth century by new leaders, notably Dr. Anna Howard Shaw and Mrs. Carrie Chapman Catt. The issue was kept before the nation by annual hearings before committees of Congress, petitions, deputations to the President, resolutions from conventions, circularization of printed matter, and speeches by both men and women.

Frustrated in their attempts to persuade Congress to amend the Constitution, suffrage leaders realized the need for political power. Political power was to be obtained by getting suffrage in the states and thereby making women voters influential in national politics. A deputation to President Roosevelt in 1908 was discouraged from making further petitions and was advised to "Go get another state." Their success in following this advice is seen in the fact that by 1919 women were entitled to vote for 339 out of a total of 531 presidential electors. The impact of this political influence, together with a general recognition of women's contribution to the war effort, helped melt opposition. On June 4, 1919, Congress approved the nineteenth amendment to the Constitution and submitted it to the states for ratification. On August 26, 1920, Tennessee, the thirty-sixth state, having ratified, universal woman suffrage became the law of the land. The fight begun in 1848 in Seneca Falls, N.Y., had at last been won.

For the Woman Suffrage Amendment

SUSAN BROWNELL ANTHONY

Born, Adams, Massachusetts, February 15, 1820; died, Rochester, New York, March 13, 1906. Reared by a Quaker father, she grew up in an atmosphere of independent thought and zeal for social reform. The family home near Rochester was a gathering place for such reformers as Phillips, Garrison, Channing, and Frederick Douglass. After a limited formal education she became a teacher and in 1846 was made head of the Female Department of Canajoharie Academy. Her interest in social issues led her to leave teaching and to take an active part in the temperance and abolitionist movements. In 1851 she met Mrs. Elizabeth Cady Stanton, and the two women formed a partnership for the promotion of woman suffrage which was to continue for half a century. President of National Woman Suffrage Association, 1892–1900. A militant leader, Susan Anthony was a propulsive force in the movement to which she consecrated her life with singleness of purpose.

$M^{r.}$ *Chairman and Gentlemen:* Mrs. Spencer said that I would make an argument. I do not propose to do so, because I take it for granted that the members of this committee understand that we have all the argument on our side, and such an argument would be simply a series of platitudes and maxims of government. The theory

Select Committee on Woman Suffrage, United States Senate, March 7, 1884. Printed as part of the debate on the woman suffrage amendment, January 25, 1887. *Congressional Record*, 49th Cong., 2nd Sess., vol. 18, pt. I, pp. 998–1002. Approximately the first two-thirds of Miss Anthony's statement is reproduced here.

of this Government from the beginning has been perfect equality to all the people. That is shown by every one of the fundamental principles, which I need not stop to repeat. Such being the theory, the application would be, of course, that all persons not having forfeited their right to representation in the Government should be possessed of it at the age of twenty-one. But instead of adopting a practice in conformity with the theory of our Government, we began first by saying that all men of property were the people of the nation upon whom the Constitution conferred equality of rights. The next step was that all white men were the people to whom should be practically applied the fundamental theories. There we halt to-day and stand at a deadlock, so far as the application of our theory may go. We women have been standing before the American republic for thirty years, asking the men to take yet one step further and extend the practical application of the theory of equality of rights to all the people to the other half of the people—the women. That is all that I stand here to-day to attempt to demand.

Of course, I take it for granted that the committee are in sympathy at least with the reports of the Judiciary Committees presented both in the Senate and the House. I remember that after the adoption of the fourteenth and fifteenth amendments Senator EDMUNDS reported on the petition of the ten thousand foreign-born citizens of Rhode Island who were denied equality of rights in Rhode Island simply because of their foreign birth; and in that report held that the amendments were enacted and attached to the Constitution simply for men of color, and therefore that their provisions could not be so construed as to bring within their purview the men of foreign birth in Rhode Island. Then the House Committee on the Judiciary, with Judge Bingham, of Ohio, at its head, made a similar report upon our petitions, holding that because those amendments were made essentially with the black men in view, therefore their provisions could not be extended to the women citizens of this country or to any class except men citizens of color.

I voted in the State of New York in 1872 under the construction of those amendments, which we felt to be the true one, that all persons born in the United States, or any State thereof, and under the jurisdiction of the United States, were citizens, and entitled to equality of rights, and that no State could deprive them of their equality of rights. I found three young men, inspectors of election, who were simple enough to read the Constitution and understand it in accordance with what was the letter and what should have been its spirit. Then, as you will remember, I was prosecuted by the officers of the Federal court, and the cause was carried through the different courts in the State of New York, in the northern district, and at last I was brought to trial at Canandaigua.

When Mr. Justice Hunt was brought from the supreme bench to sit upon that trial, he wrested my case from the hands of the jury altogether, after having listened three days to testimony, and brought in a verdict himself of guilty, denying to my counsel even the poor privilege of having the jury polled. Through all that trial when I, as a citizen of the United States, as a citizen of the State of New York and city of Rochester, as a person who had done something at least that might have entitled her to a voice in speaking for herself and for her class, in all that trial I not only was denied my right to testify as to whether I voted or not, but there was not one single woman's voice to be heard nor to be considered, except as witnesses, save when it came to the judge asking, "Has the prisoner anything to say why sentence shall not be pronounced?" Neither as judge, nor as attorney, nor as jury was I allowed any person who could be legitimately called my peer to speak for me.

Then, as you will remember, Mr. Justice Hunt not only pronounced the verdict of guilty, but a sentence of $100 fine and costs of prosecution. I said to him, "May it please your honor, I do not propose to pay it"; and I never have paid it, and I never shall. I asked your honorable bodies of Congress the next year—in 1874—to pass a resolution to remit that fine. Both Houses refused it; the committees reported against it; though through Benjamin F. Butler, in the House, and a member of your committee, and Matthew H. Carpenter, in the Senate, there were plenty of precedents brought forward to show that in cases of multitudes of men fines had been remitted. I state this merely to show the need of woman to speak for herself, to be as judge, to be as juror.

Mr. Justice Hunt in his opinion stated that suffrage was a fundamental right, and therefore a right that belonged to the State. It seemed to me that was just as much of a retroversion of the theory of what is right in our Government as there could possibly be. Then, after the decision in my case came that of Mrs. Minor, of Missouri. She prosecuted the officers there for denying her the right to vote. She carried her case up to your Supreme Court, and the Supreme Court answered her the same way; that the amendments were made for black men; that their provisions could not protect women; that the Constitution of the United States has no voters of its own.

Mrs. SPENCER. And you remember Judge Cartter's decision in my case.

Miss ANTHONY. Mr. Cartter said that women are citizens and may be qualified, &c., but that it requires some sort of legislation to give them the right to vote.

The Congress of the United States notwithstanding, and the Supreme Court of the United States notwithstanding, with all deference and respect, I differ with them all, and know that I am right and that they are wrong. The Constitution of the United States as it is protects me. If I could get a practical application of the Constitution it would protect me and all women in the enjoyment of perfect equality of rights everywhere under the shadow of the American flag.

I do not come to you to petition for special legislation, or for any more amendments to the Constitution, because I think they are unnecessary, but because you say there is not in the Constitution enough to protect me. Therefore I ask that you, true to your own theory and assertion, should go forward to make more constitution.

Let me remind you that in the case of all other classes of citizens under the shadow of our flag you have been true to the theory that taxation and representation are inseparable. Indians not taxed are not counted in the basis of representation, and are not allowed to vote; but the minute that your Indians are counted in the basis of representation and are allowed to vote they are taxed; never before. In my State of New York, and in nearly all the States, the members of the State militia, hundreds and thousands of men, are exempted from taxation on property; in my State to the value of $800, and in most of the States to a value in that neighborhood. While such a member of the militia lives, receives his salary, and is able to earn money, he is exempted; but when he dies the assessor puts his widow's name down upon the assessor's list, and the tax-collector never fails to call upon the widow and make her pay the full tax upon her property. In most of the States clergymen are exempted. In my State of New York they are exempted on property to the value of $1,500. As long as the clergyman lives and receives his fat salary, or his lean one, as the case may be, he is exempted on that amount of property; but when the breath leaves the body of the clergyman, and the widow is left without any income, or without any means of support, the State comes in and taxes the widow.

So it is with regard to all black men. In the State of New York up to the day of the passage of the fifteenth amendment, black men who were willing to remain without reporting themselves worth as much as $250, and thereby to remain without exercising the right to vote, never had their names put on the assessor's list; they were passed by, while, if the poorest colored woman owned 50 feet of real estate, a little cabin anywhere, that colored woman's name was always on the assessor's list, and she was compelled to pay her tax. While Frederick Douglass lived in my State he was never allowed to vote until he could show himself worth the requisite $250; and when he did vote in New York, he voted not because he was a man, not because he was a citizen of the United States, nor yet because he was a citizen of the State, but simply because he was worth the requisite amount of money. In Connecticut both black men and black women were exempted from taxation prior to the adoption of the fifteenth amendment.

The law was amended in 1848, by which black men were thus exempted, and black women followed the same rule in that State. That, I believe, is the only State where black women were exempted from taxation under the law. When the fourteenth and fifteenth amendments were attached to the

Constitution they carried to the black man of Connecticut the boon of the ballot as well as the burden of taxation, whereas they carried to the black woman of Connecticut the burden of taxation, but no ballot by which to protect her property. I know a colored woman in New Haven, Conn., worth $50,000, and she never paid a penny of taxation until the ratification of the fifteenth amendment. From that day on she is compelled to pay a heavy tax on that amount of property.

Mrs. SPENCER. Is it because she is a citizen? Please explain.

Miss ANTHONY. Because she is black.

Mrs. SPENCER. Is it because the fourteenth and fifteenth amendments made women citizens?

Miss ANTHONY. Certainly; because it declared the black people citizens.

Gentlemen, you have before you various propositions of amendment to the Federal Constitution. One is for the election of President by the vote of the people direct. Of course women are not people.

Senator EDMUNDS. Angels.

Miss ANTHONY. Yes; angels up in heaven or else devils down there.

Senator EDMUNDS. I have never known any of that kind.

Miss ANTHONY. I wish you, gentlemen, would look down there and see the myriads that are there. We want to help them and lift them up. That is exactly the trouble with you, gentlemen; you are forever looking at your own wives, your own mothers, your own sisters, and your own daughters, and they are well cared for and protected; but only look down to the struggling masses of women who have no one to protect them, neither husband, father, brother, son, with no mortal in all the land to protect them. If you would look down there the question would be solved; but the difficulty is that you think only of those who are doing well. We are not speaking for ourselves, but for those who can not speak for themselves. We are speaking for the doomed as much as you, Senator EDMUNDS, used to speak for the doomed on the plantations of the South.

Amendments have been proposed to put God in the Constitution and to keep God out of the Constitution. All sorts of propositions to amend the Constitution have been made; but I ask that you allow no other amendment to be called the sixteenth but that which shall put into the hands of one-half of the entire people of the nation the right to express their opinions as to how the Constitution shall be amended henceforth. Women have the right to say whether we shall have God in the Constitution as well as men. Women have a right to say whether we shall have a national law or an amendment to the Constitution prohibiting the importation or manufacture of alcoholic liquors. We have a right to have our opinions counted on every possible question concerning the public welfare.

You ask us why we do not get this right to vote first in the school districts, and on school questions, or the questions of liquor license. It has been shown very clearly why we need something more than that. You have good enough laws to-day in every State in this Union for the suppression of what are termed the social vices; for the suppression of the grog-shops, the gambling houses, the brothels, the obscene shows. There is plenty of legislation in every State in this Union for their suppression if it could be executed. Why is the Government, why are the States and the cities, unable to execute those laws? Simply because there is a large balance of power in every city that does not want those laws executed. Consequently both parties must alike cater to that balance of political power. The party that puts a plank in its platform that the laws against the grog-shops and all the other sinks of iniquity must be executed, is the party that will not get this balance of power to vote for it, and, consequently, the party that can not get into power.

What we ask of you is that you will make of the women of the cities a balance of political power, so that when a mayor, a member of the common council, a supervisor, a justice of the peace, a district attorney, a judge on the bench even, shall go before the people of that city as a candidate for the suffrages of the people he shall not only be compelled to look to the men who frequent the grog-shops, the brothels, and the gambling houses, who will vote for him if he is not in favor of executing the law, but that he shall have to look to the mothers, the sisters, the wives, the daughters of those deluded men to see what they will do if he does not execute the law.

We want to make of ourselves a balance of political power. What we need is the power to execute the laws. We have got laws enough. Let me give you one little fact in regard to my own city of Rochester. You all know how that wonderful whip called the temperance crusade roused the whisky ring. It caused the whisky force to concentrate itself more strongly at the ballot-box than ever before, so that when the report of the elections in the spring of 1874 went over the country the result was that the whisky ring was triumphant, and that the whisky ticket was elected more largely than ever before. Senator Thurman will remember how it was in his own State of Ohio. Everybody knows that if my friends, Mrs. ex-Governor Wallace, Mrs. Allen, and all the women of the great West could have gone to the ballot-box at those municipal elections and voted for candidates, no such result would have occurred; while you refused by the laws of the State to the women the right to have their opinions counted, every rum-seller, every drunkard, every pauper even from the poor-house, and every criminal outside of the State's prison came out on election day to express his opinion and have it counted.

The next result of that political event was that the ring demanded new legislation to protect the whisky traffic everywhere. In my city the women did not crusade the streets, but they said they would help the men to execute the law. They held meetings, sent out committees, and had testimony secured against every man who had violated the law, and when the board of excise held its meeting those women assembled, three or four hundred, in the church one morning, and marched in a solid body to the common council chamber where the board of excise was sitting. As one rum-seller after another brought in his petition for a renewal of license, who had violated the law, those women presented the testimony against him. The law of the State of New York is that no man shall have a renewal who has violated the law. But in not one case did that board refuse to grant a renewal of license because of the testimony which those women presented, and at the close of the sitting it was found that twelve hundred more licenses had been granted than ever before in the history of the State. Then the defeated women said they would have those men punished according to law.

Again they retained an attorney and appointed committees to investigate all over the city. They got the proper officer to prosecute every rum-seller. I was at their meeting. One woman reported that the officer in every city refused to prosecute the liquor dealer who had violated the law. Why? Because if he should do so he would lose the votes of all the employes of certain shops on that street, if another he would lose the votes of the railroad employes, and if another he would lose the German vote, if another the Irish vote, and so on. I said to those women what I say to you, and what I know to be true to-day, that if the women of the city of Rochester had held the power of the ballot in their hands they would have been a great political balance of power.

The last report was from District Attorney Raines. The women complained of a certain lager-beer-garden keeper. Said the district attorney, "Ladies, you are right, this man is violating the law, everybody knows it, but if I should prosecute him I would lose the entire German vote." Said I, "Ladies, do you not see that if the women of the city of Rochester had the right to vote District Attorney Raines would have been compelled to have stopped and counted, weighed and measured? He would have said, 'If I prosecute that lager-beer German I shall lose the 5,000 German votes of this city, but if I fail to prosecute him and execute the laws I shall lose the votes of 20,000 women.'"

Do you not see, gentlemen, that so long as you put this power of the ballot in the hands of every possible man, rich, poor, drunk, sober, educated, ignorant, outside of the State's prison, to make and unmake, not only every law and lawmaker, but every office-holder who has to do with the executing of the law, and take the power from the hands of the women of the nation, the mothers, you put the long arm of the lever, as we call it in mechanics, in the hands of the whisky power and make it utterly impossible for regulation of sobriety to be maintained in our community? The first step towards social regulation and good society in towns, cities, and villages is the ballot in the hands of the mothers of those places. I appeal to you especially in this matter.

I do not know what you think about the proper sphere of women. It matters little what any of us think about it. We shall each and every individual find our own proper sphere if we are left to act in freedom; but my opinion is that when the whole arena of politics and government is thrown open to women they will endeavor to do very much as they do in their homes; that the men will look after the greenback theory or the hard-money theory, that you will look after free-trade or tariff, and the women will do the home house-keeping of the government, which is to take care of the moral government and the social regulation of our home department.

It seems to me that we have the power of government outside to shape and control circumstances, but that the inside power, the government house-keeping, is powerless, and is compelled to accept whatever conditions or circumstances shall be granted.

Therefore I do not ask for liquor suffrage alone, nor for school suffrage alone, because that would amount to nothing. We must be able to have a voice in the election not only of every law-maker, but of every one who has to do either with the making or the executing of the laws.

Then you ask why we do not get suffrage by the popular-vote method, State by State? I answer, because there is no reason why I, for instance, should desire the women of one State of this nation to vote any more than the women of another State. I have no more interest as regards the women of New York than I have as regards the women of Indiana, Iowa, or any of the States represented by the women who have come up here. The reason why I do not wish to get this right by what you call the popular-vote method, the State vote, is because I believe there is a United States citizenship. I believe that this is a nation, and to be a citizen of this nation should be a guaranty to every citizen of the right to a voice in the Government, and should give to me my right to express my opinion. You deny to me my liberty, my freedom, if you say that I shall have no voice whatever in making, shaping, or controlling the conditions of society in which I live. I differ from Judge Hunt, and I hope I am respectful when I say that I think he made a very funny mistake when he said that fundamental rights belong to the States and only surface rights to the National Government. I hope you will agree with me that the fundamental right of citizenship, the right to voice in the Government, is a national right.

The National Government may concede to the States the right to decide by a majority as to what banks they shall have, what laws they shall enact with regard to insurance, with regard to property, and any other question; but I insist upon it that the National Government should not leave it a question with the States that a majority in any State may disfranchise the minority under any circumstances whatsoever. The franchise to you men is not secure. You hold it to-day, to be sure, by the common consent of white men, but if at any time, on your principle of government, the majority of any of the States should choose to amend the State constitution so as to disfranchise this or that portion of the white men by making this or that condition, by all the decisions of the Supreme Court and by the legislation thus far there is nothing to hinder them.

Therefore the women demand a sixteenth amendment to bring to women the right to vote, or if you please to confer upon women their right to vote, to protect them in it, and to secure men in their right, because you are not secure.

I would let the States act upon almost every other question by majorities, except the power to say whether my opinion shall be counted. I insist upon it that no State shall decide that question.

Then the popular-vote method is an impracticable thing. We tried to get negro suffrage by the popular vote, as you will remember. Senator Thurman will remember that in Ohio the Republicans submitted the question in 1867, and with all the prestige of the national Republican party and of the State party, when every influence that could be brought by the power and the patronage of the party in power was brought to bear, yet negro suffrage ran behind the regular Republican ticket 40,000.

It was tried in Kansas, it was tried in New York, and everywhere that it was submitted the question was voted down overwhelmingly. Just so we tried to get women suffrage by the popular-vote method in Kansas in 1867, in Michigan in 1874, in Colorado in 1877, and in each case the result was precisely the same, the ratio of the vote standing one-third for women suffrage and two-thirds against women suffrage. If we were to canvass State after State we should get no better vote than that. Why? Because the question of the enfranchisement of women is a question of government, a question of philosophy, of understanding, of great fundamental principle, and the masses of the hard-working people of this nation, men and women, do not think upon principles. They can only think on the one eternal struggle wherewithal to be fed, to be clothed, and to be sheltered. Therefore I ask you not to compel us to have this question settled by what you term the popular-vote method.

Let me illustrate by Colorado, the most recent State, in the election of 1877. I am happy to say to you that I have canvassed three States for this question. If Senator Chandler were alive, or if Senator Ferry were in this room, they would remember that I followed in their train in Michigan, with larger audiences than either of those Senators throughout the whole canvass. I want to say, too, that although those Senators may have believed in woman suffrage, they did not say much about it. They did not help us much. The

Greenback movement was quite popular in Michigan at that time. The Republicans and Greenbackers made a most humble bow to the grangers, but woman suffrage did not get much help. In Colorado, at the close of the canvass, 6,666 men voted "Yes." Now I am going to describe the men who voted "Yes." They were native-born white men, temperance men, cultivated, broad, generous, just men, men who think. On the other hand, 16,007 voted "No."

Now I am going to describe that class of voters. In the southern part of that State there are Mexicans, who speak the Spanish language. They put their wheat in circles on the ground with the heads out, and drive a mule around to thrash it. The vast population of Colorado is made up of that class of people. I was sent out to speak in a voting precinct having 200 voters; 150 of those voters were Mexican greasers, 40 of them foreign-born citizens, and just 10 of them were born in this country; and I was supposed to be competent to convert those men to let me have as much right in this Government as they had, when, unfortunately, the great majority of them could not understand a word that I said. Fifty or sixty Mexican greasers stood against the wall with their hats down over their faces. The Germans put seats in a lager-beer saloon, and would not attend unless I made a speech there; so I had a small audience.

Mrs. ARCHIBALD. There is one circumstance that I should like to relate. In the county of Las Animas, a county where there is a large population of Mexicans, and where they always have a large majority over the native population, they do not know our language at all. Consequently a number of tickets must be printed for those people in Spanish. The gentleman in our little town of Trinidad who had the charge of the printing of those tickets, being adverse to us, had every ticket printed against woman suffrage. The samples that were sent to us from Denver were "for" or "against," but the tickets that were printed only had the word "against" on them, so that our friends had to scratch their tickets, and all those Mexican people who could not understand this trick and did not know the facts of the case, voted against woman suffrage; so that we lost a great many votes. This was man's generosity.

Miss ANTHONY. Special legislation for the benefit of woman! I will admit you that on the floor of the constitutional convention was a representative Mexican, intelligent, cultivated, chairman of the committee on suffrage, who signed the petition, and was the first to speak in favor of woman suffrage. Then they have in Denver about four hundred negroes. Governor Routt said to me, "The four hundred Denver negroes are going to vote solid for woman suffrage." I said, "I do not know much about the Denver negroes, but I know certainly what all negroes were educated in, and slavery never educated master or negro into a comprehension of the great principles of human freedom of our nation; it is not possible, and I do not believe they are going to vote for us." Just ten of those Denver negroes voted for woman suffrage. Then, in all the mines of Colorado the vast majority of the wage laborers, as you know, are foreigners.

There may be intelligent foreigners in this country, and I know there are, who are in favor of the enfranchisement of woman, but that one does not happen to be Carl Schurz, I am ashamed to say. And I want to say to you of Carl Schurz, that side by side with that man on the battlefield of Germany was Madame Anneke, as noble a woman as ever trod the American soil. She rode by the side of her husband, who was an officer, on the battlefield; she slept in battlefield tents, and she fled from Germany to this country, for her life and property, side by side with Carl Schurz. Now, what is it for Carl Schurz, stepping up to the very door of the Presidency and looking back to Madame Anneke, who fought for liberty as well as he, to say, "You be subject in this Republic; I will be sovereign." If it is an insult for Carl Schurz to say that to a foreign-born woman, what is it for him to say it to Mrs. ex-Governor Wallace, Elizabeth Cady Stanton, Lucretia Mott—to the native-born, educated, tax-paying women of this Republic? I can forgive an ignorant foreigner; I can forgive an ignorant negro; but I can not forgive Carl Schurz.

Right in the file of the foreigners opposed to woman suffrage, educated under monarchical governments that do not comprehend our principles, whom I have seen traveling through the prairies of Iowa or the prairies of Minnesota, are the Bohemians, Swedes, Norwegians, Germans, Irishmen, Mennonites; I have seen them riding on those magnificent loads of wheat with those magnificent Saxon horses, shining like glass on a sunny morning, every one of them going to vote "no" against woman suffrage. You can not convert them; it is impossible. Now and then there is a whisky manufacturer, drunkard, inebriate, libertine, and what we call a fast man, and a colored man, broad and generous enough to be willing to let women vote, to let his mother have her opinion counted as to whether there shall be license or no license, but the rank and file of all classes who wish to enjoy full license in what are termed the petty vices of men are pitted solid against the enfranchisement of women.

Then, in addition to all these, there are, as you know, a few religious bigots left in the world who really believe that somehow or other if women are allowed to vote St. Paul would feel badly about it. I do not know but that some of the gentlemen present belong to that class. So, when you put those best men of the nation, having religion about everything except on this one question, whose prejudices control them, with all this vast mass of ignorant, uneducated, degraded population in this country, you make an overwhelming and insurmountable majority against the enfranchisement of women.

It is because of this fact that I ask you not to remand us back to the States, but to submit to the States the proposition of a sixteenth amendment. The popular-vote method is not only of itself an impossibility, but it is too humiliating a process to compel the women of this nation to submit to any longer.

I am going to give you an illustration, not because I have any disrespect for the person, because on many other questions he was really a good deal better than a good many other men who had not so bad a name in this nation. When, under the old *régime,* John Morrissey, of my State, the king of gamblers, was a Representative on the floor of Congress, it was humiliating enough for Lucretia Mott, for Elizabeth Cady Stanton, for all of us to come down here to Washington and beg at the feet of John Morrissey that he would let intelligent, native-born women vote, and let us have as much right in this Government and in the government of the city of New York as he had. When John Morrissey was a member of the New York State Legislature it would have been humiliating enough for us to go to the New York State Legislature and pray of John Morrissey to vote to ratify the sixteenth amendment, giving to us a right to vote; but if instead of a sixteenth amendment you tell us to go back to the popular-vote method, the old-time method, and go down into John Morrissey's seventh Congressional district in the city of New York, and there, in the sloughs and slums of that great Sodom, in the grog-shops, the gambling-houses, and the brothels, beg at the feet of each individual fisticuff of his constituency to give the noble, educated, native-born, tax-paying women of the State of New York as much right as he has, that would be too bitter a pill for a native-born woman to swallow any longer.

I beg you, gentlemen, to save us from the mortification and the humiliation of appealing to the rabble. We already have on our side the vast majority of the better educated—the best classes of men. You will remember that Senator Christiancy, of Michigan, two years ago, said on the floor of the Senate that of the 40,000 men who voted for woman suffrage in Michigan it was said that there was not a drunkard, not a libertine, not a gambler, not a depraved, low man among them. Is not that something that tells for us, and for our right? It is the fact, in every State of the Union, that we have the intelligent lawyers and the most liberal ministers of all the sects, not excepting the Roman Catholics. A Roman Catholic priest preached a sermon the other day, in which he said, "God grant that there were a thousand Susan B. Anthonys in this city to vote and work for temperance." When a Catholic priest says that there is a great moral necessity pressing down upon this nation demanding the enfranchisement of women, I ask you that you shall not drive us back to beg our rights at the feet of the most ignorant and depraved men of the nation, but that you, the representative men of the nation, will hold the question in the hollow of your hands. We ask you to lift this question out of the hands of the rabble.

You who are here upon the floor of Congress in both Houses are the picked men of the nation. You may say what you please about John Morrissey, the gambler, &c.: he was head and shoulders above the rank and file of his constituency. The world may gabble ever so much about members of Congress being corrupt and being bought and sold; they are as a rule head and shoulders above the great majority who compose their State governments. There is no doubt about it. Therefore I ask of you, as representative men, as men who think, as men who study, as men who philosophize, as men who know, that you will not drive us back to the States any more, but that you will carry out this method of procedure which has been practiced from the beginning of the Government; that is, that you will put a prohibitory amendment in the Constitution and submit the proposition to the several State legislatures. The amendment which has been presented before you reads:

ARTICLE XVI.

SECTION 1. The right of suffrage in the United States shall be based on citizenship, and the right of citizens of the United States to vote shall not be denied or abridged by the United States, or by any State, on account of sex, or for any reason not equally applicable to all citizens of the United States.

SECTION 2. Congress shall have power to enforce this article by appropriate legislation.

In this way we would get the right of suffrage just as much by what you call the consent of the States, or the States' rights method, as by any other method. The only point is that it is a decision by the representative men of the States instead of by the rank and file of the ignorant men of the States. If you would submit this proposition for a sixteenth amendment, by a two-thirds vote of the two Houses to the several legislatures, and the several legislatures ratify it, that would be just as much by the consent of the States as if Tom, Dick, and Harry voted "yes" or "no." Is it not, Senator? I want to talk to Democrats as well as Republicans, to show that it is a States' rights method.

Senator EDMUNDS. Does anybody propose any other, in case it is done at all by the nation?

Miss ANTHONY. Not by the nation, but they are continually driving us back to get it from the States, State by State. That is the point I want to make. We do not want you to drive us back to the States. We want you men to take the question out of the hands of the rabble of the State.

The CHAIRMAN. May I interrupt you?

Miss ANTHONY. Yes, sir; I wish you would.

The CHAIRMAN. You have reflected on this subject a great deal. You think there is a majority, as I understand, even in the State of New York, against women suffrage?

Miss ANTHONY. Yes, sir; overwhelmingly.

The CHAIRMAN. How, then, would you get Legislatures elected to ratify such a constitutional amendment?

Miss ANTHONY. That brings me exactly to the point.

The CHAIRMAN. That is the point I wish to hear you upon.

Miss ANTHONY. Because the members of the State Legislatures are intelligent men and can vote and enact laws embodying great principles of the government without in anywise endangering their positions with their constituencies. A constituency composed of ignorant men would vote solid against us because they have never thought on the question. Every man or woman who believes in the enfranchisement of women is educated out of every idea that he or she was born into. We were all born into the idea that the proper sphere of women is subjection, and it takes education and thought and culture to lift us out of it. Therefore when men go to the ballot-box they all vote "no," unless they have actual argument on it. I will illustrate. We have six Legislatures in the nation, for instance, that have extended the right to vote on school questions to the women, and not a single member of the State Legislature has ever lost his office or forfeited the respect or confidence of his constituents as a representative because he voted to give women the right to vote on school questions. It is a question that the unthinking masses never have thought upon. They do not care about it one way or the other, only they have an instinctive feeling that because women never did vote therefore it is wrong that they ever should vote.

Mrs. SPENCER. Do make the point that the Congress of the United States leads the Legislatures of the States and educates them.

Miss ANTHONY. When you, representative men, carry this matter to Legislatures, State by State, they will ratify it. My point is that you can safely do this. Senator Thurman, of Ohio, would not lose a single vote in Ohio in voting in favor of the enfranchisement of women. Senator EDMUNDS would not lose a single Republican vote in the State of Vermont if he puts himself on our side, which, I think, he will do. It is not a political question. We are no political power that can make or break either party to-day. Consequently each man is left independent to express his own moral and intellectual convictions on the matter without endangering himself politically.

Senator EDMUNDS. I think, Miss Anthony, you ought to put it on rather higher, I will not say stronger, ground. If you can convince us that it is right we would not stop to see how it affected us politically.

Miss ANTHONY. I was coming to that. I was going to say to all of you men in office here to-day that if you can not go forward and carry out either your Democratic or your Republican or your Greenback theories, for instance, on the finance, there is no great political power that is going to take you away from these halls and prevent you from doing all those other things which you want to do, and you can act out your own moral and intellectual convictions on this without let or hindrance.

Senator EDMUNDS. Without any danger to the public interests, you mean.

Miss ANTHONY. Without any danger to the public interests. I did not mean to make a bad insinuation, Senator.

I want to give you another reason why we appeal to you. In these three States where the question has been submitted and voted down we can not get another Legislature to resubmit it, because they say the people have expressed their opinion and decided no, and therefore nobody with any political sense would resubmit the question. It is therefore impossible in any one of those States. We have tried hard in Kansas for ten years to get the question resubmitted; the vote of that State seems to be taken as a finality. We ask you to lift the sixteenth amendment out of the arena of the public mass into the arena of thinking legislative brains, the brains of the nation, under the law and the Constitution. Not only do we ask it for that purpose, but when you will have by a two-thirds vote submitted the proposition to the several Legislatures, you have put the pin down and it never can go back. No subsequent Congress can revoke that submission of the proposition; there will be so much gained; it can not slide back. Then we will go to New York or to Pennsylvania, and urge upon the Legislatures the ratification of that amendment. They may refuse; they may vote it down the first time. Then we will go to the next Legislature, and the next Legislature, and plead and plead, from year to year, if it takes ten years. It is an open question to every Legislature until we can get one that will ratify it, and when that Legislature has once voted and ratified it no subsequent legislation can revoke their ratification.

Thus, you perceive, Senators, that every step we would gain by this sixteenth amendment process is fast and not to be done over again. That is why I appeal to you especially. As I have shown you in the respective States, if we fail to educate the people of a whole State—and in Michigan it was only six months, and in Colorado less than six months—the State Legislatures say that is the end of it. I appeal to you, therefore, to adopt the course that we suggest. . . .

Against the Woman Suffrage Amendment

JOSEPH EMERSON BROWN

> Born, Pickens County, South Carolina, April 15, 1821;
> died, Atlanta, Georgia, November 30, 1894. Attended
> Calhoun Academy in South Carolina; studied law, was
> admitted to Georgia bar, 1845; later was graduated from
> Yale Law School. Member of Georgia State Senate, 1849;
> judge of Superior Court of the Blue Ridge circuit, 1855.
> Governor of Georgia throughout Civil War: first elected
> 1855; reëlected 1859, 1861, 1863. Appointed chief justice
> of Supreme Court of Georgia, 1868; resigned 1870 to be-
> come president of Western and Atlantic Railroad Com-
> pany. An ardent states' rights, proslavery man, Brown
> favored secession. After the war, however, he advocated
> compliance with the will of Congress, and joined with the
> Republicans in helping put through reconstruction meas-
> ures. For this action he was denounced as a traitor to his
> state and to the South. In 1871 he returned to the Demo-
> cratic party. Appointed in 1880 to fill a vacancy in the
> United States Senate, he was elected as a Democrat in
> 1885 and served in the Senate until 1891.

*M*r. President: The joint resolution introduced by
my friend, the Senator from New Hampshire [Mr.
Blair], proposing an amendment to the Constitution of the United States,
conferring the right to vote upon the women of the United States, is one
of paramount importance, as it involves great questions far reaching in their
tendency, which seriously affect the very pillars of our social fabric, which

United States Senate, January 25, 1887. *Congressional Record*, 49th Cong., 2nd
Sess., vol. 18, pt. I, pp. 980–983.

involve the peace and harmony of society, the unity of the family, and much of the future success of our Government. The question should therefore be met fairly and discussed with firmness, but with moderation and forbearance. . . .

I believe that the Creator intended that the sphere of the males and females of our race should be different, and that their duties and obligations, while they differ materially, are equally important and equally honorable, and that each sex is equally well qualified by natural endowments for the discharge of the important duties which pertain to each, and that each sex is equally competent to discharge those duties.

We find an abundance of evidence, both in the works of nature and in the Divine revelation, to establish the fact that the family properly regulated is the foundation and pillar of society, and is the most important of any other human institution.

In the Divine economy it is provided that the man shall be the head of the family, and shall take upon himself the solemn obligation of providing for and protecting the family.

Man, by reason of his physical strength, and his other endowments and faculties, is qualified for the discharge of those duties that require strength and ability to combat with the sterner realities and difficulties of life. The different classes of outdoor labor which require physical strength and endurance are by nature assigned to man, the head of the family, as part of his task. He discharges such labors as require greater physical endurance and strength than the female sex are usually found to possess.

It is not only his duty to provide for and protect the family, but as a member of the community it is also his duty to discharge the laborious and responsible obligations which the family owe to the State, and which obligations must be discharged by the head of the family, until the male members of the family have grown up to manhood and are able to aid in the discharge of those obligations, when it becomes their duty each in his turn to take charge of and rear a family, for which he is responsible.

Among other duties which the head of the family owes to the State, is military duty in time of war, which he, when able-bodied, is able to discharge, and which the female members of the family are unable to discharge.

He is also under obligation to discharge jury duty, and by himself or his representatives to perform his part of the labor necessary to construct and keep in order roads, bridges, streets, and all grades of public highways. And in this progressive age upon the male sex is devolved the duty of constructing and operating our railroads, and the engines and other rolling stock with which they are operated; of building, equipping, and launching, shipping and other water craft of every character necessary for the transportation of passengers and freight upon our rivers, our lakes, and upon the high seas.

The labor in our fields, sowing, cultivating, and reaping crops must be discharged mainly by the male sex, as the female sex, for want of physical strength, are generally unable to discharge these duties. As it is the duty of the male sex to perform the obligations to the State, to society, and to the family, already mentioned, with numerous others that might be enumerated, it is also their duty to aid in the government of the State, which is simply a great aggregation of families. Society can not be preserved nor can the people be prosperous without good government. The government of our country is a government of the people, and it becomes necessary that the class of people upon whom the responsibility rests should assemble together and consider and discuss the great questions of governmental policy which from time to time are presented for their decision.

This often requires the assembling of caucuses in the night time, as well as public assemblages in the daytime. It is a laborious task, for which the male sex is infinitely better fitted than the female sex; and after proper consideration and discussion of the measures that may divide the country from time to time, the duty devolves upon those who are responsible for the government, at times and places to be fixed by law, to meet and by ballot to decide the great questions of government upon which the prosperity of the country depends.

These are some of the active and sterner duties of life to which the male sex is by nature better fitted than the female sex. If in carrying out the policy of the State on great measures adjudged vital such policy should lead to war, either foreign or domestic, it would seem to follow very naturally that those who have been responsible for the management of the State should be the parties to take the hazards and hardships of the struggle.

Here, again, man is better fitted by nature for the discharge of the duty—woman is unfit for it. So much for some of the duties imposed upon the male sex, for the discharge of which the Creator has endowed them with proper strength and faculties.

On the other hand, the Creator has assigned to woman very laborious and responsible duties, by no means less important than those imposed upon the male sex, though entirely different in their character. In the family she is a queen. She alone is fitted for the discharge of the sacred trust of wife and the endearing relation of mother.

While the man is contending with the sterner duties of life, the whole time of the noble, affectionate, and true woman is required in the discharge of the delicate and difficult duties assigned her in the family circle, in her church relations, and in the society where her lot is cast. When the husband returns home weary and worn in the discharge of the difficult and laborious task assigned him, he finds in the good wife solace and consolation, which is nowhere else afforded. If he is despondent and distressed, she cheers his heart with words of kindness; if he is sick or languishing, she soothes, comforts, and ministers to him as no one but an affectionate wife can do. If his burdens are onerous, she divides their weight by the exercise of her love and her sympathy.

But a still more important duty devolves upon the mother. After having brought into existence the offspring of the nuptial union, the children are dependent upon the mother as they are not upon any other human being. The trust is a most sacred, most responsible, and most important one. To watch over them in their infancy, and as the mind begins to expand to train, direct, and educate it in the paths of virtue and usefulness is the high trust assigned to the mother. She trains the twig as the tree should be inclined.

She molds the character. She educates the heart as well as the intellect, and she prepares the future man, now the boy, for honor or dishonor. Upon the manner in which she discharges her duty depends the fact whether he shall in future be a useful citizen or a burden to society. She inculcates lessons of patriotism, manliness, religion, and virtue, fitting the man by reason of his training to be an ornament to society, or dooming him by her neglect to a life of dishonor and shame. Society acts unwisely when it imposes upon her the duties that by common consent have always been assigned to the stronger and sterner sex, and the discharge of which causes her to neglect those sacred and all important duties to her children and to the society of which they are members.

In the church, by her piety, her charity, and her Christian purity, she not only aids society by a proper training of her own children, but the children of others, whom she encourages to come to the sacred altar, are taught to walk in the paths of rectitude, honor, and religion. In the Sunday-school room the good woman is a princess, and she exerts an influence which purifies and ennobles society, training the young in the truths of religion, making the Sunday-school the nursery of the church, and elevating society to the higher planes of pure religion, virtue, and patriotism. In the sick room and among the humble, the poor, and the suffering, the good woman, like an angel of light, cheers the hearts and revives the hopes of the poor, the suffering, and the despondent.

It would be a vain attempt to undertake to enumerate the refining, endearing, and ennobling influences exercised by the true woman in her relations to the family and to society when she occupies the sphere assigned to her by the laws of nature and the Divine inspiration, which are our surest guide for the present and the future life. But how can woman be expected to meet these heavy responsibilities, and to discharge these delicate and most important duties of wife, Christian, teacher, minister of mercy, friend of the suffering, and consoler of the despondent and needy, if we impose upon her the grosser, rougher, and harsher duties which nature has assigned to the male sex?

If the wife and the mother is required to leave the sacred precincts of home, and to attempt to do military duty when the state is in peril; or if she is to be required to leave her home from day to day in attendance upon the court as a juror, and to be shut up in the jury room from night to night with men who are strangers while a question of life or property is being discussed; if she is to attend political meetings, take part in political discussions, and mingle with the male sex at political gatherings; if she is to become an active politician; if she is to attend political caucuses at late hours of the night; if she is to take part in all the unsavory work that may be deemed necessary for the triumph of her party; and if on election day she is to leave her home and go upon the streets electioneering for votes for the candidates who receive her support, and mingling among the crowds of men who gather round the polls, she is to press her way through them to the precinct and deposit her ballot; if she is to take part in the corporate struggles of the city or town in which she resides, attend to the duties of his honor, the mayor, the councilman, or of policeman, to say nothing of the many other like obligations, which are disagreeable even to the male sex, how is she, with all these heavy duties of citizen, politician, and officeholder resting upon her shoulders, to attend to the more sacred, delicate, and refining trust to which we have already referred, and for which she is peculiarly fitted by nature? If she is to discharge the duties last mentioned, how is she, in connection with them, to discharge the more refining, elevating, and ennobling duties of wife, mother, Christian, and friend, which are found in the sphere where nature has placed her? Who is to care for and train the children while she is absent in the discharge of these masculine duties?

If it were proper to reverse the order of nature and assign woman to the sterner duties devolved upon the male sex, and to attempt to assign man to the more refining, delicate, and ennobling duties of the woman, man would be found entirely incompetent to the discharge of the obligations which nature has devolved upon the gentler sex, and society must be greatly injured by the attempted change. But if we are told that the object of this movement is not to reverse this order of nature, but only to devolve upon the gentler sex a portion of the more rigorous duties imposed by nature upon the stronger sex, we reply that society must be injured, as the woman would not be able to discharge those duties so well, by reason of her want of physical strength, as the male, upon whom they are devolved, and to the extent that the duties are to be divided, the male would be infinitely less competent to discharge the delicate and sacred trusts which nature has assigned to the female.

But it has been said that the present law is unjust to woman; that she is often required to pay tax on the property she holds without being permitted to take part in framing or administering the laws by which her property is governed, and that she is taxed without representation. That is a great mistake.

It may be very doubtful whether the male or female sex in the present state of things has more influence in the administration of the affairs of the Government and the enactment of the laws by which we are governed.

While the woman does not discharge military duty, nor does she attend courts and serve on juries, nor does she labor on the public streets, bridges, or highways, nor does she engage actively and publicly in the discussion of political affairs, nor does she enter the crowded precincts of the ballot-box to deposit her suffrage, still the intelligent, cultivated, noble woman is a power behind the throne. All her influence is in favor of morality, justice, and fair dealing, all her efforts and her counsel are in favor of good government, wise and wholesome regulations, and a faithful administration of the laws. Such a woman, by her gentleness, kindness, and Christian bearing, impresses her views and her counsels upon her father, her husband, her brothers, her sons, and her other male friends who imperceptibly yield to her influence many times without even being conscious of it. She rules not with a rod of iron, but with the queenly scepter; she binds not with hooks of steel but with silken cords; she governs not by physical efforts, but by moral suasion and feminine purity and delicacy. Her dominion is one of love, not of arbitrary power.

We are satisfied, therefore, that the pure, cultivated, and pious ladies of this country now exercise a very powerful, but quiet, imperceptible influence in popular affairs, much greater than they can ever again exercise if female suffrage should be enacted and they should be compelled actively to take part in the affairs of state and the corruptions of party politics.

It would be a gratification, and we are always glad to see the ladies gratified, to many who have espoused the cause of woman suffrage if they could take active part in political affairs, and go to the polls and cast their votes alongside the male sex; but while this would be a gratification to a large number of very worthy and excellent ladies who take a different view of the question from that which we entertain, we feel that it would be a great cruelty to a much larger number of the cultivated, refined, delicate, and lovely women of this country who seek no such distinction, who would enjoy no such privilege, who would with woman-like delicacy shrink from the discharge of any such obligation, and who would sincerely regret that, what they consider the folly of the state, had imposed upon them any such unpleasant duties.

But should female suffrage be once established it would become an imperative necessity that the very large class, indeed much the largest class, of the women of this country of the character last described should yield, contrary to their inclinations and wishes, to the necessity which would compel them to engage in political strife. We apprehend no one who has properly considered this question will doubt if female suffrage should be established that the more ignorant and less refined portions of the female population of this country, to say nothing of the baser class of females, laying aside feminine delicacy and disregarding the sacred duties devolving upon them, to which we have already referred, would rush to the polls and take pleasure in the crowded association which the situation would compel, of the two sexes in political meetings, and at the ballot-box.

[Senator Brown then speaks of the impropriety of adding an immense number of uneducated Negro women to the voting population.]

. . . .

It has been frequently urged with great earnestness by those who advocate woman suffrage that the ballot is necessary to the women to enable them to protect themselves in securing occupations, and to enable them to realize the same compensation for the like labor which is received by men. This argument is plausible, but upon a closer examination it will be found to possess but little real force. The price of labor is and must continue to be governed by the law of supply and demand, and the person who has the most physical strength to labor, and the most pursuits requiring such strength open for employment, will always command the higher prices.

Ladies make excellent teachers in public schools; many of them are every way the equals of their male competitors, and still they secure less wages than males. The reason is obvious. The number of ladies who offer themselves as teachers is much larger than the number of males who are willing to teach. The larger number of females offer to teach because other occupations are not open to them. The smaller number of males offer to teach because other more profitable occupations are open to most males who are competent to teach. The result is that the competition for positions of teachers to be filled by ladies is so great as to reduce the price; but as males can not be employed at that price, and are necessary in certain places in the schools, those seeking their services have to pay a higher rate for them.

Persons having a larger number of places open to them with fewer competitors command higher wages than those who have a smaller number of places open to them with more competitors. This is the law of society. It is the law of supply and demand, which can not be changed by legislation. Then it follows that the ballot can not enable those who have to compete with the larger number to command the same prices as those who compete with the smaller number in the labor market. As the Legislature has no power to regulate in practice that of which the advocates of woman suffrage complain, the ballot in the hands of females could not aid its regulation.

The ballot can not impart to the female physical strength which she does not possess, nor can it open to her pursuits which she does have the physical ability to engage in; and as long as she lacks the physical strength to compete with men in the different departments of labor, there will be more competition in her department, and she must necessarily receive less wages.

But it is claimed again, that females should have the ballot as a protection against the tyranny of bad husbands. This is also delusive. If the husband is brutal, arbitrary, or tyrannical, and tyrannizes over her at home, the ballot in her hands would be no protection against such injustice, but the husband who compelled her to conform to his wishes in other respects would also compel her to use the ballot, if she possessed it, as he might please to dictate. The ballot would therefore be of no assistance to the wife in such case, nor could it heal family strifes or dissensions. On the contrary, one of the gravest objections to placing the ballot in the hands of the female sex is that it would promote unhappiness and dissensions in the family circle. There should be unity and harmony in the family.

At present the man represents the family in meeting the demands of the law and of society upon the family. So far as the rougher, coarser duties are concerned, the man represents the family, and the individuality of the woman is not brought into prominence; but when the ballot is placed in the hands of woman her individuality is enlarged, and she is expected to answer for herself the demands of the law and of society on her individual account, and not as the weaker member of the family to answer by her husband. This naturally draws her out from the dignified and cultivated refinement of her womanly position, and brings her into a closer contact with the rougher elements of society, which tends to destroy that higher reverence and respect which her refinement and dignity in the relation of wife and mother have always inspired in those who approached her in her honorable and useful retirement.

When she becomes a voter she will be more or less of a politician, and will form political alliances or unite with political parties which will frequently be antagonistic to those to which her husband belongs. This will introduce into the family circle new elements of disagreement and discord which will frequently end in unhappy divisions, if not in separation or divorce. This must frequently occur when she becomes an active politician, identified with a party which is distasteful to her husband. On the other hand, if she unites with her husband in party associations and votes with him on all occasions so as not to disturb the harmony and happiness of the family, then the ballot is of no service, as it simply duplicates the vote of the male on each side of the question and leaves the result the same.

Again, if the family is the unit of society, and the state is composed of an aggregation of families, then it is important to society that there be as many happy families as possible, and it becomes the duty of man and woman alike to unite in the holy relations of matrimony.

As this is the only legal and proper mode of rendering obedience to the early command to multiply and replenish the earth, whatever tends to discourage the holy relation of matrimony is in disobedience of this command, and any change which encourages such disobedience is violative of the Divine law, and can not result in advantage to the state. Before forming this relation it is the duty of young men who have to take upon themselves the responsibilities of providing for and protecting the family to select some profession or pursuit that is most congenial to their tastes, and in which they will be most likely to be successful; but this can not be permitted to the young ladies, or if permitted it can not be practically carried out after matrimony.

As it might frequently happen that the young man had selected one profession or pursuit, and the young lady another, the result would be that after marriage she must drop the profession or pursuit of her choice, and employ herself in the sacred duties of wife and mother at home, and in rearing, educating, and elevating the family, while the husband pursues the profession of his choice.

It may be said, however, that there is a class of young ladies who do not choose to marry, and who select professions or avocations and follow them for a livelihood. This is true, but this class, compared with the number who unite in matrimony with the husbands of their choice, is comparatively very small, and it is the duty of society to encourage the increase of marriages rather than of celibacy. If the larger number of females select pursuits or professions which require them to decline marriage, society to that extent is deprived of the advantage resulting from the increase of population by marriage.

It is said by those who have examined the question closely that the largest number of divorces is now found in the communities where the advocates of female suffrage are most numerous, and where the individuality of woman as related to her husband, which such a doctrine inculcates, is increased to the greatest extent.

If this be true, it is a strong plea in the interests of the family and of society against granting the petition of the advocates of woman suffrage.

After all, this is a local question, which properly belongs to the different States of the Union, each acting for itself, and to the Territories of the Union, when not acting in conflict with the laws of the United States.

[Senator Brown then quotes extensively from "an able and well-written volume, entitled 'Letters from the Chimney Corner,' written by a cultivated lady of Chicago." The omitted passages contain substantially the same sentiments as those just presented by the Senator.]

. . . .

Mr. President, it is no part of my purpose in any manner whatever to speak disrespectfully of the large number of intelligent ladies, sometimes called strong-minded, who are constantly going before the public, agitating this question of female suffrage. While some of them may, as is frequently charged, be courting notoriety, I have no doubt they are generally earnestly engaged in a work which, in their opinion, would better their condition and would do no injury to society.

In all this, however, I believe they are mistaken.

I think the mental and physical structure of the sexes, of itself, sufficiently demonstrates the fact that the sterner, more laborious, and more difficult duties of society are to be performed by the male sex; while the more delicate duties of life, which require less physical strength, and the proper training of youth, with the proper discharge of domestic duties, belong to the female sex. Nature has so arranged it that the male sex can not attend properly to the duties assigned by the law of nature to the female sex, and that the female sex can not discharge the more rigorous duties required of the male sex.

This movement is an attempt to reverse the very laws of our being, and to drag woman into an arena for which she is not suited, and to devolve upon her onerous duties which the Creator never intended that she should perform.

While the husband discharges the laborious and fatiguing duties of important official positions, and conducts political campaigns, and discharges the duties connected with the ballot-box, or while he bears arms in time of war, or discharges executive or judicial duties, or the duties of juryman, requiring close confinement and many times great mental fatigue; or while the husband in a different sphere of life discharges the laborious duties of the plantation, the workshop, or the machine shop, it devolves upon the wife to attend to the duties connected with home life, to care for infant children, and to train carefully and properly those who in the youthful period are further advanced towards maturity.

The woman with the infant at the breast is in no condition to plow on the farm, labor hard in the workshop, discharge the duties of a juryman, conduct causes as an advocate in court, preside in important cases as a judge, command armies as a general, or bear arms as a private. These duties, and others of like character, belong to the male sex; while the more important duties of home, to which I have already referred, devolve upon the female sex. We can neither reverse the physical nor the moral laws of our nature, and as this movement is an attempt to reverse these laws, and to devolve upon the female sex important and laborious duties for which they are not by nature physically competent, I am not prepared to support this bill.

My opinion is that a very large majority of the American people, yes, a large majority of the female sex, oppose it, and that they act wisely in doing so. I therefore protest against its passage.

THE MISSION OF AMERICA

AMERICA'S *adventure in imperialist expansion at the end of the nineteenth century was brief but intense. The Spanish-American War, begun as a crusade to liberate Cuba from the brutalities of Spanish imperial domination, ended with the United States in possession of an empire of her own. War with Spain was declared in April, 1898, after the exploitation of the Cubans, the mysterious sinking of the battleship Maine, and the fulminations of the "yellow" press had aroused public indignation to fever pitch. News of Admiral Dewey's destruction of the Spanish fleet in Manila Bay electrified the nation and sent people to their maps to locate the hitherto unfamiliar Philippine Islands. The "splendid little war" proceeded without a setback; by August it was all over. The terms of the treaty, signed December 10, 1898, provided that Spain was to relinquish sovereignty over Cuba, and to cede outright the Philippines, Puerto Rico, and Guam to the United States. Many Americans, prompted by the jingo press and the inflated eloquence of imperialist orators, became fascinated with the idea of permanent dominion over the islands. What had been proclaimed at the outset as a war of humanity and not of conquest ended with an increasingly insistent demand to hold on to the territories so easily and so gloriously acquired.*

There can be no doubt about the intensity of the wave of patriotic fervor and imperialistic enthusiasm which swept the nation at this time. But no single explanation of its origin is entirely satisfactory. Certainly it is an oversimplification to attribute the chauvinism of the period solely to a sensational, irresponsible press—although the activities of Hearst's New York Journal and Pulitzer's New York World in competing for circulation were undoubtedly an important influence. Nor was it a case of business interests crassly fomenting war for profit. Indeed, businessmen had in general opposed the war at the beginning, although they had not been reluctant to take advantage of the possibilities which became apparent with the acquisition of new territory. The fact is that the 1890's provided an appropriate atmosphere or climate for an imperialist adventure. And this climate was the product of several factors—political, economic, religious, and purely emotional.

The closing of the western frontier made access to new lands, opening of new frontiers, especially enticing. Advocates of the strenuous life like Theodore Roosevelt, as well as certain college professors and clergymen, disturbed at the passing of the frontier, made speeches about national virility and strength and sought new outlets for the "manly virtues." Internal tensions—violent labor conflict, revolt among the farmers, concentration of wealth and power, recurring depressions—made some politicians grateful for any issue which would deflect public attention. Moreover, a serviceable rationale for imperialism had already been laid down in two very influential books, Josiah Strong's Our Country—Its Possible Future and Its Present Crisis (1885) and Alfred T. Mahan's The Influence of Sea Power Upon History (1890). Strong had argued that it was the mission of the superior Anglo-Saxon people to carry the blessings of "spiritual Christianity" to the backward areas of the earth. Mahan's thesis was that abiding national greatness rests on sea power. Sea power, he asserted, exists to promote commerce; it includes a merchant marine, a navy to protect it, and colonies to serve as trading and naval bases.

Zest for territorial expansion was not, of course, unknown prior to the 1890's. Imperialist orators made much of the argument that the republic had from its beginning embarked upon a career of expansionism. The acquisition of Louisiana, Florida, Texas, the Mexican cession, all were part of a continuous expansion which was now to be carried forward another step. But anti-imperialists were quick to distinguish between expansion and imperialism, and to point out significant differences between earlier acquisitions and the proposed Philippine policy. All former acquisitions, they said, were on this continent, and all except Alaska had been contiguous to existing borders. They had been thinly peopled when populated at all; they had not involved forcible subjection and rule of a foreign people by a greatly expanded army or navy. And there had always been the expectation that these territories would subsequently enter the Union as self-governing states.

From December, 1898, until February, 1899, the treaty with Spain and the question of the retention of the Philippines were debated in the Senate and throughout the nation. The expansionists assailed the cowardice of "hauling down the flag" and pointed out the economic and strategic advantages involved in annexation. There was much talk of destiny, the inevitability of expansion, duties thrust upon us by the hand of God, inescapable responsibilities devolving upon the Anglo-Saxon race, the necessity of taking up the white man's burden and caring for the child-like Filipinos who were incapable of self-government and in need of protection. The anti-imperialists invoked the Constitution and the Declaration of Independence, objecting to Philippine annexation

*primarily on the ground that such a policy flatly violated
the doctrine that governments "derive their just powers
from the consent of the governed." In addition to humanitarian and ethical arguments they stressed the certainty
of increased taxes, the wastefulness of the militarism
which imperialism entailed, the inevitable relationship
between an imperialist policy and war.*

*The treaty was ratified on February 6, partly as the
result of the influence of William Jennings Bryan, a leading anti-imperialist who for reasons which have never
been entirely understood, urged his Democratic followers
to support ratification. In his speech on "Imperialism"[1]
he explained that his action had been motivated by a
desire to end the war first and grant independence later.
"I thought it safer," he said, "to trust the American people
to give independence to the Filipinos than to trust the
accomplishment of that purpose to diplomacy with an
unfriendly nation." Senator Hoar, a Republican who had
fought valiantly against the treaty, and who resented
Bryan's apostasy, thought this "not a convincing argument." It was subsequently charged that Bryan wanted
the treaty accepted so that he could make imperialism a
campaign issue in 1900.*

*Ratification did not end the public debate on American
policy in the Philippines; it continued throughout 1899
and 1900. A few days before the vote in the Senate the
Filipinos, sensing that they were merely exchanging
Spanish for American masters, revolted under Emilio
Aguinaldo. This failure to appreciate the beneficence of
America's mission, and the consequent necessity for ruth-
less counter-measures by the military gave rise to considerable uneasiness in this country. Unflattering analogies to
1776 were suggested, with Aguinaldo cast as a dusky
George Washington, and President McKinley in the role*

---

[1] In a passage deleted from the speech as printed below. See
explanatory note on page 359.

of George III. Critics of forcible enlightenment sang sardonically:

> Underneath the starry flag
> Civilize 'em with a Krag.[2]

Finley Peter Dunne's Mr. Dooley, who had effectively satirized the comic-opera aspects of the war with Spain, observed in his dialogue on "Expansion":

We can't give ye anny votes, because we haven't more thin enough to go round now; but we'll threat ye th' way a father shud threat his childher if we have to break ivry bone in ye'er bodies. So come to our ar-rms. . . .

In October, 1899, the American Anti-Imperialist League, led by Carl Schurz, Moorfield Storey, and George F. Hoar, proclaimed its platform and invited the coöperation of all "who remain loyal to the Declaration of Independence and the Constitution of the United States." This platform declared:

We hold that the policy known as imperialism is hostile to liberty and tends toward militarism, an evil from which it has been our glory to be free. We regret that it has become necessary in the land of Washington and Lincoln to reaffirm that all men, of whatever race or color, are entitled to life, liberty and the pursuit of happiness. . . . We insist that the subjugation of any people is "criminal aggression" and open disloyalty to the distinctive principles of our Government.

But the tide of public opinion was running the other way; articulate spokesmen for Duty, Destiny, and Expansion like Theodore Roosevelt and Albert J. Beveridge were the heroes of the hour. Beveridge, who perhaps more than any other man deserved the title "orator of imperialism," had gained national attention with his "March of the Flag" speech delivered September 16, 1898, at the opening of the Indiana Republican congressional

[2] Army rifle in use at the time.

*campaign. This speech, which committed Indiana Repub-
licans to imperialism, became an effective campaign document and was widely circulated throughout the Middle
West. Earlier in the year in an address to the Middlesex
Club of Boston, before the war with Spain had begun
and when all eyes were fixed on Cuba, Beveridge had
displayed unprecedented candor in revealing a motive for
an imperialist policy, and uncanny prescience in predict-
ing the course of events:*

*American factories are making more than the American
people can use; American soil is producing more than they
can consume. Fate has written our policy for us; the trade
of the world must and shall be ours. And we will get it as
our mother [England] has told us how. . . .
. . . In the Pacific is the true field of our earliest operations.
There Spain has an island empire. . . . The Philippines
are logically our first target.*

*Elected to the United States Senate in January, 1899,
but not entitled to take his seat until the following December, Beveridge delivered the first of a series of
emotional political orations in support of expansion at
Philadelphia, February 15. The spirit of this address is
conveyed in its title, "The Republic That Never Retreats."
In the spring he embarked on a fact-finding tour of the
Philippine archipelago, returning in the fall with the
conviction he had held at his departure, that the Filipinos
were incapable of self-government, and that the United
States must retain control of the islands indefinitely. On
January 9, 1900, he delivered his maiden speech in the
Senate,[3] speaking in support of his own resolution introduced a few days earlier: "That the Philippine Islands are
territory belonging to the United States; that it is the
intention of the United States to retain them as such and
to establish and maintain such governmental control
throughout the archipelago as the situation may demand."*

[3] *Congressional Record*, 56th Cong., 1st Sess., vol. 33, pt. I, pp.
704–712.

In his third sentence, Senator Beveridge sounded his keynote:

The Philippines are ours forever. . . . And just beyond the Philippines are China's illimitable markets. We will not retreat from either. We will not abandon our opportunity in the Orient. We will not renounce our part in the mission of our race, trustee, under God, of the civilization of the world.

After dangling before the Senate the rich prizes to be had for the taking, he dealt vigorously and at length with attacks on imperialism. He then swept into his soaring peroration:

Mr. President, this question is deeper than any question of party politics; deeper than any question of the isolated policy of our country even; deeper even than any question of constitutional power. It is elemental. It is racial. God has not been preparing the English-speaking and Teutonic peoples for a thousand years for nothing but vain and idle self-contemplation and self-admiration. No! He has made us the master organizers of the world to establish system where chaos reigns.

Beveridge closed with a passionate appeal for the adoption of his resolution—"How dare we delay when our soldiers' blood is flowing?" When the applause had subsided, Senator Hoar rose to reply. He congratulated the speaker on his "silver speech" and his patriotism. But, he went on,

As I heard his eloquent description of wealth and glory and commerce and trade, I listened in vain for those words which the American people have been wont to take upon their lips in every solemn crisis of their history. . . . The words Right, Duty, Freedom, were absent, my friend must permit me to say, from that eloquent speech.

Despite this sober appraisal, the speech produced an immediate national sensation. Front-page stories from coast to coast lauded the magic of the speaker's eloquence, the unanswerability of his arguments. Telegrams poured

*in from all quarters, among them one from Theodore
Roosevelt, who was delighted with the speech and infuriated at Hoar's reply. Even Mr. Dooley, who had some
mordant comments to make on Beveridge's youthfulness,
florid rhetoric, and vainglorious patriotism, could not
wholly restrain his admiration for its lyric quality. It was,
he said, "a gr-reat speech. 'Twas a speech ye cud waltz to."*

The following summer the Democrats once again nominated William Jennings Bryan for the Presidency. In his
speech of acceptance, August 8, 1900, in Indianapolis,
Bryan made imperialism the paramount issue of the campaign. Systematically he took up and replied to the principal arguments advanced in defense of imperialist
expansion, and pledged that if elected he would grant
independence to the Filipinos and set up an American
protectorate over the islands. Beveridge replied at Chicago
in September with his "The Star of Empire," which was
used by the Republicans as a national campaign document. In the election which followed, the people voted
against Bryan and for the policies of the administration.
McKinley won by an electoral majority of 137, a popular
plurality of over 800,000; Bryan received twenty-one
fewer electoral votes than in 1896. Imperialism had triumphed, temporarily at least.

The sequel to this expansionist adventure in the Philippines is well known. Military government was promptly
replaced in 1901 by a civil commission under the chair-
manship of William Howard Taft. During subsequent
years, in which dramatic improvements were made in education, transportation, public health, and general preparation for self-government, the islands were administered
by a series of governors-general, some of whom favored
independence for the Filipinos, and some of whom did
not. In 1933, a bill providing for independence after a
ten-year probationary period passed Congress over President Hoover's veto, but was not ratified by the Philippine

*legislature because of certain objectionable economic pro-
visions. The following year the Tydings-McDuffie Act,
providing for complete independence in 1946, passed
Congress, was signed by President Roosevelt March 24,
1934, and was ratified by the Philippine legislature May
1, 1934. This act was not motivated entirely, or even
principally, by American altruism. The glorious visions
of 1898 had proved illusory. Dreams of opening up oriental markets via the islands had not been fulfilled; commercial expectations in the islands themselves had not
been realized; naval experts considered the archipelago
indefensible and a military liability; American sugar interests resented competition from duty-free sugar. Pursu-
ant to the terms of the Tydings-McDuffie Act, an
independent Philippine Republic was established July 4,
1946.*

*Today the perfervid speeches of the imperialists, with
their reiterated themes of racism, national destiny, and
conquest, make embarrassing reading. They are too painfully similar to the utterances of a megalomaniac German
dictator, whose dreams of world domination the American people so recently helped to frustrate.*

The March of the Flag

ALBERT J. BEVERIDGE

Born, Highland County, Ohio, October 6, 1862; died, Indianapolis, Indiana, April 27, 1927. Graduate of Asbury College (now DePauw), 1885. Admitted to bar, 1887; practiced law in Indianapolis; became celebrated as a political orator. Elected to United States Senate, 1899, at age of 36. Served two terms, defeated in 1911; never again held public office. An outspoken nationalist, even a jingoist, Beveridge was a liberal in domestic politics. One of the "insurgent" Republicans who founded the Progressive party, he delivered the keynote address to the Progressive national convention in Chicago in 1912. Unsuccessful candidate for Governor of Indiana (1912), United States Senate (1914 and 1922). Author of a four-volume life of John Marshall (1916–1919), and an unfinished biography of Lincoln.

*I*t is a noble land that God has given us; a land that can feed and clothe the world; a land whose coastlines would inclose half the countries of Europe; a land set like a sentinel between the two imperial oceans of the globe, a greater England with a nobler destiny.

It is a mighty people that He has planted on this soil; a people sprung from the most masterful blood of history; a people perpetually revitalized by the virile, man-producing working-folk of all the earth; a people imperial

Speech opening Indiana Republican Campaign, Tomlinson Hall, Indianapolis, September 16, 1898. From *The Meaning of the Times and Other Speeches* by Albert J. Beveridge, copyright © 1908, 1936, used by special permission of the publishers, The Bobbs-Merrill Company, Inc. Texts of the speech vary; *cf.* Thomas B. Reed, ed., *Modern Eloquence* (New York: American Law Book Co., 1903), XI, pp. 224–243.

by virtue of their power, by right of their institutions, by authority of their Heaven-directed purposes—the propagandists and not the misers of liberty.

It is a glorious history our God has bestowed upon His chosen people; a history heroic with faith in our mission and our future; a history of statesmen who flung the boundaries of the Republic out into unexplored lands and savage wilderness; a history of soldiers who carried the flag across blazing deserts and through the ranks of hostile mountains, even to the gates of sunset; a history of a multiplying people who overran a continent in half a century; a history of prophets who saw the consequences of evils inherited from the past and of martyrs who died to save us from them; a history divinely logical, in the process of whose tremendous reasoning we find ourselves to-day.

Therefore, in this campaign, the question is larger than a party question. It is an American question. It is a world question. Shall the American people continue their march toward the commercial supremacy of the world? Shall free institutions broaden their blessed reign as the children of liberty wax in strength, until the empire of our principles is established over the hearts of all mankind?

Have we no mission to perform, no duty to discharge to our fellow-man? Has God endowed us with gifts beyond our deserts and marked us as the people of His peculiar favor, merely to rot in our own selfishness, as men and nations must, who take cowardice for their companion and self for their deity —as China has, as India has, as Egypt has?

Shall we be as the man who had one talent and hid it, or as he who had ten talents and used them until they grew to riches? And shall we reap the reward that waits on our discharge of our high duty; shall we occupy new markets for what our farmers raise, our factories make, our merchants sell— aye, and, please God, new markets for what our ships shall carry?

Hawaii is ours; Porto Rico is to be ours; at the prayer of her people Cuba finally will be ours; in the islands of the East, even to the gates of Asia, coaling stations are to be ours at the very least; the flag of a liberal government is to float over the Philippines, and may it be the banner that Taylor unfurled in Texas and Fremont carried to the coast.

The Opposition tells us that we ought not to govern a people without their consent. I answer, The rule of liberty that all just government derives its authority from the consent of the governed, applies only to those who are capable of self-government. We govern the Indians without their consent, we govern our territories without their consent, we govern our children without their consent. How do they know that our government would be without their consent? Would not the people of the Philippines prefer the just, humane, civilizing government of this Republic to the savage, bloody rule of pillage and extortion from which we have rescued them?

And, regardless of this formula of words made only for enlightened, self-governing people, do we owe no duty to the world? Shall we turn these peoples back to the reeking hands from which we have taken them? Shall we abandon them, with Germany, England, Japan, hungering for them? Shall we save them from those nations, to give them a self-rule of tragedy?

They ask us how we shall govern these new possessions. I answer: Out of local conditions and the necessities of the case methods of government will grow. If England can govern foreign lands, so can America. If Germany can govern foreign lands, so can America. If they can supervise protectorates, so can America. Why is it more difficult to administer Hawaii than New Mexico or California? Both had a savage and an alien population; both were more remote from the seat of government when they came under our dominion than the Philippines are to-day.

Will you say by your vote that American ability to govern has decayed; that a century's experience in self-rule has failed of a result? Will you affirm by your vote that you are an infidel to American power and practical sense? Or will you say that ours is the blood of government; ours the heart of dominion; ours the brain and genius of administration? Will you remember that we do but what our fathers did—we but pitch the tents of liberty farther westward, farther southward—we only continue the march of the flag?

The march of the flag! In 1789 the flag of the Republic waved over 4,000,000 souls in thirteen states, and their savage territory which stretched to the Mississippi, to Canada, to the Floridas. The timid minds of that day said that no new territory was needed, and, for the hour, they were right. But Jefferson, through whose intellect the centuries marched; Jefferson, who dreamed of Cuba as an American state; Jefferson, the first Imperialist of the Republic—Jefferson acquired that imperial territory which swept from the Mississippi to the mountains, from Texas to the British possessions, and the march of the flag began!

The infidels to the gospel of liberty raved, but the flag swept on! The title to that noble land out of which Oregon, Washington, Idaho and Montana have been carved was uncertain; Jefferson, strict constructionist of constitutional power though he was, obeyed the Anglo-Saxon impulse within him, whose watchword then and whose watchword throughout the world to-day is, "Forward!": another empire was added to the Republic, and the march of the flag went on!

Those who deny the power of free institutions to expand urged every argument, and more, that we hear, to-day; but the people's judgment approved the command of their blood, and the march of the flag went on!

A screen of land from New Orleans to Florida shut us from the Gulf, and over this and the Everglade Peninsula waved the saffron flag of Spain; Andrew Jackson seized both, the American people stood at his back, and, under Monroe, the Floridas came under the dominion of the Republic, and the march of the flag went on! The Cassandras prophesied every prophecy of despair we hear today; but the march of the flag went on!

Then Texas responded to the bugle calls of liberty, and the march of the flag went on! And, at last, we waged war with Mexico, and the flag swept over the southwest, over peerless California, past the Gate of Gold to Oregon on the north, and from ocean to ocean its folds of glory blazed.

And, now, obeying the same voice that Jefferson heard and obeyed, that Jackson heard and obeyed, that Monroe heard and obeyed, that Seward heard and obeyed, that Grant heard and obeyed, that Harrison heard and obeyed, our President to-day plants the flag over the islands of the seas, outposts of commerce, citadels of national security, and the march of the flag goes on!

Distance and oceans are no arguments. The fact that all the territory our fathers bought and seized is contiguous, is no argument. In 1819 Florida was farther from New York than Porto Rico is from Chicago today; Texas, farther from Washington in 1845 than Hawaii is from Boston in 1898; California, more inaccessible in 1847 than the Philippines are now. Gibraltar is farther from London than Havana is from Washington; Melbourne is farther from Liverpool than Manila is from San Francisco.

The ocean does not separate us from lands of our duty and desire—the oceans join us, rivers never to be dredged, canals never to be repaired. Steam joins us; electricity joins us—the very elements are in league with our destiny. Cuba not contiguous! Porto Rico not contiguous! Hawaii and the Philippines not contiguous! The oceans make them contiguous. And our navy will make them contiguous.

But the Opposition is right—there is a difference. We did not need the western Mississippi Valley when we acquired it, nor Florida, nor Texas, nor California, nor the royal provinces of the far northwest. We had no emigrants to people this imperial wilderness, no money to develop it, even no highways to cover it. No trade awaited us in its savage fastnesses. Our productions were not greater than our trade. There was not one reason for the land-lust of our statesmen from Jefferson to Grant, other than the prophet and the Saxon within them. But, to-day, we are raising more than we can consume, making more than we can use. Therefore we must find new markets for our produce.

And so, while we did not need the territory taken during the past century at the time it was acquired, we do need what we have taken in 1898, and we need it now. The resources and the commerce of these immensely rich dominions will be increased as much as American energy is greater than Spanish sloth. In Cuba, alone, there are 15,000,000 acres of forest unacquainted with the ax, exhaustless mines of iron, priceless deposits of manganese, millions of dollars' worth of which we must buy, to-day, from the Black Sea districts. There are millions of acres yet unexplored.

The resources of Porto Rico have only been trifled with. The riches of the

Philippines have hardly been touched by the finger-tips of modern methods. And they produce what we consume, and consume what we produce—the very predestination of reciprocity—a reciprocity "not made with hands, eternal in the heavens." They sell hemp, sugar, coconuts, fruits of the tropics, timber of price like mahogany; they buy flour, clothing, tools, implements, machinery and all that we can raise and make. Their trade will be ours in time. Do you indorse that policy with your vote?

Cuba is as large as Pennsylvania, and is the richest spot on the globe. Hawaii is as large as New Jersey; Porto Rico half as large as Hawaii; the Philippines larger than all New England, New York, New Jersey and Delaware combined. Together they are larger than the British Isles, larger than France, larger than Germany, larger than Japan.

If any man tells you that trade depends on cheapness and not on government influence, ask him why England does not abandon South Africa, Egypt, India. Why does France seize South China, Germany the vast region whose port is Kiouchou?

Our trade with Porto Rico, Hawaii and the Philippines must be as free as between the states of the Union, because they are American territory, while every other nation on earth must pay our tariff before they can compete with us. Until Cuba shall ask for annexation, our trade with her will, at the very least, be like the preferential trade of Canada with England. That, and the excellence of our goods and products; that, and the convenience of traffic; that, and the kinship of interests and destiny, will give the monopoly of these markets to the American people.

The commercial supremacy of the Republic means that this Nation is to be the sovereign factor in the peace of the world. For the conflicts of the future are to be conflicts of trade—struggles for markets—commercial wars for existence. And the golden rule of peace is impregnability of position and invincibility of preparedness. So, we see England, the greatest strategist of history, plant her flag and her cannon on Gibraltar, at Quebec, in the Bermudas, at Vancouver, everywhere.

So Hawaii furnishes us a naval base in the heart of the Pacific; the Ladrones another, a voyage further on; Manila another, at the gates of Asia—Asia, to the trade of whose hundreds of millions American merchants, manufacturers, farmers, have as good right as those of Germany or France or Russia or England; Asia, whose commerce with the United Kingdom alone amounts to hundreds of millions of dollars every year; Asia, to whom Germany looks to take her surplus products; Asia, whose doors must not be shut against American trade. Within five decades the bulk of Oriental commerce will be ours.

. . . .

There are so many real things to be done—canals to be dug, railways to be laid, forests to be felled, cities to be builded, fields to be tilled, markets to be won, ships to be launched, peoples to be saved, civilization to be proclaimed and the flag of liberty flung to the eager air of every sea. Is this an hour to waste upon triflers with nature's laws? Is this a season to give our destiny over to word-mongers and prosperity-wreckers? No! It is an hour to remember our duty to our homes. It is a moment to realize the opportunities fate has opened to us. And so it is an hour for us to stand by the Government.

Wonderfully has God guided us. Yonder at Bunker Hill and Yorktown His providence was above us. At New Orleans and on ensanguined seas His hand sustained us. Abraham Lincoln was His minister and His was the altar of freedom the Nation's soldiers set up on a hundred battle-fields. His power directed Dewey in the East and delivered the Spanish fleet into our hands, as He delivered the elder Armada into the hands of our English sires two centuries ago. The American people can not use a dishonest medium of exchange; it is ours to set the world its example of right and honor. We can not fly from our world duties; it is ours to execute the purpose of a fate that has driven us to be greater than our small intentions. We can not retreat from any soil where Providence has unfurled our banner; it is ours to save that soil for liberty and civilization.

Imperialism

WILLIAM JENNINGS BRYAN

*Born, Salem, Illinois, March 19, 1860; died, Dayton, Ten-
nessee, July 26, 1925. Graduate of Illinois College
(1881), and Union College of Law, Chicago (1883).
Practiced law in Jacksonville, Illinois; moved (1887) to
Lincoln, Nebraska. United States Representative, 1891–
1895. Unsuccessful candidate for United States Senate,
1894, and for Presidency, 1896, 1900, 1908. Edited
weekly* Commoner, *1901–1913. Secretary of State under
Wilson; resigned June, 1915. A perennial Chautauqua
lecturer, his most famous lecture was "The Prince of
Peace." Devoted final years to a defense of religious fun-
damentalism; appeared for the prosecution in Scopes trial
in Tennessee (1925); died shortly after close of this trial.*

M*r. Chairman and Members of the Notification Committee:* I shall, at an early day, and in a more
formal manner, accept the nomination which you tender, and shall at that
time discuss the various questions covered by the Democratic platform. It
may not be out of place, however, to submit a few observations at this
time upon the general character of the contest before us and upon the
question which is declared to be of paramount importance in this campaign.

When I say that the contest of 1900 is a contest between Democracy on
the one hand and plutocracy on the other I do not mean to say that all
our opponents have deliberately chosen to give to organized wealth a
predominating influence in the affairs of the Government, but I do assert

Speech accepting Democratic nomination for the Presidency, Indianapolis, Indiana,
August 8, 1900. *Speeches of William Jennings Bryan* (New York: Funk & Wagnalls
Company, 1909), II, pp. 17–49.

that on the important issues of the day the Republican party is dominated by those influences which constantly tend to substitute the worship of mammon for the protection of the rights of man.

[Bryan continues his observations upon "the general character of the contest" by contrasting the Republican and Democratic parties. He then explains that he voted for the Philippine treaty because he thought it better to end the war first, and then to give the Filipinos their independence. He then takes up the question of imperialism.]

. . . .

Those who would have this Nation enter upon a career of empire must consider, not only the effect of imperialism on the Filipinos, but they must also calculate its effects upon our own nation. We cannot repudiate the principle of self-government in the Philippines without weakening that principle here.

Lincoln said that the safety of this Nation was not in its fleets, its armies, or its forts, but in the spirit which prizes liberty as the heritage of all men, in all lands, everywhere, and he warned his countrymen that they could not destroy this spirit without planting the seeds of despotism at their own doors.

Even now we are beginning to see the paralyzing influence of imperialism. Heretofore this Nation has been prompt to express its sympathy with those who were fighting for civil liberty. While our sphere of activity has been limited to the Western Hemisphere, our sympathies have not been bounded by the seas. We have felt it due to ourselves and to the world, as well as to those who were struggling for the right to govern themselves, to proclaim the interest which our people have, from the date of their own independence, felt in every contest between human rights and arbitrary power.

Three-quarters of a century ago, when our nation was small, the struggles of Greece aroused our people, and Webster and Clay gave eloquent expression to the universal desire for Grecian independence. In 1898 all parties manifested a lively interest in the success of the Cubans, but now when a war is in progress in South Africa, which must result in the extension of the monarchical idea, or in the triumph of a republic, the advocates of imperialism in this country dare not say a word in behalf of the Boers.

Sympathy for the Boers does not arise from any unfriendliness towards England; the American people are not unfriendly toward the people of any nation. This sympathy is due to the fact that, as stated in our platform, we believe in the principles of self-government and reject, as did our forefathers, the claims of monarchy. If this nation surrenders its belief in the universal application of the principles set forth in the Declaration of Independence, it will lose the prestige and influence which it has enjoyed among the nations as an exponent of popular government.

Our opponents, conscious of the weakness of their cause, seek to confuse imperialism with expansion, and have even dared to claim Jefferson as a supporter of their policy. Jefferson spoke so freely and used language with such precision that no one can be ignorant of his views. On one occasion he declared: "If there be one principle more deeply rooted than any other in the mind of every American, it is that we should have nothing to do with conquest." And again he said: "Conquest is not in our principles; it is inconsistent with our government."

The forcible annexation of territory to be governed by arbitrary power differs as much from the acquisition of territory to be built up into States as a monarchy differs from a democracy. The Democratic party does not oppose expansion when expansion enlarges the area of the Republic and incorporates land which can be settled by American citizens, or adds to our population people who are willing to become citizens and are capable of discharging their duties as such.

The acquisition of the Louisiana territory, Florida, Texas and other tracts which have been secured from time to time enlarged the Republic and the Constitution followed the flag into the new territory. It is now proposed to seize upon distant territory already more densely populated than our own country and to force upon the people a government for which there is no warrant in our Constitution or our laws.

Even the argument that this earth belongs to those who desire to cultivate it and who have the physical power to acquire it cannot be invoked to justify the appropriation of the Philippine Islands by the United States. If the islands were uninhabited American citizens would not be willing to go there and till the soil. The white race will not live so near the equator. Other nations have tried to colonize in the same latitude. The Netherlands have controlled Java for three hundred years and yet today there are less than sixty thousand people of European birth scattered among the twenty-five million natives.

After a century and a half of English domination in India, less than one-twentieth of one per cent of the people of India are of English birth, and it requires an army of seventy thousand British soldiers to take care of the tax collectors. Spain had asserted title to the Philippine Islands for three centuries and yet when our fleet entered Manila bay there were less than ten thousand Spaniards residing in the Philippines.

A colonial policy means that we shall send to the Philippine Islands a few traders, a few taskmasters and a few office-holders and an army large enough to support the authority of a small fraction of the people while they rule the natives.

If we have an imperial policy we must have a great standing army as its natural and necessary complement. The spirit which will justify the forcible annexation of the Philippine Islands will justify the seizure of other islands and the domination of other people, and with wars of conquest we can expect a certain, if not rapid, growth of our military establishment.

[Mr. Bryan warns against the dangers of a large standing army. He then discusses the future status of the Filipino, implying that since he is not to be a citizen, he must necessarily be a subject.]

. . . .

What is our title to the Philippine Islands? Do we hold them by treaty or by conquest? Did we buy them or did we take them? Did we purchase the people? If not, how did we secure title to them? Were they thrown in with the land? Will the Republicans say that inanimate earth has value but that when that earth is molded by the divine hand and stamped with the likeness of the Creator it becomes a fixture and passes with the soil? If governments derive their just powers from the consent of the governed, it is impossible to secure title to people, either by force or by purchase.

We could extinguish Spain's title by treaty, but if we hold title we must hold it by some method consistent with our ideas of government. When we made allies of the Filipinos and armed them to fight against Spain, we disputed Spain's title. If we buy Spain's title we are not innocent purchasers.

There can be no doubt that we accepted and utilized the services of the Filipinos, and that when we did so we had full knowledge that they were fighting for their own independence, and I submit that history furnishes no example of turpitude baser than ours if we now substitute our yoke for the Spanish yoke.

Let us consider briefly the reasons which have been given in support of an imperialistic policy. Some say that it is our duty to hold the Philippine Islands. But duty is not an argument; it is a conclusion. To ascertain what our duty is, in any emergency, we must apply well-settled and generally accepted principles. It is our duty to avoid stealing, no matter whether the thing to be stolen is of great or little value. It is our duty to avoid killing a human being, no matter where the human being lives or to what race or class he belongs.

Every one recognizes the obligation imposed upon individuals to observe both the human and the moral law, but as some deny the application of those laws to nations, it may not be out of place to quote the opinions of others. Jefferson, than whom there is no higher political authority, said: "I know of but one code of morality for men, whether acting singly or collectively."

Franklin, whose learning, wisdom and virtue are a part of the priceless legacy bequeathed to us from the revolutionary days, exprest the same idea in even stronger language when he said:

Justice is strictly due between neighbor nations as between neighbor citizens. A highwayman is as much a robber when he plunders in a gang as when single; and the nation that makes an unjust war is only a great gang.

Many may dare to do in crowds what they would not dare to do as individuals, but the moral character of an act is not determined by the number of those who join it. Force can defend a right, but force has never yet created a right. If it was true, as declared in the resolutions of intervention, that the Cubans "are and of right ought to be free and independent" (language taken from the Declaration of Independence), it is equally true that the Filipinos "are and of right ought to be free and independent."

The right of the Cubans to freedom was not based upon their proximity to the United States, nor upon the language which they spoke, nor yet upon the race or races to which they belonged. Congress by a practically unanimous vote declared that the principles enunciated at Philadelphia in 1776 were still alive and applicable to the Cubans. Who will draw a line between the natural rights of the Cubans and the Filipinos? Who will say that the former has a right to liberty and that the latter has no rights which we are bound to respect? And, if the Filipinos "are and of right ought to be free and independent," what right have we to force our government upon them without their consent? Before our duty can be ascertained their rights must be determined, and when their rights are once determined it is as much our duty to respect those rights as it was the duty of Spain to respect the rights of the people of Cuba or the duty of England to respect the rights of the American colonists. Rights never conflict; duties never clash. Can it be our duty to usurp political rights which belong to others? Can it be our duty to kill those who, following the example of our forefathers, love liberty well enough to fight for it?

Some poet has described the terror which overcame a soldier who in the midst of the battle discovered that he had slain his brother. It is written "All ye are brethren." Let us hope for the coming of the day when human life—which when once destroyed cannot be restored—will be so sacred that it will never be taken except when necessary to punish a crime already committed, or to prevent a crime about to be committed.

It is said that we have assumed before the world obligations which make it necessary for us to permanently maintain a government in the Philippine Islands. I reply first, that the highest obligation of this nation is to be true to itself. No obligation to any particular nations, or to all the nations combined, can require the abandonment of our theory of government, and the substitution of doctrines against which our whole national life has been a protest. And, second, that our obligation to the Filipinos, who inhabit the islands, is greater than any obligation which we can owe to foreigners who have a temporary residence in the Philippines or desire to trade there.

It is argued by some that the Filipinos are incapable of self-government and that, therefore, we owe it to the world to take control of them. Admiral Dewey, in an official report to the Navy Department, declared the Filipinos more capable of self-government than the Cubans and said that he based his opinion upon a knowledge of both races. But I will not rest the case upon the relative advancement of the Filipinos. Henry Clay, in defending the right of the people of South America to self-government said:

It is the doctrine of thrones that man is too ignorant to govern himself. Their partizans assert his incapacity in reference to all nations; if they cannot command universal assent to the proposition, it is then demanded to particular nations; and our pride and our presumption too often make converts of us. I contend that it is to arraign the disposition of Providence himself to suppose that he has created beings incapable of governing themselves, and to be trampled on by kings. Self-government is the natural government of man.

Clay was right. There are degrees of proficiency in the art of self-government, but it is a reflection upon the Creator to say that he denied to any people the capacity for self-government. Once admit that some people are capable of self-government and that others are not and that the capable people have a right to seize upon and govern the incapable, and you make force—brute force—the only foundation of government and invite the reign of a despot. I am not willing to believe that an all-wise and an all-loving God created the Filipinos and then left them thousands of years helpless until the islands attracted the attention of European nations.

Republicans ask, "Shall we haul down the flag that floats over our dead in the Philippines?" The same question might have been asked, when the American flag floated over Chapultepec and waved over the dead who fell there; but the tourist who visits the City of Mexico finds there a national cemetery owned by the United States and cared for by an American citizen.

Our flag still floats over our dead, but when the treaty with Mexico was signed American authority withdrew to the Rio Grande, and I venture the opinion that during the last fifty years the people of Mexico have made more progress under the stimulus of independence and self-government than they would have made under a carpet-bag government held in place by bayonets. The United States and Mexico, friendly republics, are each stronger and happier than they would have been had the former been cursed and the latter crushed by an imperialistic policy disguised as "benevolent assimilation."

"Can we not govern colonies?" we are asked. The question is not what we can do, but what we ought to do. This nation can do whatever it desires to do, but it must accept responsibility for what it does. If the Constitution stands in the way, the people can amend the Constitution. I repeat, the nation can do whatever it desires to do, but it cannot avoid the natural and legitimate results of its own conduct.

The young man upon reaching his majority can do what he pleases. He can disregard the teachings of his parents; he can trample upon all that he has been taught to consider sacred; he can disobey the laws of the State, the laws of society and the laws of God. He can stamp failure upon his life and make his very existence a curse to his fellow men, and he can bring his father and mother in sorrow to the grave; but he cannot annul the sentence, "The wages of sin is death."

And so with the nation. It is of age and it can do what it pleases; it can spurn the traditions of the past; it can repudiate the principles upon which the nation rests; it can employ force instead of reason; it can substitute might for right; it can conquer weaker people; it can exploit their lands, appropriate their property and kill their people; but it cannot repeal the moral law or escape the punishment decreed for the violation of human rights. . . .

Some argue that American rule in the Philippine Islands will result in the better education of the Filipinos. Be not deceived. If we expect to maintain a colonial policy, we shall not find it to our advantage to educate the people. The educated Filipinos are now in revolt against us, and the most ignorant ones have made the least resistance to our domination. If we are to govern them without their consent and give them no voice in determining the taxes which they must pay, we dare not educate them, lest they learn to read the Declaration of Independence and Constitution of the United States and mock us for our inconsistency.

The principal arguments, however, advanced by those who enter upon a defense of imperialism are:

First—That we must improve the present opportunity to become a world power and enter into international politics.

Second—That our commercial interests in the Philippine Islands and in the Orient make it necessary for us to hold the islands permanently.

Third—That the spread of the Christian religion will be facilitated by a colonial policy.

Fourth—That there is no honorable retreat from the position which the nation has taken.

The first argument is addrest to the nation's pride and the second to the nation's pocket-book. The third is intended for the church member and the fourth for the partizan.

It is sufficient answer to the first argument to say that for more than a century this nation has been a world power. For ten decades it has been the most potent influence in the world. Not only has it been a world power, but it has done more to shape the politics of the human race than all the other nations of the world combined. Because our Declaration of Independence was promulgated others have been promulgated. Because the patriots of 1776 fought for liberty others have fought for it. Because our Constitution was adopted other constitutions have been adopted.

The growth of the principle of self-government, planted on American soil, has been the overshadowing political fact of the nineteenth century. It has made this nation conspicuous among the nations and given it a place in history such as no other nation has ever enjoyed. Nothing has been able to check the onward march of this idea. I am not willing that this nation shall cast aside the omnipotent weapon of truth to seize again the weapons of physical warfare. I would not exchange the glory of this Republic for the glory of all the empires that have risen and fallen since time began.

The permanent chairman of the last Republican National Convention presented the pecuniary argument in all its baldness when he said:

We make no hypocritical pretense of being interested in the Philippines solely on account of others. While we regard the welfare of those people as a sacred trust, we regard the welfare of the American people first. We see our duty to ourselves as well as to others. We believe in trade expansion. By every legitimate means within the province of government and constitution we mean to stimulate the expansion of our trade and open new markets.

This is the commercial argument. It is based upon the theory that war can be rightly waged for pecuniary advantage, and that it is profitable to purchase trade by force and violence.

. . . .

The pecuniary argument, the more effective with certain classes, is not likely to be used so often or presented with so much enthusiasm as the religious argument. If what has been termed the "gunpowder gospel" were urged against the Filipinos only it would be a sufficient answer to say that a majority of the Filipinos are now members of one branch of the Christian church; but the principle involved is one of much wider application and challenges serious consideration.

The religious argument varies in positiveness from a passive belief that Providence delivered the Filipinos into our hands, for their good and our glory, to the exultation of the minister who said that we ought to "thrash the natives (Filipinos) until they understand who we are," and that "every bullet sent, every cannon shot and every flag waved means righteousness."

We cannot approve of this doctrine in one place unless we are willing to apply it everywhere. If there is poison in the blood of the hand it will ultimately reach the heart. It is equally true that forcible Christianity, if planted under the American flag in the far-away Orient, will sooner or later be transplanted upon American soil.

If true Christianity consists in carrying out in our daily lives the teachings of Christ, who will say that we are commanded to civilize with dynamite and proselyte with the sword? He who would declare the divine will must prove his authority either by Holy Writ or by evidence of a special dispensation.

Imperialism finds no warrant in the Bible. The command, "Go ye into all the world and preach the gospel to every creature," has no Gatling gun attachment. When Jesus visited a village of Samaria and the people refused to receive him, some of the disciples suggested that fire should be called down from Heaven to avenge the insult; but the Master rebuked them and said: "Ye know not what manner of spirit ye are of; for the Son of Man is not come to destroy men's lives, but to save them." Suppose he had said: "We will thrash them until they understand who we are," how different would have been the history of Christianity! Compare, if you will, the swaggering, bullying, brutal doctrine of imperialism with the golden rule and the commandment, "Thou shalt love thy neighbor as thyself."

Love, not force, was the weapon of the Nazarene; sacrifice for others, not the exploitation of them, was His method of reaching the human heart. A missionary recently told me that the Stars and Stripes once saved his life because his assailant recognized our flag as a flag that had no blood upon it.

Let it be known that our missionaries are seeking souls instead of sovereignty; let it be known that instead of being the advance guard of conquering armies, they are going forth to help and uplift, having their loins girt about with truth and their feet shod with the preparation of the gospel of peace, wearing the breastplate of righteousness and carrying the sword of the spirit; let it be known that they are citizens of a nation which respects the rights of the citizens of other nations as carefully as it protects the rights of its own citizens, and the welcome given to our missionaries will be more cordial than the welcome extended to the missionaries of any other nation.

The argument made by some that it was unfortunate for the nation that it had anything to do with the Philippine Islands, but that the naval victory at Manila made the permanent acquisition of those islands necessary, is also unsound. We won a naval victory at Santiago, but that did not compel us to hold Cuba.

The shedding of American blood in the Philippine Islands does not make it imperative that we should retain possession forever; American blood was shed at San Juan Hill and El Caney, and yet the President has promised the Cubans independence. The fact that the American flag floats over Manila does not compel us to exercise perpetual sovereignty over the islands; the American flag floats over Havana to-day, but the President has promised to haul it down when the flag of the Cuban Republic is ready to rise in its place. Better a thousand times that our flag in the Orient give way to a flag representing the idea of self-government than that the flag of this Republic should become the flag of an empire.

There is an easy, honest, honorable solution of the Philippine question. It is set forth in the Democratic platform and it is submitted with confidence to the American people. This plan I unreservedly indorse. If elected, I will convene Congress in extraordinary session as soon as inaugurated and recommend an immediate declaration of the nation's purpose, first, to establish a stable form of government in the Philippine Islands, just as we are now establishing a stable form of government in Cuba; second, to give independence to the Filipinos as we have promised to give independence to the Cubans; third, to protect the Filipinos from outside interference while they work out their destiny, just as we have protected the republics of Central and South America, and are, by the Monroe doctrine, pledged to protect Cuba.

A European protectorate often results in the plundering of the ward by the guardian. An American protectorate gives to the nation protected the advantage of our strength, without making it the victim of our greed. For three-quarters of a century the Monroe doctrine has been a shield to neighboring republics and yet it has imposed no pecuniary burden upon us. After the Filipinos had aided us in the war against Spain, we could not honorably turn them over to their former masters; we could not leave them to be the victims of the ambitious designs of European nations, and since we do not desire to make them a part of us or to hold them as subjects, we propose the only alternative, namely, to give them independence and guard them against molestation from without.

When our opponents are unable to defend their position by argument they fall back upon the assertion that it is destiny, and insist that we must submit to it, no matter how much it violates our moral precepts and our principles of government. This is a complacent philosophy. It obliterates the distinction between right and wrong and makes individuals and nations the helpless victims of circumstance.

Destiny is the subterfuge of the invertebrate, who, lacking the courage to oppose error, seeks some plausible excuse for supporting it. Washington said that the destiny of the republican form of government was deeply, if not finally, staked on the experiment entrusted to the American people.

How different Washington's definition of destiny from the Republican
definition!

. . . .

I can conceive of a national destiny surpassing the glories of the present
and the past—a destiny which meets the responsibilities of to-day and
measures up to the possibilities of the future. Behold a republic, resting
securely upon the foundation stones quarried by revolutionary patriots
from the mountain of eternal truth—a republic applying in practise and
proclaiming to the world the self-evident propositions that all men are
created equal; that they are endowed by their Creator with inalienable
rights; that governments are instituted among men to secure these rights,
and that governments derive their just powers from the consent of the
governed. Behold a republic in which civil and religious liberty stimulate
all to earnest endeavor and in which the law restrains every hand uplifted for
a neighbor's injury—a republic in which every citizen is a sovereign, but
in which no one cares or dares to wear a crown. Behold a republic standing
erect while empires all around are bowed beneath the weight of their own
armaments—a republic whose flag is loved while other flags are only feared.
Behold a republic increasing in population, in wealth, in strength and in
influence, solving the problems of civilization and hastening the coming of
an universal brotherhood—a republic which shakes thrones and dissolves
aristocracies by its silent example and gives light and inspiration to those
who sit in darkness. Behold a republic gradually but surely becoming the
supreme moral factor in the world's progress and the accepted arbiter of the
world's disputes—a republic whose history, like the path of the just, "is as
the shining light that shineth more and more unto the perfect day."

Notes on Sources and
Supplementary Reading

This is in no sense a comprehensive bibliography. These suggestions are intended only to open up opportunities for further study of the issues presented in this volume. Hence this list is restricted to a few outstanding biographies, specialized studies, and additional speeches. We have omitted mention of all general histories, unpublished studies such as dissertations and manuscripts, and most other materials not readily available in any reasonably well-stocked library.

RATIFICATION OF THE FEDERAL CONSTITUTION

Moses Coit Tyler, *Patrick Henry* (1887) is a corrective to William Wirt's earlier biography. Henry's speaking is analyzed in Louis A. Mallory, "Patrick Henry," in *A History and Criticism of American Public Address* (2 vols., 1943), edited by W. N. Brigance. Irving Brant, *James Madison, Father of the Constitution, 1787–1800* (1950) is one of a series of books on Madison by this author.

See Carl Van Doren, *The Great Rehearsal* (1948) for a dramatic account of the making and ratification of the Constitution. Hamilton's speaking is discussed in Bower Aly, *The Rhetoric of Alexander Hamilton* (1941), and in Aly's essay on Hamilton in *A History and Criticism of American Public Address* (1955), III, edited by Marie K. Hochmuth. See also Ralph H. Gabriel, ed., *Hamilton, Madison and Jay on the Constitution; Selections From the Federalist Papers* (1954) in the American Heritage Series.

The extended debate between Henry and Madison is found in Jonathan Elliot, *The Debates in the Several State Conventions on the Adoption of the Federal Constitution* (5 vols., 1901), III. Frank Moore, ed., *American Eloquence* (2 vols., 1881) has speeches on the Federal Constitution by Henry, Madison, and Hamilton.

THE BASIS OF POLITICAL SOCIETY: A SPECTRUM OF VIEWS

For David Daggett see *Dictionary of American Biography*. The standard biography of Jefferson is Dumas Malone, *Jefferson and His Times* (2 vols.,

1948–1951). Richard N. Current, *Daniel Webster and the Rise of National Conservatism* (1955) is useful here, as is Russel B. Nye, *George Bancroft: Brahmin Rebel* (1944). Valuable for background on men, ideas, and period are Albert J. Beveridge, *The Life of John Marshall* (4 vols., 1916–1919); Vernon L. Parrington, *Main Currents in American Thought* (3 vols., 1927); and Arthur M. Schlesinger, Jr., *The Age of Jackson* (1946).

Other speeches advancing conservative doctrine are Daggett, "An Oration on the Eleventh Anniversary of the Independence of the United States" (1787) and "Count the Cost" (1804); Timothy Dwight, "The Duty of Americans, at the Present Crisis" (1798)—all pamphlets; Seth Ames, ed., *The Works of Fisher Ames* (2 vols., 1854); Daniel Webster, "First Settlement in New England" (1820) in standard editions of his works.

Abraham Bishop, a New Haven Jeffersonian, carried on a running political debate with Daggett is his "Oration on Connecticut Republicanism" (1800) and "Oration Delivered in Wallingford" (1801)—both pamphlets. Frances Wright, a woman orator and crusader, attacked many cherished beliefs and institutions in her *Course of Popular Lectures* (1829). For speeches by Jacksonians, see Joseph Blau, ed., *Social Theories of Jacksonian Democracy* (1947). Relevant also are Ralph Waldo Emerson's "Man the Reformer" (1841) and "The Conservative" (1841) in standard editions of his works; and Henry David Thoreau's lecture on "Civil Disobedience" (1849), now published as an essay in various collections of his works.

RELIGIOUS LIBERALISM VS. ORTHODOXY

Biographical works on Channing, which contain treatments of the controversy, are: Arthur W. Brown, *Always Young for Liberty* (1956); William H. Channing, *Memoir of William Ellery Channing* (3 vols., 1848). Elizabeth Peabody, *Reminiscences of Rev. Wm. Ellery Channing, D.D.* (1880), concerns the years 1816–1842 and contains a number of Channing's letters. Chief source of information on Lyman Beecher is the *Autobiography and Correspondence of Lyman Beecher, D.D.*, edited by Charles Beecher (2 vols., 1865). Popular essays on Beecher are to be found in Constance M. Rourke, *Trumpets of Jubilee* (1927), and Lyman Beecher Stowe, *Saints, Sinners, and Beechers* (1934).

Representative accounts of the controversy are to be found in Joseph H. Allen and Richard Eddy, *A History of the Unitarians and the Universalists in the U.S.*, American Church History Series (13 vols., 1894), X; Earl M. Wilbur, *History of Unitarianism* (1945); William W. Fenn, "How the Schism Came," *Proceedings of the Unitarian Historical Society* (1925), vol. I, Pt. I. A tract by Charles H. Lyttle, *The Pentecost of American Unitarianism* (1920), deals with the Baltimore Sermon; orthodox reaction to this sermon is found in Moses Stuart, *Letters to the Rev. Wm. E. Channing* (1819), and Leonard Woods, *Letters to Unitarians* (1822). Also useful in presenting orthodox views are James K. Morse, *Jedidiah Morse* (1939); and Sam W. Worcester, *The Life and Labors of Rev. Samuel Worcester, D.D.* (2 vols., 1852).

Channing's major statements during the controversy are published in his

Discourses, Reviews, and Miscellanies (1830); see the preface for his justification for entering the dispute. Theodore Parker, "The Transient and Permanent in Christianity" (1841), in a volume of his sermons bearing that title, reveals a later development of Unitarian ideas. Relevant also are speeches by Edwards, Channing, Emerson, and Parker in Joseph L. Blau, ed., *American Philosophic Addresses, 1700–1900* (1946); and Timothy Dwight, *Sermons* (2 vols., 1828).

THE ESSENTIAL NATURE OF THE CONSTITUTION

Charles M. Wiltse, *John C. Calhoun* (3 vols., 1944–1951), particularly vol. II; Claude M. Fuess, *Daniel Webster* (2 vols., 1930), I; Clement Eaton, *Henry Clay and the Art of American Politics* (1957). Consult W. N. Brigance, ed., *A History and Criticism of American Public Address* (2 vols., 1943) for Ernest J. Wrage, "Henry Clay"; Herbert Curry, "John C. Calhoun"; Wilbur S. Howell and Hoyt H. Hudson, "Daniel Webster."

For background, Frederic Bancroft, *Calhoun and The South Carolina Nullification Movement* (1928); Richard Hofstadter's essay on Calhoun in *The American Political Tradition* (1948); Vernon L. Parrington, *Main Currents in American Thought* (3 vols., 1927), particularly sections on Calhoun and Webster with surrounding discussion.

The Calhoun-Webster exchange, of February 15–16, 1833, while the high point in strictly constitution debate, was but one episode in a protracted controversy over sectionalism and the Union. Other key speeches in sequence are Calhoun, "On the Tariff Bill" (April 6, 1816); Henry Clay, "On American Industry" (March 30–31, 1824); Daniel Webster, "The Tariff" (April 1–2, 1824); Webster, "Second Speech on the Tariff" (May 9, 1828); the Hayne-Webster debates (January 19–27, 1830); Clay, "Nullification and Other Topics" (August 3, 1830); Calhoun, "States Rights" (February 26, 1833). For Clay, Calhoun, and Webster, the final struggle occurred in the debate over Clay's compromise resolutions in 1850. See appropriate volumes of the following sources: Calvin Colton, ed., *The Works of Henry Clay* (10 vols., 1904); Richard Crallé, ed., *The Works of John C. Calhoun* (6 vols., 1853); *The Writings and Speeches of Daniel Webster* (18 vols., 1903); *Register of Debates in Congress*; and *Congressional Globe*.

A HOUSE DIVIDED

Ulrich B. Phillips, *The Life of Robert Toombs* (1913); Russel B. Nye, *William Lloyd Garrison and the Humanitarian Reformers* (1955). Ralph Korngold, *Two Friends of Man* (1950) is a double biography of Garrison and Wendell Phillips. Benjamin P. Thomas, *Abraham Lincoln* (1952) and Carl Sandburg, *Abraham Lincoln* (1954) are fine one-volume studies. George Fort Milton, *The Eve of Conflict: Stephen A. Douglas and the Needless War* (1934), belongs to the school of historical revisionism. W. N. Brigance, ed., *A History and Criticism of American Public Address* (2 vols., 1943), has studies of speakers: Willard H. Yeager, "Wendell Phillips"; Rexford S. Mitchell, "William L. Yancey"; R. Elaine

Pagel and Carl Dallinger, "Charles Sumner"; Mildred F. Berry, "Abraham Lincoln"; Earl Wiley, "Abraham Lincoln"; Forest L. Whan, "Stephen A. Douglas." Richard Hofstadter, *The American Political Tradition* (1948) has informative essays on Phillips, Calhoun, and Lincoln.

Russel B. Nye, *Fettered Freedom* (1949) is fine on civil liberties and slavery. Gilbert H. Barnes, *The Anti-Slavery Impulse* (1933) puts abolitionism in a new context, though it may overcorrect older interpretations. See Harry V. Jaffa, "Expediency and Morality in the Lincoln-Douglas Debates," *The Anchor Review*, no. 2 (1957) and *Crisis of the House Divided: An Interpretation of the Lincoln-Douglas Debates* (1959).

For speeches, see Calhoun, "On the Reception of Abolition Petitions" (February 6, 1837) in Richard K. Crallé, ed., *Speeches of John C. Calhoun* (6 vols., 1853), II; Wendell Phillips, *Speeches, Lectures, and Letters* (1st ser., 1894)—particularly "The Murder of Lovejoy" (1837), "Public Opinion" (1852), "Philosophy of the Abolition Movement" (1853), and "Disunion" (1861); William H. Seward, "The Irrepressible Conflict" (1858) in Samuel Harding, ed., *Select Orations Illustrating American History* (1909). Paul Angle, *Created Equal?* (1958) is splendid for the Lincoln-Douglas debates and five preliminary speeches. Edwin Sparks, *The Lincoln-Douglas Debates* (1908) has texts and newspaper reports on the debates. Roy P. Basler and others, eds., *The Collected Works of Abraham Lincoln* (9 vols., 1953) supersedes earlier collections.

RECONSTRUCTION OF THE FEDERAL UNION

Radically different views of Stevens are found in Ralph Korngold, *Thaddeus Stevens* (1955) and Richard Current, *Old Thad Stevens* (1942). Raymond's journalistic career is traced in Augustus Maverick, *Henry J. Raymond and the New York Press* (1870) and Ernest F. Brown, *Raymond of the Times* (1951). Information on his political activities may be found in several of the Stevens biographies and in W. H. Barnes, *History of the Thirty-Ninth Congress of the United States* (1868).

For accounts of the Reconstruction period see Claude Bowers, *The Tragic Era* (1929) and George Fort Milton, *The Age of Hate* (1930). Paul H. Buck, *The Road to Reunion, 1865-1900* (1937) is particularly useful in tracing shifting sectional attitudes. James G. Blaine gives a vivid account of the Congressional debate in the second volume of his *Twenty Years of Congress* (2 vols., 1886).

See Roy Basler, ed., *Abraham Lincoln: His Speeches and Writings* (1946) for Lincoln's last public address (1865). Johnson's Message to Congress (1865) and Stevens' speech of January 3, 1867, on the First Reconstruction Bill are reproduced in Samuel B. Harding, ed., *Select Orations Illustrating American Political History* (1909). Also in Harding is Carl Schurz, "Plea For General Amnesty" (1872). Lucius Q. C. Lamar, "Eulogy of Charles Sumner" (1874), is in Chauncey M. Depew, ed., *The Library of Oratory* (15 vols., 1902), X. Henry Grady's "The New South" (1886) is readily available in standard anthologies. A running debate on reconstruction measures may be followed in the *Congressional Globe*. Note especially speeches by Sumner, Stevens, Raymond, and Finck.

RUGGED INDIVIDUALISM AND SOCIAL PROTEST

Harris E. Starr, *William Graham Sumner* (1925); A. G. Keller, *Reminiscences (Mainly Personal) of William Graham Sumner* (1933). Maurice R. Davie, ed., *Sumner Today* (1940) suggests continuing interest in Sumner. Charles A. Barker, *Henry George* (1955). Daniel Aaron, *Men of Good Hope* (1951) has good essays on George and contemporary reformers.

For background, see appropriate chapters in Richard Hofstadter, *Social Darwinism in American Thought* (1944); Ralph Gabriel, *The Course of American Democratic Thought* (1940); Robert G. McCloskey, *American Conservatism in the Age of Enterprise* (1951). See standard works on agrarian and labor movements, particularly John Hicks, *The Populist Revolt* (1931). Robert G. Gunderson, "The Calamity Howlers," *The Quarterly Journal of Speech*, XXVI (1940), pp. 401–411 is good on populist orators. Finally, George's *Progress and Poverty* (1879), Edward Bellamy's *Looking Backward* (1888), Henry Demarest Lloyd's *Wealth Against Commonwealth* (1894), and other writings of the period are invaluable.

For a bibliography of Sumner's writings and speeches, see A. G. Keller, ed., *The Forgotten Man and Other Essays* (1918). Seven of Henry George's addresses are included in "Our Land and Land Policy," in *The Complete Works of Henry George* (10 vols., 1904–1906), VIII. *Edward Bellamy Speaks Again!* (1937) has some of Bellamy's speeches on Nationalism. Eight of Henry Demarest Lloyd's speeches are in his *Men the Workers* (1909).

THE GOSPEL OF WEALTH VS. THE SOCIAL GOSPEL

There are no satisfactory biographies of Conwell or Herron. See the *Dictionary of American Biography* and *Encyclopedia Americana* for sketches. Useful bits of information may be winnowed from Agnes Burr, *Russell H. Conwell and His Work* (1917), and Robert Shackleton, *Acres of Diamonds* (1915). The Shackleton biography contains an "Autobiographical Note" by Conwell and a text of the lecture. For an unfriendly treatment, see W. C. Crosby, "Acres of Diamonds," *The American Mercury*, XIV (1928), pp. 104–113.

The following books are valuable for men and background: Andrew Carnegie, *Autobiography* (1920); Ralph H. Gabriel, *The Course of American Democratic Thought* (1940), particularly chs. 13 and 24; Charles H. Hopkins, *The Rise of the Social Gospel in American Protestantism, 1865–1915* (1940); Henry F. May, *Protestant Churches and Industrial America* (1949); Eric F. Goldman, *Rendezvous with Destiny* (rev. ed., 1956); Irwin G. Wyllie, *The Self-Made Man in America* (1954); Robert G. McCloskey, *American Conservatism in the Age of Enterprise* (1951).

See Maurice F. Tauber, "Russell Herman Conwell: A Bibliography" (1935). This is an extensive though incomplete mimeographed list of Conwell's sermons, lectures, and writings, as well as writings about Conwell, issued by Temple University library. Some of Herron's important speeches appear under the titles

Between Caesar and Jesus (1893) and *The Christian State* (1895). The latter volume contains his highly controversial commencement oration given at the University of Nebraska. Representative of Washington Gladden's statements are his *Working People and Their Employers* (1876) and *Social Salvation* (1902). The foremost theologian of the Social Gospel Movement was Walter Rauschenbusch. Several of his lectures were published in elaborated form under the title, *A Theology for the Social Gospel* (1918).

REVEALED RELIGION VS. THE RELIGION OF HUMANITY

C. H. Cramer, *Royal Bob* (1952) is the best life of Ingersoll. There are no satisfactory biographies of Talmage; see, for example, Louis A. Banks, *T. DeWitt Talmage: His Life and Work* (1902) and a sketch in Clarence E. Macartney's *Six Kings of the American Pulpit* (1942). Consult W. N. Brigance, ed., *A History and Criticism of American Public Address* (2 vols., 1943) for Lionel Crocker, "Henry Ward Beecher"; W. M. Parrish and A. D. Huston, "Robert G. Ingersoll." See Marie Hochmuth, ed. *A History and Criticism of American Public Address* (1955), III, for Robert Huber, "Dwight L. Moody."

For background, consult Washington Gladden, *Who Wrote the Bible?* (1891); Andrew D. White, *A History of the Warfare of Science with Theology* (2 vols., 1896); Arthur M. Schlesinger, "A Critical Period in American Religion, 1875–1900," *Proceedings of the Massachusetts Historical Society*, LXIV (June, 1932); Bert J. Loewenberg, "Darwinism Comes to America, 1858–1900," *Mississippi Valley Historical Review*, XXVIII (December, 1941); Ralph Gabriel, *The Course of American Democratic Thought* (1940), especially chs. 14–16; Merle Curti, *The Growth of American Thought* (1943), especially chs. XXI–XXII.

Ingersoll's best known lectures on religion and speeches on sundry subjects arranged for publication, are contained in *The Works of Robert G. Ingersoll*, Dresden Edition (12 vols., 1900). Talmage's six sermons attacking Ingersoll and his beliefs are in *The Brooklyn Tabernacle* (1884). See also, Henry Ward Beecher, *Evolution and Religion* (1885).

CRUSADE FOR THE BALLOT

The best biographies of Miss Anthony are Ida Husted Harper, *The Life and Work of Susan B. Anthony* (3 vols., 1898–1908); and Katherine Anthony, *Susan B. Anthony* (1954). For a discussion of her speaking career see Doris Y. Twitchell, "Susan B. Anthony," in *A History and Criticism of American Public Address*, Marie K. Hochmuth, ed. (1955), III. Louise B. Hill, *Joseph E. Brown and the Confederacy* (1939), concerns the Civil War and Reconstruction periods, but contains nothing on Brown's Senate career.

Nearly all chroniclers of the suffrage movement rely heavily upon the bulky *History of Woman Suffrage* (6 vols., 1881–1922) prepared by E. C. Stanton, S. B. Anthony, M. J. Gage, and I. H. Harper. A clearer and less cluttered outline of the movement is presented in *Woman Suffrage and Politics* (1923) by C. C. Catt and N. R. Shuler. Useful also are *Victory, How Women Won It* (1940), a symposium published by the National Woman Suffrage Association; and Ida H. Harper, *Story of the National Amendment for Woman Suffrage* (1919). Horace Bushnell, *Woman Suffrage: the Reform Against Nature* (1869) is a calm, detailed presentation of an opposing point of view. There are numerous autobiographies and biographies of woman suffrage leaders, particularly of Mrs. Stanton; see, for example, Alma Lutz, *Created Equal* (1940); Harriet Stanton Blatch and Theodore Stanton, *Elizabeth Cady Stanton As Revealed in Her Letters, Diary, and Reminiscences* (2 vols., 1922); and Mrs. Stanton's own *Eighty Years and More* (1898).

Brown's Senate speech against woman suffrage is printed in part in *History of Woman Suffrage* (IV, pp. 93–100), together with a pointed and often amusing commentary provided by Stanton, Anthony, and Gage in footnotes and italicized passages. Frederick C. Hicks, ed., *Famous Speeches By Eminent American Statesmen* (1929) contains speeches by Miss Anthony and Mrs. Catt. See also *Orations and Addresses of George William Curtis* (3 vols., 1894), I, for several speeches on women's rights, and Wendell Phillips' lecture on "Woman's Rights" in his *Speeches, Lectures, and Letters* (2 vols., 1894), I.

The Mission of America

Claude G. Bowers, *Beveridge and the Progressive Era* (1932). Paxton Hibben, *The Peerless Leader, William Jennings Bryan* (1929); William J. Bryan and Mary B. Bryan, *The Memoirs of William Jennings Bryan* (1925). See essays on the speaking careers of Beveridge and Bryan by Herold T. Ross and Myron G. Phillips in William Norwood Brigance, ed., *A History and Criticism of American Public Address* (2 vols., 1943).

For background see Julius W. Pratt, *Expansionists of 1898* (1936); Walter Millis, *The Martial Spirit* (1931); Theodore P. Greene, ed., *American Imperialism in 1898* (1955), Problems in American Civilization Series. See also appropriate sections in biographies by Bowers, Hibben, and others.

See Warren C. Shaw, *History of American Oratory* (1928), pp. 570–579, for an excellent brief bibliography of speeches on imperialism. See also *Speeches of William Jennings Bryan* (2 vols., 1909); Albert Beveridge, *The Meaning of the Times* (1908), especially "Our Philippine Policy" (1900) and "The Star of Empire" (1900). *Republic or Empire? The Philippine Question* (1900) is a collection of speeches by prominent public figures. Other relevant speeches are: George Hoar, "The Filipino War" (1902) in Frederick C. Hicks, ed., *Famous Speeches By Eminent American Statesmen* (1929); Theodore Roosevelt, "The Strenuous Life" (1899) in *The Strenuous Life* (1910); Carl Schurz, "The Policy of Imperialism" (1899) in T. B. Reed, ed., *Modern Eloquence* (15 vols., 1903).